# IMPERIALISM

Established in the belief that imperialism as a cultural
phenomenon had as significant an effect on the dominant
as on the subordinate societies, Studies in Imperialism
seeks to develop the new socio-cultural approach which
has emerged through cross-disciplinary work on popular
culture, media studies, art history, the study of education
and religion, sports history and children's literature.
The cultural emphasis embraces studies of migration and
race, while the older political, and constitutional,
economic and military concerns will never be far away.
It will incorporate comparative work on European and
American empire-building, with the chronological focus
primarily, though not exclusively, on the nineteenth and
twentieth centuries, when these cultural exchanges were
most powerfully at work.

Mount Kenya from the south
From J. G. Millais, *Life of Frederick Courtenay Selous, D.S.O.*, London, 1919

# STUDIES IN IMPERIALISM

general editor John M. MacKenzie

# The Empire of Nature

## HUNTING, CONSERVATION AND BRITISH IMPERIALISM

### John M. MacKenzie

**MANCHESTER
UNIVERSITY PRESS**
Manchester and New York

Distributed exclusively in the USA and Canada
by ST. MARTIN'S PRESS

Copyright © John M. MacKenzie 1988

Published by **MANCHESTER UNIVERSITY PRESS**
OXFORD ROAD, MANCHESTER M13 9PL
and **ROOM 400, 175 FIFTH AVENUE, NEW YORK, NY 10010, USA**
*Distributed exclusively in the USA and Canada by*
**ST. MARTIN'S PRESS, INC.**
**175 FIFTH AVENUE, NEW YORK, NY 10010, USA**

*British Library cataloguing in publication data*
MacKenzie, John M. (John MacDonald), 1943-
  The empire of nature: hunting, conservation and British imperialism.
  — (Studies in imperialism).
  1. British Colonies. Big Game. Hunting. 1700-1900
  I. Title II. Series
  799'.2'6'09171241

*Library of Congress cataloging in publication data*
MacKenzie, John M.
  The empire of nature : hunting, conservation, and British
  imperialism / John M. MacKenzie.
      p. cm. — (Studies in imperialism)
      Bibliography: p. 328.
      Includes index.
      ISBN 0-7190-2227-4 : $35.00 (U.S. : est.)
      1. Hunting—History. 2. Hunting—Great Britain—History.
  3. Great Britain—Africa—Administration—History. 4. Great
  Britain—Asia—Administration—History. I. Title. II. Series:
  Studies in imperialism (Manchester (Greater Manchester))
  SK21.M33 1988
  333.95'4'0917124—dc19        88-5301

ISBN 0-7190-2227-4

Typeset in Trump Mediaeval by
Koinonia Limited, Manchester

Printed in Great Britain
by Bell & Bain Limited, Glasgow

# CONTENTS

# ILLUSTRATIONS

# GENERAL INTRODUCTION

Imperialism was more than a set of economic, political and military phenomena. It was a habit of mind, a dominant idea in the era of European world supremacy which had widespread intellectual, cultural and technical expressions. The series is designed to explore, primarily but not exclusively, these relatively neglected areas. Volumes are planned on the scientific aspects of imperialism, on education, disease, the theatre, literature, art, design and many more. But in redressing the balance in favour of these multi-disciplinary and cross-cultural studies it is not intended that the economic, political and military dimensions should be ignored. There will be books in these fields too and the series will seek to examine colonial and imperial developments in a variety of periods and in diverse geographical contexts. It is hoped that individually and collectively these works will illumine one of the most potent characteristics of modern world history.

Changing approaches to hunting constitute an important theme in human history. The pursuit and killing of animals has invariably developed ideological overtones and both literature and the pictorial arts have tended to stress the mythic, courtly and martial rather than the purely practical aspects of the chase. Many European hunters in the nineteenth century were aware of this rich tradition and turned hunting into a symbolic activity of global dominance. Thus hunting became part of the culture of imperialism. It was closely connected with the study of natural history, a central area of scientific debate in the period. It performed important economic and social functions. It was subject to complex legislation and was much influenced by technical developments in firearms. As Europeans restricted access to the animal kingdom to themselves they developed notions of conservation which had a powerful effect on the landscape of imperial territories. This book uses hunting as one focus for the complex interaction of Europeans with Africans and Indians. It seeks to illuminate the nature of imperial power when exercised in the relationship between humans and the natural world.

J.M.M.

# ABBREVIATIONS

| | |
|---|---|
| *BJSH* | *British Journal of Sports History* |
| BSAC | British South Africa Company |
| CAP | Central Africa Protectorate (later Nyasaland, now Malawi) |
| CO | Colonial Office |
| EAP | East Africa Protectorate (later Kenya) |
| EIC | East India Company |
| FO | Foreign Office |
| GEA | German East Africa |
| IBEAC | Imperial British East Africa Company |
| ICS | Indian Civil Service |
| *Int. J. Af. Hist. Studs.* | *International Journal of African Historical Studies* |
| IO | India Office |
| *JAH* | *Journal of African History* |
| *JICH* | *Journal of Imperial and Commonwealth History* |
| *JSPFE* | *Journal of the Society of the Preservation of the (Wild) Fauna of the Empire* |
| KAR | King's African Rifles |
| PP | Parliamentary Papers |
| RCS | Royal Commonwealth Society |
| SPFE | Society for the Preservation of the (Wild) Fauna of the Empire |
| UP | United Provinces (later Uttar Pradesh), India |

# PREFACE

The phrase 'hunting, shooting and fishing' was transformed long ago from a conventional description of recreations in *Who's Who* into a joke. It was emblematic of a specific class at a particular time, a class whose interests and pastimes soon seemed eminently satirisible. P. G. Wodehouse, inevitably, made fun of them, and 'big-game hunters' flitted uproariously across the variety stage as well as appearing in entertainments ranging from Mary Dunn's *The Memoirs of Lady Addle* to the BBC's radio soap opera 'The Archers'. This has made it difficult for scholars to take hunting seriously and has led to the devaluation of the significiance of the hunting ethos in the period when Europe dominated much of the world. In any case a liberal intellectual tradition in the twentieth century has generally found the suspected assault upon and destruction of animals in the recent past thoroughly repugnant, and that aversion has tended to induce a certain amount of scholarly silence.

Anyone attempting to break that silence faces a number of problems. The primary sources for hunting are legion, the secondary ones almost non-existent. The range of expertise required to understand the human and animal relationships in hunting in the imperial setting is daunting, virtually beyond the competence of one individual. Such a study requires some consideration of anthropological, economic, sociological and cultural dimensions. Moreover the hunting of wild animals has long given rise to a great range of complex legislation, and this is particularly true of the British Empire. A large number of colonial legislatures produced an extensive body of laws that has never been fully studied. Further, an understanding of hunting requires an attempt to come to grips with the technical development of firearms in the nineteenth century, with the directions taken by the study of natural history in the period, and even a nodding acquaintance with zoology, with the habits, habitats and anatomies of the animals themselves. Additional hazards are presented by the myth and controversy attendant upon the modern concern for international conservation – which has its origins in the imperial period – and the pressure groups that promote it.

Three areas of the human relationship with animals in Africa and Asia have received some attention. The ivory trade has been subjected to a good deal of analysis, though the results have often been inconclusive and the sources conflict at many points. Despite all this work we still await a definitive study. Second, scholars and practitioners from several disciplines have examined wildlife conservation from a variety of standpoints. But their approach has generally been Whiggish, assuming the positive nature of the onward march of the conservationist ideal, worrying about setbacks, and attempting to prescribe future developments. Third, some modern ethnographers, breaking with their predecessors, have noted the importance of hunting in many precolonial societies formerly classified as predominantly 'pastoral' or 'agricultural'. There has, however, been no attempt to bring this fragmentary material together.

The ivory trade is not central to this study, though some discussion of elephant hunting is unavoidable. The approach to conservation will be critical, though far from negative. There will be some attempt to establish the significance of hunting in African economies, though the material here will necessarily be patchy and the conclusions tentative. The main concern of the book is with hunting in general, the full range of animal products, the significance of game meat in the African diet and to conquest and settlement, and the social and cultural dimensions of the chase in both traditional and imperial societies. It attempts to place the hunting ethos, as developed in the imperial period, into a deeper historical perspective, relating it to a long tradition of social relations, to the ecological ideas of 'experts' in the late nineteenth and early twentieth centuries, to colonial notions about settlement patterns and to the origins and early development of conservation.

Through this approach hunting and conservation become part of a complex network of economic, social, racial, legal and cultural relationships. This opens up almost limitless possibilities, so some definitions, terminological, chronological and geographical are necessary. In the book 'hunting' will be used in its general sense, avoiding the technical usage derived from fox hunting that has been current in England over the past 150 years or so. 'Hunting' will therefore encompass the pursuit, driving, ambushing and trapping of wild animals of all species with the intention of killing them for meat, other animal products, or purely for sport. Thus the full range of animals – from elephant to rabbit – of techniques and hunters will be subsumed under the term. The principal focus will be on land animals, and there will be only marginal references to fishing. The main concern throughout will be with the replacement of indigenous techniques by European hunting methods, objectives and ideas about the natural world in an age of imperialism.

In the examination of hunting in almost all societies it is necessary to distinguish between the utilitarian and the ritualistic. Many forms of hunting contain elements of both, but the proportions tend to change

[ 2 ]

according to the class involved. In this study general and utilitarian aspects will be covered by the words 'hunting', 'shooting' and 'the chase', while the strongly ritualised will be identified by the term 'the Hunt'. 'Sport' can be a component throughout the hunting spectrum, though increasing emphasis upon it marks the shift from the practical to the pleasurable. Sport and ritual overlap at many points, but they also diverge according to the degree of risk involved. Sport often seeks risk, while ritual can attempt to avoid it.

The book will concentrate on the nineteenth and twentieth centuries, although there will be allusions to other periods, particularly in the first chapter. The main geographical emphasis will be on southern, Central and East Africa, as well as South Asia, but reference will be made to other parts of Africa and Asia and to the effects of white settlement elsewhere. The territories examined will be mainly in the British imperial system, although the hunting practices, or lack of them, of other empires will also be mentioned.

Even with these limitations the information is diffuse and there are many possible routes through the material. The problem of organisation and analysis are rendered more difficult by the fact that there are few if any tracks to follow. Scarcely any scholars have attempted such a cultural approach and there are virtually no specialist studies on which to build an overview. There are some signs that such projects are currently being developed, examining the interaction between indigenous and imperial hunting in specific territories. Perhaps a preliminary exploration of a world-wide problem will help to stimulate their appearance and provide scholars with an outline map, however rudimentary, into which they can set their more detailed surveys.

Hunting has invariably been a communal activity, and the writing of this book has followed that pattern. Although I have sometimes felt that I was advancing on trackless wastes, colleagues have been tireless in beating out new pieces of information or offering ideas. In the history department at the University of Lancaster I have benefited from discussions with Lee Beier, Martin Blinkhorn, Bob Bliss, Peter Broks, John Brooke, Stephen Constantine, Eric Evans, Ralph Gibson, Sandy Grant, Jeffrey Richards and Michael Winstanley. David Arnold has encouraged me by offering fruitful lines of enquiry, much information, and many ideas on South Asia. David Omissi read the entire manuscript and made many helpful suggestions. I have also received help of various sorts from Dave Anderson, Bill Baker, Frank Bell, Scott Bennett, Peter Blight, J. K. Brigg, Jim Casada, Richard Cashman, Phillip Dalziel, Brian Durrans, John Flenley, Robert Fox, Richard Grove, Lawrence James, Tony Lemon, David Lowenthal, John Lowerson, John McCracken,

Tony Mangan, Willie Milne, Mike Pearson, Terry Ranger, Andrew Roberts, David Rubinstein, John Springhall, Murray Steele, Ed Steinhart, Brian Stoddart and Frank Willett. That I have still got lost despite all this help is entirely my own fault.

As always, the book could not have been written without the help of several key libraries. Donald Simpson, Terry Barringer, Pauline Foster and Sue Bradley supplied books, journals and illustrations from the unrivalled collections of the Royal Commonwealth Society Library. Thelma Goodman and her staff at the inter-library loans office of the University of Lancaster Library have seen a constant stream of hunting books passing through their hands over the past two years. The Bodleian Law Library, Oxford, was an invaluable source of colonial legislation and my labours were lightened by the efficient photocopying service. Ann Datta of the Zoology Library of the British Museum (Natural History) supplied useful information and helped me to use its resources, as did the librarians of the High Commissions of Canada, India and New Zealand.

Game books and other hunting materials have been tracked down to Dunrobin Castle (with thanks to the Countess of Sutherland and Lord Strathnaver for correspondence and help), Hopetoun House (with thanks to the administrator, Major Drummond-Brady), Kedleston House, the National Army Museum and the National Library of Scotland. The information officer of Tatton Park, Iris Hickman, and the archivist of Blair Castle, Jane Anderson, offered helpful advice, while Andrew Sherratt of the Ashmolean Museum in Oxford made available his extensive knowledge of Ancient and Medieval hunting. The Endangered Species Branch of the Department of the Environment supplied information on their work.

The University of Lancaster provided two terms' sabbatical for the completion of the book, and I am grateful to Keith Morgan for approving it. I have been greatly encouraged by the support of Alistair MacKenzie, Alexander MacKenzie (who saw safari firms at work in Nairobi in the 1920s) and the dedicatee.

*For N. R. D.*

# CHAPTER ONE

# Hunting: themes and variations

The significance of hunting in the imperialism of the nineteenth and twentieth centuries has never been fully recognised. This is curious for the exploitation of animals is everywhere in the imperial record. In many areas of the world, the colonial frontier was also a hunting frontier and the animal resource contributed to the expansionist urge. In the era of conquest and settlement animals sometimes constituted a vital subsidy to an often precarious imperial enterprise, while in the high noon of empire hunting became a ritualised and occasionally spectacular display of white dominance. European world supremacy coincided with the peak of the hunting and shooting craze, and that conjunction can be found in a great range of contemporary publications. Accounts of exploration, missionary activity and military campaigns, together with biographies, memoirs and popular and juvenile fiction, abound in descriptions of the imperial chase. In addition, soldiers, administrators, professional hunters and wealthy travellers produced a seemingly endless stream of specialised hunting books, many of them dressed up as natural history.

A cultural characteristic may be rendered nebulous by its very ubiquity. Where historians have noticed the exploitation of the animal resource – in ivory and skins in eastern, central and southern Africa – it has been primarily through the lens of international trade. The animals themselves, hunting techniques, and the complex sets of social relations surrounding them, have inspired little interest. The economic, sociological and natural historical dimensions of hunting, set within a wider cultural context, have perhaps proved dauntingly complex. Moreover, it may be that we have continued to be influenced by Social Darwinian classifications. A discussion of hunting is clearly vital to the understanding of hunting and gathering societies, but it seems to be merely a marginal mode to the pastoral, agricultural or industrial. In economic evolution, hunting appears to be transformed into a purely sporting and symbolic activity. Perhaps this misconception more than any other has ensured that the hunting and consumption of game have been either ignored or much oversimplified as an element in the economies and diets of many indigenous societies and in white interaction with them. Yet much has been written about the role of hunting in the development of early humankind. Hunting is an activity for which the human is physically ill-adapted. He can neither kill nor prepare meat without the aid of weapons and tools. Hunting has therefore long been recognised as a prime stimulus to the creation of artefacts, the origins of material culture. It is known too that hunting developed sociological significance, became subjected to rules and rights, at a very early period.

Moreover, hunting in Europe and the Mediterranean world is a

[ 7 ]

relatively well worked field. It is impossible to avoid the prominence of the Hunt in Middle Eastern archaeology and in the daily activities and values of Greece and Rome, in the assertion of the medieval royal prerogative and the vesting of property rights in game by several centuries of legislation, in the romantic attachment to the chase in both the Celtic and the Germanic world and in the idealised oriental world of Arab and Persian. These connections between the classical and the chivalric, the Celtic and the orientalist were enthralling to nineteenth-century Europeans and fed the wild enthusiasm for the chase by both the aristocracy and the *nouveaux riches* in the era of imperial ascendancy. The interest of modern scholars has inevitably been more fragmentary and there has perhaps been a sharp distinction between studies of ancient and medieval hunting and the more radical examination of the game laws in Britain, with their extensive social and political implications.

Images of the Hunt are everywhere in Eastern and European art. As each culture and each medium has successively turned to man's relationship with wild animals as a central theme first of human survival, then of human dominance, the art has become more self-conscious, more overlaid with symbolic meaning. Stone Age cultures represented hunting and the animal kingdom as the basic fact of existence, whether on the great cave paintings like those of Lascaux (with their later parallels in many part of Africa) or in the carving of bone and antlers. Animals and hunting scenes appear on Egyptian artefacts ranging from ivory wands and combs to stone scarabs, from pottery to slate palettes. The great Assyrian carved friezes depict the lion hunt raised to a central act of state. Greek pottery documents the Hunt as it does so many other aspects of Greek life.[1] The virtues of the dead have been represented in heroic hunting encounters from the shaft-grave tombs of Mycenae to Roman sarcophagi. One of the twelve labours of Hercules, often given sculptural expression, was his struggle with the Nemean lion. Roman mosaic art provided a perfect medium for the colour and life of the Hunt, which can also be found etched into Roman glass or used as a lively decoration for samian and caster ware.[2]

So dominant was the hunting theme that it came to be identified with Christian art. In the late Roman Empire hunting scenes became an allegory of Christian virtue and a symbol of the victory of Christ over the forces of darkness.[3] Later, hunting was associated with dramatic conversions, as in the cases of St Eustace and St Hubert, who were alleged to have seen the miraculous appearance of a cross between the antlers of a stag when hunting.[4] The foundation story of Holyrood Abbey in Scotland, which contains an excellent description of a medieval game drive, suggests that King David I was saved from attack by a stag through the appearance of such a cross in its antlers. The representation of elaborate hunts on Pictish stones and on the great Celtic crosses in Scotland may have had allegorical or religious significance, but it may be that they merely extol the exploits of notable hunters. Such is the likely explanation of the Hunt on the beautiful fifteenth-century Macmillan Cross (showing Christ crucified on the reverse side) at Kilmory in Argyll or the detailed hunting accoutrements on the early sixteenth-century tomb of Alexander MacLeod at Rodel in Harris.[5] These are but two examples of an extensive sculptural tradition, many crosses and stones depicting epic hunts that have their literary counterparts in medieval Gaelic poetry and in its romantic recreation in Macpherson's *Ossian*.

Elsewhere medieval depictions of the chase appear in a host of sculptures and carvings in architectural contexts as well as across a wide range of artefacts. Animals of the Hunt, real and mythical, became a central part of heraldry, sometimes linked with the appropriation of the attributes of the Hunt in an aristocratic name like Grosvenor (Great Hunter). But the most striking medieval representations were in new media, in tapestries and in manuscript illuminations. Among the finest examples of the first are the Devonshire hunting tapestries or those of the Burrell collection;[6] of the second, the illustrations to some of the copies of the *Book of Hunting* of Gaston Phoebus, Count of Foix.[7] These have their Eastern counterparts in the elegant and intricate paintings of the Persian and Mughal court.[8]

The extraordinary persistence of hunting scenes in Western art is amply evidenced by the continuation of the tradition in ivory, wood and other forms of carving from the late medieval and early modern period, particularly in Germany, in ceramic decoration, and in other art forms. The English school of sporting painting, depicting the English fascination with animals and humans in the landscape, represents an almost continuous tradition from Tudor and Stuart times reaching a great climax in the pictorial arts of the nineteenth century.[9] Sir Edwin Landseer was but the most famous of a wave of painters and engravers fascinated by the animal world, and in particular human power over it.[10] Because Landseer is so representative of the nineteenth-century cast of mind, with its ambivalent approach to gory violence and romantic beauty, cruelty and sentimentality, it will be necessary to examine his work in greater detail below.

There are perhaps a number of reasons for the extraordinary popularity of hunting images in so many cultures and so many centuries. For Stone age man hunting represented a primary economic mode, a basic fact of subsistence. In depicting his natural environment he often concentrated on the extraordinary (the larger animals, for example) rather than the ordinary, but he was grappling with basic and useful facts. Much of the rest of hunting art has dealt with a narrow band of hunting activity, and has been laden with class and moral significance. Thus in the ancient world the hunting of the lion and the boar, elite and kingly preoccupations, have been illustrated rather than the mundane hunting of the plain man. Both here and in Celtic sculpture the treatment of the Hunt is epic rather than as a matter of everyday survival. Peasants appear as auxiliaries in some medieval representations, but, as in the Persian and Mughal tradition, it is the Hunt as a spectacular and elegant courtly pursuit that reigns supreme. In the work of Landseer and other nineteenth-century artists nature as property, dominated and tamed, at least in death, comes to the fore. But in all these traditions the artist clearly revels in the opportunity to present man within the natural world (and in these works it is generally man rather than woman), using auxiliary animals – horses, dogs, elephants – elaborate clothing and weapons to assist his authority over it. It is true that there is a world of difference between ancient sculpture showing gods in human form, naked but for shield and sword, in a dangerous and heroic struggle with lion or boar and a seemingly safe and elaborate medieval equestrian and courtly pursuit of boar or deer (with perhaps the Celtic stag hunt as a mid-way point), but the attractions of movement, drama, the combination of human and natural elements, and the opportunity for allegorical meaning clearly attracted the artists in all these cases. They were also attracted by patronage. Each elite seemed to find this the most powerful and appealing way to present itself. The Hunt, in short, constituted propaganda: it showed emperor, king, or lord exhibiting power, enjoying the privilege that went with it and asserting prestige within widespread territorial bounds.

It is indeed the progressive restriction of social access to hunting that constitutes the enduring theme of hunting in a wide range of societies. This upward exclusiveness tends to mark a shift from utility to inutility, and often from edibility to inedibility. The symbolic and normative content is emphasised, and strict rules of procedure are followed. In 'sport' the rules are often designed to increase difficulty, in ritual to minimise it. Not that the Hunt entirely drives out hunting. Hunting usually survives, continuing to perform its humble subsistence role, but it is despised by the elite and their apologists. It fails to exhibit the character-forming, moral attributes of the Hunt. Because it is concerned with basic survival or baser commercial motives it takes the shortest route to destruction. In hunting the end is all-important, the death and utilisation of the animal. In the Hunt the means are all. The subsistence hunter is concerned with the ease with which his purpose can be achieved. The sportsman indulging in the Hunt is concerned with the difficulty. The greatest joy to the practical hunter is when the animal falls into a pit, is ensnared or simply lies down and dies. The sportsman regards the first two as base and unacceptable techniques, the latter eventuality as a disaster denying him his 'sport'. In the Hunt the animal is most to be valued, and by extension the hunter who slays it, according to the fight it puts up. In securing its death he follows strict rules of procedure and endangers himself in the process. If ritual tends to eliminate danger, then it is because the status of the sportsman is such that he must appropriate the attributes of the Hunt without the risk.

In the Greek Bronze Age hunting seems to have been of the practical variety. Deer were taken in nets or hunted on foot with hounds; wild goats were hunted with bow and with javelin. Homer's heroic hunters slew stags and boars to eat rather than as sport. But with the emergence of the Greek aristocracy the Hunt became the perquisite of the elite.[11] The role of the chase as a builder of physical fitness, stamina and courage required in war was emphasised by Xenophon in arguments that were to be used down to modern times. When Xenophon wrote that 'when men used to hunting make difficult marches under arms, they will not give in, but will endure hardships, because it is with hardship that they are accustomed to take wild beasts' he laid out a prospectus that was to be repeated by Baden-Powell at the end of the nineteenth century. Xenophon, appealing to history as an exemplar, as propagandists will, went on:

> Our ancestors knew that hunting was the source of their success over their enemies and made the young men practise it. For though they were short of agricultural produce in primitive times, they decreed nonetheless that hunters should not be restrained from hunting through any sort of standing crop; in addition, that there should be no hunting within many furlongs of town, so that those who possessed this skill should not destroy the sportsmen's game. For they saw that the pleasure that young men take in hunting provides in itself many benefits. It makes them self-restrained and just, through education in true principles; and our ancestors recognised that to these they owed their success, especially in war.[12]

In other words, the practical hunting of the townsmen should be restrained in order to preserve 'sport' as character training for war. Such a programme for training the young as officers and leaders of men received the approval of Plato, who also contributed to the obverse tradition that was to survive to the twentieth century, the depreciation of the ordinary man's hunting. There was, in his view, no virtue at all in the fowling and snaring of small game by the poorer classes, particularly if it was undertaken for the market.[13]

The same distinction was promoted by the Romans. The hunting of the early republic had been largely practical, but by the later republic the class and moral overtones are in evidence. In the second century B.C. Scipio Aemilianus took up hunting as part of his admiration for Greek culture. Scipio hunted extensively during and after the Macedonian wars. He brought his enthusiasm back to Rome and built his reputation on daring and memorable feats in the chase. Some older Romans may have looked askance, but by imperial times the Hunt was a central part of Roman life. Cicero had admired the disciplines of the Hunt as a preparation for war, but he could not stomach the spectacular circus hunts arranged by Pompey the Great and Julius Caesar. Significantly, aristocratic hunting was encouraged by the emperor Augustus in the peace following the civil wars, although he himself may not have hunted. It was not long before Roman moralists were regarding the position of the Hunt and the relationship of the emperor to it as a sort of fever chart of the health of the imperial state. Nero's spectacles, which he sometimes opened by slaying an animal himself, were regarded as degenerate, as was Domitian's practice of killing large numbers of driven game in his game park outside Rome. Domitian's interest was considered oriental, akin to the release of caged lions before the Assyrian king. Pliny saw Trajan's return to a seemingly more noble hunting as indicative of his virtue, and Hadrian was to make propagandist capital out of the Hunt. He admired the heroic hunts of the Greeks, and emphasised his own prowess against the most 'noble' and dangerous beasts, the lion, the boar and the bear. His exploits were commemorated on sculptured medallions and turned into propaganda on the coinage. He was followed in these pursuits by Marcus Aurelius (who also issued hunting coinage) and Antoninus Pius. The image of the emperor as heroic hunter was carefully fixed in the minds of the subjects of imperial Rome, just as Persian, Assyrian and Egyptian rulers had portrayed themselves as brave protectors of their people against the ferocious animals that beset them.[14]

These ancient examples cannot have been lost on the classically educated elite of a new imperial State, Britain, in the nineteenth century. In this we can detect a distinct shift in intellectual emphasis from the eighteenth to the nineteenth centuries. Gibbon implied that the hunting of animals, the fighting back of the wild, was essential to an early stage of human survival, prerequisite for the formation of civilisation, but he saw no reason why the civilised, no longer threatened by the natural world, should hunt. He reserved his special distaste for the spectacular and bloody events of the amphiteatre.[15] In this he reflected eighteenth-century notions of cultivated manners, a developing refinement which was, however, a false dawn in the human approach to animals. The aristocratic and intellectual disdain for hunting that was briefly displayed in that period was soon replaced by a wholehearted adoption of the Hunt and its values by all branches of the elite – with individual exceptions – in the nineteenth century. That shift produced another reaction involving perceptions of the Middle Ages. The Normans had introduced the notion of the Hunt as an essential element of the royal prerogative and reserved vast forest tracts for the purpose. The great eighteenth-century jurist Blackstone had seen this as the point at which the Norman yoke had chafed most painfully. He contrasted Norman prohibitions on hunting with Saxon liberties, when all had had access to the fruits of the chase. The sharpness of the distinction may have been partly a myth, but it is certainly true that the Normans developed the hierarchical approach to hunting and rules about social access to an extraordinary degree.[16] By the nineteenth century, significantly, the Normans were more highly regarded in popular historiography. As an imperial people, as law-givers, bringing peace and civilisation to an allegedly primitive and war-torn land, they seemed, no less than the Romans, to be worthy models for a new imperial age.

It may well be that we can identify the same shift from the practical to the sporting and ritualistic, from hunting to the Hunt, in Saxon and Norman England as in Bronze Age and classical Greece, republican and imperial Rome. The touchstone of this lies in an important legal distinction. Roman law had seen game as *res nullius*, the rights lying with him who slew it rather than with the landowner on whose land it was slain. The principle of *res nullius* seems to have survived in Anglo-Saxon England and also in early medieval Wales, although it was already being abandoned in Scandinavia and there is evidence to suggest that it was not adhered to in Ireland. Cnut established a royal hunting preserve in his Secular Ordinance of 1020-23, but it was the Normans who introduced the full-scale *foresta* system, first developed in Europe by the Franks in the seventh century.[17]

It is certainly clear that Norman hierarchies and their complexities of forest law were more concerned with sport, class privilege and the assertion of royal status than with the food supply. Declining areas of privilege were expressed in the fourfold division of forest, chase, park and warren. The king or his delegated officers, coveted positions, had sole right of access to the forest with its five beasts of venary – hart and hind (red deer), hare, boar and wolf. The chase and park, areas of unenclosed and enclosed land respectively, were the preserves of the great Norman lords who held the franchises, for the hunting of buck and doe (fallow deer), fox, marten and roe. The warren, with its hare, coney, pheasant and partridge was also held by a franchise from the king, and all these franchises were not necessarily coterminous with land ownership.[18] Thus the distinction between possession by killing and ownership through the land, as laid out in *res nullius*, was overlaid by a severely restricted franchise for the right of killing.

The Norman concept of forest reserves was introduced into Scotland by King David, probably in the 1130s. From now on the Pictish tradition of hunting with nets and the ordinary hunter's use of snares were despised.[19] Only the aristocratic hunts, using a variety of breeds of hounds in driving (the traditional system of Celtic Ireland and Scotland), coursing or *par force* hunting (in which hounds were slipped in relays) of deer received social and cultural acceptance. Moreover, in the great drives it was only the king or the greatest lords who could command the hundreds of people who were sometimes involved. The figures may well be inflated, but some of the medieval sources describe extraordinary numbers used in such hunts, with a correspondingly high number of kills. For example, a hunt described in an early sixteenth-century Gaelic poem suggests that 3,000 men with as many hounds killed 6,000 deer. Bishop Lesley, also in the sixteenth century, stated that 500 to 1,000 men with as many hounds might drive deer from a radius of ten to twenty miles to a narrow valley where the noble hunters waited.[20]

In the taking of wildfowl similar distinctions between the practical simplicity of the techniques of the common man and the elaboration of aristocratic hunting emerged. Old techniques of luring and netting were despised as entirely unsuitable for those of higher social standing. The latter pursued wildfowl with hawks, a sport learnt in part from the East. Long-winged hawks like the peregrine, the kestrel and the merlin, and the short-winged, such as the goshawk, sparrowhawk and buzzard, were used for different prey in different conditions. Hawks required special quarters and expensive establishments, and it was alleged that ownership was regulated in a strictly hierarchical fashion. The Boke of St Albans of 1486 tells us that eagles were for emperors, peregrine falcons for princes and earls, merlins for ladies, goshawks for yeomen, sparrowhawks for priests and kestrels for knaves.[21] The Book of Howlett, a fifteenth-century Scottish poem, produced a variant on this by personifying the hawks as eagle for emperor, erne for king, gerfalcon for duke, falcon for earl marshal, goshawks for chieftains in war, sparrowhawks as knights.[22] In fact the peregrine was the most valued bird and the goshawk the most common and the most efficient killer. A great hawking establishment would have had examples of many different sorts of hawks, each trained for a different quarry.

The forest laws were certainly one of the great sources of friction of the Norman system. The forests ebbed and flowed according to a variety of external factors. They were reduced, for example, to pay for crusades or other campaigns. King John was forced to make concessions in a forest charter in 1217. After the depopulation of the Black Death the forests made a brief resurgence in the late fourteenth and fifteenth centuries, which some see as a golden age of medieval hunting. It was certainly a period of considerable literary activity connected with hunting. Soon the forests were being despoiled to supply timber for the navy. But the ancient themes survive. The monarch's authority in the land is represented by his or her role as the greatest hunter, a prerogative reasserted in practical terms by the Tudors, notably Henry VIII and Elizabeth. The early Stuarts attempted to extend and develop their hunting rights, and, after a period when popular access to animals was possible during the interregnum, the hunting prerogatives were re-established at the Restoration.[23]

Thus, with the exception of the Cromwellian period, 'subsistence' hunting was frowned upon and hunting was viewed as an inappropriate activity for the lower orders except as auxiliaries in the hunts of the nobility. The Abbess of Sopwith, a fifteenth-century authority on heraldry, hawking and fishing, stressed this, the problem being that the lower orders were incapable of adhering to the unwritten rules, i.e. the 'sporting' code.[24] Hunting and fishing had the effect of debilitating them morally, while it uplifted the superior classes. Gaston Phoebus, Count of Foix, also emphasised the class and organisational characteristics of the nobleman's hunt. In describing the hunting down of wolves attacking the villagers' sheepfolds, he made it clear that this was a noble obligation, a source of social dependence.[25] In the early fifteenth century Edward Plantagenet, Duke of York, wrote a work entitled *The Master of Game*. He too stressed the noble and character-forming qualities of the Hunt, though he urged its adoption by all classes – no doubt in their appropriate stations in the 'sporting' hierarchy.[26]

The early Stuarts were fervent hunters, positioning their Scottish palaces, like Falkland, in areas of good hunting. The progresses of Mary Queen of Scots around the country involved much hunting, and her son, James VI and I, was eager to introduce Scottish practices to

England to re-emphasise the royal prerogative. He revealed his classical education by invoking Xenophon. The most notable painting of his son, the short-lived Henry, Prince of Wales, depicts him in the act of killing a stag. Saxton's maps in Elizabethen times had shown 700 deer parks throughout the land, maintained largely for pleasure, and there were probably more parks in England than in the whole of Europe.[27] In 1614 Francis Bacon wrote, 'Forests, parks, chases, they are a noble portion of the King's prerogative; they are the verdure of the King, they are the first marks of honour and nobility, and the ornament of a flourishing kingdom.'[28]

Game laws were to act as the litmus of class conflict into the twentieth century. During the interregnum the fierce resentments against the royal and aristocatic parks led to the breaking down of fences and the near extermination of the deer. The taking of hares, the animal most assiduously coursed and hunted throughout the ages, also greatly increased.[29] This seems to have had little effect on hare stocks, but it took some time for the deer to recover. From the late seventeenth century deer were often coursed by hounds in a drive, and by the eighteenth carted deer were being used for the purpose.[30] It was a sport clearly designed to take account of the availability of smaller numbers. With the Restoration game laws had been reimposed. Although access was soon to be improved for people of rank, more severe attempts were made to destroy the hunting opportunities of the common people.

From 1671 the royal prerogative was modified to favour the superior landed gentry, placing, as Blackstone put it, a little Nimrod in every manor instead of one mighty hunter. But the landowning qualification was high and the status of qualified person did not necessarily coincide with specific areas of land. The complexities of game legislation were compounded in three ways: first, through the distinction between wild animals which were nonetheless bred and nourished for hunting, the unlawful killing of which constituted 'stealing', since they were property, and truly wild animals which were available only to the qualified, the unlawful killing of which was poaching; second, by repeated adjustments to the precise definition of 'game'; third, through the development of penalties for 'poaching' which at times turned the taking of game into a political and near revolutionary act.[31]

In all the discussions of game-law reform in the late eighteenth and early nineteenth centuries it was the boundary of qualification that was at issue, particularly bringing it more closely into line with proprietorial rights. The Game Reform Act of 1831 extended the social range of access to game, but only by making game the property of the landowner, who had sole right of access.[32] Tenant farmers' rights were improved only later in the century under pressure from the distress caused by the agricultural depression. By producing more readily enforceable laws the reformers were concerned to ensure the more effective exclusion of the ordinary subsistence hunter. During the long period in which the reform of the game laws had been under consideration, Pitt the Younger had divided society into three groups for the purposes of game legislation. The gratification of the higher orders of society claimed prior attention because the right to kill game was better suited to their station in life. Occupiers of land might be given some right of participation, but only to a limited degree, while the lower classes (and here Pitt echoed Plato) 'for their own sake, and the sake of society, should not be encouraged to engage in such diversions'.[33]

It is important to understand this historical and metropolitan background, because many of these perceptions were to be applied to colonial game legislation later in the century. A number of other themes also need to be understood in the development of nineteenth-century ideas about the Hunt. In these we shall once more be focusing on British experience. First we need to look at the notion of 'protection' and the status of 'vermin'; second, at the concept of 'preservation'; third, at the idea of maintaining areas separate from cultivated land as preserves for game, to maintain stocks and provide regions suitable for hunting; and fourth, at the image of the Hunt as an essentially male pursuit.

The great hunters of the ancient world offered protection to their subjects' life and limb and to their crops by destroying wild predators. In Greek myth Meleagor slew the famous Calydonian boar because it was attacking fields and orchards after King Oinens had neglected the sacrifices to Artemis. Lion hunts at Mycenae and in many other parts of the ancient world were intended to resolve the incompatibility of human settlement and dangerous predators. In Assyria, where the lions were captured and released for the king and his court to kill from chariots, the protective role of the monarch had become ritualised.[34] Such protective hunting implied that the ultimate aim was to eliminate the crop eater or predator altogether. Lions were indeed gradually exterminated over large areas of the Mediterranean and Middle Eastern world (as they were in India at a later date). Yet extermination also removed the ritual aspect of such hunting, necessitating the use of captive animals. The Romans took this to extraordinary lengths by introducing exotic animals such as lions and elephants, even giraffes, that had never been indigenous to Italy. In the Roman spectacles, however, combat between man and beast for the purpose of entertainment had departed a long way from the notion of royal or lordly protection. That extermination lay in the logic of the protective hunt was, however, borne out by the elimination of the wolf and the wild boar from Britain.

The protective hunt, with its symbolic dependence, was to be very important in the imperial setting, as was the definition of certain animals as 'vermin' against whom every man's hand could legitimately be turned. Yet the status of vermin soon involved curious contradictions. First, despite the animal being singled out as a prime enemy of mankind, its destruction might nonetheless only be undertaken by certain hands. The emergence of fox hunting in Britain as the most popular equestrian hunt from the late eighteenth century makes this abundantly clear. The fox was a danger to all domestic poultry and to the eggs and young of pheasants reared for slaughter, yet farmers and gamekeepers who killed them were dubbed 'vulpicides', people who failed to comply with the elaborate rules of the countryside, the restricted access and ritualised forms of vermin destruction. But, like the Assyrian lion hunt, the sport developed its own dynamic, its own expansive needs. Far from being exterminated, foxes were encouraged, even being bagged from one part of the country to another to perform their function. Some were imported from the Continent by merchants of the Leadenhall Market in order to be bagged.[35] Thus the logic of 'protective' hunting had been inverted. The ritual of protection against vermin had become so necessary to rural social relations that the vermin had to be preserved and increased. The sporting needs of the 'Hunt' had turned the 'vermin' into a protected species.

While foxhunting was emerging as the premier English hunting technique, increasingly surrounded by rules and ritual, the shooting of birds underwent an extensive process of development. The 'walking-up' and shooting of partridges had been greatly encouraged by the appearance of hedgerows in the eighteenth-century enclosures. Shooting partridges in the stubble of harvested fields is a common pictorial image of the late eighteenth century. But the partridges were shot relatively haphazardly – on the ground, roosting or on the wing. As shotguns improved, particularly with the introduction of the cartridge in 1808, sporting rules developed. The partridge could no longer be shot on the ground by any self-respecting hunter; a bird had now to be shot in its most difficult aspect, on the wing. Moreover, to increase the range of the sport, the French partridge was introduced from across the Channel.[36] In the course of the nineteenth century the partridge was to be replaced as the prime quarry by the pheasant, formerly a relatively rare bird, shot by 'walking up' techniques. From the 1820s it was reared and driven, and many exotic species were introduced from Asia.[37] From the 1850s the northern moorland grouse rose dramatically in status, and when it did so there was a shift of attention to the destruction of its predators.[38] The hawks, the enemies of the grouse, were attacked by men in the later nineteenth century, at a time when hawking had virtually died out, and their numbers in the wild were drastically reduced.

In game 'preservation' the shooting fraternity interfered with the processes of natural reproduction. Although the animals (usually birds and generally the pheasant) remained in theory wild, they were carefully bred. Nature was modified to provide perfect conditions for breeding and roosting. Woodlands were carefully managed, trees coppiced and undergrowth was encouraged. New copses were planted for shelter and rhododendrons introduced as coverts. The eggs of the birds were taken for incubation by other birds, such as domestic chickens, later by artificial incubation, and the young were hand-fed.[39] Yet their 'wildness' had also to be preserved so that on the appointed day of the shoot they would fly and could be shot as wild, not domesticated animals. The great advantage of the system was not just the maintenance of numbers but the fact that at the appointed hour the quarry came to the hunters rather than the other way round. Fox hunting, developing in its modern form at the same time, seemed perfectly in tune with this system, since the fox was the prime predator of game birds. But as fox hunting built up to its great peak between 1830 and 1870, and the need to preserve and supply foxes grew, the strains between the 'hunting' and 'shooting' fraternities (using the terms in their English sense) increased.[40]

Generally, however, tensions arose not between the respective sporting groups (which did of course overlap) but between the practitioners of incompatible land use. In several English countries agricultural land was converted into pheasant-rearing shooting estates. The most notable examples were the series of Rothschild estates in Buckinghamshire and the Prince of Wales's Sandringham estate in Norfolk.[41] The greatest resentment arose from the fact that the preservers of game, in protecting its 'wild' status while greatly increasing its numbers, were in effect feeding it on their neighbours' and tenants' crops. As in Scotland, the elite Hunt had turned from protection to destruction. It had become a form of surplus extraction in which the animals gathered the rent.

In Scotland the reversal of protection took even more striking forms. Vast tracts of land which had been converted from a crofting mixed economy to pastoralism in the Highland Clearances of the 1820s were now reconverted from sheep walks to deer runs. Heather moorland was carefully managed – it was allowed to spread and subjected to periodic burning – to encourage the grouse. War was declared on the predators of grouse. In other words, a landowning elite decided to permit the re-encroachment of the wild in the interests of sport. No fewer than three million acres of Scotland were converted from pasture to moor and forest in the nineteenth century.[42] These conversions were prompted partly by a collapse in wool and mutton prices, to a certain extent affected by imperial imports, but the direction taken by land usage was heavily influenced by the specific interests of the elite in the period, and the particular forms of display their conspicuous expenditure led them to. These concerns of the Victorian elite will be examined in chapter two, but it should be noted in this context that the elite hunter has ceased to protect human settlement and has come to protect animals instead.

The conversion of English agricultural land and Scottish pasture had the effect of creating game reserves in all but name. The idea of separating productive human settlement from areas demarcated for the use of animals and the pursuit of the hunt was admittedly an ancient one. By this technique a ruling elite could draw its revenue and human following from the one while exhibiting its prestige, securing its recreation and symbolically establishing its authority over the natural world in the other. As is well known, the Achaemenid Persians had kept game in a great park called a 'paradise'. Xenophon describes the game park where Cyrus the Great hunted and exercised his horses. This was but one of many reserves owned by the king and other noble Persians. Alexander the Great hunted in such parks in central Asia, enjoying a particularly grand hunt in a 'paradise' somewhere near Samarkand that had remained undisturbed for four generations. The Roman emperor Domitian kept such a park and a number of sources indicate that noble Romans established game preserves.[43] The tradition was maintained by the Arabs and passed on to the Normans in Sicily. From Persia and central Asia it reached India with the Mughals. The Norman forests in England were a form of game reserve, although, unlike their oriental and Roman counterparts they were not stocked with exotic or captive wild game. Although vestiges of forests survived to be the scene of social disorder in the era of the Black Acts, by the eighteeenth century the carefully controlled deer park was the more characteristic expression of the English preserve before the development of the even more carefully nurtured shooting estate.[44] The reconversion of large tracts of Scotland to the wild therefore represented a nineteenth-century return to an ancient idea, now funded by industrial wealth.

The progressive restriction of social access to hunting and the elaboration of its rules and etiquette had a tendency to transform hunting into a predominantly male pursuit. The myth of 'man the hunter' is an oft repeated one, yet it flies in the face of much evidence to the contrary. It may be argued that it is essentially a perception of the nineteenth and early twentieth centuries, linked with the severe separation of the masculine and feminine worlds in that period, and to the valuation of the Hunt as the promoter of supposedly distinctive male virtues. In many hunting and gathering societies any tendency to a sexual division of labour was overridden by the demands made by the chase upon sheer numbers of human participants. Hunting was essentially labour-intensive, and in consequence men, women and children frequently participated together. In a subsequent chapter I shall endeavour to demonstrate that this was also true of the hunting activities of some agricultural societies in central and southern Africa. The evidence for the participation of women in ancient hunting is rather more ambiguous. The deities of the Hunt, Artemis and Diana, did of course take female form. Huntresses like Atalanta appear in myth, and women may well have taken part in Greek Bronze Age hunting. Some Roman women may have hunted, and a girl certainly appears in a hunting scene on a Roman mosaic in North Africa.[45] In medieval times women participated in falconry, one hawk, at least theoretically, being demarcated for their use. Occasionally women held high forest office, and, while noble women would customarily have been spectators at hunting parties some actually took part. The Abbess of Sopwith contributed to hunting lore, though more particularly with regard to fishing, while at a later period Elizabeth I's exploits with driven game are celebrated. She secured her prerogative and prestige in this area just as her father had done. Noble women may have refrained from the roughest hunting pursuits of the eighteenth century (as indeed did many of their more refined menfolk) but the courts throw up instances of female poachers.[46] Women have probably always played a part, if a minority one, in trapping and snaring.

Foxhunting started life as a distinctively male pursuit, associated with the wild drinking and whoring of the young hunting bloods at Melton Mowbray. But by the 1850s women were asserting a striking equality in the foxhunting field.[47] In equestrian skills they yielded nothing to the men, especially after they changed from the side to the

[ 21 ]

cross-saddle. During the golden age of fox hunting it became a woman's sport *par excellence*, and though they were rare there were even one or two female masters of fox hounds.

It is an interesting fact that fox hunting was also seen as socially conciliatory, a sporting milieu where all rural classes could mix as spectators and participants, even though each was in his or her allotted place. This was also true of hare coursing and the Cumbrian hunts on foot. As a result William Cobbett, a fierce opponent of the game laws, approved of fox hunting because of its capacity to bring classes together.[48] In fact fox hunting was severely hierarchical and had its own complex patterns of patronage and dependence. They emerged in the organisational and social sides of the sport, together with such practices as the 'walking' of hound pups to be fed and brought up by estate tenants and servants.

But the other hunting obsessions of the nineteenth century tended towards social and sexual separation. The *battue*, the often competitive, apparently compulsive, and hugely destructive shooting of birds at stationary butts, a fascination largely acquired from Germany, was chiefly a male preserve. Some women did shoot, but generally they were spectators and conversed with the men at the butts. The role of the women in provoking or restraining the men's competitiveness was explored in Isobel Colegate's novel *The Shooting Party* and the film of the same name. Moorland grouse shooting and above all Scottish stag hunting (often involving day-long stalks) were an almost exclusively male preserve.[49] So were the various forms of hunting developed for equestrian training and recreation among the military outposts of empire. There were some exceptions, but the imperial hunt was a largely male affair and extolled as such. Its rituals and its alleged character-forming qualities were depicted as being 'manly', a masculine training for imperial rule and racial domination.

As the nineteenth century progressed hunting became a central part of imperial culture. For the first time a dominant elite assumed a global significance and the various historical themes explored in this chapter were translated to a world stage. An imperial and largely masculine elite attempted to reserve for itself access to hunting, adopted and transformed the concept of the Hunt as a ritual of prestige and dominance, and set about the separation of the human and animal worlds to promote 'preservation' (later 'conservation') as a continuing justification of its monopoly. A world-wide legislative authority, backed by military and technical power, enabled Europeans to take elite policies in existence intermittently from ancient times and attempt their global application. That attempt and its relative success or failure will be surveyed in the ensuing chapters. But first it is necessary to examine the distinctiveness of the nineteenth-century impulse. This existed in two main areas, the drive to classify and order the natural world through a new scientific understanding, and the emergence of hunting not only as a dominant pursuit of the elite but also as an ethos to be respected and admired by subordinate social classes. The next chapter considers the hunting cult in Britain, the related study of natural history and the cultural forms through which hunting ideals filtered downwards.

## *Notes*

1 Andrew Sherratt, 'The chase, from subsistence to sport' *The Ashmolean*, 10 (summer 1986), pp. 4-7. Some of the artefacts mentioned here were in Mr Sherratt's exhibition on the chase in the Ashmolean Museum, Oxford, in 1986.

2 J. K. Anderson, *Hunting in the Ancient World*, Berkeley, Cal., 1985, contains many illustrations that provide useful evidence for the techniques and social dimensions of hunting.

3 Anderson, *Hunting*, p. 130.

4 John M. Gilbert, *Hunting and Hunting Reserves in Medieval Scotland*, Edinburgh 1979, pp. 75-6.

5 Gilbert, *Hunting Reserves*, pp. 52, 62-6, 75. See also Graham Ritchie and Mary Harman, *Exploring Scotland's Heritage: Argyll and the Western Isles*, Edinburgh, 1985, and J. W. M. Bannerman and K. A. Steer, *Late Medieval Monumental Sculpture in the West Highlands*, Edinburgh, 1977.

6 Richard Marks *et al.*, *The Burrell Collection*, Glasgow, 1983, pp. 181-9.

7 Gaston Phoebus, Count of Foix, *The Hunting Book*, reprinted with text by Gabriel Brise, London, 1984.

8 There are many sources for Mughal court art, but see especially the collections of the Victoria and Albert Museum and *The Indian Heritage: Court Life and Arts under Mughal Rule*, the catalogue of a V & A exhibition in 1982.

9 Anthony Vandervell and Charles Coles, *Game and the English Landscape; the Influence of the Chase on Sporting Art and Scenery*, London, 1980.

10 Richard Ormond, *Sir Edwin Landseer*, London, 1981.

11 Anderson, *Hunting*, chapters 1–3.

12 Anderson, *Hunting*, p. 18.

13 Anderson, *Hunting*, pp. 19-22.

14 Anderson, *Hunting*, chapters 5–7.

15 Edward Gibbon, *The Decline and Fall of the Roman Empire*, abridged by D. M. Low, London, 1960, pp. 52-4. 'Ethiopia and India yielded their most extraordinary productions; and several were slain in the amphitheatre which had been seen only in the representations of art, or perhaps of fancy. Commodus killed a cameleopardalis or giraffe, the tallest, the most gentle, and the most useless of the large quadrupeds.'

16 Charles Chenevix Trench, *The Poacher and the Squire*, London, 1967, pp. 19-23.

17 Gilbert, *Hunting Reserves*, pp. 5-9.

18 Trench, *Poacher*, pp. 36-9, Sherratt, 'The chase'.

19 Gilbert, *Hunting Reserves*, pp. 12-13.

20 Gilbert, *Hunting Reserves*, pp. 52, 55. 'In medieval Scotland barons probably spent more time, effort, and thought on hunting than any other activity', Gilbert, p. 1.

21 Vandervell and Coles, *Game*, pp. 30-1.

22 Gilbert, *Hunting Reserves*, p. 74.

23 Trench, *Poacher*, pp. 99-106. Vandervell and Coles, *Game*, p. 84.

24 Trench, *Poacher*. p. 76.

25  Phoebus, *Hunting Book*, pp. 58, 79.
26  Trench, *Poacher*, p. 62.
27  Vandervell and Coles, *Game*, p. 25.
28  Quoted in Vandervell and Coles, *Game*, p. 15.
29  Trench, *Poacher*, pp. 106-8.
30  Vandervell and Coles, *Game*, p. 28.
31  P. B. Munsche, *Gentlemen and Poachers: the English Game Laws, 1671-1831*, Cambridge, 1981. E. P. Thompson, *Whigs and Hunters: the Origin of the Black Act*, Harmondsworth, 1977. Harry Hopkins, *The Long Affray: the Poaching Wars in Britain, 1760- 1914*. London, 1985. Munsche attempts to argue that game laws bore down only lightly on rural society, but Hopkins provides a useful and convincing antidote to this revisionism.
32  Munsche, *Gentlemen*, pp. 6, 156-8.
33  Munsche, *Gentlemen*, p. 129.
34  Sherratt, 'The chase'. Anderson, *Hunting*.
35  David C. Itzkowitz, *Peculiar Privilege: a Social History of English Foxhunting, 1753-1885*, Hassocks, 1977, pp. 12, 50, 117, 148, 152-4.
36  Vandervell and Coles, *Game*, pp. 100-1.
37  Hopkins, *Long Affray*, pp. 70-3.
38  Willie Orr, *Deer Forests, Landlords and Crofters*, Edinburgh, 1982.
39  Vandervell and Coles, *Game*, pp. 109-11.
40  Itzkowitz, *Peculiar Privilege*, pp. 115-30.
41  Hopkins, *Long Affray*, pp. 246-50, 270-3, 284. Information about and pictures depicting the Rothschilds' hunting enthusiasms can be seen at Dalmeny House, near Edinburgh.
42  Orr, *Deer Forests*, pp. 6-8, 22. In 1883 there were 1.9 million acres of deer forest; in 1892 2.4 million acres; in 1906 3.5 million.
43  Anderson, *Hunting*, pp. 58-60, 78-80, 100.
44  Thompson, *Whigs and Hunters*.
45  Anderson *Hunting*, pp. 138, 168.
46  Munsche, *Gentlemen*, p. 200.
47  Itzkowitz, *Peculiar Privilege*, pp. 48, 55-6.
48  Itzkowitz, *Peculiar Privilege*, pp. 23-5. Leonore Davidoff, *The Best Circles: Society, Etiquette, and the Season*, London, 1973, pp. 28-9. Thomas Assheton Smith considered that fox hunting served 'to retain the moral influence of the higher over the lower classes of society' (in his memoirs of 1859). I am grateful to Stephen Constantine for this reference.
49  By the 1920s Sir Iain Colquhoun of Luss was putting down the declining popularity of stag hunting to the revolt of women. John Ross (ed.), *The Book of the Red Deer*, London, 1925, pp. 109-10.

# CHAPTER TWO

# The nineteenth-century hunting cult

In Britain the nineteenth-century hunting cult had an extraordinary range of cultural manifestations. As the shooting elite converted arable land and hill pasture into a new form of planned wilderness they not only changed the landscape, they also created fresh topographical perceptions for the nineteenth century. Victorian artists and travel writers transformed this carefully arranged natural world into nature itself. Pheasant covert, grouse moor and deer forest, explored and dominated by humans in the Hunt, became prime elements in nineteenth-century Romanticism. While the cult rearranged the landscape it also influenced architecture and interior decoration, creating a more rigid separation between the sexes as it did so. As the century progressed the hunting cult was transferred overseas, often searching for a genuine wilderness, and generated an entire ethos which distinguished certain characteristics of the Hunt as markers of civilisation and gentlemanly conduct. The study of a global natural history became closely related to this, and the combination of science and ethic, nature study, human control and moral code began to take a central role in popular fiction and juvenile training.

The relationship between these developments and Romanticism is complex. Keith Thomas has seen the developing study of natural history in the late eighteenth century and its relationship with the Romantic movement as effecting a transformation in the relationship between man and animals which constituted 'a great revolution in modern western thought'.[1] The professional middle classes acquired a whole range of sensibilities which made them unsympathetic to hunting. In glorifying the natural world the Romantics sought respect through preservation rather than abuse through killing. There were greater anxieties about meat-eating and the revolution culminated in the foundation of the Society for the Prevention of Cruelty to Animals in 1824 and in nineteenth-century legislation on animal welfare. By 1887 Queen Victoria was congratulating her subjects that 'among other marks of the spread of enlightenment' she had noticed 'with real pleasure the growth of more humane feelings towards the lower animals'.

The explanation for this 'revolution in perceptions' lay in the benevolent effects of science: 'The detached study of natural history had discredited many of the earlier man-centred perceptions. A closer sense of affinity with the animal creation had weakened old assumptions about human uniqueness. A new concern for the suffering of animals had arisen.'[2] Two other distinguishing characteristics of this revolution were that it was distinctively English and it set a sympathetic understanding of animals on a track that was to lead to the squeamish sensitivities of modern times:

These developments were but aspects of a much wider reversal in the relationship of the English to the natural world. They were part of a whole complex of changes which, by the later eighteenth century, had helped to overthrow many established assumptions and to create new sensibilities of a kind which have gained in intensity ever since.

These are large claims, combining the concept of detached scientific study with national uniqueness and an unbroken historical development.

There are a number of problems with Thomas's reassuring Romantic climacteric. The era of his new sensibilities coincided with the creation of the *battue*, the large-scale slaughter of carefully reared birds, the renewal of aristocratic enthusiasm for the chase and the incorporation of other classes, including the professional middle class, into that interest and the extension of the hunting cult to the rest of the world, all contributing to a fascination with cruelty and death that increasingly infused nineteenth-century art and popular literature. While legislation put an end to working-class pastimes like bear-baiting and cock-fighting, or attempted to regulate the treatment of draught horses and other domestic animals, it did nothing to fetter aristocratic forms of the chase or the use of auxiliary animals to effect kills on other species.[3] Neither the RSPCA nor the Humanitarian League, regarded in its day as a more radical body, attacked the blood sports which became the dominant ethic of the elite.[4] Fox hunting, otter hunting, hare coursing, the shooting of pheasant and grouse, deer driving and stalking all entered upon a golden age. In short, Victorian legislation brought the same class distinctions to the treatment of animals as had Xenophon, Plato or the younger Pitt. Moreover, the gentleman's code of hunting behaviour was not fully formulated until the end of the nineteenth-century and its framing had a great deal more to do with technological developments in firearms and the need to exclude a new under-class, the Africans and Asians of the empire, from access to hunting. A close examination of the works of Edwin Landseer and his many imitators, the illustrations of juvenile literature, the hunting descriptions of popular fiction and the close alliance between the worlds of hunting and of natural history create many difficulties for Thomas's progressive development of sensibilities down to the twentieth century.

One of the manifestations of Romanticism, after all, was Gothic fantasy and horror. The rediscovery of forests and mountains, particularly those in the genuine wild, brought human beings face to face with, and forced them to participate in, nature in the raw. Its violence and cruelty had to be appropriated in order to control and tame it. In doing so an increasing distinction was made between the pursuits suitable for male and female within the natural environment. The activities of Victoria and Albert in Scotland and the representations of them by Landseer and Winterhalter perfectly symbolised this and set the tone for much of the rest of society. Even diet conveyed these overtones of sexual separation. The diet of the Victorian elite was highly carnivorous, and indeed meat-eating was seen as 'manly', particularly within the empire.[5] Each of these themes will be explored in the chapters that follow.

The best way for us to approach the hunting cult in this new landscape is perhaps through its architectural expression and the influence of animals on interior decoration. The relationship betweeen hunting and sexual separation did indeed take architectural forms. The romantic rediscovery of the remoter regions of the British Isles and the hunting potential of moors and mountains led to the acquisition of shooting estates and the building of hunting lodges throughout the Highlands and Islands, northern England and some parts of Wales and the West Country.[6] The royal family, heavily influenced by Albert's German upbringing, was prominent in this. Balmoral may have been a family home in a marginal area between the cultivated and the wild, and of mixed architectural parentage, but for most of the lodges and country seats of the period Gothic was deemed the appropriate medium. The lodges were like monastic retreats devoted to the chase, their dark woods, ornate fenestration, immense stone fireplaces and gloomy high ceilings designed to evoke a medieval and supposedly masculine environment. The contrast with the cultivated and ordered world of eighteenth-century architecture and landscape is striking. Their significance far outran the confines of Scotlnd. They were re-created across the world, from the Rockies to Simla, and their canons of taste penetrated other architectural environments to which they were much less suited. The most obvious of such transfers was the trophy.

It is difficult to establish exactly when the passion for trophies began.[7] They had no doubt been used for practical purposes and as decoration in an earlier period, but not in any systematic way, neither as mementos of specific hunting occasions nor in the pursuit of records. The eighteenth-century interior was surely innocent of them. The craze for them was a product of the Romantic period. Roualeyn Gordon Cumming, who was born in 1820, relates in his memoirs that he had adorned the bedroom of his parental home at Altyre in Morayshire with trophies of his youthful, and presumably local, hunting exploits before he went to Eton.[8] Later in life Cumming contributed to the use of horns, heads and skins as part of the spectacular showmanship of the nineteenth century. He hunted in southern Africa between 1843 and 1848 and made a large collection of both animal trophies and African artefacts. He, and others before and after him, hoped that these would have the power to astonish the public as much as exotic animals had done in ancient and medieval times.

Even on the edge of hunting territory trophies could make a sensation. Cumming claimed that the whole town came to see and marvel at his trophies when he laid them out for public view in Colesberg, on the frontier of Cape Colony.[9] On his return to Britain Cumming continued to turn his hunting feats into sensational showmanship. He exhibited his trophies at the 1851 Great Exhibition in the Crystal Palace and later in other sites in London; he employed a Khoisan hunter called Ruyter, who had returned to Britain with him, to walk up and down Piccadilly advertising his show. It must be said that Cumming was an avid self-publicist who was suspected of much exaggeration by his fellow hunters, but his success with the public cannot be denied. It should perhaps be remembered that many of the animals being presented in this way were genuinely new. New species of large mammals continued to be 'discovered' up to at least the First World War, and representations of many known ones were discovered to be inaccurate by nineteenth-century travellers.

Thus the display of animal trophies was in both the public and the private domain from the start of the craze. To a certain extent the fashion for bedecking interiors with such trophies was another nineteenth-century attempt to reinvoke the Middle Ages. The great stairwells of the Gothic house, the appearance of specific male sanctums like the billiard room or the smoking room, the effort to recreate the medieval 'hall', all lent themselves to adornment with trophies. In an age when most middle-class and aristocratic families had some members serving in India, later in Africa, or some other part of the world, it was not long before the local stags were joined by the heads and horns of exotic animals. By the end of the century such tophies were the fruits of upper-class tourism. Fine skins, particularly of the great cats, appeared on floors and walls. Like all collecting interests, it stimulated a desire to possess representative collections from specific areas and a desire for rarities to fill gaps. Soon bourgeois stay-at-homes were aping the taste, and trophies began to appear in homes further down the social scale, if only as hat racks. This effort to bask in the reflected glories of the Hunt generated a considerable trade in trophies which was to stimulate legislative action in African colonies in the early twentieth century.

Many examples can still be seen today. The walls of Blair Castle, one of the centres of the hunting cult, are filled with trophies from around the world.[10] They added to the general clutter, the accumulated cultural detritus, of the Sutherlands at Dunrobin (the fourth duke, as well as owning over 100,000 acres of Scottish deer forest, became a notable big-game hunter), the Bowes-Lyons at Glamis, the MacLeods of Dunvegan, the Hamiltons at Brodick.[11] A host of other greater and lesser homes attempted to compete, and the trophies were matched by appropriate paintings, carvings, silverwork, plates, and natural history collections of stuffed birds and animals. Just as the castles and great homes of Scotland were far removed from the tiger-shooting of India or big-game hunting of Africa, so were many English country houses apparently remote in culture and architecture from the new romantic hunting cult. Yet they too were swept up in the craze and entrammelled with trophies. At Tatton Park in Cheshire the Egertons built a tenants' hall and festooned it with trophies from their hunting trips in the British Empire.[12] They entertained the tenantry in the midst of the symbols of their hunting exploits, evidence of their status and conspicuous expenditure on foreign travel. Servants' halls, billiard room extensions, smoking rooms and studies were similarly adorned. Foreign service and hunting prowess, social status and 'manly' pursuits, together with an intelligent interest in natural history, were all symbolically captured in this form of interior decoration. As the century progressed the hunting cult and imperial power met on the walls of country houses.

Some collections were so remarkable as to merit the status of private museums. William Cotton Oswell, who had accompanied and partly financed David Livingstone on his first expeditions to Lake Ngami and the Zambezi, amassed a great collection of trophies which he placed in his home in Kent. Schoolchildren and apprentices were brought from nearby Tunbridge Wells to see his animal heads and other African memorabilia.[13] The second Lord Rothschild, whose family had moved to its several estates in Buckinghamshire to combine banking with healthy rustic pursuits, established a private museum at Tring, now part of the Natural History Museum, and many of the great hunters at the end of the century collected for him.[14] One such was Frederick Selous, who had his own museum of trophies at his house in Worplesden.[15] Perhaps the most remarkable was P. H. G. Powell-Cotton, who hunted in Asia and Africa betweeen 1887 and 1939 and built extensions to his home, Quex House at Birchington in Kent, to house a vast number of trophies, remarkable examples of the taxidermist's art, in dioramas illustrative of different African and Indian habitats, as well as African weapons and artefacts.[16] This combination of the ethnic and the natural historical was characteristic, a sweeping-up of exotic taxonomies, both human and zoological.

This had indeed become a traditional combination by the end of the century. In Paris a close connection had been established between the Jardin d'Acclimatation and ethnic shows. As William Schneider has demonstrated, the bringing of exotic peoples to Paris to be displayed at the Jardin from 1877 stimulated a great deal of public interest and saved the fortunes of that institution.[17] The same combination of exotic humans and animals was similarly successful at the exhibitions which were a central aspect of the imperial spectacles in Britain in the period 1886 to 1938. 'Native villages' were a common feature of such exhibitions and they were joined by a 'jungle' at the Empire of India Exhibition of 1895. It was inhabited by live animals from the sub-continent and the guide to the display was written by the famous taxidermist and publisher Rowland Ward.[18] There was also a jungle at the 1911 Coronation Exhibition at the Crystal Palace, and many other exhibits of heads, trophies and stuffed animals appeared over the years, the work of the taxidermist being regarded as one of the crafts most worthy of display.[19]

When the contents of Sir Edwin Landseer's house were sold after his death in 1873 the catalogue listed thirty pairs of stags' heads and antlers, bulls' horns, rams' heads, a wild boar's head, the skeleton of his favourite deerhound, bison and tiger skins and a stuffed swan.[20] They reflected both his passion for the chase, and the search for anatomical accuracy in his paintings. They also illustrated his love of Scotland, his profound effect on Victorian sensibilities and his commensurate influence on interior decoration. Landseer painted images that dominated an age. He decorated the homes of the hunting aristocracy, painted for the royal family, and very nearly left his imprint on Parliament itself. He received the approval of Victoria and Albert, Sir Walter Scott, John Ruskin (for a time), and the leading connoisseurs and hunters of the day. Moreover he secured popular acclaim. More than half his income came from the sale of engravings. His most famous paintings were issued as popular prints, appeared on plates and packagings, tins and trays, and were emblematic of their period. Landseer brought together the study of natural history, the contemporary passion for projecting human values and characteristics on to animals, and the Romantic fascination with violence, extremes of emotion and fatalism. He studied animals at Mr Cross's menagerie at Exeter 'Change and dissected animal carcasses (including one of a lion which was sent to him). Later in life he kept a menagerie in his garden, containing horses, dogs, deer, sheep, foxes, a chained eagle and a raven.

As soon as Landseer's immense talent for animal painting was recognised he was sucked into the hunting fascinations of aristocratic circles. From his first visit to Scotland in 1824 he was enthralled. He spent several months (usually the classic hunting season from September to November) in Scotland each year, though he was said to be an erratic shot. One of his earlier successes was *The death of the stag in Glen Tilt* painted for Blair Castle, the Highland mansion of the Duke of Atholl and one of the principal shrines of the hunting cult. From 1850 to 1853 he was at Balmoral each autumn – before being displaced by Winterhalter – painting the Queeen at her sketching, the Prince Consort with his stags and other products of the chase.

His three great passions were dogs, stags and lions. It was an animal trinity that was to fascinate many of the celebrated nimrods of the nineteenth century and after, from Gordon Cumming to Frederick Selous, Sir Samuel Baker to Sir Alfred Pease. The dog represented devotion and obedience but also a cruel hunting auxiliary. J. G. Lockhart, the son-in-law and biographer of Sir Walter Scott, found Landseer and his circle to be 'utter boobies', their conversations 'all dog and horse, stag and Queen'.[21] The artist and his friends discussed the rat-catching capacities of various dogs, and they were duly painted at work. When he wished to depict *High Life* and *Low Life* he contrasted the noble deerhound with the plebean terrier. Dogs were a vital component of many of his hunting pictures.

The stag, so often humbled and brought to bay by dogs, nonetheless represented a romantic ideal – wild, powerful, independent, sexually dominant, tamed in death and transformed into venison by human hunting prowess. The sexual imagery was perfectly conveyed by his painting of two fighting stags under the title (quoting Dryden's *Alexander's Feast*) *None but the brave deserve the fair*. He painted frescoes of deer on the walls of the Scottish shooting lodges of the Duke of Abercorn and the Duchess of Bedford. They represented the living animals of the surrounding landscape just as the antlers on the adjacent walls were representative of the dead. It was proposed that he should paint three hunting subjects for panels in the refreshment room of the House of Lords. The Commons, however, struck the amounts out of the estimates and the only painting executed passed into private hands.

It was *The monarch of the glen,* which one commentator has described as reflecting in its 'haughty authority' the 'quintessential Victorian mood', its 'imperious and proud' face exulting in its 'secure majesty'.[22] On the other hand his painting *The Hunted Stag* and the drawing *The wounded stag swimming* present the epitome of apprehension and fear, while paintings like *The hunting of Chevy Chase* (where the fallow deer of the Borders is transformed into a red deer for greater effect), *The Highlanders returning from deerstalking, Return from the stag hunt,* and *The drive* all represent the hunter's desire to humble that 'secure Majesty'. 'Who does not glory in the death of a fine stag?' Landseer wrote. He expressed some regret for 'the assassination', but his love of the animal, he went on, got the better of 'such tenderness'. The picturesque and graceful quality of the stag was 'too great a quality to sacrifice to common feelings of humanity'.[23]

With lions he embraced the national and imperial icon, exploring their majesty and cruel potential in a range of media from paintings and drawings to his most obvious legacy, the sculptures of the Nelson monument. He had a recurrent dream in which he was attacked by a lion, and several of his paintings reveal his obsession with violence. In *The cat's paw* he took the La Fontaine fable and added the element of extreme cruelty. There is a pitiless character about his *Last run of the season,* the terrified but defiant fox about to be killed, while *The otter hunt,* technically brilliant as it is, is a supreme evocation of violence. The terrifying *Swannery invaded by eagles* loses nothing of its horror by its impracticality in terms of natural history. Even his use of colour was indicative, his favourite juxtaposition being red and green, symbolising blood and nature. Thus Landseer heightened existing violence and added it where none existed. But neither his life style nor the internal interpretive elements indicated that he did so to decry human participation in the raw cruelty of the natural world. Human involvement is, rather, glorified as an imperative of command over nature, perfectly conveyed in *The otter hunt.*

In all these ways Landseer epitomised the role of hunting in nineteenth-century culture, transforming the innocence and easy self-confidence of eighteenth-century sporting paintings into a deeply self-conscious and often troubled response to the natural world. Humans made contact with it in both creative and destructive ways, conscious of a whole range of historical, moral and allegorical overtones to their relationship with and exploitation of animals. He successfully conveyed the sensuality of killing and converted gore into an everyday sacramental experience. Yet his many paintings of dead animals also seemed to express the Victorian desire to elevate and beautify death. Occasionally he sentimentalised it, as in *A random shot*, where a fawn desperately tries to suckle a dead hind killed by mistake. He also contrasted the sentimental world of the domestic animal with the violent terror of the wild. That contrast was, perhaps, an allegory of Victorian perceptions of 'Civilisation' and 'barbarism', and it was the hunter who moved between the two, bringing the values of the one to bear upon his activities in the other. That was an allegory implicit in many of the hunting works surveyed in this book. Yet Landseer was in the end overwhelmed by the vivid and violent images of his imagination. He took to drink and began to lose control of his reason. He was reduced to the demented drawing of animals, and his last painting, *The swannery invaded by eagles*, which Victoria disavowed, was a consummation of his obsession with violence, aggression, blood and death.

Landseer and his successors provided a visual stimulus for the keeping of game books and the growing passion for anatomical records. Game books began in their modern form in the mid-eighteenth century, and by the nineteenth all those participating in hunting and shooting were encouraged to keep one.[24] They were the sporting equivalent of the diaries and journals that were *de rigueur* for all intelligent travellers. Some game books were kept in the great hunting houses and lodges. They were primarily a record of visitors, numbers of guns, and the quantity of game shot on each day of the season. Others were kept by individuals and were more idiosyncratic. As in the best journals, there might be drawings, miniature water colours, records of natural history observation, comment on the weather and the particular conditions of the season, as well as a record of game encounters, near misses and game shot. Military and administrative officers serving overseas, professional hunters of higher social standing or superior education, and rich sporting travellers might all keep them.[25] The uppermost reaches of the imperial elite, colonial governors or Indian viceroys might have a particularly opulent, but largely statistical, version kept for them.[26] Visits to remote regions or to Indian princes would be recorded, with the records of game shot and of the achievements of each gun printed before binding.

There were two forms of record. One, used in pheasant, partridge, grouse or wildfowl shooting, was merely a record of kills. The great shots of the day, like Lord Walsingham and the Marquess of Ripon, or the notable shooting houses, vied for the highest number of kills of specific species in particular seasons.[27] The Indian princes and their guests were swept up into a similar competitive slaughter in the shooting of duck, snipe and other wildfowl on the lakes and tanks of the princely states. The other form of record was the careful measuring of anatomical dimensions, particularly the lengths of the great cats, or, above all, the size of horns. In stags (red deer) the numbers of points to the antlers was an indication of age. An animal with fewer than a particular number was not worthy of being shot and would be left alone by any self-regarding sportsman. All tried for a 'royal' with ten-point antlers, and hoped for the ultimate achievement in the 'imperial' or twelve-pointer. So far as the buffalo, antelope and deer of Africa and India were concerned, the horns could be measured in a number of ways – length on the curve, the distance between points, girth at thickest point, and other measurements appropriate to the species. With elephants the length of outstanding tusks might be recorded, but it was of course weight and therefore commercial value that was crucial.

Hunting books in the early nineteenth century claimed animals of record dimensions shot, but these were purely informal claims established largely by word of mouth among the as yet relatively small fraternity of hunters. By the end of the century such claims were, in effect, registered with the taxidermist and wildlife publisher Rowland Ward. Ward was not only the proprietor of the most successful taxidermy business of the age, with premises in Piccadilly, but was also a publisher, a writer on natural history subjects and a contributor to exhibitions and museum displays. He did much to stimulate the collecting mania and competitive cult by publishing a number of practical handbooks and books of records. In 1880 he issued the *Sportsman's Handbook to Practical Collecting ... Preserving of Trophies and Specimens*. It reached its tenth edition in 1911 and was reissued after the First World War in 1923. *Horn Measurements and Weights of the Great Game of the World, being a Record for the Use of Sportsmen and Naturalists* appeared in 1892 and was the forerunner of his celebrated *Records of Big Game*, which was first published in 1896. It was an extensive compendium which grew from 325 pages in its first edition to 532 in its seventh in 1914. The African and Asiatic sections wre published separately in 1935 and there were further editions in 1962, 1969, 1971 and 1973 (the fifteenth).

Most of those who subscribed to Ward's publications would have claimed to be natural historians and would have justified their collecting mania on those grounds. The study of natural history and the collecting of specimens had been seen as a worthy interest of the elite for some time, starting perhaps with the famous cabinets of curiosities of the seventeenth century. But in the second half of the nineteenth century the study of natural history changed dramatically in scope. The great debates about Darwinian evolution brought it to the forefront of intellectual discourse. The number of scientists concerned with natural history increased dramatically with the expansion of museum services, the appearance of a separate Natural History Museum in London and other European capitals, and the opening of new universities. At the same time natural history continued to increase its geographical range and its social penetration. On the one hand natural history became part of the imperial impulse; on the other it came to be propagated as an appropriate hobby for all social classes.

D. E. Allen has suggested that natural history 'is an area of cultural behaviour rather than a network of ideas'.[28] It should be set into an institutional and sociological framework, a 'social geography' of natural history knowledge.[29] This approach has, however, only begun to be developed among historians of science, and Allen's own work on British natural historians is purely domestic, thereby lacking the global and racial dimensions crucial to an understanding of the natural history of the late nineteenth century. The study of natural history in this period has surely to be placed in an imperial context. Imperial visions pervaded all cultural forms and most intellectual endeavour of the time. The emergence of natural history specialisms, the division and ordering of the scientific effort, reflected the accelerating urge to order the world of nature, which was itself both an impulse towards and a symptom of the developing yearning to order and classify human affairs through imperialism.

In fact taxonomies never entirely conceal the human social and cultural relationships that lie behind them. This can be readily illustrated in examining the connections between hunting, hunters and natural history displays in the late nineteenth and early twentieth centuries. Classification meant killing, and the collection of specimens for scholarly examination and public display involved killing on a large scale. The viewer of the resulting zoological exhibits, the large and small-scale participants in the collecting craze, and the scholarly users of the national specimen collections were all aware in one way or another of the justificatory ideas implicit in these activities, above all the curiosity, classificatory power and destructive capacity of the hunter in the service of a scientific knowledge which epitomised Western man's command of a global natural world. That command was, of course, 'race'-specific. It was the preserve of Europeans and Americans, and among Europeans it was, in Treitschke's words, only the 'virile nations' who had made themselves colonial powers. Thus, on a world-wide scale, assumptions about the hunter and identifier of species carried implicit representations of the humans among whom the animals lived. The classification of zoological exotica helped to define the ethnic exotica to which they were related. Private displays, like those of Gordon Cumming, Cotton Oswell and Powell Cotton, invariably combined the two.

Indeed the prime mover behind the creation of a separate Natural History Museum, Richard Owen, the celebrated anti-Darwinist, made the connections between zoology and empire explicit. In his address to the British Association for the Advancement of Science in 1858 he argued that British collections should be 'worthy of this great Empire':

> Our colonies include parts of the earth where the forms of plants and animals are the most strange. No empire in the world had ever so wide a range for the collection of the various forms of animal life as Great Britain. Never was there so much energy and intelligence displayed in the capture and tranmission of exotic animals by the enterprising travel- ler in unknown lands and by the hardy settler in remote colonies, as by those who start from their native shores of Britain.[30]

Hunters made the connections between empire and natural history even more explicit. Denis Lyell suggested that the building of the British Empire had been largely due to a love of travel and adventure, 'for in most cases the traveller has been drawn to a country because it is the home of wild game',[31] while for Hugh Gunn 'the spirit of the chase has been equally responsible for the adventures and enterprises that have led . . . to the exploration and settlement of unknown and pagan lands'.[32] These views, however exaggerated, were repeated in much popular literature.

Richard Owen's great rival, J. E. Gray, advocated the separation of study and display areas in museums, the latter providing for the 'diffu- sion of instruction and rational amusement among the mass of the people'. It is characteristic of the second half of the nineteenth century that these very Victorian twin ideals of 'instruction' and 'rational amusement' took off in natural history studies.[33] It was asserted before the 1860 Select Committeee on the British Museum that both the middle and working classes were making natural history collections and were consulting the Britsh Museum on classification.[34] Even if the image of the working class spending its holidays collecting insects is a little far-fetched, there is considerable evidence of a developing natural history craze in the period. It seems to have become an import- ant part of the downward percolation of elite values and ideals which was such a characteristic of the time.

In the development of both the study and display areas of the natural history museums the scientists and museum curators were dependent upon imperial hunters. Many of the most famous hunters of the day collected for them, and the museums, through boards of trustees, tended to fall into the hands of the hunting elite. Prince Albert asked Richard Owen to teach natural history to the royal family. The Prince Consort had already led the way in the conversion of sheep runs in Scotland to deer forest, while one of Owen's pupils, the Prince of Wales, the future Edward VII, was to convert large tracts of Norfolk farmland into pheasant coverts.[35] The Prince of Wales became a trustee of the British Museum (Natural History) after its move to South Kensington in 1881 and frequently made private visits to its exhibits. Lord Walsingham, who coveted the title of the greatest shot of his day and brought down countless thousands of carefully reared birds to prove it, was another trustee.[36] These were but two of the most notable hunters of the day who had a powerful influence upon the study of natural history.

The great hunters and collectors like F. C. Selous, C. H. Stigand, Denis Lyell and Richard Meinertzhagen gained an *entrée* both into the aristocratic elite and into the scientific circles of natural history museums through their hunting prowess. Selous indeed secured a place of honour in an imposing monument on the stairs leading from the great hall of the South Kensington museum. Another group who fed specimens, ideas and a particular ethos into the natural history establishment were colonial governors. A large number of the early African governors based their political power, in effect, on their hunting abilities. They were swept up into the imperial enterprise because they happened to be in the right place at the right time, often on hunting or natural history expeditions. This was true of Sir Frederick Lugard, Sir Alfred Sharpe, Sir Robert Coryndon, Sir Frederick Jackson and Sir Geoffrey Archer, among others. Sir Harry Johnston, one of the main instigators of the scramble for Africa on the ground, considered himself a naturalist above all else. His most important works – the same was true of Sir Frederick Jackson – were in the field of zoology and ornithology.[37] All these imperial administrators also contributed to the literature of 'sport', the very word synonymous with hunting in the period.

Moreover, natural history offered explorers, hunters and governors a route to immortality quite apart from their historical roles. The discovery and naming of a species, usually after themselves, was one of the great prizes of the period. This activity was greatly facilitated by the introduction of trinomials into natural history classification and the extensive, indeed excessive, elaboration of sub-species. These were often no more than regional variants, but the repeated subdivision of the classificatory systems perfectly represented the passion for refined codification that was one of the marks of the age. Explorers like Joseph Thomson and Harry Johnston could have important species named after them. So did Cotton Oswell, Livingstone's companion, and his distant relative, Powell Cotton. Sir Alfred Sharpe gave his name to a duiker. The railway engineer and hunter H. S. Varian had two small antelopes named after him. E. S. Grogan contrived to name a new variant after his girlfriend. Richard Meinertzhagen discovered a hitherto unknown forest pig in Kenya. These examples could be multiplied many times.

This proliferation of species dramatically accelerated the process of collecting. The Natural History Museum in South Kensington, the Smithsonian Institution in Washington and a host of other museums and private collections employed hunters to supply examples of every conceivable species and sub-species. Zoos were beginning to build up live stocks, and prominent figures in the Scramble for Africa, following long-established Indian practice turned small zoological collections into symbols of successful dominance. Rhodes kept one at Groote Schuur in Cape Town, while also building up the specimen collection of the Cape Town Museum.[38] So did Sir Harry Johnston in the grounds of his residence at Zomba in the British Central African Protectorate (Malawi). All this activity could actually place species at risk, just as the contemporary passion for the collection of birds' eggs and butterflies seriously reduced the numbers of some rarities. F. C. Selous perfectly combined a range of hunting activities. He was a commercial hunter who turned to specimen collecting for museums in the 1880s, built up a large personal collection at his house in Worplesden, and acted as adviser to many other hunters and collectors, ranging from Theodore Roosevelt to Lionel Rothschild. The cavalier approach to endangered species is perfectly represented by the hunter and administrator Robert Coryndon, who shot what were then thought to be the last two white rhinoceros in Mashonaland in 1893.[39] They were carefully mounted and sold, one to the Rothschild collection at Tring, at a suitably inflated price for its rarity value, the other to Cape Town.

The passion for classification, the same combination of science and showmanship, and a mixture of professional and amateur, elite and popular, interests were also applied to the human world. Indeed, it was the scientific and classsificatory urges that helped to identify 'advanced' peoples. This emerges in a section on 'primitive mentality' in the British Museum *Handbook to the Ethnographic Collections* of

1910:

> The mind of primitive man is wayward, and seldom capable of continuous attention. His thoughts are not quickly collected, so that he is bewildered in an emergency; and he is so much the creature of habit that unfamiliar influences such as those which white men introduce into his country disturb his mental balance. His powers of discrimination and analysis are undeveloped, so that distinctions which to us are fundamental need not be obvious to him. Thus he does not distinguish between similarity and identity, betweeen names and things, between the events which occur in dreams and real events, between the sequence of ideas in his mind and of things in the outer world to which they correspond. His ideas are grouped by chance impressions, and his conclusions often based on superficial analogies which have no weight with us.[40]

The phraseology – 'discrimination and analysis', 'similarity and identity', 'chance impressions' and 'superficial analogies' – the lack of correspondence between 'ideas' and 'things in the outer world' clearly contrast the 'primitive mind' with the supposedly ordered, classificatory urges of the European scientific one. Turning to hunting, the handbook noted the connections between the chase and the development of weapons and tools, described its importance in the diet, social relations, dress and ornamentation of traditional economies, and also observed that great hunting skills could be combined with extreme primitiveness in culture.[41] These were the skills that the white hunter could bend to his more elevated scientific ends, offering meat as a by-product, an act of patronage, rather than as the prime objective of the hunt.

This concern with science and public display, study and mass re-creation, which were the mark of civilised society, filtered downwards from the great national institutions. As we have seen, the Natural History Museum, resplendent in its Alfred Waterhouse terracotta plumage, was opened in 1881, a critical date in the development of the new imperialism. It was also an important time in the development of civic institutions. The establishing of museums was an important part of local pride in cities and towns throughout the land. In late Victorian and Edwardian times they proliferated in a manner only matched by the post-industrial enthusiasm for museums apparent in recent years. They were dedicated everywhere to the Victorian concern for study and rational recreation, and inevitably they reflected contemporary tastes and interests. Few were without galleries of stuffed animals, a dead zoo designed to bring the Natural History Museum in miniature to every city and town. As a result of the existence of so much private, civic and national patronage taxidermy was a highly visible trade.

[ 40 ]

Many high streets throughout the country boasted a taxidermist, while the two great London firms of Rowland Ward and Edward Gerrard of Camden Town vied for the trade of the aristocrat, professional hunter, imperial soldier and administrator. In the census of 1891 there were no fewer than 369 people (247 male and 122 female) employed as animal and bird preservers in the establishments of taxidermists in London. Elsewhere there were more than 500 similarly employed. Interestingly they were listed in the category of occupations described as 'house decorations'.

The connection between the multifarous natural history collections in private houses throughout the country and the great 'Temple of Nature' in South Kensington was perfectly expressed by H. G. Wells in *Tono Bungay*: '"By Jove," said I, "but this is the little assemblage of cases of stuffed birds and animals upon the Bladesover staircase grown enormous . . ."'[42] The relationship between hunting, natural history, the gratification of trophy collecting and the yearning for public instruction were still coming together as late as the 1930s in the Westmorland town of Kendal. A local landowner, Colonel Edgar Harrison, had amassed a large collection of trophies, heads and skins from foreign campaigns and hunting trips. Many had been stuffed and mounted by Ward's of Piccadilly, Gerrard's of Camden Town, P. Spicer of Leamington Spa and a local firm, H. Murray of Carnforth. The whole collection, together with the money to build a large extension to house it, was given to the Kendal Museum and opened in 1939.[43] It remains the larger part of that museum to this day, where it is displayed together with information on his firearms, the taxidermists he used, and his examples of bullets distorted by impact with various parts of his quarry's anatomy. Nothing better illustrates the development of twentieth-century ideas about the natural world than the contrast between this and another important display in the museum. It is a survey of the natural history of the Lake District. It contains a prominently displayed sign which informs visitors that all the exhibited animals died of natural causes. It is a bewildering juxtaposition, lacking chronological or social explanation, yet it encapsulates the connections between the study of natural history and the dominant social ideas of the age, the hunting ethos in the one and the conservationist, anti-blood sports in the other.

It also illustrates a transformation in moral perceptions. The popularisation of natural history in the nineteenth century was intended for specific moral ends, and killing for character formation, study, collecting and display was part of that moral purpose. Charles

Kingsley was but one among many influential figures who argued for the value of natural history and urged its acceptance in the education and training of the young.[44] After the 1870 Education Act natural history became a compulsory school subject, and schools made collections of specimens. Youthful collecting, usually on the manageable scale of insects, butterflies, and birds' eggs, was encouraged and the memoirs and biographies of the period are redolent of such experiences. The ease with which hunters might graduate to larger specimens can be readily understood.

Kingsley believed that moral conviction was served by the promotion of courage and health through physical strength. The study of natural history served these ends by taking boys and men into nature: uncovering the infinite complexities of creation revealed to its practitioners the divine pattern of the moral as well as the physical universe. But it was also a study which reflected the semi-divine role of man revealed in Genesis 1:28 when God commanded Adam and Eve to 'have dominion over the fish of the sea, and over the fowls of the air, and over every living thing that moveth upon this earth'. The complex of ideas embodied in Kingsley's Muscular Christianity was used to promote and justify the collection and study of specimens by the young, a pursuit impossible without hunting and killing. The more articulate among adult imperial hunters also used the study of natural history to justify their activities, but among them Darwin invariably exercised a powerful influence. They saw sexual selection everywhere in nature and often regarded themselves as intervening to promote the emergence of the fittest. By killing the older dominant males (bearing their finest trophies) they offered reproductive opportunities to younger, more vigorous animals. The evolutionary theorising of the hunters will be examined in subsequent chapters.

Connections, some explicit some implicit, can also be made with human sexuality. Trophies were themselves sexual emblems, representing the war of males for sexual conquest. The more immediate phallic symbolism of horns and antlers was not lost on contemporaries. In searching for the largest and best proportioned the hunter was studying and appropriating eugenic processes. The Hunt itself was occasionally recognised as a pseudo-sexual act. Hunting works are full of descriptions of the physical agonies of the Hunt, of 'the exaltation no civilised world can supply', the tensions induced by great risk, and the ecstasy of release when the hunter prevails and stands over his kill.[45] Some of this can readily be interpreted as sexual sublimation, while the sexual analogue of the gradual building up of the chase and the orgasmic character of the kill had long been recognised in writings about and pictorial representations of the Hunt.[46] Hunting released primeval urges. For Theodore Roosevelt it created a link with man's distant past, with 'matters primitive and elemental'.[47] Yet the courage and vigour required in its pursuit created the physical qualities that made the hunter an appropriate human procreator in the present. Many hunters implied this, and it lay behind the hero-worship of the physical attributes of a great hunter like Selous. Such men became emblems of the ideal male, human counterparts of the animal versions celebrated in the record books of Rowland Ward. It is ironic that trophy hunting, like all forms of collecting, may well have been an emotional substitute. There is an ambiguity in all these sexual and emotional connections betweeen the sublimation and the actuality.

Hunting indeed seems rich in such ambiguities, primitive and elemental on the one hand, morally uplifting on the other, a source of both physical training and scientific understanding, character formation and mental instruction. Charles Kingsley and others like him would have recognised no such ambiguity, for he emphasised the connections between physical passions and divine love, between bodily exertions and moral purpose, between domination of nature, following Genesis, and an understanding of creation through scientific study. Nor would the hunting elite have found anything odd about the other apparent paradoxes of the hunting code; preserve to be killed, kill to conserve.

If showmanship inspired interest and excitement, if museums developed scientific observation as a rational recreation, then literature, contemporary iconography and juvenile training were designed to transmit the moral superstructure of the hunting and natural history ethos to the masses, above all the young. Tales and images of hunting represented adventure, travel, excitement. They offered yarns with a moral purpose, and they presented a rural – and, in many cases, essentially frontier – ideal, much favoured by the elite, to a mainly urban, industrialised society.

The late Victorian elite was remarkably successful in establishing itself as a model for other social classes.[48] The ideas and methods of the recently reformed public schools were held up for emulation in the State system after 1870. The Volunteer Movement, the new youth organisations, and the most successful political organisatioon of the day, the Primrose League, all played a part in the downward filtration effect.[49] Above all, juvenile literature and popular fiction portrayed public school-educated heroes as pursuing national duties, character-forming interests and 'manly' sports appropriate for all. G. A. Henty, the most successful children's writer of the period, and other authors of juvenile fiction produced a succession of heroes who were educated at public schools or service colleges, who valued intellectual and cultural attainment far less than sporting prowess, who exhibited a blind loyalty, faith in leadership, and an ambition to put duty before personal survival.

Willingness to take life was an important part of this ethos, and hunting was seen as a necessary preparation and training for Europen expansion and conflict with other peoples. Henty dictated his books to an amanuensis in a study filled with guns, spears, skins and other animal trophies, constant reminders of adventure.[50] For him, hunting lay at the centre of the imperial experience, and he had a horror of lads who shrank from shedding blood.[51] 'Natives,' he wrote, were 'uninterested in learning or intelligence: it was pluck and fighting power' that impressed them.[52] Moreover sportsmen could speedily diminish the numbers of wild beasts that were the scourge of cultivators. The attributes of the hunter, therefore, were crucial both in establishing mastery of the environment and in creating patterns of patronage. It comes as no surprise to find that Henty had a considerable natural history collection and that Gordon Stables, another popular boys' writer, collected natural history specimens all his life.

Henty and the other juvenile writers were merely developing a traditional theme, adapting frontier images to imperial purposes. The works of the American Fenimore Cooper illustrate this tradition of pioneering and adventure. They date from the 1820s and '30s and were invariably set in the eighteenth century, but at the end of the nineteenth they entered a new period of immense popularity. Cheap editions of Fenimore Cooper from a variety of publishers became a favourite staple of the prize and present market. Cooper's description of young Deerslayer, dressed in his deerskins, was the image all hunters liked to convey: he stood six feet tall in his moccasins, his frame 'comparatively light and slender; showing muscles, however, that promised unusual agility, if not unusual strength'.[53] His facial expression was that of 'guileless truth, sustained by an earnestness of purpose, and a sincerity of feeling, that rendered it remarkable'. The code of the hunting gentlemen was there too. When Deerslayer's companion offers him some venison, the manly young hunter responds 'Nay, nay, Hurry, there's little manhood in killing a doe, and that, too, out of season.' An illustrated Collins edition which enjoyed large sales early this century had colour pictures not only of Red Indian foes but also of stags attempting to escape the hunters' bullets. At the end of Cooper's *The Pioneers* the old hunter stands on the verge of the wood, the symbolic edge of civilisation, before disappearing for ever. 'He had gone far towards the setting sun – the foremost in that band of Pioneers who are opening the way for the march of the nation across the continent.'[54]

Youth and age, guileless, noble, self-reliant, killing to survive and to spread civilisation, illustrating at every turn the mastery that was wrought by technical advance, environmental knowledge and moral worth; these were the images conveyed by a host of works written for children in the late nineteenth century.[55] W. H. G. Kingston, himself a propagandist for emigration and settlement in the empire, pioneered this taste for the British market.[56] His works included *Peter the Whaler, Hendricks the Hunter, In the Wilds of Africa* and *In the Wilds of Florida*. R. M. Ballantyne, who had spent his early career as a clerk and factor in the Hudson's Bay Company, incorporated hunting into almost all his works.[57] Many of his titles were explicit: *The Gorilla Hunters, The Walrus Hunters, The Buffalo Runners, Hunting the Lion*. Captain Mayne Reid, another of the classic boys' writers from the third quarter of the nineteenth century, was equally obsessed with hunting. *The Boy Hunters, The Young Voyageurs, The Young Yagers, Bruin or the Grand Bear Hunt, The Giraffe Hunters* and *The Wild Horse Hunters* are but a selection from his hunting titles. Contemporary obsessions with all forms of natural history were reflected in his *The Plant Hunters*. In the later period H. Rider Haggard's books, a popular staple until at least the 1950s, are full of hunting. His principal characters are based on famous hunters of the day: Allan Quatermain on F. C. Selous and Captain Good on Sir Frederick Jackson.[58] Haggard's brother was a vice-consul in East Africa, and Jackson – a family friend and Norfolk neighbour who went to Africa as a hunter, was employed by the Imperial British East Africa Company and later became Governor of Uganda – fed Haggard with hunting incidents for inclusion in his novels.

The historian of the cult of athleticism in the English public school tells us that school magazines abounded in stories of big-game hunting in which the courage and hunting abilities of old boys were held up as role models for the current generation.[59] In their rural localities public school boys were celebrated for their hunting and poaching activities, in which they were sometimes encouraged by their masters. William Cotton Oswell was nearly expelled from Rugby for such an exploit, and it was common for them to have a feud with the local game-keepers.[60] In these ways the public schools offered an 'antidote to effeminacy'.[61] One hunter in Africa, Denis Lyell, suggested more than once that every boy's prime excitement in adolescence consisted of bagging his first blackbird with a catapult or taking potshots with a shotgun at local cats, imagining they were lions or tigers. 'In later years,' he and his collaborator, C. H. Stigand, wrote, 'we have experienced the same feelings in securing a good kudu or pair of tusks as we did in knocking over our first blackbird with a catapult or bagging our neighbour's cherished cat with our new rook rifle.'[62] For Lyell this was typical boy's behaviour of the time:

> The first thing a boy does when he gets home for his holidays is to rush off to his own den to see if his fishing-rod, gun, butterflies or stuffed birds are all right; then he goes off to the kennel to see his spaniel and ferrets. His first question will be whether there are lots of rabbits and trout about, and whether any rats have come back to the hayloft since he left home. That boy in his spare time will pore over books of sport and travel, and it will be his dearest wish to visit the countries he has read so much about, when he is a man. At nights his dreams will be about shooting elephants and lions, or getting to a country where no white man has been.[63]

It was very much the image of the upper middle-class public school boy, but journals, books and schools attempted the downward percolation of these values. In South Africa Lyell noted with approval that Boer children fought each other for the right to kill fowls.

According to E. S. Grogan (celebrated for walking the length of Africa and subsequently as a Kenyan settler) it was 'the norm of adventurous life which was the general ambition of Victorian youth'.[64] The use of books of heroes as material for moral emulation was designed to the same end. Boys should be given 'manly' rather than 'refined' books, which should help to create 'manly boys, uttering manly thoughts, and performing manly actions'.[65] Pioneering and hunting activities, supremely manly actions, constituted a training for war and were 'the antipodes of an effeminate sentimentalism'.[66] Popular anthologies of hunting stories carried these ideas to a wider audience. The coloured frontispieces of *Pictorial Sport and Adventure*, just such an anthology, are a tigress on one page and Landseer's African lion on the other.[67] *The Romance of Modern Pathfinders*, published in the early 1930s, was filled with accounts of hunting, from Africa to Kamchatka, Baffin Land to the Amazon.[68]

Even greater currency was provided for this tradition by the boys' journals which struck a winning formula after the founding of the *Boy's Own Paper* in 1879. Patrick Dunae, who has closely studied juvenile periodicals, notes their obsession with hunting, continuing the Ballantyne tradition, which never spared any gory detail.[69] The moral and 'sporting' code of hunting was repeatedly laid out for junior edification. Detailed descriptions of taxidermy were offered just as the natural history craze was reaching schools and local museums everywhere. Such hunting material offered a bloody substitute for the penny dreadfuls, which one hunter described as 'manlier stuff' than the melodrama of the twentieth-century cinema.[70] Jacqueline Bratton has also identified hunting as a central theme of the juvenile literature of the time.[71] Kipling's heroes, she notes, 'define themselves by birth, by the profession of arms, by the practice of certain sports and games, notably hunting, and by adherence to a set of rules of personal behaviour which can loosely be designated chivalric.' The hunting code readily fitted these chivalric notions, and the fascination with the Middle Ages also tended to stimulate hunting images. The covers of juvenile journals were frequently adorned with 'pictures of big game in furious conflict with white hunters', while 'St George slaying the dragon' was 'associated with the aristo-military pastime of hunting, much used for pictorial and fictional excitement in boys' magazines'.[72]

The iconography of St George was indeed ubiquitous in the period, and often represented a conscious link with the hunting tradition. Many a literary Nimrod summoned up St George as his exemplar. St George slaying the dragon was the ultimate Hunt, the victory of good over evil, the epitome of saint-like courage against an abnormally fearsome foe. Hunters set about appropriating not only his military and equestrian heroism, together with his moral and physical courage, but also the sexually protective, chivalric overtones. By analogy, big-game hunting represented the striving and victory of civilised man over the darker primeval and untamed forces still at work in the world. The lion was the second icon of that struggle. It lies at the centre of hunting books, the most fearsome foe, a dragon substitute, a source of awe and fascination to most African hunters. All were proudest of their careful tally of lion kills. They had contributed to the successful annexation of the 'king of beasts' as a national and imperial symbol. The lion was everywhere in pioneering and hunting images, in a whole variety of moods, the epitome of empire itself. It was as though the virile imperialist and the lion − in India the tiger − were locked in deadly combat for control of the natural world.

Though Landseer's lions, often reproduced in juvenile literature, retained their hold on the late Victorian imagination, as did most of his other animal pictures, many of the animal artists of the later period turned to a realistic yet idealised representation of nature. Painters like John G. Millais (son of Sir John Everett), Charles Whymper and Archibald Thorburn (whose father, Robert Thorburn, had been a personal painter to the Queen) contributed to the classification of species by their minutely detailed attention to every physical characteristic of their subjects.[73] Millais visited Africa, painted African wildlife, was himself a hunter and wrote a biography of Frederick Selous.[74] Thorburn gave up hunting after hearing the squeal of a hare he had wounded, but he still painted deer and game birds for hunting patrons. He remained enraptured by the savage mystery of the sport, by the hunter's desire to do more than admire beauty, to possess it in death. As one student of Thorburn's work put it, the cock pheasant, the ptarmigan and the mighty capercailzie deserved their 'kingly place' only by being 'cursed with all the danger and adventure of high office; to earn the finery of its plumage and the splendour of its deportment, it must have a great terror in its life. It must be struck down, sacrificed.'[75]

All these painters were given wider currency through engravings. The vast late Victorian literature of natural history and sport was filled with illustrations, some of the 'classificatory' type, but many showing humans in conjunction with animals, so that the moral of human dominance and danger through discovery and understanding could be drawn. Well authenticated events, like the attack upon David Livingstone by a lion, were repeatedly illustrated to demonstrate the heroism of the missionary–explorer. As we have seen, juvenile literature, journals and 'annuals' were filled with such material. It is perhaps not surprising, given this pervasive cultural influence, that the study and representation of natural history should have been transformed into a whole system of youth training in the early twentieth century.

In this R. S. S. Baden-Powell holds the premier position. He perfectly brings together the fascination with natural history and the sketching tradition with military and hunting exploits on the imperial frontier. He contributed, at least for a period, to the strict separation of sexual roles that the frontier tradition promoted. In *Scouting for Boys* he set about transforming frontier ideals into a complete system of juvenile training for an industrial society. His injunction that 'every boy ought to learn how to shoot and to obey orders, else he is no more good when war breaks out than an old woman' in the first camp-fire yarn of the 1908 edition of *Scouting* epitomises concepts of manliness derived from that frontier.[75] B.-P.'s ideas on the training of boys emerged from Lord Edward Cecil's boy-scout troop formed in Mafeking during the siege of 1899-1900. Drawing upon that experience, he believed that discipline and character formation for the young should take precise forms: obeying orders from elders and superiors, training in firearms, acceptance of violence as part of the natural order, preparation for war and a strict separation of sexual roles.

He distinguished between war and peace scouts, and derived almost all his examples of the latter from the colonial frontier. He defined them as 'men who in peacetime carry out work which requires the same type of abilities' as in war:

> These are frontiersmen of all parts of our Empire. The 'trappers' of North America, hunters of Central Africa, the British pioneers, explorers, and missionaries over Asia and all the wild parts of the world, the bushmen and drovers of Australia, the constabulary of North West Canada and of South Africa – all are peace scouts, real *men* in every sense of the word, and thoroughly up in scout craft, i.e. they understand living out in the jungles, and they can find their way anywhere, are able to read meaning from the smallest signs and foot tracks; they know how to look after their health when far away from doctors, are strong and plucky, and ready to face any danger, and always keen to help each other. They are accustomed to take their lives in their hands, and to fling them down without hesitation if they can help their country by doing so.[77]

They give up their personal comforts and desires, he went on, because it is their duty to their King, and the history of the empire has been made by such men. Pioneering attributes appear on many other pages of *Scouting for Boys*. The men who come from the farthest frontiers of the empire, wrote B.-P., are 'the most generous and chivalrous of their race'. Their moral worth was acquired through their 'contact with Nature'. They cultivate 'truth, independence, and self-reliance'. Boxing, wrestling and Japanese martial arts were recommended to Scouts in pursuit of these virtues, as was, above all, the importance of marksmanship: 'The Colonial boys consider marksmanship the most important thing to practise, because it is for their country. They put cricket and football second, because these are for their own amusement.'[78]

*Scouting for Boys* became one of the twentieth century's best-sellers, and several generations were initiated into frontier lore through secret signs, animal names and calls, woodcraft, stalking and spooring. The current edition (1981) contains the paragraph on frontiersmen quoted above almost in its entirety, with a few geographical adjustments and with all mention of the empire excised. The passage is now accompanied by a drawing of 'frontiersmen' that modern boys would immediately associate with the 'wild west'. This indeed aptly represents the transformation wrought in the image of the frontier by popular culture, primarily the cinema, in the twentieth century.

Britain's imperial frontier was not a continental one, like the American, but a highly dispersed phenomenon in different continents and highly varied environments. B.-P.'s own experience had been mainly in India and southern Africa, but he was at pains to include examples from North America, Australasia and other parts of the empire. Yet a composite image was established in which different conditions contributed to a set of characteristics which he wished to inculcate. There was indeed a close interaction between British and American concepts of the frontier, and no one created the bridge betweeen them more effectively than Theodore Roosevelt. Rancher, soldier, big-game hunter, as well as President, Roosevelt seemed to typify the frontier spirit and was an untiring propagandist for it. B.-P. referred to his example and his works with approval. For Roosevelt the pioneer and cowboy 'possesses, in fact, few of the emasculated, milk-and-water moralities of the pseudo-philanthropist; but he does possess, to a very high degree, the stern, manly qualities that are invaluable to a nation'.[79] Above all, the pioneer is a hunter, and the hunter is 'the archetype of freedom'. He is self-sufficient not just in food but if need be in clothing and deerskins for his bunk. Roosevelt was an anglophile whose admiration for the British Empire is apparent in a number of his works. His closest contacts were with British big-game hunters, for whose works he supplied an apparently endless stream of introductions, and he liked to compare himself as a naturalist with them.[80]

There was, however, another paradox in B.-P.'s admiration of hunting as the essence of the pioneering spirit, as exemplified by 'peace scouts' and Roosevelt. Hunting developed self-reliance, yet B.-P. wished to bend these qualities to group loyalties, to the supreme expression of the State in imperial rule. Most of the imperial hunters whose works will be examined in subsequent chapters depicted themselves as serving both ideals. But B.-P. also wanted to make hunting a source of fun and adventure, the sugar on the pill of imperial defence.

> All the fun of hunting lies in the adventurous life in the jungle, the chance in many cases of the animal hunting *you* instead of you hunting the animal, the interest of tracking him up, stalking him and watching all that he does and learning his habits. The actual shooting the animal that follows is only a very small part of the fun.[81]

Thus B.-P. and Roosevelt seemed to imply that hunting represented the most perfect expression of global dominance in the late nineteenth century. Hunting required all the most virile attributes of the imperial male – courage, endurance, individualism (adaptable to national ends), sportsmanship (combining the moral etiquette of the sportsman with horsemanship and marksmanship), resourcefulness, a mastery of environmental signs, and a knowledge of natural history. It was indeed that scientific dimension, the acquisition of zoological, botanical, metereological and ballistical knowledge, and the associated ordering and classifying of natural phenomena which helped to give hunting its supreme acceptability among late Victorians.

## Notes

1 Keith Thomas, *Man and the Natural World: Changing Attitudes in England, 1500-1800*, London, 1983, pp. 15, 300-3, 149.
2 Thomas, *Natural World*, p. 243.
3 Peter Bailey, *Leisure and Class in Victorian England: Rational Recreation and the Contest for Control, 1830-85*, London, 1978, Thomas, *Natural World*, pp. 149, 158-60.
4 David C. Itzkowitz, *Peculiar Privilege*, Hassocks, 1977, pp. 142-5.
5 Little work has been done on diet and sexual separation. See chapter 11 and Julia Twigg, 'Vegetarianism and the meaning of meat', in Anne Murcott (ed.), *The Sociology of Food and Eating*, London, 1983, pp. 18-30, and Thomas, *Natural World*, pp. 288-91.
6 Clive Aslet, *The Last Country Houses*, London, 1982.
7 I am grateful to Clive Aslet for discussion of the use of horns in interior decoration.
8 Roualeyn Gordon Cumming, *Five Years of a Hunter's Life in the Far Interior of South Africa*, 2 vols., London, 1850, Vol. 1, p. vii.
9 Cumming, *Hunter's Life*, Vol. 1, p. 215.
10 Blair Archives. See the Blair Castle guide book. I am grateful to Mrs Jane Anderson of the Blair Castle archive for further information.
11 Dunrobin Museum and the Dunrobin Castle guide book. A museum was built in the grounds of Dunrobin to house the duke's collections. See also the guide books of Glamis, Dunvegan and Brodick. Dunvegan contains the collections of Norman Magnus MacLeod, twenty-sixth chief (1839-1929), a big-game hunter who was given a record tusk weighing 116 lbs by the elephant hunter Arthur Neumann. Neumann dedicated his book on elephant hunting to MacLeod, who had given him hospitality at Dunvegan while he was writing it.
12 The Egerton hunting diaries are deposited in the County Records Office in Chester. Iris Hickman, information officer of Tatton Park, supplied information.
13 W. Edward Oswell, *William Cotton Oswell, Hunter and Explorer*, London, 1900, Vol. II, pp. 167, 233.
14 Peter Whitehead, *The British Museum (Natural History)*, London, 1981, pp. 16-17; William T. Stearn, *The Natural History Museum at South Kensington*, London, 1981.
15 J. G. Millais, *The Life of Frederick Courtenay Selous*, London, 1918 pp. 60, 205-6.
16 See the guide book to the Powell-Cotton Museum and Quex House, Quex Park, Birchington, Kent; also P. H. G. Powell-Cotton, *In Unknown Africa*, London, 1904, and *A Sporting Trip through Abyssinia*, London, 1902.
17 William G. Schneider, *An Empire for the Masses: the French Popular Image of Africa, 1870-1900*, Westport, Conn., 1982, pp. 128-39.
18 Rowland Ward, *Empire of India Exhibition: an Illustrated Guide to the Jungle*, London 1895; John M. MacKenzie, *Propaganda and Empire*, Manchester, 1984, pp., 102-6.
19 See the leaflet on taxidermy issued by the Glasgow Museums and Art Galleries Natural History Department; also Carl E. Akeley, *In Brightest Africa*, London, 1924.

**20** Richard Ormond, *Sir Edwin Landseer*, London, 1982, p. 12. Ormond's book was published for the Landseer exhibition at the Tate Gallery in 1982. The examples of Landseer's art analysed here appeared in that exhibition.

**21** Ormond, *Landseer*, p. 17. Landseer illustrations began to appear on decorative game cards: Harry Hopkins, *The Long Affray*, London, 1985, pp. 163, 216.

**22** Ian Barras Hill, *Landseer*, Aylesbury, 1973, p. 35.

**23** Hill, *Landseer*, p. 15.

**24** Hopkins, *Long Affray*, p. 163. Examples of such game books can stil be seen in many country houses.

**25** Several travelling and hunting accounts appeared in the exhibition on Scotland and India in the National Library of Scotland in 1986. Alex M. Cain, *The Cornchest for Scotland: Scots in India*, Edinburgh, 1986.

**26** The game book of the Earl of Minto is in the collection of the National Library of Scotland, that of the Marquess of Linlithgow at Hopetoun House, near Edinburgh.

**27** Jonathan Garner Ruffer, *The Big Shots: Edwardian Shooting Parties*, London, 1984.

**28** Quoted in James A. Secord, 'Natural history in depth', *Social Studies of Science*, 15 (1985), p. 184.

**29** David Elliston Allen, *The Naturalist in Britain: a Social History*, London, 1976.

**30** Stearn, *Natural History Museum*, p. 35.

**31** C. H. Stigand and D. D. Lyell, *Central African Game and its Spoor*, London, 1906, p. 2.

**32** Hugh Gunn, 'The sportsman as an empire builder', in Hugh Gunn and John Ross (eds.), *The Book of the Red Deer and Empire Big Game*, London, 1925. p. 138.

**33** Stearn, *Natural History Museum*, p. 37.

**34** Stearn, *Natural History Museum*, p. 42.

**35** Hopkins, *Long Affray*, Willie Orr, *Deer Forests, Landlords and Crofters*, Edinburgh, 1982.

**36** Stearn, *Natural History Museum*, pp. 79, 99-100.

**37** Sir Harry Johnston, *The Uganda Protectorate*, London, 1902, contains a great deal of zoological and ornithological material. Johnston was a principal contributor to the *Harmsworth Natural History*, of 1910. Sir Frederick Jackson, *The Birds of Kenya Colony and the Uganda Protectorate*, London, 1938 (completed and edited by W. L. Sclater).

**38** The Indian princes had traditionally kept menageries and the Governor General continued the custom at the Calcutta country residence at Barrackpur. Marcus Daly collected animals for Rhodes. Daly, *Big Game Hunting and Adventure*, London 1937, p. 1.

**39** H. Marshall Hole, *Old Rhodesian Days*, London, 1928, p. 83.

**40** British Museum, *Handbook to the Ethnographic Collections*, London, 1910, p. 31.

**41** B. M. *Handbook*, p. 109.

**42** Leonore Davidoff, *The Best Circles*, London, 1973, p. 31.

**43** I am grateful to Phillip Dalziel for information on Colonel Harrison.

**44** Norman Vance, *The Sinews of the Spirit*, Cambridge, 1985; Allen, *Naturalist in Britain*, p. 180.

**45** Denis D. Lyell, *Memoirs of an African Hunter*, London, 1923, pp. 129-30; Stigand and Lyell, *Central African Game*, p. iv.

**46** Thomas, *Natural World*, p. 146.

**47** Theodore Roosevelt, *African Game Trails*, London, 1910, p. 3; Denis D. Lyell, *The African Elephant and its Hunters*, London, 1924, p. 97.

**48** MacKenzie, *Propaganda*.

**49** Hugh Cunningham, *The Volunteer Force*, London, 1975; John Springhall, *Youth, Empire, and Society*, London, 1977; Martin Pugh, *The Tories and the People*, Oxford, 1986.

**50** Patrick A. Dunae, 'British Juvenile Literature in an Age of Empire, 1880-1914', University of Manchesteer unpublished PhD thesis, 1975, p. 182.

**51** Dunae, 'British Juvenile Literature', p. 179.

**52** When Charlie Marryat was fitted out for India by his uncle, Joshua Tufton, he was given 'a brace of pistols, a rifle and a double-barrel shotgun', which he would find useful 'in the pursuit of game'. G. A. Henty, *With Clive in India*, London, n.d., p. 27.

53 J. Fenimore Cooper, *The Deerslayer*, London, n.d., pp. 8-9.
54 J. Fenimore Cooper, *The Pioneers*, London, n.d., p. 386.
This theme is explored further in John M. MacKenzie, 'Hunting and juvenile literature', in Jeffrey Richards (ed.), *Imperialism and Juvenile Literature*, Manchester, 1988.
56 J. S. Bratton, *The Impact of Victorian Children's Fiction*, London, 1981, pp. 115-33.
57 Eric Quayle, *R. M. Ballantyne: a Bibliography of First Editions*, London, 1968.
58 Sir Frederick Jackson, *Early Days in East Africa*, London, 1969 (first published 1930), pp. vi, 1, 124.
59 J. A. Mangan, *Athleticism in the Victorian and Edwardian Public School*, Cambridge, 1981, p. 137.
60 Oswell, *Oswell*, Vol. 1, p. 54.
61 Dunae, 'British Juvenile Literature', p. 475. The remark was made by Edmund Warre, headmaster of Eton, in 1898.
62 Stigand and Lyell, *Central African Game*, pp. 1, 4.
63 Lyell, *Memories*, p. 44.
64 Preface by Grogan to H. F. Varian, *Some African Milestones*, Oxford, 1953, p. vii.
65 Dunae, 'British Juvenile Literature', p. 39.
66 This phrase was used by Dr Hutchison to describe the stories and books of Talbot Baines Reed. Dunae, 'British Juvenile Literature', p. 294.
67 *Pictorial Sport and Adventure, being a Record of Deeds of Daring and Marvellous Escapes by Field and Flood*, London, n.d. (1890s?) A copy in the author's possession was given as a Sunday School prize in Shipley in 1900.
68 Norman J. Davidson, *The Romance of Modern Pathfinders*, London, n.d.
69 Dunae, 'British Juvenile Literature', pp. 157, 179, 182, 245, 327, 375-6.
70 Lyell, *Memories*, p. 14.
71 J. S. Bratton, 'Of England, home and duty', in John M. MacKenzie, *Imperialism and Popular Culture*, Manchester, 1986, p. 81.
72 Bratton, 'Of England', pp. 77, 90.
73 Anthony Vandervell and Charles Coles, *Game and the English Landscape*, London, 1980, pp. 68-9.
74 J. G. Millais, *A Breath from the Veld*, London, 1899.
75 *The Field*, 23 November 1985, pp. 64-7.
76 R. S. S. Baden-Powell, *Scouting for Boys*, London, 1908, p. 3.
77 Baden-Powell, *Scouting*, p. 5.
78 Baden-Powell, *Scouting*, p. 248.
79 Theodore Roosevelt, *Ranch Life and the hunting Trail*, Gloucester, 1985, (reprint of 1896 edition), pp. 56, 83.
80 Roosevelt wrote introductions to books by Selous and Stigand, among others.
81 Baden-Powell, *Scouting*, p. 90.

# CHAPTER THREE

# Hunting and African societies

Hunting was an important part of the pre-colonial economy and diet of many African peoples. The disappearance of game from some parts of the continent by the end of the nineteenth century, the imposition of game legislation, the attempt to separate human settlement from animal habitat and the reduction in the range of African occupations resulting from increasing agricultural specialisation and migrant labour all led to the decline of hunting as a significant sector of the African economy. Ethnographers, arriving several decades after the hunting mode had been largely eliminated (particularly in southern Africa), discounted its importance if they noticed it at all. More recently some anthropologists (notably Thayer Scudder and Stuart Marks working in Zambia) have noted the significance of both gathering and hunting among agriculturalists, but historians have generally studied African societies in terms of their principal mode of production. The coexistence of a range of productive processes, each important in the overall pattern of African subsistence, has been largely ignored.

Historians who have referred to hunting have tended to see it merely as a survival mechanism, a subsistence fall-back in times of great stress. The implication has always been that it was an inferior form of economic activity. Thus Leonard Thompson, writing of the disruption of the Sotho by the Nguni migrations and raids of the 1820s, described 'demoralised survivors' wandering around, 'contriving to live on game or veld plants', which, together with the emergence of cannibalism, served to illustrate 'the collapse of the social and moral order'.[1] William Beinart has suggested that in Pondoland hunting became particularly important in times of stress, providing 'a major source of meat in the 1820s and 1830s'.[2] Peter Delius, writing of the economy of the Pedi, has noted that the cattle losses they experienced in the 1820s 'presumably increased the importance of hunting, and by 1839 they lived "chiefly by the chase, on millet and on beans"'.[3] More contentiously, the historian of the Shona of Zimbabwe has asserted that hunting was taken up only in time of famine.[4]

No doubt hunting did become more important when other forms of subsistence failed. But this should not obscure the fact that it could be a significant source of meat and domestic commodities, as well as of trade goods, even in normal times. Beinart and Delius, reflecting a new sensitivity to the full range of African economic opportunities, both seem to accept this, the latter in particular recognising an ambiguity in the expected balance of Pedi activities: 'The gradual re-accumulation of cattle reduced this dependence on the hunt, but in accounts of the region in the 1860s, hunting is given equal prominence with agriculture and cattle-keeping as constituting the economic bases of local societies.' Delius sees the continuing importance of hunting as being related to the use of guns and to the significance of animal products, 'skins, horns, feathers and ivory', in Pedi trade, although he acknowledges that it is difficult to draw clear distinctions between hunting for trading purposes and its role in everyday subsistence.

It remains difficult, if not impossible, to establish which was the primary motive for the chase – meat, domestic items or trade goods. Perhaps this very combination of opportunity ensured the continuing popularity of hunting while animals were still available. Clearly, different priorities prevailed at various times, depending on the scale and social organisation of the particular hunt. The various products were redistributed or appropriated according to the status of the participants. The large-scale hunt was a vital arena of social and political relations. It was labour-intensive and, if successful, immediately productive in a manner which contrasted strikingly with the slower processes of herding or cultivation. It was the equivalent of the raid, although it was nature that was raided rather than fellow humans. Philip Bonner has argued, most suggestively, that the Swazi and Zulu aristocracies were able to control the size and reproduction of individual homesteads through, among other things, 'the organisation of "hunts" which provided for a more substantial proportion of subsistence than is normally ackowledged'.[5]

A survey of African hunting, however brief, needs to examine function, technique, the role of animal products in subsistence, crafts and trade, as well as the complex social relations associated with the chase. In pursuing this prospectus we need to avoid a number of pitfalls. One is an excessive concentration on the use of firearms, which has often obscured the great range of traditional techniques used by African societies in sub-Saharan Africa, some remaining in use into the twentieth century. Another is the obsession with trade which has marked much historical scholarship. Hunting involved not only the spectacular pursuit of large game but also the taking of rodents, rabbits and birds as a food source.

The evidence seems to indicate that most peoples in southern and eastern Africa hunted in one way or another, and function and technique were as varied as the animals pursued, snared or trapped. The functional categories would include defensive hunting to protect humans, stock or growing crops; hunting for export (mainly ivory, but also horns, hides and pelts), and hunting as a domestic resource, a supplier of meat, skins, ornaments and receptacles. Method can be divided into the social and the technical. The social incorporates auxiliary and opportunist hunting (inert, small-scale and individualist) and great communal hunts; while the technical includes weaponry, (from bows and arrows through spears to firearms), artefacts and structures (from snares and traps to pits).

There can be no doubt that wild animals constituted a great threat as well as a great opportunity. In some places the threat outweighed the opportunity: crops might be destroyed, inducing famine, or villages might be forced to move away from the haunts of dangerous animals. Herders had to protect their stock from carnivores and some who did not hunt for food were nonetheless forced into defensive hunting to rid themselves of lions or other predators. Cultivators used a variety of scaring techniques – drums, rattles, and so on – or defensive precautions like ditches, fences or pits around their crops. The agriculturalist might well move on to the offensive, in effect using the lure of his ripening crops to bring his quarry to him.

Various forms of auxiliary and opportunist hunting are described in the sources. Predators, mainly the big cats, might be scared off their prey, which could then be used for human consumption. As European hunters became a more familiar part of the landscape African hunters were often able to follow them and kill the animals that had been wounded. Individuals and small groups might well seize their chance when animals unexpectedly presented themselves, for the instruments of the hunt – assegais, spears, bows and arrows, axes, clubs – were invariably carried at all times, since they were useful for a variety of purposes. 'Inert' hunting involved the use of pitfalls in game trails, deadfall suspended spears or logs activated by trip wires, and a wide variety of traps and snares. These were designed to catch all forms of game, from elephant to guinea fowl, and would be inspected from time to time.

More active forms of hunting might be conducted on a very different scale. Individuals, children or small village groups might hunt with dogs, stalk or drive into nets animals of diverse sizes. But among many peoples large numbers might be gathered together periodically for a great communal hunt. Such a hunt would be declared and organised by the chief or headman, and the participants, often both sexes as well as children, would be carefully marshalled as beaters, drivers, hunters, and so on. Such a hunt might be used to drive animals towards pitfalls or nets. Sometimes fire was used to force animals out of game-rich bush.

Hunting had a much wider significance than simply the supply of protein or trade goods for export. It stimulated crafts and local trade in the manufacture of weapons, nets, snares and poisons. Animal products were in turn manufactured into clothing, ornamentation, receptacles, musical instruments and symbolic or magical items. Horns were used as signal clarions in both war and the hunt, while the smaller ones were turned into receptacles for gunpowder or gold dust. Some peoples believed that particular parts of certain animals' anatomies, when eaten, conveyed virtues like courage or had special curative powers. Others with totemic taboos forbade the consumption of specific animals by particular clans.

The social relations and ritualistic powers associated with hunting were complex. Hunting tales and ancestor figures who were great nimrods feature in the myths of origin and explanatory stories of many peoples. Kings, chiefs and headmen were frequently credited with special hunting significance, if only as the controllers of the hunt and keepers of its ritual. Among some peoples, particularly in the Central African regions that are now Zaire and northern Zambia, specialised hunting guilds existed, while specialist hunters were highly regarded in many societies. Expertise in the hunt was often one of the prime means to meritocratic advance. Kings and chiefs levied extensive tribute from the products of the hunt and often exercised sumptuary laws with regard to the wearing and symbolic use of animal products. The labour time of regiments and of people seasonally underemployed could be utilised for the hunt. In some places, particularly in Botswana, hunting grounds and pastoral lands might be territorially distinct, with a subordinate people exploiting and offering tribute from the former. It is also clear from many accounts, both of travellers and of anthropologists, that hunting was an important source of training, recreation and understanding of natural phenomena for many Africans.

An adequate survey of the economic, social and dietary significance of hunting to the pre-colonial economy in Africa would require a separate book. Given the space available, the approach must be selective. The social and economic significance of the ivory trade, as the most visible result of African hunting, has received most attention. It will receive proportionately less space in this study. This chapter is particularly concerned to offer some examples, derived from nineteenth-century travellers' accounts, a few anthropological studies, and some oral evidence of the relative importance of hunting among pastoral and agricultural peoples. Its purpose is to demonstrate that hunting was a sufficiently prominent pre-colonial activity for the European usurpation of and legal restrictions upon African hunting rights to have a significant effect on diet, economic and social relations, recreation, and the association with the natural world of many African peoples. At the risk of repetition it will be divided into three geographical areas; southern, central and eastern Africa.

*Southern Africa*. Nowhere do evolutionary categories and distinct modes of production break down more effectively than in southern Africa. Hunting and gathering peoples were widely dispersed throughout the sub-continent until the nineteenth century. Some remained independent groups, but many had adopted either a symbiotic relationship with or a client status towards other peoples. As they become economically interconnected, so too did they become genetically and linguistically intermingled. Both herders and cultivators often had hunting clients, and they exchanged the products of their different production processes, although that did not preclude the herders and cultivators from hunting themselves, sometimes using the skills of associated hunting groups.

It has become customary to refer to the peoples formerly known as 'Hottentots' and 'Bushmen' collectively as the Khoisan, since it has proved impossible to find a satisfactory physical, economic or cultural basis on which to separate them. While some linguistic distinctions can be drawn, the interaction between them over many centuries was so extensive that many of their cultural characteristics became shared. Although the Khoikhoi (Hottentots) distinguished between themselves and the San it may be that the latter term denoted a different social class rather than a distinct ethnic group. In support of this Richard Elphick has emphasised the fluidity of status and economic activity among them. The old notion that the Khoikhoi were herders and the San hunters has broken down. Herders became hunters and hunters herders according to changing human and natural fortunes. Moreover the herders always hunted.

The striking ambivalence about hunting is well conveyed by the attitudes of the Khoikhoi. On the one hand hunting had high prestige among them. Because Khoikhoi women tended the stock, male labour time was released for hunting, and since they rarely slaughtered their stock most meat supplies came from hunting. Chiefs preferred to dress in the skins of wild animals, like leopard, rather than cowhides or sheepskins. In some places at least chiefs levied tribute from the products of the chase. Yet those who were solely hunters (and gatherers, of course) were looked down on and the greatest misfortune that could befall a Khoikhoi stockholder was to lose his cattle or sheep and be forced back into a purely hunting and gathering subsistence.[6]

It seems clear from this that hunting had a high status when it was discretionary (or apparently so), communal in its mode of operation, and bearing an ideological and social superstructure. When it became simply a method of survival, pursued by individuals and small groups, it lost all prestige. This would probably be equally true of Bantu-speaking cultivators, and there is also an interesting parallel with European attitudes. Travellers in the nineteenth century noted the continuing hunting activities of the Khoikhoi. One source suggests that they referred to the great southern African herds of springbok as their 'sheep', indicating that they hunted them at will.[7] Some acquired guns and became professional hunters, providing a new respectability for individualist hunting. On the eastern Cape Andrew Steedman met a celebrated 'Hottentot' hunter of elephants called Skipper.[8] His horse had recently been killed under him by a rhino. He was a 'bold and successful' marksman, and large numbers of animals had fallen to his gun.

European observers in the nineteenth century made a clear distinction between 'Hottentot' and 'Bushman'. But, whether the hunters were clients of the Khoikhoi or independent, Europeans were always impressed by the range and effectiveness of their techniques. Their incomparable eye for tracking and their capacity to stalk their prey when it was sighted led to their being employed as ideal auxiliaries for European hunters. Steedman, who encountered 'Bushmen' in the north-eastern Cape in 1830 greatly admired their marksmanship and the efficiency of their poisons.[9] Several travellers noted that 'Bushmen' dressed themselves in ostrich skins and feathers in order to stalk ostriches and other game or alternatively carried a decoy, designed to look like an ostrich, in front of them.[10] In addition to the skilful use of bows and arrows they dug pits, particularly in the Kalahari. They sometimes secured a large quantity of game by poisoning waterholes, a technique which damaged neither the flesh nor the skins of the victims.[11]

'Bushmen' had long been accustomed to aiding others in their hunting, but with the arrival of threatening new settlers in the territory they also took to 'hunting' domestic stock – sheep, cattle and horses. As a result they became the object of the hunt themselves. Boer commandos had indeed been hunting them down since the late seventeenth century. Steedman encountered such a commando in 1830,[12] and Sir Arthur Cunynghame, the General Officer Commanding of the Cape Colony in the late 1870s, noted the same practice still occurring during his residence in the country. Bushmen, he wrote, are hunted like game: 'Last year a number of men and women were killed in an expedition sent out against them by the Boers under circumstances which appeared almost like a slaughter in cold blood.'[13]

As the 'Bushmen' – many of whom had formerly hunted in a land of plenty[14] – were increasingly marginalised they became more dependent on African or European exploiters of their hunting skills. By then Europeans had begun to appreciate their cave paintings as the greatest hunting art of the sub-continent. H. A. Bryden used it as evidence for the more extensive distribution of the great game of the region before the nineteenth century. As more and more cave paintings were found, particularly the great abundance of them on the granite formations north of the Limpopo, they offered evidence of the wider distribution of the 'Bushmen' and of their hunting arts until comparatively recent times.[15]

One survey has suggested that 30 per cent of Khoikhoi economic activity was devoted to hunting, possibly a larger amount of labour time than the 'Bushmen' gave to the hunting sector of their economy.[16] The same survey, using published ethnographic sources, suggests that hunting constitued only 0-10 per cent of the economic activity of Bantu-speaking peoples in southern Africa. These figures are, however, highly problematic. The principal ethnographic studies were conducted after hunting opportunities had seriously declined in the late nineteenth century. The reports of European travellers suggest that hunting was a much more important part of the economies of the Nguni and the Sotho than a figure of 10 per cent or under would indicate.

Hunting had long been an important activity among the southern Nguni. From the turn of the seventeenth and eighteenth century Dutch settlers had been buying ivory from them, indicating that they were capable of exploiting the elephant resources of the region by that time.[17] But hunting was probably even more significant in their domestic economy, supplying food, clothing and artefacts. They hunted in the expanses of unpopulated country between chieftaincies, a characteristic approach to 'hunting preserves' that occurs elsewhere in Africa. The missionary John Brownlee described the Xhosa as 'passionately fond' of the chase 'as an active and animating amusement'. They indulged in highly organised communal hunts for elephants, rhino, hippo, buffalo and lion. They drove antelope and other game to a narrow pass where 'long files of hunters stationed on either side' hurled showers of assegais at the animals as the herd rushed through. The Xhosa were prodigal of game but sparing of their cattle, and venison from the one and milk from the other constituted the main components of their diet.[18] To a certain extent hunting was conditioned by poor soil and uncertain rainfall, but it was also 'a preferred way of life'. They dressed themselves in the pelts of wild animals, and the chiefs and their families reserved to themselves the finest cat skins. Hunting also performed a ritualistic and purificatory role, for example at the end of mourning for a chief or headman.

In the 1820s large game animals were still to be seen in the eastern Cape, though rapidly declining in numbers, and European travellers observed great African hunts. Steedman described an elephant hunt which had taken place near Mount Coke in 1826.[19] Large numbers of men and dogs had participated, and the main weapons were assegais. The elephants were hamstrung and when immobilised were subjected to a shower of spears. As in most parts of Africa the chief took one

[ 61 ]

tusk of each animal and also received the tuft of hair on the tail which was later suspended from his cattle kraal. That event was already becoming rare so close to the Colony. Most ivory came from the interior, where Africans were stepping up supplies to feed the voracious demand of the coast. In the 1820s hippos were still encountered in a few rivers of the eastern Cape and were much prized by African hunters because of the large quantities of meat they yielded, but they too were rapidly disappearing.[20]

Further north, in Natal, the balance between cultivation and hunting varied according to the nature of the land, the quantity of game, and the degree to which other elements of production had been put under stress. Some are said to have been much more diligent cultivators than hunters.[21] But most of the northern Nguni displayed a predilection for hunting both on a small scale and as a great communal activity through which the chief or king exercised his control over an important area of natural production and used up the peace time or seasonal under-employment of army regiments and cultivators. Good hunting grounds may have been one cause of the movements of the northern Nguni in the late eighteenth century. Nguni hunting methods were transferred to other parts of south central Africa as a result of the Mfecane, the migrations of the northern Nguni in the 1820s and 1830s.

W. C. Baldwin, who hunted in Zululand in the 1850s, described 'a great Kaffir hunt' at which 'all the natives from far and near turned out. They were delighted with their sport.'[22] He also saw many pitfalls in Zululand and in Tonga country, farther north. The most celebrated description of a Zulu hunt, however, comes from E. A. Ritter's *Shaka Zulu*.[23] While Ritter added an ideological superstructure of 'sportsmanship' clearly derived from European ideas (for example, he alleged that Shaka disliked the use of poisons, an 'unmanly technique' learned from the Bushmen) there is no reason to doubt his general description of the hunt. It took place about 1819 as part of the celebrations of a great victory, and was 'planned as a military expedition'. It used the natural trap of the confluence of the White and Black Umfolozi rivers to pen the animals. A complex of fences (*isengqelo*) were built with pits (*igebe*) six feet wide, nine feet deep and twelve to fifteen feet long at openings. Large numbers of troops drove the game while others acted as spearsmen. Shaka, who was positioned in a favourable spot to which the game was driven, himself participated in hamstringing and killing elephants, rhinoceros and buffaloes. Eland, wildebeest, sable, roan, giraffe, zebra, kudu, waterbuck, impala and bushbuck were all trapped and speared. Large numbers of dogs were used and there were also confrontations with lions and leopards. There were a number of human fatalities, but vast quantities of meat resulted from the drive and it

[ 62 ]

was followed by a great feast. Much of the meat was dried for future used.

Ritter also described the use of pits with sharpened stakes known as *iveku*, and suggested that neither hippos nor wild pigs were eaten by the Zulus, although they were killed in order to protect crops. In 1827 the Port Natal hunter-trader Henry Francis Fynn recorded that forty-eight elephants were killed in a single Zulu national hunt. Beyond the Cape frontier to the north and west the various Sotho Tswana people, who inhabited a region notably rich in game, were also avid hunters. It has been suggested that their remarkably large settlements may have resulted in part from the importance of trade in animal products, notably skins, karosses, feathers and ivory, as well as metals.[24] The positioning of these settlements may have been conditioned by the availability of metals and the convenience of routes in channelling hunting products towards their markets. Moreover, as the quantities of game rapidly declined around the edges of the Cape Colony the Sotho were still able to draw on the great resources of the desert regions to the west or, in the case of the northern Tswana, the Lake Ngami area.

The Tlhaping, Rolong and Ngwaketse from the northern Cape and southern Botswana, who had formerly traded ivory to the north, became part of the network of the Griquas, the people of mixed race who established themselves under patriarchal leadership between the Orange and the Vaal, utilising their strategic position to mix herding with hunter-trading.[25] Well mounted and armed, they were able to use their Cape wagons to reach well stocked hunting grounds in three to four-month trips. They took wagons loaded with trade goods and established a pattern of hunting-trading that would also be followed by Europeans. Of the ivory, feathers and skins they brought back often less than half would result from their own hunting, the rest being made up from trading with Africans.[26] By 1804 a Griqua called Solomon Kok was trading with the Tswana, and as it developed such hunter trading became an important component of Griqua power, for it offered rich pickings. It was this trade which led to their involvement in the struggles between Mzilikazi's Ndebele kingdom, one of the Nguni offshoots of the Mfecane which settled in the western Transvaal, and his neighbours the Tswana. Within a few decades the Griqua had been supplanted by Europeans, and the loss of their trade was one of the factors in the decline and fall of their communities as independent political entities.

Each of the Tswana groups had clearly defined western hunting grounds inhabited by client hunters. Some of these herded for their Tswana overlords; all offered hunting tribute in exchange for protection and commodities of the Tswana could supply to them. These clients were

[ 63 ]

of both Khoisan and Bantu-speaking groups. An indication of the scale and expertise of their hunting was provided by Francis Galton, who travelled in the Kalahari in 1851. He

> passed a magnificent set of pitfalls, which the Bushmen who live about these hills had made; the whole breadth of the valley was staked and bushed across. At intervals the fence was broken, and where broken deep pitfalls were made. The strength and size of timber that was used gave me a great idea of Bushman industry, for every tree had to be burned down and carried away from the hills, and yet the scale of the undertaking would have excited astonishment in far more civilised nations. When a herd of animals was seen among the hills the Bushmen drove them through this valley up to the fence; this was too high for them to jump so that they were obliged to make for the gaps, and there tumbled into the pitfalls.[27]

Whether the San had learned to use the pitfalls from the Tswana, or the other way round, they were clearly one of the most important of hunting techniques throughout Tswana country, and immense labour was devoted to their construction. One of the earliest European hunters in the interior, Cornwallis Harris, offers several descriptions of them, as well as testimony to their effectiveness.

> After crossing the Saltpan, we passed a long line of pitfalls used for entrapping game. Upwards of sixty of these were dug close together in a treble line; a high thorn fence extending in the form of a crescent a mile on either side, in such a manner that gnoos, quaggas and other animals may easily be driven into them. They are carefully concealed with grass, and their circumscribed dimensions render escape almost impossible. Heaps of whitened bones bore ample testimony to the destruction they had occasioned.[28]

On one occasion he became trapped in a labyrinth of thorn fences newly constructed to capture game. W. C. Baldwin, who travelled in Tswana country in the 1850s, saw pitfalls arranged in a 'honeycomb . . . all shapes, round oval, oblong, square, and there are generally about fifty in one pass, and fifteen or twenty passes in a space of two miles of country'.[29] As elsewhere, 'a strong fence on each side confines the game, which have thus no opportunity to escape'.

David Livingstone described the single pit or *hopo* used by the people around his mission station in Kolobeng.[30] Large herds of game gathered at the water holes there, and Livingstone saw the *hopo* frequently in use. The hedges formed a V shape over a mile long, 'very high and thick' near the angle, where it funnelled into a lane fifty yards long. At the end of the lane was one very large pit, with trees forming an overlapping border on the far side rendering escape almost impossible.

The people 'making a circle three or four miles round the country adjacent to the opening, and gradually closing up, are almost sure to enclose a large body of game'. 'Driving it up with shouts to the narrow part of the hopo, men secreted there throw their javelins into the affrighted herds, and on the animals rush to the opening presented at the converging hedges, and into the pit till that is full of a living mass.' Unlike most of his contemporaries, Livingstone found the spectacle distasteful: 'It is a frightful scene. The men, wild with excitement, spear the lovely animals with mad delight: others of the poor creatures, borne down by the weight of their dead and dying companions, every now and then make the whole mass heave in their smothering agonies.'

By this system, Livingstone tells us, sixty or seventy head of large game were killed at the different *hopos* each week, and 'the meat counteracted the bad effects of an exclusively vegetable diet'. Despite his anxieties about the painful death of the animals, Livingstone often wrote of the importance of meat to his own and the African diet. He noted the constant craving for meat exhibited by most African peoples throughout his travels. He encountered more pits on the river Zouga or Botletle.[31] These were dug into the sloping grassy banks of the river, where the animals came to drink. They were wedge-shaped and usually arranged in pairs, with a wall a foot thick left uncut between the ends of each 'so that if the beast, when it feels its fore legs descending, should try to save itself from going in altogether by striding the hind legs, he would spring forward and leap into the second with a force which insures the fall of his whole body into the trap.' All the excavated earth was removed to a distance so as not to excite the suspicion of the animals, and the traps were carefully covered with reeds, grass and sand. Several of Livingstone's party fell into these pits while searching for them to open them so that the oxen might not fall in.

This question of the opening of pitfalls was indeed a great bone of contention between European travellers and African chiefs. Oxen, horses and humans frequently fell into them.[32] The Scottish hunter Roualeyn Gordon Cumming, never squeamish, beat a chief in order to force him to open pitfalls.[33] Here hunting methods were in conflict, the passive technique of the African with the highly mobile arrangements of armed and mounted Europeans. Gordon Cumming offers many descriptions of African hunting and found one system similar to that used in his native Highlands. The chief Mahura held a hunting party on the old Scottish principle of the ring, 'a common and successful mode of hunting among the South African tribes', but 'on this occasion the ring was mismanaged and the game broke through'.[34]

[ 65 ]

Cumming also saw Mahura's people running across the plain bearing parasols of black ostrich feathers which they brandished on high to press the panic-stricken herds on. He claimed that some 6,000 zebra, wildebeest, blesbok and springbok were in sight being driven towards a range of pitfalls. Wherever these techniques were used grass was often burnt in order to encourage fresh young growth to attract the game.

The importance of hunting was very apparent at the court of Mzilikazi, king of the Ndebele. Animal products were everywhere, and Mzilikazi's heralds praised the king in terms of hunting exploits, making both visual and aural animal imitations.

> Advancing slowly towards the waggons, he opened the exhibition by roaring and charging, in frantic imitation of the king of beasts – then placing his arm before his mouth, and swinging it rapidly in pantomimic representation of the elephant, he threw his trunk above his head and shrilly trumpeted. He next ran on tiptoe imitating the ostrich; and lastly, humbling himself into the dust, wept like an infant. At each interval of the scene he recounted the matchless prowess and mighty conquests of his illustrious monarch, and made the hills re-echo with his praise.[35]

The hunting prowess of the king was perhaps extolled because of its importance to his people. Harris saw the products of the chase as more important to the subsistence of ordinary people than the products of herding.

> The wealth of this barbarous sovereign may be said almost to consist in his innumerable droves of horned cattle. These are herded in various parts of the country, and furnish employment to a considerable portion of his lieges, who are precariously maintained by his bounty, but depend chiefly for support upon their success in hunting.[36]

Harris found that the Ndebele were intrepid in their attacks on elephants with nothing more than assegais, often trapping them in defiles. They caught rhinos in the same way, but normally snared them in pitfalls provided with sharpened stakes. Mzilikazi himself usually led 'the great hunting expeditions which frequently take place'.

> On these occasions he is attended by a retinue of several thousand men, who extend themselves in a circle, enclosing many miles of country, and gradually converging so as to bring incredible numbers of wild animals within a small focus. Still advancing, the ring at length becomes a thick and continuous line of men, hemming in the game on all sides, which, in desperate efforts to escape, display the most daring and dangerous exhibition of sport that can be conceived. As the scene closes, the spears of the warriors deal death around them, affording a picture thrilling to the sportsman, and striking in the extreme.[37]

Harris showed none of the scruples of Livingstone. It is clear that large quantities of meat could result from such hunts, and throughout Africa it was preserved for future use by cutting into strips and sun-drying.

Such natural bounty inevitably led to a whole range of crafts associated with animal products. The Sotho indulged in highly skilled ivory carving as well as superb leatherwork.[38] Tanning and sewing were a masculine employment, and the high regard in which it was held is evidenced by the fact that men of superior status participated in stitching karosses. The results were of excellent quality, soft and beautifully sewn. Almost everywhere the poor wore antelope skins and the rich garments made up of jackal and cat furs. According to Gordon Cumming the Tswana wore a *tsecha* or skin on their loins and a kaross of skins.[39] Their sandals were made of buffalo or giraffe hide, as were their shields, while the women wore a kaross and kilt, generally of impala skin. The finest karosses were always desirable and invariably expensive. Ostrich-feather parasols were made and the feathers were also used as hat plumes.[40] Here is an interesting example of the adoption of an African fashion by Europeans.

By 1890 when H. Anderson Bryden hunted in Botswana and carefully observed the trade in animal products the finest karosses were fetching over £6 each.[41] Even then the kaross industry of the Tswana remained very important. 'No other people can so deftly shape and sew them.'

> Hunting and snaring is systematically conducted; the long grass of the desert is periodically set on fire, so that hunting with dogs may be more readily pursued; and throughout the Kalahari, the Vaalpense and Bushmen, vassals of the various Bechuana tribes, are always at work collecting skins, which in turn are gathered together by a chief or headman from headquarters on his annual visitation.[42]

Bryden gave a detailed account of the various hunting grounds of the Sotho-Tswana chieftaincies and described them as 'loving passionately . . . the chase of game'.

Khama, king of the Tswana, had a particularly strong love of hunting and remembered the days when Gordon Cumming hunted in his area. Khama had become alarmed at the decline of game and imposed hunting restrictions on the northern and western parts of his territory. Boer hunters were not permitted to enter, and 'even Englishmen have to obtain permission.' 'The hunting parties of the tribe . . . are regulated by the chief himself.' Indeed, because of fear of the Ndebele the northern areas had been left untouched and the game had consequently increased. Bryden estimated that Khama had some 8,000 to 10,000 armed men under his control, 2,000 to 3,000 of them with Martini-Henry, Snider or Westly Richards rifles, the rest with smooth-bores,

Enfields and Tower muskets.[43]

The importance of hunting of the Tswana and the anxieties of Khama are well represented in a letter he wrote to the British after their annexation of Bechuanaland.

> My people enjoy three things in our country; they enjoy their cultivated lands, and their cattle stations, and their hunting grounds. We have lived through these three things. Certainly the game will come to an end in the future, but at the present it is in my country, and while it is still there I hold that it ought to be hunted by my people.
>
> What I wish to explain is that my people must not be prevented from hunting in all the country, except where the English shall have come to dwell.[44]

Clearly hunting had a particular significance to the Sotho peoples, but it seems to have been no less important to the Nguni, and evidence could be adduced from elsewhere in southern Africa to indicate the prominence of hunting in subsistence. The views of Bonner, Beinart and Delius have been quoted earlier. When James Stevenson-Hamilton set about establishing the vast Sabi reserve, later the Kruger National Park, in the north-western Transvaal, he found it inhabited by African hunters.

> In those days the native inhabitants of the low-veld looked upon game as their natural food, in fact as their chief support, and every track within miles of a habitation was dotted at short intervals with every variety of snare and other device for entrapping birds and beasts known to kaffir ingenuity. Besides this every kraal contained a horde of nondescript dogs, usually of the lurcher type, used solely for hunting, and a considerable number of the men were in possession of firearms of one kind or another. It may therefore be realised that the initial task was no sinecure.[45]

The task was of course to transform these hunters into 'poachers' in order to frustrate their hunting activities.

In the light of all this evidence it is hard to accept the contention of Schapera and Goodwin that hunting 'is nowhere a regular occupation', that 'it is carried out fairly sporadically' and that its products could not be described in any way as 'a staple food'.[46] It is true that they made a partial though qualified exception of Botwana, where 'game may be an important source of food'. It may well have been true that by the 1930s game had become only a marginal source for most African peoples, but this should not be permitted to obscure its much greater significance in the past. By the 1930s, as we shall see, game had been destroyed in many areas or had been confined to reserves. Moreover, Africans had become 'poachers', themselves ensnared in a whole range of hunting legislation.

*Central Africa.* When the Ndebele crossed the Limpopo to their new territory in Zimbabwe they took their hunting practices with them. The misssionary T. M. Thomas suggested that hunting was a means of using up the surplus energies of Ndebele warriors when they were not fighting or raiding.[47] Thomas, like Harris earlier in the century, observed thousands of the Ndebele hunting by driving the game forward in an immense circle miles in circumference. The animals so enclosed were speared when trying to escape or when trapped in the ever reducing circle of beaters and hunters. The resulting meat, Thomas asserted, was all taken to the king and disposed of by him. The Ndebele also used pitfalls, wedge-shaped and with pointed stakes, in the game trails, but according to Thomas 'their most destructive game trap' was the *muhopo,* the equivalent of the Tswana *hopo* described by Livingstone. The Ndebele placed their trap between the game's pasturage and the watering place, the funnel of the hedge leading from the water towards the pit. Thomas saw rhinoceros, eland, wildebeast, zebra, tsessebe and reed buck all caught in this way. Mzilikazi's son, Lobenguala, attempted to create his own private hunting ground. Able hunters could rise rapidly in royal favour.

The Ndebele also hunted in small parties, which travellers frequently encountered, and levied tribute in animal products from subordinate peoples.[48] Such tribute was levied from the Shona chieftaincies that were pulled into the orbit of the Ndebele kingdom, and the Shona were accustomed to hunting where the game was available and the country permitted it. They set traps and snares, and training in their use was an important part of the education of the young.[49] They had nets called *mambure,* made of long strips of bark, which were used in conjunction with large numbers of beaters. Karl Mauch saw the Shona of the Chibi district using these nets and provides a detailed description of the hunt. Each net was 10-12 ft high and 100-200 ft long, and could just be carried by one man.

> The chief of the district announces the hunt. If he feels a desire for game meat he persuades the neighboring chiefs to join him in the hunt and to call out men with their mampulas. Little persuasion is needed, for who among the blacks is not keen on meat?[50]

The people set out heavily laden with *mambure,* assegais, bows and arrows.

> It took almost ¼-hour's walking to pass those nets already erected and to reach the next set. The heavy load, certainly between 60-80 lb., is

thrown to the ground, the net is unrolled, the sticks or thin poles are freed from the ropes which tied them together and the erection begins. The last hunter rolls out the end of his mampula from its last pole to which presently the net of the next arrival is attached. An 8 ft long, thin pole, which is forked at its top, is put up, sloping forward, at an interval of about 20 ft, so that the upper edge of the net reaches the height of about 8-10 ft. Care is taken that the lower part of the net lies slack on the ground on the side from which the game is expected.

The hunters concealed themselves, and the women and children arrived with food, since the hunt was expected to last several days. One of the chief's sons took control, organising the women beaters. The nets formed a semi-circle of three miles, almost completely surrounding the mouth of a small valley. The blowing of the horn of a harrisbuck signalled the start of the beat. When the first beat was relatively unsuccessful, a second line of nets five miles long was established. This secured a few animals and a third hunt was instituted. Thomas Baines drew a *mambure* hunt which he witnessed farther north, in the Lomagundi district.

Mauch's description is interesting because it indicates the expenditure of a great deal of labour in the making of the stakes and nets, the laying out of the great line in the hunt, and the marshalling of the beaters. There is no mention of famine, and it is indeed an activity likely to be undertaken by people in good heart. The chief's decision is represented as an elective one, eagerly accepted by the hunters, not one to which they were driven *in extremis*.

Theodore Bent, the first excavator of the ruins of Great Zimbabwe, saw the people of that area using bows with finely barbed arrows to shoot mice, 'a delicacy greatly beloved of them'.[51] They also collected caterpillars, which they 'eat in enormous quantities, and what they cannot eat on the expedition they dry in the sun and take home for future consumption'. Here, as elsewhere in the continent, Africans collected and ate locusts, sometimes pounding them into a paste.

Hunting was also eagerly pursued throughout the region that constitutes modern Zambia. Livingstone commented on the avid hunting tastes of the Lozi and their Kololo aristocracy in the upper Zambezi valley. He stayed with one chief, Santuru, a great hunter who also (unusually) enjoyed taming wild animals. The Lozi and their associated peoples pursued water antelopes like lechwe and nakong (a type of water buck), spearing them from fast-moving canoes. These antelopes, wrote Livingstone, existed in 'prodigious herds', 'feeding quite heedlessly over the flats', although the numbers killed annually 'must be enormous'.[52] The Lozi also hunted hippos from canoes, trapping them in an ever decreasing area of shallows near the river bank where they could be attacked by large numbers of spear carriers.[53]

In Barotseland the king commanded a great annual elephant hunt, involving hundreds of participants in which elephants were trapped in the angle of the Chobe and Zambezi rivers and as many despatched as possible. In 1875 the hunt was led by King Sipopa, and took place in late October. The elephants were driven by fire and by beaters to the trapping point, where they were caught between 200 canoes and over a thousand hunters on foot. Two thousand men were said to have participated in all. The 1875 hunt was a comparative failure, but in another year no fewer than ninety elephants were killed.[54]

Sipopa's successor, Lewanika, similarly took command of the hunt. As well as the elephant hunts there was an annual antelope hunt to supply domestic needs. Each year Lewanika organised it when the waters of the Zambezi were high. At this time the animals were trapped on islands which were surrounded by canoes, and the game was slaughtered in thousands to provide skins and meat for the coming winter. In 1887 the flood was slight and the animals escaped over the plain, which was considered a great disaster.[55] Under European influence Lewanika seems to have increased the scale and frequency of the hunts as well as elaborating the ritual associated with them. The hunt became a central part of State ceremonial. In 1889 he gave a Martini-Henry rifle to his son Letia, and the prince's first kills were met with congratulations from around the kingdom.[56] The hunt had became a rite of passage to the chieftaincy. Lewanika reserved a particular area for his exclusive use and had a hunting lodge built within it.[57] In 1895 three great hunting expeditions took place. The king commanded one of the hunts from an anthill, where he waited while the animals were surrounded and beaten towards him by hundreds of men. He insisted on making the first kill, piercing the animal with a weapon in his own hand. 'Alas!' wrote the missionary François Coillard, 'the pretensions of royalty multiply in an alarming manner; ceremonies are becoming more and more complicated . . .'[58] Lewanika was inventing tradition in the middle of Africa. The last of these great Barotse hunts took place in 1913.

Hunting had become closely bound up with Lozi ceremonial. Each hunter erected an altar 'where he dedicates the first-fruits of his hunting and some of the vertebrae or horns of the animals'. Lewanika's great village, before he ascended the Lozi throne, was full of 'heaps of heads and horns of every kind of animal' while on its edge was a shrub loaded with vertebrae. Every hunter's tomb was decorated with skulls, horns or tusks, depending on the animal he most favoured in the hunt. Sewing was a masculine prerogative and 'it was the hunter's privilege to dress and stitch the skins of the animals he chased and to embroider a garment for his bride'.[59]

Farther down the Zambezi Valley the Gwembe Tonga had a complex and important relationship with hunting. When David Livingstone visited them in 1860 hunting was still a major aspect of their economy, and hunting artefacts constituted a significant part of their material culture. A variety of shrines and rituals were devoted to different forms of hunting, from hippo harpooning to the use of snares, pits and guns. A number of crafts, including the manufacture of poisons, were associated with hunting, and dogs were kept in every village. There were elaborate rules for the distribution of meat and a distinction was drawn between one group of animals, mostly the larger, over which the ritual leader or chief exercised rights to meat and other products and another, usually the smaller, to which the hunters themselves had sole claim. By the 1950s, a period of intense anthropological activity among the Tonga because of the threatened inundation of their territory by Lake Kariba, hunting had become a minor part of the Tongan economy, although libations were still poured and rituals practised to honour hunting ancestors.[60]

Elsewhere the work of anthropologists has suggested 'a widespread enthusiasm for hunting in many areas of rural Zambia'.[61] Certainly the accounts of travellers and early administrators in the region abound in descriptions of African hunting. For example, when 'Chirupula' Stephenson arrived in the Hook of the Kafue, in central Zambia, to establish the British South Africa Company administration at the turn of the century he found a land in which there were numerous game traps, freshly set, camouflaged pits and log deadfalls set in trees for elephants. This was Lala country, where the chiefs, as in the south, arrogated to themselves the right to wear jackal and leopard skins. The Lala were one of a whole complex of chieftaincies which traced their origins from Luba migrants. The Luba and their neighbours the Lunda, occupying a large area of Zaire and north-western Zambia, were celebrated hunters who had specialised hunting guilds expert in procuring ivory and game meat or in defending the people against the great carnivores. The European hunter Dugald Campbell and other travellers encountered large hunting parties when visiting their territory.[62] Many of the Luba migrants may have been attracted to new lands by hunting opportunities, and the notion of the specialised guilds of hunters survived in some of the societies claiming origin from them. The historic relationship of many of the peoples of Zambia to the Luba-Lunda is complex, but a high ideological commitment to hunting seems to have been a common characteristic. The Luvale and Ndembu of the west, the Bemba and Bisa of the east, all claimed to value hunting more than agriculture, despite being fundamentally agricultural peoples.

Stuart Marks's study of hunting among the Bisa of the Luangwa Valley indicates why this might be the case.[63] The Bisa inhabited an area infested with tsetse fly, which precluded their keeping domestic stock, but their region was rich in game. The threat to their crops was neatly reflected in a saying (attributed to Europeans rather than the Bisa themselves) which suggested that they had to plant three seeds in each hole, one for the elephants, one for the guinea fowl and one for themselves. In actual fact the main damage to crops was probably caused by rodents. The Bisa were assiduous in crop protection and successfully used the game as a supply of meat. They had specialised guilds to hunt elephant, hippo, ant-bears and others, while non-guild hunters pursued animals like warthogs and impala. They maintained hunting shrines 'decorated with the skulls of mammals symbolizing an individual's prowess' rather like those of the Lozi. The Bisa deployed a great deal of magic in their hunting and used it as a central aspect of divination.

In the course of the nineteenth and twentieth centuries Bisa hunting underwent significant changes. The appearance of muzzle-loaders made hunting a much more individual activity and helped to kill the guilds. The shrines were abandoned, partly as a result of European disapproval. Game laws attempted to eliminate some traditional practices, such as game pits, and may have helped to change Bisa tastes (for example, hippo meat, formerly favoured, came to be rejected), though the game laws, interestingly, were more stringently enforced after 1960. Yet in 1966-67 when Marks conducted his research among the Bisa, hunting remained central to their subsistence. Hunters still had high prestige (and were often headmen). A great range of techniques remained in use, and children were trained by snaring birds. Wild meat composed, according to season, between 33 per cent and 53 per cent of dishes in the diet of one village, and similar figures were obtained in others. Success rates were fairly high and yields good, though the time devoted to hunting, in comparision with other economic activities, was relatively low. Here is one explanation of the high regard in which hunting was held – its high productivity in terms of the relative effort involved.

If hunting was particularly important to the Bisa, its continuing significance to modern times was conditioned by the relative remoteness of the Luangwa Valley, the intermittent character of colonial rule in the area, and its supremely game-rich ecology. Indeed, the Bisa of the valley believed that the numbers of game had increased in the decade before Marks's arrival, and the growing game population in the two reserves, Luangwa North and South, on either side of their corridor of land, may well have contributed. Perhaps some allowance should be made for the fact that Marks was himself an avid hunter who took a rifle and a shotgun on his field research, actively participated in Bisa hunting and lent his weapons to a Bisa hunting friend. He was by no means an impartial observer, but brought American hunting passions, in an academic guise, to Central Africa. Nevertheless, even if hunting has seldom survived elsewhere as such a successful component of subsistence, its role for the Bisa offers some clue to its importance among other peoples in the past.

The Bemba of north-eastern Zambia provide an example of high commitment to hunting no longer matched by performance. The anthropologist Audrey Richards, conducting research on their diet and economic life in the 1930s, discovered a 'passionate enthusiasm' for hunting. Chieftaincies were valued and country was classified according to the richness of the game resources or the size of the rivers for fishing. Both men and women were interested and commented on the nature of the country and the habits of the game as they travelled about. The Bemba hunted with nets, rather like the Shona. The men staked the nets and waited behind them to effect the kills when the children beat the bush. Richards suggested that women did not take part (as did Marks for the Bisa). Among the Bemba such hunting was on a smaller scale than that of the Shona, with only five or six men participating. The Bemba also used the full range of snares, traps, weighted spears and pits, although by Richards's time these techniques had been banned by the colonial government. They blew a 'magic' whistle said to attract duiker by imitating their call, hunted with dogs, and used spears, bows and muzzle- loaders as weapons.[64]

Hunting played a notable part in Bemba ceremonies. The Bemba used hunting rituals when selecting a new village site, following tree-cutting ceremonies (part of their *citemene* system of agriculture, which involved the pollarding of trees and the burning of the branches), and to discover whether their gardens were going to be blessed. Richards saw hunting as a source of romance and delight to the Bemba, more surrounded by magic than any other activity. But her observations suggest that it was not very effective. She was sceptical when they looked back to a golden age of plentiful game or when Bemba migrant workers on the Copperbelt referred to hunting as one of the joys of home; and she was noncommittal when they blamed the whites for the disappearance of game, pointing out that whites equally blamed blacks.[65]

The past tends to become more golden through the lens of memory, but other evidence indicates that at a time of bountiful game African techniques could be effective, yielding large quantities of meat. It is hard to imagine that such a range of techniques, some of them making heavy demands on labour time, and so many stories, myths, rituals and ceremonies could have been evolved for an economically marginal activity low in productivity compared with others. Richards wrote in an age when intellectuals were reacting against hunting. She was tempted to see it more as ritual than as a means of dominating and controlling the African fauna and supplying meat.

*East Africa.* Hunting was also widespread and varied in technique throughout East Africa. Elephants had long been hunted and there were a number of peoples, like the Kamba and the Nyamwezi, who were celebrated as elephant hunters and ivory traders. In the course of the nineteenth century more and more people were sucked into the ivory trade. For many elephants had been more important as a source of meat than of ivory, but as the trade build up and new sources were sought people like the Lango and Jie of northern Uganda or the Kimbu and Shambaa of Tanzania were drawn into its grip.

But although ivory has, as always, received the lion's share of attention, there is ample evidence that the majority of East African peoples viewed game as an important source of meat. There are a number of examples in East Africa of specialist hunters maintaining symbiotic relationships with neighbouring herders and cultivators, but most of the latter two groups also hunted for themselves. The Ndorobo of Kenya and northern Tanzania were celebrated specialist hunters who used a variety of techniques, different clans favouring different hunting methods.[66] Some used hides of branches near water holes. Richard Meinertzhagen considered the Ndorobo to be so successful as to be placing the game at risk, but he was a master of overstatement. Near one of their encampments he saw the ground strewn with rhino skulls (twenty-five in all), as well as the heads of impala, zebra and bushbuck.[67] The Ndorobo of both Kenya and northern Tanzania also manufactured poisons particularly prized for their speed of action, often selling them at a great profit.[68] Boni hunters in Tanaland in northern Kenya bought poison either directly or indirectly from the Ndorobo as did the Kamba.

The Kamba were famous elephant hunters and ivory traders who from the eighteenth century established hunting and trading settlements away from their own homeland – for example, in the Shambaa country of Tanzania. But despite being herders and cultivators, they also hunted for meat. Between their country and that of the Masai, their long-standing enemies, lay largely unpopulated plains teeming with animals where they hunted assiduously and successfully in the dry season.[69] The game resource was particularly important in times of famine, for many of them lived in an area of doubtful rainfall, and, as we shall see in a later chapter, one of the objectives of early European rulers and game administrators was to frustrate Kamba hunting.

To the west the Kikuyu inhabited a richer land, but they too hunted. When Frederick Lugard arrived to establish the Imperial British East Africa Company's administration in their territory he found game pits along the fringes of the forest.

> These forest paths are full of deep pits for buffalo, elephant, etc., which are concealed with such consummate skill that though I was aware there were many about, and was on the look-out, and considered myself by no means a novice in jungle-craft, it was not long before I precipitated myself into one! The common custom is to dig the pit close to where a trunk of a tree has fallen across the path. To step over this involves a lengthened pace, and consequently, when the foot descends through the thin covering of twigs and grass which conceals the pit on the far side, it is impossible to recover one's balance and withdraw it. If the trunk is a large one, wild animals would carry both fore feet over together, and thus go headlong into the trap.[70]

Although the Masai did not normally hunt for meat they did indulge in defensive hunting. Lions and other predators were a contant threat to their cattle and were courageously faced by groups of young men. When rinderpest destroyed the Masai herds in the early 1890s they did, however, turn to hunting to avert famine.[71]

In Tanzania there were areas of wilderness between the chieftaincies which acted as game preserves in which hunting could take place. The driving of game by fire, a technique much disapproved of by colonial authorities, was practised in many places. The Shambaa, who inhabited territory just inland from the coast established their settlements on the margin of mountain and plain so that they could combine agriculture with hunting. Their myths of origin, as with so many peoples, involved a great hunter, in this case called Mbegha, who ingratiated himself with the local people by gifts of meat (as Europeans were to do in imperial exploration, conquest and settlement) and who made the transition from a nomadic hunter of wild pig to a noble and protective slayer of lions (a transition again to be followed by Europeans in Africa and India). Game meat was an important part of the diet of the Shambaa in pre-colonial times and when a hunter made a large kill he was able to trade his surplus. In the later nineteenth century the Shambaa became progressively sucked into Kamba ivory trading.[72]

The peoples of central Tanzania also hunted extensively. The Ukimbu forests were a constant lure to Kimbu hunters, who found 'the call of the forest stronger than that of the fields'. The Kimbu established hunting camps in the forest in the dry season and hunted the full range of game with pitfalls, weighted spear traps, snares, spear, and bows and arrows. The meat was dried for future use in the villages. Until the 1860s they dressed in skins, and it was only from this later period that they began to hunt elephants for ivory as well as for meat. The chiefs reserved ivory to themselves, and the lion was regarded as 'royal game' to be killed as part of the chief's prerogative of protection. Most of the Kimbu myths of origin involved hunters.[73]

When the missionary Alfred Swann visited Mirambo, chief of the Nyamwezi, in the early 1880s, the latter expressed his friendship by offering to 'give you my country to hunt in' in exchange for the use of the Swann's boat to bring ivory across Lake Tanganyika. When Swann left Urambo, Mirambo's capital, he found that 'game was abundant everywhere, but the numerous pits dug for the capture of wild animals made it risky to hunt, except with great care'.[74] A traveller in Tanzania in the 1920s saw a highly effective and presumably long-standing technique for netting game taking place among the Nyamwezi. Hunting was a village undertaking, each family providing a line of nooses 150 ft in length, suspended four feet from the ground, so arranged that each open noose touched the next. A great drive was organised into a total area of nooses, covering at least five acres, and 'result was a game trap as devilish as any devised by the mind of man. It caught practically everything that entered the area, whether they came in singles or hundreds.' The rope, made of sanseviera fibre, was yellow, like the grass, and few of the animals succeeded in breaking through. The hunt was highly successful, as the European observer, G. Lister Carlisle noted:

> We saw tons of meat ready for transport. There were remnants of all local animals from Thompson's gazelles to zebra, giraffe, and we even counted five striped unborn eland calves. Such slaughter is supposed to be illegal ... My estimate of the animal life taken by all these native

hunters from the surrounding country then filled with herds in their dry season migration is 300 per day.[75]

Alfred Swann also encountered game pits on the shores of Lake Tanganyika, near Ujiji, and himself participated in an African hippo hunt near the lake.[76] The hunters taunted the hippos to induce them to attack, whereupon they attempted to spear them from their canoes. Swann was astonished at the risky nature of the venture and the bravery of the hunters. Indeed, the intrepidity of African hunters was frequently remarked by European travellers, particularly the manner in which Africans fearlessly hunted dangerous beasts like rhino and buffalo.[77]

There were also grand *battues* of hippos on the upper Nile, and the entire Nile region in northern Uganda was important hunting country. The Lango, who inhabited a vast tract of territory north of Lake Kioga, regarded hunting as one of the most important parts of their economy. The quest for game had been significant both in their migration to the area and in their establishment of control, with a relatively small population, over a country of some 5,000 square miles. Game was an important factor in the founding of village sites, and was a prime source of disputes, internally between clans and externally in relations with the Bunyoro kingdom. They hunted in the dry season, often driving game by firing the bush. The country was carefully divided into game tracts, or *arum*, and each great hunt was controlled by a master of the hunt, or *won arum*, a hereditary office distinct from the clan elders. While a great hunt, involving the participation of large numbers of people, might take place only once a year, smaller groups would hunt more frequently at other times. By these means the Lango relied on game meat for an important part of their diet, and they were probably more expert hunters than their neighbours, the Acholi. From the 1860s they became more concerned with the ivory trade as a result of being subjected to the raiding and trading of the Sudanese in search of ivory.[78]

Hunting was also integral to the economy of the Jie, a people to the east of the Lango. They too lived in a land rich in game and used throwing sticks, spears, snares and traps. Large hunts were organised by whole territorial divisions, and smaller co-operative hunts were arranged by the young men. They too based their history of migration and settlement on the search for game and also derived many place names from hunting incidents. From the 1880s they were drawn into the ivory trade of Abyssinian and Swahili ivory dealers, with whom they maintained an amicable relationship. They had shown little inclination for elephant hunting until that time. During the great disasters of the 1890s, the failure of crops through drought and the destruction of stock by rinderpest, they were forced to fall back on the hunting and gathering sector of their economy in order to survive.[79] John Lamphear's summing up of the significance of hunting to the Jie would probably apply to many other African peoples. Hunting and gathering were indulged in constantly, but 'their importance ranges from merely that of a rather pleasant pastime and a means of collecting additional dietary variation in a "good" year to that of a grim economic necessity in years of crop failure and livestock disaster'. [80]

In many other parts of East Africa the full range of hunting techniques was pursued. Traps and snares were almost universal. On one of his expeditions to Uganda Lugard noted that his porters set traps every afternoon to enhance their diet on the march.[81] There was an infinite gradation in hunting, from this snaring and trapping of rodents to the great hunts. Some peoples favoured different techniques. For example, Henry Faulkner, a member of an expedition to find David Livingstone, noted that the Nyanja people of southern Malawi used pits, while the Yao preferred to hunt with bows and arrows and guns.[82] Around the northern shores of Lake Nyasa (Malawi) the Konde people seem to have used every possible technique. One observer in the early twentieth century said that game laws had made hunting a thing of the past, but before the arrival of Europeans 'hunting was an important and regular part of the year's work'.[83] Hunting trips took from four to eight weeks; each tribe had its own hunting ground, and territorial infringements could lead to war. Every form of trap, pit and drive was used; hippos were speared from canoes; poisons were effectively employed; and meat, half cooked, could be kept for many months. In the Sudan, at the other end of East Africa, the Hamran Arabs, made famous by Sir Samuel Baker, hunted elephant, giraffe and buffalo on horseback, using only swords.[84] With these they hamstrung the animals at speed before closing in to deliver the coup de grâce.

As in southern Africa, important crafts were associated with hunting and animal products. An important part of the production of iron-workers was devoted to the manufacture of the blades of spears, axes, knives and arrowheads. Smiths also repaired muzzle-loaders and produced ammunition, while other peoples made gunpowder. In some places rhino and giraffe hides were greatly favoured for the manufacture of shields. Skins were widely worn, though cloth rapidly penetrated many parts of East Africa. As we have seen, poisons were produced by specialists and traded widely.

*Conclusion.* Almost all African peoples hunted in one form or another. The animals ranged from mice to elephants, and the three main categories of hunting – for defence, for export, and for domestic use – were common almost everywhere, though in varying prominence. Hunting was undertaken by individuals, small groups and large centralized communal gatherings. Techniques, varied as they were, show a remarkable similarity over wide areas of the continent. Since meat could be salted and dried it could be kept for long periods, and the scale of the hunt was not restricted by the capacity to consume in the short term. Herding, cultivation and hunting coexisted in varying proportions, but game meat may well have been a more important component of many people's diet than many ethnographers or historians have noticed.

Hunting was partly a product of necessity. For people in the low-veld of the Transvaal, for example, where soils were poor and rainfall scarce, game was the main resource of the area. The same is partly true of the Luangwa Valley of Zambia, where the Bisa were heavily dependant on game meat to supplement or sometimes replace an otherwise meagre subsistence. An interesting contrast may be supplied by the Kikuyu and Kamba in Kenya. The Kikuyu land is richer and its rainfall superior to that of their neighbours, the Kamba. Hunting may have been less important to the economy of the Kikuyu because they had little need of game meat. The Kamba seem to have hunted at all times, but when their crops failed necessity drove them to hunt in neighbouring territory. This background may explain the fact that they were more assiduous 'poachers' than the Kikuyu in the colonial period.[85] But while some people may have hunted like the Masai only when forced to by famine, many did so frequently and by inclination when the game and the labour time were available and the season permitted. We know from Richards, Shorter, Lamphear and others that many people hunted from choice. It was not just a function of necessity, but a preference involving excitement and romance, recreation and training.

As well as a popular choice, it may well have been an elite preference for pleasure, profit and patronage, a fascination closely related to function. Hunting offered the elite, as it was to offer imperial rulers, a symbolic dominance of the environment, a means of asserting boundaries of territory, action and behaviour. It gave them an opportunity to centralise and control the labour time of large numbers of people, and its results offered not only profit, and the power that profit confers, through the export trade, but also opportunities to assert their domestic authority through the redistribution of meat and skins. The communal hunt offered the speediest recycling of natural resources in which the fervour of the participants was related to the expectation of feast and fable, and the leadership role was connected with ancestral achievement, protection and patronage in the present, and the expectation of further feats in the future. It acted as 'the image of war', a builder of courage and a means of military training, an opportunity to gain rank and a source of competition for leadership. Its importance in ritual is illustrated by the Gwembe Tonga of Zambia, among whom ceremonies connected with hunting survived even when the game had gone or game laws had restricted activity.[86] The importance of hunting may lie precisely in its range, from humble survival mechanism for individuals and small groups to a communal pursuit laden with ritual and political, social and economic significance.

With the arrival of colonial rule game was swiftly supplanted by the store as the source of a variety of domestic commodities – clothing, blankets, jewellery, ritual objects and receptacles. But it may be that colonial rule did not compensate for the loss of nutrition. Even if we cannot be sure of the proportionate significance of game meat in the pre-colonial diet – though the Bisa offer a clue – we can at least suggest that the destruction of game or its removal to remote reserves (sometimes cleared of humans to make way for animals, as we shall see) and the denial of hunting rights to Africans must have had a significant effect not only on indigenous economic and social relations but also on African nutrition.

One member of the Society for the Preservation of the Fauna of the Empire, R. W. G. Hingston, neatly reflected the views of the white hunter-preservationists and some at least of colonial officaldom when he asserted categorically that 'Meat is not part of the routine diet of the African native.' Securing meat by hunting 'is the stamp of primitiveness' from which Europeans should lead him by teaching him 'the meat-securing methods which are practised by more cultured races'. This would involve a 'discouragement of native slaughter' and 'teaching of the keeping and breeding of domestic animals such as cattle, pigs, goats, sheep, fowls and ducks'.[87] Some of the chapters that follow (with a somewhat different emphasis in the contrasting Asian experience) are devoted to establishing the manner in which the African relationship with game was modified or destroyed by the extension of white settlement and imperial conquest, and with them the application of Hingston's views.

## Notes

1 Monica Wilson and Leonard Thompson (eds.), *The Oxford History of South Africa*, Oxford, 1969, Vol. I, p. 395.
2 William Beinart, 'Production and the material basis of chieftainship', in Shula Marks and Anthony Atmore (eds.), *Economy and Society in Pre-industrial South Africa*, London, 1980, p. 128.
3 Peter Delius, 'Migrant labour and the Pedi, 1840-80', in Marks and Atmore, *Economy and Society*, p. 301.
4 D. N. Beach, 'The Shona economy', in R. Palmer and R. Parsons, *The Roots of Rural Poverty*, London, 1977, pp. 39-40.
5 Philip Bonner, 'Classes, the mode of production and the State in pre-colonial Swaziland', in Marks and Atmore, *Economy and Society*, p. 85.
6 Richard Elphick, *Khoikhoi and the Founding of White South Africa*, Johannesburg, 1985, pp. 31-2, 37-8.
7 H. A. Bryden, *Gun and Camera in Southern Africa*, London, 1893, p. 390.
8 Andrew Steedman, *Wanderings and Adventures in the Interior of South Africa*, 2 vols., London, 1835, Vol. I, pp. 69-70.
9 Steedman, *Wanderings*, Vol. I, p. 149.
10 William Cornwallis Harris, *The Wild Sports of Southern Africa*, London, 1852, p. 260; Roualeyn Gordon Cumming, *Five Years of a Hunter's Life in the far Interior of South Africa*, 2 vols., London, 1850, Vol. I, p. 114; Robert Moffat, *Missionary Labours and Scenes in Southern Africa*, London, 1846, p. 17.
11 Steedman, *Wanderings*, Vol. II, p. 91.
12 Steedman, *Wanderings*, Vol. I, pp. 107 ff.
13 General Sir Arthur Cunynghame, *My Command in South Africa, 1874-78*, London, 1879, p. viii.
14 For visions of plenty see Harris, *Wild Sports*, pp. 55, 67, 69, 72, 247, 253.
15 Bryden, *Gun and Camera*, pp. 323-4; Roger Summers (ed.), *Prehistoric Rock Art of the Federation of Rhodesia and Nyasaland*, Salisbury, Rhodesia, 1959.
16 G. P. Murdock, *Ethnographic Atlas*, Pitsburgh, Penn., 1967.
17 Wilson and Thompson, *Oxford History*, Vol. I, p. 234.
18 Wilson and Thompson, *Oxford History*, Vol. I, pp. 110, 235, 254.
19 Steedman, *Wanderings*, Vol. I, pp. 21-5.
20 Steedman, *Wanderings*, Vol. I, p. 254.
21 Marks and Atmore, *Economy and Society*, pp. 124-6.
22 W. C. Baldwin, *African Hunting and Adventure from Natal to the Zambezi*, London, 1894, pp. 42, 74.
23 E. A. Ritter, *Shaka Zulu*, London, 1955, pp. 205-15.
24 Wilson and Thompson, *Oxford History*, pp. 153, 179.
25 Robert Ross, *Adam Kok's Griquas*, Cambridge, 1976, pp. 14-16.
26 For descriptions of Griqua hunters see Harris, *Wild Sports*, pp. 48-9, and Cumming, *Five Years*, Vol. I, pp. 138-9 and 141-2.
27 Wilson and Thompson, *Oxford History*, pp. 48-9.
28 Harris, *Wild Sports*, pp. 49, 94.
29 Baldwin, *African Hunting*, p. 145.
30 David Livingstone, *Missionary Travels in South Africa*, London, 1857, p. 26.
31 Livingstone, *Missionary Travels*, pp. 69-70.
32 Baldwin, *Africa Hunting*, pp. 318, 381.
33 Cumming, *Five Years*, Vol. II, p. 202.
34 Cumming, *Five Years*, Vol. II, p. 209.
35 Harris, *Wild Sports*, p. 96.
36 Harris, *Wild Sports*, pp. 114-15.
37 Harris, *Wild Sports*, pp. 138-40.
38 Wilson and Thompson, *Oxford History*, p. 147.
39 Cumming, *Five Years*, Vol. I, pp. 230-1.
40 Harris, *Wild Sports*, p. 52.

**41** Bryden, *Gun and Camera*, pp. 60-2.
**42** Bryden, *Gun and Camera*, p. 62.
**43** Bryden, *Gun and Camera*, pp. 268-9.
**44** Bryden, *Gun and Camera*, pp. 271-2.
**45** J. Stevenson-Hamilton, *Our South African National Parks*, Cape Town, 1940, p. 25.
**46** I. Schapera and A. J. H. Goodwin, *Work and wealth*, in I. Schapera (ed.), *The Bantu-speaking Tribes of South Africa*, London, 1937, p. 141.
**47** T. M. Thomas, *Eleven Years in Central South Africa*, London, 1893, pp. 116-17, Harold Child, *The Ndebele*, Salisbury, Rhodesia, 1968, pp. 68-72.
**48** J. R. D. Cobbing, 'The Ndebele under the Khumalos, 1820-96', unpublished Ph D thesis, University of Lancaster, 1976, pp. 174-5.
**49** Charles Bullock, *The Mashona and the Matabele*, Cape Town, 1950, pp. 40-1.
**50** E. E. Burke (ed.), *The Journals of Karl Mauch*, Salisbury, Rhodesia, 1969, pp. 159-61; F. O. Bernhard (ed.), *Karl Mauch*, Cape Town, 1971, p. 220.
**51** J. Theodore Bent, *The Ruined Cities of Mashonaland*, London, 1892, pp. 51-2.
**52** Livingstone, *Missionary Travels*, pp. 204-5, 217.
**53** François Coillard, *On the Threshold of Central Africa*, London 1897, p. 600. E. C. Tabler, *Trade and Travel in Early Barotseland*, London, 1963, p. 43.
**54** Tabler, *Trade and Travel*, p. 110; E. C. Tabler (ed.), *To the Victoria Falls via Matabeleland: the Diary of Major Henry Stabb*, 1875, Cape Town, 1967, p. 173.
**55** Coillard, *Threshold*, p. 287; Gervas Clay, *Your Friend Lewanika*, London, 1968, p. 22.
**56** Coillard, *Threshold*, pp. 365-6.
**57** Tabler, *Trade and Travel*, p. 67.
**58** Coillard, *Threshold*, p. 591.
**59** Coillard, *Threshold*, p. 598, C. W. Mackintosh, *Coillard of the Zambezi*, London, 1907, pp. 342, 346.
**60** Thayer Scudder, *The Ecology of the Gwembe Tonga*, Manchester, 1962, pp. 189-201.
**61** Stuart A. Marks, *Large Mammals and a Brave People*, Seattle, Wash., 1976, pp. 198, 219, quoting Richards on the Bemba, Turner on the Ndembu, White on the Luvale and Stefaniszyn on the Ambo.
**62** K. S. Rukavina, *Jungle Pathfinder*, London, 1951, p. 75. Dugald Campbell, *Wanderings in Central Africa*, London, 1929, pp. 56, 72.
**63** The following account is based on Marks, *Large Mammals*, passim.
**64** Audrey I. Richards, *Land, Labour and Diet in Northern Rhodesia*, London, 193, pp. 18, 233, 344-7.
**65** Richards, *Land, Labour and Diet*, pp. 283, 343, 350, 366.
**66** Arthur H. Neuman, *Elephant Hunting in East Equatorial Africa*, London, 1898, pp. 13-15.
**67** Richard Meinertzhagen, *Kenya Diary, 1902-6*, Edinburgh, 1957, p. 111.
**68** Marcus Daly, *Big Game Hunting and Adventure, 1897-1936*, London, 1937, p. 45.
**69** Useful material on Kamba hunting can be found in the reports by Frederick Jackson and Blayney Percival enclosed in Sadler to Elgin, 12 March and 28 September 1906, Cd 3189. See also Frederick Jackson, *Early Days in East Africa*, London, 1969, pp. 298-300, and Ian Parker and Mohamed Amin, *Ivory Crisis*, London, 1983.
**70** F. D. Lugard, *The Rise of our East African Empire*, 2 vols., London, 1893, Vol. I, pp. 323-4.
**71** Lugard, *East African Empire*, Vol. I, p. 340. Sir Charles Eliot, *The East Africa Protectorate*, London, 1905, pp. 138, 144. Jackson, *Early Days*, p. 131.
**72** Steven Feierman, *The Shambaa Kingdom; a History*, Madison, Wis. 1974, pp. 23, 40-1, 44, 79, 125-7, 168, 185-6.
**73** Aylward Shorter, *Chiefship in Western Tanzania; a Political History of the Kimbu*, Oxford, 1972, pp. 40, 46, 55, 136, 193.
**74** Alfred J. Swann, *Fighting the Slave Hunters in Central Africa*, London, 1910, pp. 61, 65, 187.
**75** *JSPFE*, XI (1930), pp. 50-1.
**76** Swann, *Slave Hunters*, pp. 205-7.
**77** W. D. M. Bell, *The Wanderings of an Elephant Hunter*, London, 1958, p. 156.

THE EMPIRE OF NATURE

78 Josh Tosh, *Clan Leaders and Colonial Chiefs in Lango*, Oxford, 1978, pp. 22-3, 29-31, 47, 53-4, 85-6, 96-7.
79 John Lamphear, *The Traditional History of the Jie of Uganda*, Oxford, 1976, pp. 7, 11, 115.
80 Lamphear, *Jie*, p. 12.
81 Lugard, *East African Empire*, Vol. I, p. 251.
82 Henry Faulkner, *Elephant Haunts*, London, 1968, p. 46.
83 D. R. Mackenzie, *The Spirit-ridden Konde*, London, 1925, pp. 132-45.
84 Sir Samuel W. Baker, *Wild Beasts and their Ways*, 2 vols. London, 1890, Vol. I, p. 116; Vol. II, pp. 73, 152. See also Ian Cunnison, 'Giraffe hunting among the Humr tribe', *Sudan Notes and Records*, XXXVII (1956), pp. 49-60.
85 Parker and Amin, *Ivory Crisis*, pp. 11-13, 128.
86 Scudder, *Gwembe Tonga*, p. 193.
87 *JSPFE*, XII (1930), p. 56.

# CHAPTER FOUR

# Hunting and settlement in southern Africa

Until the nineteenth century the fauna of southern Africa was richly diverse, highly prolific, and widely dispersed. Humans had interacted with animals throughout the region's history exploiting them as a food source and defending their stock and crops against predators, carnivorous or herbivorous. As we have seen, indigenous hunting techniques were varied and effective and game meat constituted a source of protein for almost all the peoples of the sub-continent. For some, particularly the Sotho-Tswana peoples living on the eastern fringes of the Kalahari, it was a central area of economic and social relations. But with white expansion in the eighteenth and nineteenth centuries the southern African fauna was sent into rapid retreat.

It is possible to identify a number of phases in the white exploitation and destruction of game. Game constituted a vital expansionist resource, a ready source of meat, a means of paying labour, and an item of trade to supplement other forms of economic activity. Hunters had always crossed the frontiers of settlement in search of animals, and as the game frontier receded such hunters were drawn deeper into the interior, often acting as the vanguard of a further extension of the settlement frontier. Wild animal products were among the most important traded goods between black and white, most of the frontier hunters acting also as traders. Game was a vital subsidy to the Boers during their Great Trek after 1835. In the ensuing decades the high veld was rapidly cleared of game and the hunting frontier was extended into Zululand and southern Mozambique, westwards into the Tswana hunting grounds of the Kalahari, and eventually northwards beyond the Limpopo into the territory of the modern Zimbabwe. In this period a succession of hunters whose publications made them famous revealed the animal resources of the region to the outside world. They offer so many insights into the retreat of game and the hunting ethos that their careers are worth following in some detail. By the 1890s the game populations of the Cape, Natal, the Orange Free State and the South African Republic had been almost completely worked out. This was to stimulate the first pressure for conservation.

When the Dutch arrived at the Cape in 1652 wild animals inhabited the entire region. Several of the large antelope, many small gazelles, zebras and accompanying predators were to be found in the vicinity of the Cape itself. Elephant and rhinoceros were discovered in the immediate interior, and hippos inhabited the rivers and streams of the eastern Cape. White rhino and giraffe, long associated with the further interior beyond the Orange river, may well have existed in the northern Cape. Ostriches must have been found close to the Cape too, for a lively trade in eggs and feathers developed from the earliest days of Dutch settlement. The first settlers, having come from one of the most densely populated areas of Europe, where little or no hunting was to be found, can have seen animals only as dangerous competitors, to be beaten back from the enclave of civilisation. Nevertheless, their value as a cheap source of food must soon have been evident, and as the Dutch embarked upon their rapid process of environmental adaptation the opportunities for exploiting animal resources became more apparent. From the early eighteenth century freeburghers repeatedly went out on hunting parties, particularly in pursuit of hippos and eland.[1] These animals were an excellent source of meat for the colonists and their slaves.

As the Dutch spread into the interior, specific places became associated with animals to be seen there and place names developed accordingly. These names, many of them still to be found on the map today, testify to the richness of the Cape's game before the nineteenth century. They include Elandsberg, Rhenoster (rhinoceros) Kop, Oliphant's Vlei, Quagga Fontein, Gemsbok Laagte, Leeuw (lion) Spruit, Wildebeespan, Hartbeeskuil, and many others. By the second half of the nineteenth century few, if any, such animals could be found in the Cape at all. David Livingstone remarked that place names commemorated animals that were not to be found for hundreds of miles.[2] In 150 years the settlers, Boers and later British, aided by African hunters, had cleared the entire Colony of game. They had done so before the era of the breech-loading rifle and cartridge, using only muskets (particularly the large Boer variety, or 'roer'), muzzle-loaded with powder and home-made balls.

Dutch hunting parties were leaving the Colony for hunting grounds in the eastern Cape from the early eighteenth century, and a number of freeburghers made a career as professional hunters. They went mainly for ivory, but other animal products were brought back too. In 1736 two expeditions, one of six wagons and the other of thirteen, traded ivory with the Thembu and the Xhosa. Several of the members of one of these expeditions led by Hurmanus Heupenaer, were killed in a clash with the Xhosa.[3] The number of such parties increased during the century, although their activities were often more or less clandestine, and by 1770 a regular wagon road led to the Fish river. Hunting was combined with trade, and the 'hunters' probably obtained more ivory from Africans than they shot themselves. These hunter-traders, or *togtgangers*, also exchanged European goods, including arms and ammunition for cattle. The itinerant traders, or *smouse*, of the interior and frontier districts likewise obtained products of the hunt, ostrich feathers, biltong (dried meat), and sometimes hides and skins. The importance of game to the frontier has long been recognised. The travellers of the late eighteenth and early nineteenth centuries noted

[ 87 ]

the extent to which the frontier graziers subsisted on it while establishing themselves, using venison and buffalo beef to avoid slaughtering their own animals. In the 1770s the Swedish botanist Carl Peter Thunberg described the manner in which the frontier colonists used Khoikhoi hunters to feed themselves and their employees.

> The whole roof in the kitchen was hung with thick slices of buffalo's flesh, which, being dried and smoked, they ate as hung beef . . . Buffaloes were shot here by a Hottentot, who had been trained to this business by the farmer, and in this manner found the whole family in meat, without having recourse to the herd. The balls were counted out to him every time he went shooting, and he was obliged to furnish the same number of dead buffaloes as he received of balls. Thus the many Hottentots that lived here were suported without expense, and without the decrease of the tame cattle, which constituted the whole of the farmer's wealth. The greatest part of the flesh of the buffalo falls to the share of the Hottentots, but the hide to that of the master.[4]

Indeed, animals skins and hides supplied many of the articles essential to frontier life: thongs and whips, saddle blankets and sacks, covering of all sorts in the home, even clothes among the poorest. They were thus a valuable trade item. In the 1790s John Barrow noted the importance of the springbok to the frontier farmer.

> He also has to purchase a musquet and a small quantity of powder and lead which will procure him as much game as his whole family can consume . . . The springboks are so plentiful on the borders of the colony, and so easily got at, that a farmer sends out his Hottentot to kill a couple of these deer with as much certainty as if he sent him among his flock of sheep. In a word, an African [i.e. Boer] peasant of the lowest condition never knows want; and if he does not rise into affluence, the fault must be entirely his own.[5]

In 1809 another traveller, Collins, reported on the area around Rhinocerosberg. It contained not only fine pasturage and good water but also the third necessity of the frontier colonist, an abundance of game.[6] There were many hippos and plenty of antelopes and springboks. Moreover, in this period of expension, the frontier trade, often in animal products, was as important as it had been in the eighteenth century. Thus, 'The graziers who combined stock farming with hunting and trading formed the vanguard of the expansion movement'.[7] Moreover, hunting added impetus to frontier expansion, since hunting was, of course, exceptionally land extensive. Inevitably, hunting was to be an even more important support system to the Voortrekkers of the Great Trek than it had been to the Trekboers of the frontier.[8]

Hunting was in fact a characteristic of the 'open' frontier. Giliomee has defined the 'closed' frontier as one in which authority is established and the frontiersman's freedom of action inhibited; there is greater population pressure on the land, and the status of non-whites deteriorates.[9] One might add that as the frontier closes the game is frozen out beyond the area of human settlement. The hunter was therefore the distinctive figure of the open frontier. No authority was required, or at least authority – in the shape of Bastard or African political systems – could be flouted. Hunting and trading often shaded into raiding in the freebooting conditions. Indeed, it has been suggested that the Boer commando was but the military form of hunting and trading parties.[10] In many ways the Great Trek set out to reproduce over a large area the conditions of the open frontier.

The game was, of course, a wasting asset. It offered a temporary subsidy to the frontier settler or trekker. As settlement was consolidated the game was shot out or, disturbed, moved on. Nor was this necessarily a disadvantage to the farmers. As herds were built up, the balance between the pastoral and the hunting sectors of the frontiersman's economy changed. It was no longer in his interest to have animal competitors for the grazing. Migratory herds, particularly of springbok, might still appear and could be shot at will in order to protect the pasturage. Once the Boer republics had been established, many farmers, together with some on the frontiers of the Cape Colony and Natal, alternated between farming in the growing season and more distant hunting expeditions in the dry winter. Some moved their stock to winter grazing where game might still be found. By the turn of the nineteenth century game had already been successfully driven back from all the cultivated areas of the Cape. In 1768 one traveller noted that the semi-independent Khoikhoi had given up their circular camping formation in some parts of the Colony because of the decrease in danger from wild animals.[11] By 1800 the fast-retreating game frontier had seen the first extinction of a species. The blaaubok or bluebuck had been exterminated by about 1798.[12]

The first few decades of the nineteenth century saw a tremendous quickening of the destruction of game in southern Africa. The British brought the Cape more closely into contact with the international economy, and it was swiftly responsive to new demands based on developing tastes in Europe. The fate of the ostrich illustrates this well. Its feathers had been exported from the Cape in the early eighteenth century and the value of ostrich eggs had long been recognised. Eggs were purchased by Royal Naval officers at the turn of the nineteenth century because they could be kept at sea for some time, certainly much longer that hens' eggs (and each ostrich egg was equivalent to twenty-four hens' eggs). Feathers were beginning to fetch high prices and swiftly became an important element of Cape trade.[13] Frontier Boers hunted the ostrich and traded beads for feathers with Africans on the eastern Cape. For the first thirty years of the century the supply of wild feathers was maintained, and it was only when wild sources were beginning to be exhausted that the domestication of the ostrich was undertaken. The wild ostrich frontier retreated into the continent while the tame ostrich was reared in the settled areas.

In the early 1820s ostriches were still relatively numerous on the Cape frontier, where they were assiduously hunted by the Boers. In that period the finest plumes fetched 6d to 1s each, while the skin could be sold for 15s – 25s.[14] Since an ostrich could bear forty-five plumes of the best quality, one bird could bring the hunter from £1 17s 6d (£1.87) to £3 10s (£3.50). Steedman saw wild ostriches as close to the Cape as the Hex river and the Zwartberg mountains in 1831. He saw tame ostriches stalking about at Griqua's Town, a better indicator of the future of the ostrich in southern Africa.[15] By the 1890s, the wild ostrich could be found only in the region around and to the north of the Limpopo. By that time the plumage from an ostrich could fetch £22 10s (£22.50), which made its continued hunting a lucrative proposition despite its widespread domestication farther south.[16]

As we shall see in chaper eight, the first British game legislation was introduced to the Cape in 1822. It was partly a response to the realisation that game was being progressively exterminated. Thomas Pringle, who led a Scottish settlement to Glen Lyndon on the Baavians river between 1820 and 1822, provides some valuable insights into the survival and decline of game on the Cape frontier. The settlers had to defend themselves against lions and hyenas, and there were still many elephants in the area, though Pringle and his followers never saw any.[17] Boer farms were sometimes subject to attack, their crops being destroyed and inhabitants chased. Members of Pringle's settlement attempted to shoot quaggas, wildebeest and wild boars for meat, but they did not always have much success. In fact Pringle stressed the sharp decline of game. Quagga, zebra, hartebeest and all the antelopes were seldom seen because of the 'incessant pursuit of the huntsman'. Eland, kudu and wildebeest, formerly numerous, had almost entirely disappeared, while the 'poor quagga' was often pursued for sport alone, since 'man delights to *destroy* for the mere sake of pastime'. Hippos had become 'scarce and shy', though they continued to 'abound in the larger rivers to the east and north of our frontier'. Many local place names – Buffelskloof, Buffelshock, Buffelsfontein – indicated that buffalo had previously been numerous, but hunting was so 'passionately followed' that they were 'nearly extirpated in the Colony'[18] In 1831 Andrew Steedman had to leave the Colony to collect natural history specimens. He shot gemsboks between Griqua country and Kuruman and noted that the giraffe, formerly quite common in the Colony, could now be found only to the north of Kuruman, while kudus had been driven beyond the Fish and Orange rivers.[19]

The prices of ivory, ostrich feathers and hides were buoyant in the early years of British rule and there was a considerable growth in the export of ivory and hides (at this point mainly ox and horse from around Cape Town). At the end of the Napoleonic wars, in 1815, a mere £59 worth of ivory was exported from the Cape. In 1816 the figure had already risen to £282 and by 1825 it had reached £16,586, although it was halved the following year when depression set in. Hides and skins had formerly been supplied free by meat contractors, but by the 1820s they were beginning to be an important item of export trade. Exports of hides rose from £2,324 in 1820 to £23,544 in 1825. It was not long before the skins and hides of wild animals were beginning to feature in this export trade, although they were always to remain more important in the domestic market for the manufacture of karosses. From the middle 1820s a trade in horns developed at the Cape and grew rapidly in the ensuing years. A 'keen-sighted merchant' had discovered that there was a growing demand for them in England. Whether this demand reflects the development of the fashion for decorating housing with animal horns, which must have arisen from this period, or the growing use of horn for handles in the manufacture of cutlery is not clear. The trade in horn reached an initial peak, by value, of £6,621 in 1829.[20]

Animal products dominated the trade of Albany, the English settlement on the eastern Cape which grew rapidly after the arrival of the settlers in the 1820s. By 1831, out of a total trade of £51,290, animal products accounted for £38,738 or more than 75 per cent. The latter was made up of ivory, hides, horns, skins and ostrich feathers. Andrew Steedman, surveying the market register at Grahamstown, discovered that 1,906 wagon loads of mainly animal products had entered the market between October 1831 and 30 September 1832. At this market the visitor could see:

the farmer from the most distant extremities of the Colony, with his waggon laden with curiosities, such as skins of wild animals, ostrich feathers, ivory, and the rude but deadly weapon of the Bushmen and Bechuanas. Here also is to be seen the enterprising settler, just returned

[ *91* ]

from a six months' trading journey to the interior, with a cargo of hides and ivory, together with the rich fur dresses or cloaks of the natives of distant regions, visited by him in his peregrinations.[21]

The appearance of the wool-bearing merino sheep and the rapid growth of wool exports from the Cape hastened the retreat of the game frontier. Exports of wool from the Cape Colony rose from 113,000 lb in 1833 to 5,447,000 lb in 1851. Sheep farmers from Albany took up land vacated by Boers, and immigrants and capital were attracted from Britain. Neither humans nor game were permitted to compete with intensive sheep farming. Many Bastard grazier-hunting communities of the frontier were dispossessed and the land was taken up by white farmers.[22] The merino sheep confirmed the closing of the Colony's frontier, the diminution of game, and the re-location of hunting enterprise deeper in the interior.

As the animal resources of southern Africa became more important to the international economy in the first decades of the nineteenth century they came to be studied and hunted for science and sport. The first published observations of the fauna of the region came from botanists, who supplemented their collection and description of specimens with geographical, zoological and ethnographic material. The most distinguished of these was the Swedish botanist Carl Peter Thunberg, who made three visits to the interior of the Cape between 1772 and 1775.[23] His compatriot, Anders Sparrmann, visited the Cape in the same period.[24] The Frenchman François Le Vaillant, an avid hunter, made two journeys in the Cape in 1780-82 and 1783-85.[25] He concentrated rather more on the fauna, although he was primarily an ornithologist. Further information about the interior was added by the mathematician and cartographer John Barrow, who mapped the Cape in 1797 and 1798,[26] and the German naturalist Martin Heinrich Lichtenstein, travelling between 1803 and 1806.[27] W. J. Burchell explored the interior on the eve of the re-establishment of British rule, while Pringle and Steedman observed animals while pursuing other objectives. The publications of these scientists and settlers helped to introduce to southern Africa a new breed of literate traveller for whom hunting was the primary objective. Several of the hunters published amounts of their experiences, and their works, many of them bestsellers, made the animal life of southern Africa better known to a wider audience, particularly as zoological gardens in Europe were obtaining live specimens at the same time. By increasing knowledge of the interior they stimulated speculation about its natural, including animal, resources. Above all, they contributed to the developing hunt-

ing cult of the nineteenth century. The exploits of a succession of celebrated hunters were avidly read by their successors later in the century.
By then the technology and the opportunities had both changed, but
the classic works of the 1830s, 1840s and 1850s inspired later hunters
to emulate their famous predecessors. The transition from the
naturalist observers, representatives of the scientific renaissance of the
turn of the eighteenth and nineteenth centuries, to the great Nimrods
of the middle decades of the nineteenth is well represented by the
careers of Burchell, Smith, Cornwallis Harris, and their hunting successors. Each pushed farther out of the Colony to reach the retreating game
riches of the region.

The activities of William John Burchell (1782?-1863) illustrate the
diverse scientific interests of the early travellers. In 1805 he was
appointed schoolmaster and acting botanist on St Helena in the service
of the East India Company. There he became acquainted with General
Janssens, the last Dutch governor of the Cape, and the great naturalist
Martin Lichtenstein. In 1810 he went to the Cape and travelled in the
interior between 1811 and 1815. He visited Adam Kok, leader of one
of the Bastard communities, and reached Latakum (Dithakong). On his
return to Britain he published the astronomical, meteorological, botanical and natural historical observations derived from his expeditions.
He brought back skulls and skins of all the larger mammals to the
British Museum. He published two volumes on his travels, illustrated
by himself, (a third was projected but did not appear), as well as pamphlets on Cape emigration.[28] Later he was employed by Kew to collect
plants in South America.

Andrew (later Sir Andrew) Smith (1797-1872) was an army medical
officer at the Cape from 1821 to 1837. A graduate of the University of
Edinburgh, he later became the Director General of the Army and
Ordnance Medical Departments and was severely censured for the
failures of the army medical department in the Crimean War. At the
Cape he compiled reports on the Bushmen (1828) and on the Zulu and
Port Natal (1831), but he is best known for the scientific expediton he
led into the interior between 1834 and 1836. He was authorised to
negotiate treaties with African chiefs and kings, but his main objective
was to study the flora and fauna of the region beyond the Cape frontier,
primarily in what was later to be Bechuanaland. He brought back
numerous specimens for museums (his example of a giraffe was still
on display in the Natural History Museum in South Kensington at the
end of the century)[29] and published his five-volume *Illustrations of the
Zoology of South Africa* between 1838 and 1847.[30] For several years he

held the post of honorary director of the government civil museum in Cape Town.

His expedition and his published work were to influence the new breed of hunter that now arrived in southern Africa. The latter set out to combine the study of natural history with hunting, conferring on adventure and butchery an air of scientific respectability. Several of them were Indian Army Officers who had their first experience of the Cape on the long voyage out to India. While the ship was re-victualling and re-fitting they were often able to indulge in a brief visit to the immediate interior of the Cape and enjoy their first taste of African 'sport'. Moreover, Indian medical boards began to use the Cape as a 'sanatorium'. Officers of the Indian Army whose health was impaired by fever were advised to convalesce at the Cape. This was what brought the first of the celebrated international pseudo-scientific hunters to the region.

Captain (later Major Sir) William Cornwallis Harris (1807-48) joined the service of the Honourable East India Company in 1825 as a second lieutenant in the Bombay establishment (engineers). In 1836 he was invalided to the Cape. On the voyage across the Indian Ocean he met Richard Williamson, a 'noted shikari' of the Bombay civil establishment, and they resolved to go hunting together in the interior. At the Cape they met Andrew Smith, just returned from his expedition, and discussed with him their route and the animals they would encounter. In his account of the journey, published in Bombay in 1838 and London in 1841, Harris described his qualifications for the chase. 'From my boyhood upwards I have been taxed by the facetious with shooting madness, and truly a most delightful mania I have ever found it.'[31] He fired a blunderbuss at the age of six. He shot his neighbour's ducks and geese with a crossbow of his own construction, and acquired a musket with his Christmas present money. In India he shot buck and tiger from elephant-back and attempted to shoot the lions of Gujerat (none of which, he asserted, reached adulthood because they were all shot — by the end of the century they were almost extinct). He set out for southern Africa in the hope of fulfilling his 'desire to add to Geography and Natural History'· He 'stalked the forest and scoured the plain' in pursuit of his 'passion for venerie and natural history observation' and wrote his account for 'brother officers equally passionate for the chase'.

Harris and his party set out from Port Elizabeth and his route took him via Grahamstown, Somerset, Graaf Reinet and Kuruman to the residence, in the north-west of the Transvaal, of King Mzilikazi of

Ndebele. He was well received by the king, was granted permission to hunt elephants, and headed north towards the Limpopo. He travelled back to the Colony by a more easterly route for which the king had not given permission, and returned to India at the end of 1837. Harris employed a cook who had previously worked for another hunting party from India, so it is clear that the tradition of East India Company officers using the Cape as a hunting ground was already established. Moreover, at Grahamstown he met 'two Indian gentlemen' (meaning, of course, Europeans from India) returning from the interior with ivory. Later he referred to the expedition of Mr Kinloch of the East India Company, who had been shooting in the Cashan mountains, north of the Vaal. He also met, in Griqua territory, Captain Sutton of the 75th Foot, 'a mighty Nimrod', returning from a successful expedition after elephants.[32] An elite hunting tradition, self-financing when ivory was secured, was already well established.

Harris lamented the decline and disappearance of game in the Cape Colony, and suggested that African hunters, confronted with vast herds in the interior, were bent on extermination. Nevertheless, his descriptions of game-rich areas were to enthral subsequent hunters confronted with an ever retreating game frontier. He saw a trek of springbok early in his journey. On the way to Mzilikazi's capital the landscape was 'a moving mass of game'. Later he saw a 'perfect panorama of game', with, at one point, 300 elephants in view at one time. He shot quaggas, wildebeest, hartebeest, hippos, rhino, impala and waterbuck in large numbers. Once he reached the area where they could be found he shot many elephant and was particularly ecstatic when killing giraffe. Shooting his first giraffe produced in him a 'tingling excitement', for the 'summit of hunting ambition' was 'actually obtained'; it took him seventeen shots, given the muzzle-loading firearms of the period. On another occasion he described the fifty wounds he had had to inflict in order to bring down a bull elephant. Wherever he went large numbers of camp followers and local people attached themselves to him to take advantage of the quantities of meat he left behind.

There can be no doubt that he was a profligate hunter. He filled his wagons with so much ivory that he was 'reluctantly compelled to leave the ground strewed with that valuable commodity'. Soon afterwards he found it so easy to kill elands that he salted their tongues and briskets for his homeward journey, leaving the carcases to the vultures. Others were able to take advantage of his trigger happy approach. On his journey from Kuruman to Mzilikazi's capital he left so many quaggas and wildebeest wounded that local hunters could emerge to

[ 95 ]

finish them off with their spears. Before the expedition was over his tally of big game passed the 400 mark.[33]

Harris recovered his costs from the sale of ivory, although the neglect of his 'Hottentot' servants caused him a loss, he claimed, of £800. His followers, indeed, did business on their own account by collecting hippo teeth and ostrich feathers for subsequent sale (at a time when the value of hippo ivory remained high). He offered advice to subsequent Indian expeditions on the manner in which they could finance their expeditions from the sale of ivory. He had hoped to reach Lake Ngami, but when it proved impossible on his first journey he expressed a desire to return to southern Africa to lead an expedition to the lake. That achievement later fell to David Livingstone and William Cotton Oswell. Harris contented himself with communicating an account of his travels to the Geographical Society of Bombay and the Royal Geographical Society in London. Like so many travellers of the time, he was also an amateur artist. In addition to *The Wild Sports of Southern Africa* he published a folio volume of lithographs in 1840, *Portraits of the Game Animals of Southern Africa, drawn from Life in their Natural Haunts*. He published papers in the *Proceedings of Zoological Society of London* in 1838 and in the same society's *Transactions* in 1842.

Roualeyn Gordon Cumming, perhaps the most celebrated of all nineteenth-century hunters in southern Africa, also first reached the Cape by courtesy of the East India Company.[34] Born in 1820, the second son of Sir William Gordon Gordon Cumming of Altyre and Gordonstoun, second baronet, he developed an interest in 'sport' and natural history from his earliest days. In 1839, after Eton, he sailed to India as a subaltern in the 4th Madras Light Cavalry. On the way he touched at the Cape of Good Hope and hunted smaller antelopes, obtaining 'a foretaste of the splendid sport I was in after years so abundantly to enjoy'. In India he collected a large number of specimens of natural history and 'laid the foundation of a collection' which later 'swelled to gigantic proportions'. (He also described himself as a passionate oologist, building up one of the finest collections of birds' eggs). He soon found the Indian climate disagreeable and left. He devoted some time to stag hunting in Scotland and procured a 'fine collection of select heads'. But he found the presence of keepers and foresters restricting and resolved to try for bison and wapiti in North America. He joined the Royal Veteran Newfoundland Companies, soon discovered he would get little time off for hunting, and transferred to the Cape Riflemen in 1843. At the Cape he realised once again that soldiering would get in the way of hunting and brought himself out.

He embarked on a series of five expeditions between late 1843 and 1848 on which he built the rest of his career. He was clearly never short of a private income and was able to fit himself out with several wagons, Khoikhoi servants (on two occasions he was also accompanied by a white servant), an extensive armament, trade goods, and all the horses, dogs and oxen he required. He was a colourful figure. He weighed fourteen stone (a grave handicap to his horses) and invariably hunted in the kilt and 'Badenoch brogues'. He exploited his Scottish origins with the Boers, by hinting that the Scots should make common cause with them against the English. He also traded on his national origins in seeking hospitality, advice and introductions to African kings from his compatriots, the missionaries Robert Moffat and David Livingstone.

He gives us an interesting description of the hunting activities of frontier Boers, their residences often surrounded by hundreds of skulls and horns, their conversation all on the hunt, whether of gemsbok, lions or Bushmen. He visited one, Hendrik Strydom, who lived entirely by hunting and soap manufacture. He also hunted with the Griquas and observed Tswana hunts. He encountered *smouse*, frontier traders bringing back cattle in exchange for their trade goods and bearing ivory, karosses and ostrich feathers on their wagons. In his repeated forays back and forth across the Colony's borders he described the sporting hunts of the frontier towns. The Nimrods of Grahamstown indulged in wild boar and porcupine hunting. A Captain Hogg kept a pack of foxhounds to course the few springbok that were left. At Colesberg Colonel Campbell of the 91st went out shooting to provide meat for his men, combining sport with utility.

In his first two expeditions he progressed only a short distance across the Vaal, but on the next three he penetrated beyond Kuruman to the northern Tswana regions. He combined hunting with trade, selling muskets, powder and other goods to the northern Tswana peoples in exchange for ivory, karosses and ostrich feathers. He also made large collections of African arms, crafts, ornaments and dress, which he termed 'curiosities'. At the end of his first journey he sold ivory and ostrich feathers worth £1,000.

He was even more profligate in his hunting that Harris had been. Like all hunters of the period he was influenced by the apparent fecundity of nature. He saw 'plains teeming with game', a 'hunter's elysium'. When he reached the richest hunting lands to the north he saw 'a never-ending succession of every species of noble game'. He felt they were

[ 97 ]

his, that he could exercise 'undisputed sway' over them in hunting which compared dramatically with 'the tame and herded narrow bounds of the wealthiest European sportsman'.[35] Confronted by a trek-bok, he killed thirty to forty springboks in company with Boers who shot hundreds. He killed at least 105 elephants on his journeys and, judging by his descriptions of daily exploits, innumerable other game. For example, he nonchalantly describes killing thirty hippos in a few days. Once when he encountered a herd of eight bull and cow elephants he killed them all. He seldom, if ever, expressed regret, as his successors fifty years later were to do. He was even profligate with his own animals. Forty-five horses and seventy oxen died in his service, presumably from the rigours of climate and disease as well as hunting and travelling. He was never without large packs of dogs which he used in every form of the hunt. As well as coursing antelope they also brought elephants to bay, distracting them while the hunter was reloading, and even pursued lions. The latter was a particularly dangerous exploit, and it is not surprising that seventy dogs were killed in the course of Cumming's hunting activities.

His techniques, his descriptions of them, and the reception he and his works received cast a curious light on Keith Thomas's contention, quoted in chapter two, that by the end of the eighteenth century 'a new concern for the suffering of animals had arisen', helping 'to create new sensibilities of a kind which have gained in intensity ever since'.[36] By the late nineteenth century a hunting code had developed, and adherence to it was the mark of the gentleman sportsman . Cumming flouted every provision of that as yet unformulated code. He fired indiscriminately into herds; he shot females as often, or more often, than males; he indulged in long shots with little hope of success. He frequently shot at a water hole at night. He shot to lame rather than to kill, a technique dictated by his muzzle-loading, powder-and-ball (the balls cast from a store of lead he carried with him) firearms. The meat was often left for scavengers, although it is true that anything up to 200 African camp followers accompanied him to take advantage of the remains he left in his wake. Often, however, there was more than people could eat.

Given the primitiveness of his technology it often took up to fifty-seven balls to kill an elephant. He never seemed particularly anxious to put an animal out of its pain. On one occasion he declined to kill a sable antelope he had wounded until he had tested his dogs on the blood spoor. On another he lamed an elephant with a ball in the shoulder blade. Then:

[ 98 ]

> I resolved to devote a short time to the contemplation of this noble
> elephant before I should lay him low; accordingly, having off-saddled the
> horses beneath a shady tree which was to be my quarters for the night
> and ensuing day, I quickly kindled a fire and put on the kettle, and in a
> very few minutes my coffee was prepared. There I sat in my forest home,
> coolly sipping coffee, with one of the finest elephants in Africa awaiting
> my pleasure behind a neighbouring tree.[37]

His descriptions of the death throes of animals are frequently harrowing.

> I gave him thirty-five balls, all about and behind his shoulder, and dis-
> charged at distances varying from fifteen to thirty-five yards, before he
> would halt and die. At length he reduced his pace to a very slow walk;
> blood flowed from his trunk and all his wounds, leaving the ground
> behind him a mass of gore; his frame shuddered violently, his mouth
> opened and shut, his lips quivered, his eyes were filled with tears; he
> halted beside a thorny tree, and having turned right about he rocked for-
> wards and backwards for a few seconds, and, falling heavily over, his
> ancient spirit fled.[38]

Nor was he squeamish about his servants and domestic animals. He
administered corporal punishment to the first and was surprised when
they decamped. He believed the Boers were too soft on their oxen, and
did not recognise the necessity of heavy flogging. On several occasions
he described his oxen as 'running down with gore' from the whip. His
attitude to his dogs is interesting. He became attached to many of
them, but he consciously forced them into danger, lost three animals
on one hunt, and described their injuries and death throes in detail.[39]

These instances are offered not to transmit condemnation from a
more squeamish age but to demonstrate the problematic character of
Keith Thomas's Whiggish belief in the beneficent effects of Romanticism and the study of natural history. Cumming was not condemned
by his contemporaries, although some professed to find his exploits
rather far-fetched and found the subsequent showmanship distasteful.
On the contrary, his two-volume A Hunter's Life in the far Interior of
South Africa, published in 1850, was an immense success and, according to the Dictionary of National Biography, made him 'the lion of
the season'. His trophies and 'curiosities', which had filled nine wagons
when shipped home, were exhibited first at his 'South African
Museum' in the Chinese Gallery in London, and later with great success at the Great Exhibition in the Crystal Palace in 1851.[40] He travelled the country lecturing and exhibiting his lion-skins under the
sobriquet 'The Lion Hunter', and in 1856 brought out a condensed

version of his book under the title *The Lion Hunter in South Africa*. New editions appeared later in the century and it remained an influential work with the leaders of the hunting cult. In 1858 he established his collections in his own museum at Fort Augustus, on the Caledonian Canal, where it became 'a great attraction to tourists'. All these activities brought him a good deal of popularity and a lot of money.

Some more restrained hunters (though it is a matter of degree) were rather dubious about some of his methods, but he seems to have maintained a good relationship with David Livingstone, who asked Cumming to kill game to feed workers who were thatching the mission church. Cumming seems to be the practical hunting and literary equivalent of Landseer. His descriptions are frequently ecstatic; his favourite adjective for all game was 'noble'; and he often linked, in direct proportions, the beauty of the prey to his desire to kill and possess. On one occasion he encountered 'an antelope of the most exquisite beauty'. It was a 'princely old buck' (in fact a bushbuck):

> On beholding him I was struck with wonder and delight. My heart beat with excitement. I sprang from my saddle, but before I could fire a shot this gem of beauty bounded into the reeds, and was lost to my sight. At that moment I would have given half what I possessed in this world for a broadside at that lovely antelope, and I at once resolved not to proceed farther on my expedition until I had captured him, although it should cost me the labour of a month.[41]

The passage well represents the ambiguities of the Victorian attitude towards animals. It may be that a distinction was drawn between the domestic and the wild, between a man's responsibility and man's opportunity, but, as Cumming reveals, there was an ambivalence towards domestic animals too. Taking potshots at the neighbour's birds or cats was to be a favourite preoccupation of youthful hunters, from Harris to the admiring successors of Cumming at the end of the century. What would today be regarded as criminal would in Victorian times be seen as no more than a jolly jape, judging by the number of figures who confessed to it. The study of natural history, far from introducing 'new sensibilities', in fact offered justification for the study of the anatomical processes of death.

If Gordon Cumming's activities and the public reaction to them tell us something of mid-Victorian attitudes to hunting, natural history and showmanship, his exploits and observations are indicative of the withdrawal of the hunting frontier in southern Africa. He provides evidence of the depredations of those who did not publish their experiences or game bags. Boer, Griqua and Tswana hunters were hacking away at the game resource as at a coal face. They no longer hunted to survive, but to supply the demands of trade in skins, ivory and feathers. Two of Cumming's contemporaries, William Cotton Oswell and David Livingstone, were also to observe and participate in this process.

Late in life Oswell (1818-93) urged his sons to read the works of Harris and Gordon Cumming. Harris's book, he wrote in a letter in 1874, had induced him to go to Africa and was the best account of African travels. 'He did not go in very far, but in those days all the big game was close at hand; now it is far, far away. Where he left off shooting, I began'.[42] Oswell's family on his mother's side had served the East India Company, and after Rugby he was sent to Haileybury to prepare himself for the civil branch of the company's service. He had been a poacher at Rugby and had been involved in ducking the local gamekeeper in the river, an exploit which nearly led to his expulsion. He had a passion for dogs and horses, and hunting was his chief delight. He read the novels of Captain Marryat and Fenimore Cooper until he knew them by heart. He left for India in 1837 and was posted to the southern division of Arcot. He soon established himself as a hot-tempered official who delivered summary punishments of flogging, and he joined his younger colleagues in pig sticking, hunting and shooting. In letters home he described the manner in which bouts of work punctuated sport rather than the other way round. He contrasted his pursuit of bison, deer and boar with shooting in England:

> Why the Gentlemen of England don't know what sport is. The knocking over a brace or two of partridges, and a hare or two in a little bit of a plantation, or an unromantic grain field, called by them *sport*, is not to be compared with Indian shooting. The one is confined in extent, the other boundless; the one dull and tame, the other exciting to a degree.[43]

But he contracted fever, partly, his son and biographer thought, as a result of too much hunting. In 1844 he was given fifteen months' sick leave and resolved to go to South Africa rather than home . There he joined the hunter Mungo Murray and resolved to head for the interior to hunt. He reached Kuruman in 1845, where Moffat advised him – as he seems to have advised all hunters – to go 220 miles farther north to the mission of his son-in-law, David Livingstone. The encounter with Livingstone was, in effect, to destroy Oswell's career. Livingstone not only advised him on hunting opportunities but also stimulated his interest in further exploration. Oswell rejoiced in the abundance of game still to be seen in Tswana country, spent twelve hours of every day in the saddle hunting and feared to give a full account of his exploits in his letters home lest he disgust his mother. He spent several weeks on the Limpopo and was joined in the hunt by some 600 famine-starved people. He claimed that he supplied them with 60,000 lbs of meat. His second expedition was accomplished in the company of Captain Frank Vardon in 1846-47 and took him to the same region. They returned with wagons piled high with ivory and received the approval of the Boers because they did not trade, as Cumming had done, placing muskets and powder in the hands of Africans. By the time he returned to India he had overstayed his leave to such an extent that he lost his job. He briefly became superintendent of the government Coopum or Kheddah, the stable of tame elephants, and returned to England in late 1847. By the end of the following year he was back at the Cape, spending £600 on fitting out another expedition.

This time he teamed up with Livingstone and his family, and set out to reach Lake Ngami. This expedition, and two subsequent ones, were partly financed from Oswell's hunting exploits. When Livingstone expressed his gratitude for the subsidy, Oswell said that he was merely offering the fruits of the 'game of Mrs. Livingstone's preserves'.[44] At Lake Ngami and on the river Zouga or Botletle Oswell again found a great abundance of game. He not only fed the exploring party but smoothed the way with local peoples by offering them meat in large quantities. He wrote that one gun could keep 800 people in meat for months. At one stage on this expedition he saw a herd of 400 elephants. He did not use dogs in elephant hunting and came to closer grips with his quarry than Cumming had done. He was proud that every animal killed was eaten and no meat was wasted. They returned to Lake Ngami the following year, and Oswell later joined Livingstone on his expedition to the Zambezi, though he left the missionary before the latter began his journey down the river, and returned to England in 1851.

On his return he refused to publicise himself in any way. He declined to give lectures or write articles, and later he even burnt his notebooks. His family felt that he had not received his due as an explorer, but it was Livingstone who made their discoveries more widely known. Oswell was lazy as a writer and correspondent, and although he was on the council of the Royal Geographical Society he seldom attended its meetings. He had lost much of his family fortune, largely through generosity, and gave away most of his skins, heads, horns and curiosities to relatives and friends. He visited the Crimea during the war, North and South America and the West Indies. His extensive and wealthy family connections helped him to recover both his fortune and his trophies; he married in 1860 and had a house built (by Norman

Shaw) in Kent. He formed a close friendship with Sir Samuel Baker, revisited India for a hunting trip late in life and at last committed his hunting experiences to paper when he contributed the South African big-game section to the Badminton Library, published in 1892, the year before his death.

There can be little doubt that Livingstone held Oswell in high regard. His daughter wrote that her father had regarded Oswell as 'the kindest friend I had in Africa'.[45] Oswell helped finance Livingstone's earliest journeys, kept the expedition fed, and bought clothes for Livingstone's family when they were returning to Britain. Livingstone himself had a complex and ambivalent approach to hunting that was typical of the man. He recognised its necessity to exploration and all frontier activity. He frequently recorded, with his sharp observer's eye, descriptions of African hunts, and he had a great admiration for Bushmen and their relationship with the natural world. But he had many scruples about the slaughter of animals. In passing through the Cape Colony he noticed the disappearance of species from places whose names indicated their former presence. He described how two gentlemen hunting in the same area as Gordon Cumming had killed in one season no fewer than seventy-eight rhinoceros alone, and 'as guns are introduced among the tribes all these fine animals melt away like snow in spring'. He deprecated hunting at water holes – 'It is mere wanton cruelty to take advantage of the necessities of these poor animals' – and he refused to allow either his men or himself to indulge in the practice.[46] When he writes of comparative hunting prowess, it is difficult to establish whether his tone is negative or positive. Hunting the elephant, he asserted, is 'the best test of courage this country affords':

> The Bushmen choose the moment succeeding a charge when the elephant is out of breath, to run in and give him a stab with their long-bladed spears. In this case the uncivilised have the advantage over us, but I believe that with half the training Englishmen would beat the Bushmen. Our present form of civilization does not necessarily produce effeminacy, though it unquestionably increases the beauty, courage, and physical powers of the race. When at Kolobeng I took notes of the different numbers of elephants killed in the course of the season by the various parties which went past our dwelling, in order to form an idea of the probable annual destruction of this noble animal. There were parties of Griquas, Bechuanas, Boers and Englishmen. All were eager to distinguish themselves, and success depended mainly on the courage which leads the huntsman to go close to the animal, and not waste the force of his shot on the air. It was noticeable that the average for the natives was under one per man, for the Griquas one per man, for the Boers two, and

for the English officers twenty each. This was the more remarkable, as the Griquas, Boers, and Bechuanas employed both dogs and natives to assist them while the English generally had no assistance from either. They approached to within thirty yards of the animal, while the others stood at a distance of a hundred yards, or even more, and of course spent all the force of their bullets on the air. One elephant was found by Mr. Oswell with quite a crowd of bullets in his side, all evidently fired in this style, and they had not gone near the vital parts. It would thus appear that our more barbarous neighbours do not possess half the courage of the civilised sportsman.[47]

On the one hand he seems anxious about the destruction of the elephant, yet he is keen to identify courage and effectiveness in humane killing as a mark of civilisation, even if that civilisation carried with it ten to twenty times the destructive power.

Livingstone himself was forced to hunt for his party on all his expeditions and often portrayed himself as submitting to a craving for meat. He sometimes persuaded his men to hunt for him, and when one day, north of the Zambezi, he watched his followers kill a cow and a calf elephant he was prompted to these thoughts:

> I regretted to see them killed, and more especially the young one, the meat not being at all necessary at that time; but it is right to add, that I did not feel sick when my own blood was up the day before. We ought perhaps to judge these deeds more leniently in which we ourselves have no temptation to engage. Had I not been previously guilty of doing the very same thing, I might have prided myself on superior humanity, when I experienced the nausea in viewing my men kill these two.[48]

His feelings were 'not relieved by the recollection that the ivory was mine, though that was the case'. Perhaps this ambivalence was communicated to Oswell, for he felt that the missionary did not fully appreciate the efforts of the hunter.

> I am afraid he despised the role of a sportsman and no doubt believed, as he has stated, that the Kafirs looked upon us as weaklings to be used for providing them food. Perhaps he was right; but I think he overlooked that we, with no knowledge of the language, should have found it very difficult to make our way if we had only come to see the country, without shooting. He could talk to the Kafirs' ears and hearts, we only to their stomachs; but I would fain believe that his grand work was occasionally made a little smoother by the guns.[49]

However ambivalent Livingstone felt, hunting was one of the imperatives of the frontier and neither exploration nor expansion could take place without it.

Livingstone's debate with himself is, like so many other things about him, a rare instance of the recognition of the moral and environmental complexities of the hunting frontier. The speed of destruction of game in southern Africa is well illustratred in another classic of the hunting canon, William Charles Baldwin's *African Hunting and Adventure from Natal to the Zambezi*, first published in 1863, and reaching its third edition in 1894.[50] The late nineteenth-century hunters often depicted Harris, Cumming and Baldwin as the trinity of their cult. Like the others, Baldwin was fascinated by dogs, horses and the chase from an early age. He tells us that he played truant from school in order to join the local harriers in their pursuit of hares. As a young man he took work on a West Highland farm in the hope of being able to fish and shoot, but he soon found that tame and decided to emigrate. He thought of Canada or the United States, but Cumming's book induced him to go to South Africa, and he decided to land in Natal. His luggage consisted almost entirely of guns, rifles, saddles and seven deerhounds. He arrived in December 1851 and began a career as a hunter and adventurer that lasted from 1852 to 1860. He went on seven hunting expeditions, three to the north of Natal and four west to Tswana country, finally reaching the Victoria Falls. Each journey was longer than the last, the final one covering some 2,000 miles.

After his arrival he sought out 'Elephant' White, a celebrated hunter, and applied to join an expedition to shoot hippos in St Lucia Bay. Hippo hide secured a high price for making sjamboks and whips. Seven Europeans and a large number of Africans left on this trip, each European carrying 10lb of powder to comply with the strict powder laws for expeditions proceeding across the Tugela into Zulu country. Two other Europeans eventually joined them. They had three wagons, two to trade (mainly hoes, four, each worth 1s 6d, being exchanged for an ox). Baldwin's main function was to shoot meat for the party. They went out in the wet malarial season, and no fewer than seven of the nine hunters died of fever. Nevertheless, fifty-five hippos and one elephant were shot. When they became over supplied with meat they simply sank the carcasses, and the local Africans were shocked at the waste. He himself suffered from fever and returned from the trip with his health broken. He settled on a 9,600 acre farm, twenty-two miles from Durban. There he traded cattle to Africans, the cattle having been brought down from Zululand by 'Elephant' White.[51]

Finding this a monotonous existence, he set out on his second expedition to Zululand, loading up a wagon with 3,000 lb of picks (or hoes). His shooting operations were, however, restricted by the fact that Mpande, king of the Zulus, carefully regulated the entry of Europeans to the shooting areas. Nevertheless, Baldwin frequently hunted with parties of Zulus, supplying them with large quantities of meat (on one occasion, he claimed, five tons), always taking the delicacies for himself – the sumptuary law of the hunter. He encountered George Shadwell, another hunter, returning from the north, having shot 150 hippos and ninety one elephants. Baldwin traded mainly for ivory. On one occasion, in Tsonga country, he secured ivory worth ten times the gun he offered for the tusks. The heavy weighting of the terms of trade on the side of the European trader is a theme that recurs frequently in Baldwin's work. He seems to have made contact with a number of African hunters on this trip and proceeded to operate a 'putting out' system. They hunted and he traded, offering them a proportion of the profits. It was a system that was to be much used in southern Africa, by the Boers of the Zoutpansberg in the northern Transvaal and by the hunters Westbeech and Phillips on the Zambezi. It was still in use in the Congo in the 1920s and '30s. Baldwin brought back 350 lb of ivory from this trip and attempted to make up his load with twenty-five buffalo hides, for which there was a considerable market. His account is repeatedly punctuated with shooting game for meat for local people, and for his own amusement he hunted bushpig with dogs.

In 1856 he made his third trip to Zulu country to look up his hunters and take them fresh ammunition. He frequently shot for local Africans, and was offered presents of meal, rice, eggs and beer by 'pretty girls' to induce him to do so. He shot meat for the starving Tsonga and over supplied his own party to such an extent that his dogs were useless from excessive feeding. His operations were restricted, however, by the fact that a Zulu *impi* was out. Nevertheless he collected a larger number of hides, describing a good day's sport as three hartebeests, an eland bull and two buffalo bulls. Whether the difficulties in Zululand were becoming too great or he sought fresh excitements, he resolved to commence his expeditions into the interior.

In 1857 he left Natal via Ladysmith and Harrismith. He joined a party of Boers who were heading for Merico country to hunt giraffe, and encountered a Boer called Swartz who claimed to have traded 141 lb of ivory for 8 lb of beads and two bullets. He also descibes Africans parting with valuable black ostrich feathers for buttons in the mistaken belief that the latter were money. The Merico country was discovered to be fertile but virtually denuded of game, so the party decided to head northwards to Mzilikazi's country. They painted a wagon as a gift for the Ndebele king. They visited the Tswana kings Sechele and Sicomo *en route* and discovered that they were as eager to trade as they had been in Cumming's time. Sechele's people had 'no end of guns' and were in consequence eager to trade powder, lead and caps for karosses and ostrich feathers. Sechele himself bought the wagon intended for Mzilikazi for 800 lb of ivory worth £250.

Baldwin's party attempted to secure permission from Mzilikazi to hunt elephants in his country. One hunter, Collins, did get the king's permission, but he found no elephants. Mzilikazi was suspicious because Zoutpansberg Boers were already hunting north of the Limpopo in what he regarded as his territory. Mzilikazi kept Baldwin's group waiting for months and (since they had reached the fly country) their horses began to die. They sold wagons to Mzilikazi for twenty tusks; they continued to trade ivory with the northern Tswana, and they hunted for sport when they could. In the end Baldwin concluded that Mzilikazi 'has completely humbugged us, and got all he wanted from us. . . The wily old fox completely got the better of us.'[52] Baldwin resolved never to travel with Boers again, as their sole topic of conversation was their hunting exploits. Although they had failed to hunt in Ndebele country they must still have returned with a large quantity of ivory (on one occasion Baldwin described a transaction involving 1,300 lb), karosses and ostrich feathers.

It was not long before he returned to Sechele's country. He visited Swartz in the Merico region and they trekked together to Letloche. There they parted, Swartz for Mzilikazi's territory once more, Baldwin north-west to Lake Ngami. Baldwin lamented the retreat of the elephant. 'Elephants are, indeed, hard to come at now. I am very much farther north and west than Gordon Cumming ever went, and have only seen one spoor, and expect that I shall not be fairly amongst them for another three weeks.'[53] Everyone knew the value of ivory, he wrote, and a party of Bamangwato even demanded payment for permission to hunt. Nevertheless, Baldwin continued to secure very favourable trading terms. He sold a horse, which had cost him £9, for ivory worth £60 and on his return secured 100 lb of ivory from Sechele on which he could make 100% profit. He found Lake Ngami disappointing. Even in Lechulatebe's country, on the lake shore, the game was scarce:

> Today is the third day we have been without flesh meat of any kind or sort; the game is entirely exterminated: guns, pitfalls, and poisoned arrows have done their work, and last year's drought and famine had left the natives nothing to live on but the spoils of the chase.[54]

It should be remembered that Gordon Cumming and Oswell had been hunting little more than ten years before Baldwin. The speed with which the elephant frontier had retreated and the great teeming herds of game had disappeared is remarkable. Still, Baldwin left Lake Ngami with 700 lb of ivory plus skins and 'rubbish of the Kaffirs' which he would throw away if he could secure more ivory. He did indeed obtain more from Sechele on his way south.

He returned to Lake Ngami in 1859 and this time seems to have had better luck as a hunter. He employed eight Bushmen to spoor elephant and, as usual, obtained the services of many Africans for meat. On one occasion he killed eight elephants in half an hour. Two or three weeks later he shot six bulls and secured 250 lb of ivory. As usual, he gained more from trade than from the hunt. He sold one wagon and a large quantity of stores in order to load up one of his other wagons with ivory. On his return he overtook two famous Boer hunters, Jan Viljoen and Piet Jacobs. They had shot ninety-three elephants only a few days' journey farther north from Baldwin's northernmost limit. He had 'no cause to complain, however', as he had some 5,000 lb of ivory on his two wagons. His account of his trading of this load of ivory is interesting:

> I am now ouspanned before the Vaal River, four days on my road to Natal from Mooi River Dorp. I found there ivory at a very low price, in consequence of the rumoured war, or some other reason; but I was obliged to sell part of my stock there. I got 5s. 6d. per lb. for 1,000 lb., and only 3s. 6d. for 500 lb. more; but what with feathers at £7 10s. per lb., and a few karosses and rhinoceros horns, I sold to the tune of about £430, a trifle more or less, and have still a waggon-load of the finest ivory left, which I am taking to Natal, and all the best of the karosses. I have become a transport-rider, and am taking in one waggon 3,000 lb. of wool and ivory down to Natal, for which I am to receive, however, only 9s. per 100 lb.[55]

Baldwin's final journey took him to the Victoria Falls, where he met David Livingstone. He found the prospects depressing. He met an Englishman called Polson who had reached the interior from Walvis Bay fourteen months earlier and had still not got a load of ivory. Elephants were so persecuted that they were difficult to spoor, but he and several African hunters he employed managed to shoot sufficient elephants (many of them cows) to make up a load. He indulged in some night shooting and received four tusks as a present from a 'Maccalacca' chief for whom he shot large quantities of meat. Baldwin hunted on horseback, while his men hunted on foot, but one of them, Adonis, taken on at Sechele's, doubled Baldwin's kills. 'Adonis has killed four more large bulls; he runs with the speed and endurance of an ostrich and is one of the very best shots in all Africa.' But Baldwin was beginning to weary of hunting – 'it is no longer sport.'[56] Polson had at last secured 4,000 lb of ivory, but Baldwin had only one load, so he loaded up his other wagon with trophies. He endured considerable privations on the return journey and thought he had lost one of his wagons. It turned up in Natal, in charge of his servant Boccas and some hunters, six weeks after himself. His employees had found elephants in tsetse country, shot a large number, abandoned his trophies, and filled the wagon with ivory. Unfortunately, Baldwin gives us no information on his final trading prices or the method of remunerating his employees.

Baldwin proves excellent evidence of the speed with which the hunting and trading fontier moved northwards together with the retreat of the elephant. It is clear that Africans were in some respects the more effective hunters, responding swiftly to demand, and ensuring that the white 'hunters' traded more than they shot themselves. The retreat of the elephant was followed by the rapid extermination of other game, partly for hides and trophies, partly for the support system, and partly by African hunting (both for subsistence and for trade). The Lake Ngami region provides a valuable test for the disapearance of game in the space of a mere decade or two, Baldwin's evidence being confirmed by a number of other expeditions which, stimulated by the observations of Oswell and Livingstone, went there in these and subsequent years. Baldwin encountered some of the celebrated hunters of the day who left no records of their own, and heard a great deal of the reputation of the Zoutpansberg Boers. Mzilikazi was alarmed at their operations, and on one occasion Sechele was in a rage because they had confiscated guns from several of his hunters. Baldwin himself used the subcontracting system in which they excelled, and above all provides good examples of the adverse terms of trade the white hunter–traders were able to inflict on their African sources of ivory and other game products.

The Zoutpansberg hunting and trading community, with its capital at Schoemansdal, was established as one of the three Boer republics in the Transvaal region in 1847.[57] In effect it was a breakaway from the Ohrigstad or Lydenberg community. In the Zoutpansberg the Boers led a precarious existence, with the Ndebele to the west, the Gaza Ngoni to the east and a dense African population in their immediate vicinity. The elephants of the area were soon shot out and it became necessary to hunt in the fly zone, where the usual hunting technique on horseback was impossible. The Zoutpansberg Boers were soon penetrating Ndebele territory and Sechele's country, but they also developed the sub-contracting system that Baldwin had used in northern Natal. They employed African hunters on foot to take the elephants of the fly country and attempted to control the resulting trading networks. But in distributing guns and sending African hunters into adjacent areas they set in train processes which in the end they could not control. Many of the black marksmen 'deserted', and Africans began to win back control of the hunting resource. The Boers were unable to maintain command of political changes among the neighbouring Venda people, themselves heavily influenced by the black hunters, and Schoemansdal was burnt in 1867. It later bacame a more conventional agricultural settlement. Here was an organised hunting community that overreached itself. Its numbers were too small to cope with the adjacent African hunters, and its collapse was inevitable when the elephant frontier began to retreat beyond its range.

Further evidence of the rapid diminution of game comes from Andrew Anderson. Anderson was farming in Natal in 1860 when he resolved to explore and trade beyond the colonial frontiers in order, as he put it, to add to the knowledge of the physical geography of Africa. He prepared himself by studying geology and natural history, and set out to become involved in the trade in skins and hides which seemed to him a lucrative activity among his contemporaries. During the succeeding twenty years he crossed the Transvaal, spent some time hunting on the Vaal, visited the Griquas and the diamond fields, progressed northwards through the Tswana peoples, and crossed the Kalahari to Namaqualand, Damaraland and Ovamboland. He traded in Mashonaland and Matabeleland before proceeding to Portuguese East Africa. Anderson published an account of his travels in two volumes in 1887; it was reprinted in one volume the following year.

He started by describing the almost total disappearance of game from Natal in the period 1860-85. The antelope had been 'cleared from the face of the earth by the rifle, so that scarcely one is left, and those preserved that they should not be entirely exterminated'. Elephants, which had once inhabited the Berea close to Durban, had disappeared entirely; only a few small herds of buffalo survived; and a mere handful of hippo, five of them in the Umgeni river on a sugar estate. The Boers had shot out all the animals of the north-eastern Transvaal for their skins, often leaving the carcasses to be devoured by lions and hyenas. In 1864 he encountered a Boer family on the Vaal who traded skins from Africans. He found there was a great deal of game between the Vaal and Griqualand West, but by the 1880s no game was to be seen at all between Kimberley and Pretoria. The game of the Orange Free State had been wiped out in the space of twenty years. Now 'only a few blesbok, wildebeest and springbok are to be met with. Some of the farmers have now begun to preserve them on their farms, otherwise they would long since have disappeared from the country.' Lions had all been destroyed and only a few hyenas were left. The disappearance of the game matched wider environmental change. The demand for wood at the diamond fields had been so great that scarcely a tree survived over a vast area. As each Boer township had been laid out – Potchefstroom, Pretoria, Origstad, Lydenberg – the surrounding areas had been completely cleared of game. The same was true of the Rustenberg and Merico districts in the north-western Transvaal. In the 1840s they had been teeming with game, but by the time the towns of Rustenberg and Zeerust were laid out (the latter from 1868) it had been almost exterminated.[58] One of his sources for this information was John or Jan Viljoen, who had settled in the Merico district in 1848 and told him that :

> The whole of that district swarmed with elephants and every other kind of large game, as also the neighbourhood of Rustenberg, Pretoria, and other localities more south; now they are seldom seen south of the Limpopo, except in the country to the east, under the chief Umzela.[59]

Farther west the story was the same. Old Bushmen told him of the disappearance of game, and therefore of their subsistence, from Griqualand West, and the extermination of hippos in the Vaal and Orange rivers. It had happened too in Sechele's country, partly because of the effectiveness of the great Tswana hunters who could entrap as many as 1,200 head of game in pits at a time, partly because of the interest of Europeans in the area. The considerable market for karosses had appreciably helped to promote the slaughter. Game had also declined in the country north and west of Khama's, where formerly it had been very plentiful. There were still game-rich regions in Damara, Ovambo, Shona and Ndebele country, as well as in Portuguese East Africa, but guns were arriving, and whites were trying to trade and hunt in regions formerly dominated by African hunters. Mzilikazi and Lobengula had done their best to frustrate white hunters, receiving immense quantities of presents from those eager to hunt.

It may be that Anderson's picture is a little overdrawn, and it is true that he was scathing about all aspects of the Boer lifestyle. But he himself indulged in the skin trade, hunted for meat for his employees, sometimes employed them to hunt for him, and continued to travel over some of the same routes for a period of twenty years. The contrasts he drew between the 1860s and the 1880s have an authentic ring about them, and he secured oral evidence from white and black alike about the previous decades.

Indeed, the 1870s may well have been the crucial years. General Sir Arthur Cunynghame was able to secure a good deal of 'sport' during his command in South Africa, although occasionally he found himself hunting in an emparked landscape on the European model, as at Bushey Park, eight miles from Port Elizabeth. A good deal of game was still to be found in the northern Free State and in parts of the Transvaal, though he noted its steep decline. In many places Boers continued to subsist on a diet of 'rough meal, and venison'.[60] In Durban he saw a large number of skins ready for export, while in the Orange Free State the skin trade had reached destructive proportions:

> Mr. Adler told me that he had purchased more than 70,000 skins during the last year alone, and he was but a single merchant. The aggregate exportation of skins amounts to nearly one million in the year. These come generally now from the neighbourhood of Kronstadt or from eighty to a hundred miles north of Bloemfontein. The Westley Richard, and now the Martini-Henry, rifle are very busily at work. Possibly within the next ten years not a single head of game will exist on this side of the Vaal river. Everywhere we went we found the plains strewed with the skulls of blesbok and wildebeest, showing the thousands that must be destroyed yearly.[61]

Just as antelopes were being reintroduced to 'parks' and farms, so the ostrich was making a reappearance in Cunynghame's day. He described ostrich farming as 'one of the most profitable occupations on the face of the globe'. The numbers of tame birds in the Cape had risen from eighty in 1865 to 32,000 in 1875, and the value of feathers exported had increased from £65,600 in 1865 to £205,500 in 1874.[62]

Nevertheless, the trade in animal products from the north was to remain active to the 1890s. The firm of Francis & Clarke, which operated in northern Bechuanaland between 1872 and 1887, sent large quantitites of ivory, ostrich feathers and karosses south each year. In one year the total value of these commodities reached £10,000 from this partnership alone.[63] J. G. Wood, on an expedition to Matabeleland in 1887, found game still reasonably plentiful on the route to Shoshong (mainly wildebeest, kudu and guinea fowl), but he noted the destructiveness of Boer hunters. Parties of Boers were attempting to secure permission from Lobengula to hunt, leave which was not granted. Wood was not surprised at this, 'as several hunters had destroyed a large quantity of game, making no use of the flesh, merely in order to get possession of the hides. Certainly there was some reason for putting a stop to this wholesale destruction.' Later Wood met the hunter Cornelis van Rooyen, who provided him with a statistical breakdown of his annual hunts around Tati and northwards into Matabeleland and Mashonaland, starting from the age of thirteen, when he first accompanied his father.[64] The incursions of Boer hunters across the Limpopo continued to occur in the Chartered Company period after 1890: one of the officers involved in the Ndebele war of 1893 was furnished with a warrant to arrest some hunters who had crossed the Limpopo to hunt in Rhodesia, as they had been accustomed to for many years.[65]

Further detailed evidence on the decline of game is supplied by H. A. Bryden, who later became active in the preservationist lobby in Britain. Bryden spent over a year on a farm near Vryburg in 1890-91, visited the western Transvaal, and went on a hunting trip to Lake Ngami and the Botletle river (formerly known as the Zouga). There was little or no game left in Griqualand West, southern Bechuanaland or the Transvaal by the time of Bryden's visit, although the first efforts at preservation were being made. A number of neighbouring farmers had a self-denying ordinance not to touch a troop of hartebeest near Vryburg. One or two farmers preserved small herds of game on their land. As a result the traveller became much more dependent on feathered game to satisfy daily subsistence needs. In the western Transvaal Bryden found several illustrations of the decline of Boer hunting systems. In the Merico, Boer hunters like Jan Viljoen (who still survived as a very old man) had formerly spent the winter hunting in the north and the summer looking after their farms. A few still trekked as far away as Ovamboland, but the majority now stayed at home all the year round. Zeerust, where the hunters had fitted out and traded on their return, had been almost a boom town, but by Bryden's day it had become much quieter.[66] Indeed, there was almost certainly a decline in prosperity among the citizens of the Transvaal around 1870, which was partly linked with the decline of game.[67] Those who had formerly augmented their income from hunting sold their farms, and the absence of hunting opportunity helped to depress the status of poor whites.

Bryden held that the disappearance of game was changing Boer shooting habits. They had taken to target practice, and President Kruger was encouraging them by offering Martini rifles at the low price of £4 1s 9d to replace their inferior weapons.

> But the practice at targets is, after all, a very different matter from that best of all practice at game, which every Boer until these last ten or fifteen years had his fill of. The new generation of young Dutchmen now rising to manhood are not what their fathers were – some hardly touch a gun at all – and it is not too much to say that another dozen years will see

the Transvaal burghers very different shots (far less formidable in time of war) to their forefathers.[68]

The Boer War may have shown Bryden's prognostications on the decline of Boer marksmanship to have been, from the British point of view, sanguine, but the evidence for the disappearance of game is clear.

Bryden carried a letter of introduction from the Rev. John Mackenzie to King Khama and as a result received the co-operation of that monarch for his journey to Lake Ngami.[69] Bryden's party seem to have been reasonably restrained. They secured thirty-eight head of game in a month's shooting. Boer skin hunters were still encountered and had a devastating effect on the game of any area where they settled. When Bryden and his companions were about to embark on their expedition a Boer offered to buy all their skins from them. He was surprised when they announced that they wished to keep them all. For his part Bryden was surprised that Boers placed no value on trophies. 'A Boer is not yet educated to the idea of decorating his house in this way' and usually had a pile of rotting horns around his homestead.[70] A few, however, were beginning to discover the value of horns and were bringing them down with the skins.

The demands of the market could have drastic effects on the fortunes of specific animals. Formerly hippopotamus and rhinoceros hide had furnished ox whips and sjamboks, but with the near extermination of these animals attention had turned to the giraffe. 'A few years back, there happened a dearth of sjambok hide, the price of whips rose immensely, and a giraffe skin sold readily for five pounds and more. Forthwith, parties of Dutch and native hunters flocked into the Kalahari, and scores upon scores of giraffe were slaughtered.' The slaughter was overdone, the market oversupplied and prices fell rapidly, but in Bryden's day a giraffe skin was still fetching from £2 10s to £4 10s at Khama's town, Palapye.[71] Giraffe hide was also used by the Tswana for making sandals and Bryden feared that the giraffe's days were numbered.

Bryden concluded his book with a chapter on the distribution and decline of the great game of southern Africa. He was well informed, although his forebodings on the complete extermination of species – which he took to his lobbying activities in London – were to prove largely groundless. The elephant, as always, was the prime example. At the beginning of the century a Dutch hunter had enriched himself by shooting elephant near Kuruman. Cumming's exploits had been performed mainly in the hills around Shoshong, 400 miles farther north. Livingstone had seen an abundance of elephant on the Botletle (300 miles north-west of Shoshong) in 1849 and as many as 900 were shot there in the following year. In 1877-78 the trek-Boers completed the destruction of elephant in that region.[72]

In 1894 Bryden repeated his warnings with greater force in an article in the *Fortnightly Review*.[73] He was quite clear about where the responsibility for destruction lay. It was with Europeans and the introduction of breech-loading firearms. The game of the Orange Free State was destroyed between 1840 and 1875, particularly with the development of the skin trade, which accelerated from 1850. The decline of the elephant was illustrated by the collapse in the ivory trade of Cape Colony. In 1875 it was still worth over £60,000, but by 1885 it was valued at just a little over £2,000. As recently as 1860 a drive of game had been organised for the Duke of Edinburgh, then Prince Alfred, in the Orange Free State. 'It was computed that some 25,000 herd (*sic*; head?) of game were enclosed by natives and driven in. Thousands – some say 6,000 – were shot, and several natives were trampled to death by the charge of a terrified herd of Burchell's zebra.' Over the same plains no game could now be seen. He claimed that quite recently a party of Boer hunters had driven a herd of 104 elephants into a marsh in the Okavango country and killed every one. Where formerly noble game could be hunted around Vryburg and Mafeking, English sportsmen were reduced to hunting the jackal and duiker with English foxhounds. Bryden's apocalyptic vision was influential in pressing the conservationists to action in the 1890s. He supported the introduction of game regulations in Bechuanaland in 1892 and proposed the creation of a game reserve in Mashonaland. As we shall see in chapters eight and nine these were to be the two main weapons of the conservationists.

The extraordinary migrations of the springbok (*trekbokke*) provide further evidence that the 1890s was the final decade of crises for southern African game. In Steedman's day, the early 1830s, the *trekbokke* had been much dreaded by the Boer farmers of the Sneeuwberg district of the Cape.[74] At the end of the century S. C. Cronwright-Schreiner charted from family and personal memory the disappearance of game in general and the springbok in particular.[75] His maternal grandmother, an 1820 settler, remembered elephants and buffalo between Grahamstown and the coast. His father saw springboks in lower Albany in the 1850s, but by the time of Schreiner's boyhood in the 1870s there was none left. Springbok had been seen near Cradock until the 1880s. In 1880, as a youth of eighteen, Schreiner worked on a farm at Kuilfontein, near Colesberg. Wild game was still to be seen and vultures swarmed (indicating the presence of game on which they could feed). By 1890 there were few if any vultures in the area. The *trekbokke* had been seen by the early hunters, including Gordon Cumming and David Livingstone. There were four treks between 1887 and 1896. In 1892 W. C. Scully, the magistrate at Springfontein, in Namaqualand, had to issue 100 rifles and thousands of cartridges to farmers to protect their crops.[76] Many wagons carried full loads of dead animals into the town, but even so the migration broke through the line of defence and reached cultivated land. In 1896 Schreiner himself saw the last great trek. A drought in Namaqualand sent millions of springboks into the Colony north of Kimberley near the Orange river. The Boers mounted a huge hunting operation to prevent them damaging the veld and hundred of thousands were shot. Each animal fetched 2s 6d, the skin selling for 5d or 6d and the meat converting into large quantities of biltong. Schreiner saw vast numbers 'as beautiful as it was wondrous', and estimated that half a million were in view at one time. The trek covered an area 138 miles by fifteen miles. It was the last. The survivors probably died of rinderpest, and the few springbok that continued to live in the Cape Colony were preserved by farmers who were 'as jealous of them as if they were thoroughbred cattle'.

Few regions of the world had richer and more exploitable game resources than southern Africa. Even fewer witnessed such a dramatic decline in the space of half a century. Two unique species, the blaubok and the quagga, were exterminated completely. Others were eliminated within the territories of white settlement. It is almost possible to construct charts of the retreating frontiers of individual species – the elephant always in the vanguard, closely followed by rhinos and hippos, then by the more favoured antelope like eland, by the formerly prolific wildebeest and hartebeest, and with the little springbok retreating in the face of drought, hunting and rinderpest in the 1890s. The game was simply worked out, like a mineral seam. It was a vital support to European expansion in a complex combination of trade, relations with Africans, and the important meat subsidy. The European conquest of southern Africa would have been a great deal more difficult without this mobile resource. Hunting went hand in hand with exploration. It was the essential concomitant of missionary endeavour and the initial survival mechanism of the frontier. Stock-rearing and cultivation may have rested uneasily with the continued presence of game, but the wiping out of the game constituted the initial natural asset-stripping that made settlement possible. 'International' hunting produced a wave of publications which contributed to the southern

African myth, drawing new figures to the frontier, and helping to stimulate further incursions into the continent. The exploitation of game was to be equally important in the exploration, conquest and settlement of Central and East Africa.

## Notes

1 Leonard Guelke, 'White Settlers, 1652-1780', in Richard Elphick and Hermann Giliomee (eds.), The Shaping of South African Society, Cape Town, 1979, p. 53.
2 David Livingstone, Missionary Travels in South Africa, London, 1857, p. 101.
3 Monica Wilson and Leonard Thompson, Oxford History of South Africa, Oxford, 1969, Vol. I, pp. 234-5. S. Daniel Neumark, Economic Influences on the South African Frontier, Stanford, Cal., 1957, pp. 97-8.
4 Quoted in Neumark, Economic Influences, pp. 64-5.
5 Quoted in Neumark, Economic Influences, p. 37.
6 Quoted in Neumark, Economic Influences, p. 119. See also E. A. Walker, The Great Trek, London, 1934, pp. 41-2.
7 Neumark, Economic Influences, p. 136; see also pp. 107, 178.
8 Walker, Great Trek, passim.
9 Hermann Giliomee, 'The eastern frontier, 1770-1820', in Elphick and Giliomee, Shaping of South African Society, pp. 316-17.
10 Martin Legassick, 'The northern frontier to 1820', in Elphick and Giliomee, Shaping of South African Society, p. 247; Walker, Greak Trek, p. 54.
11 Richard Elphick, 'The Khoisan to c. 1770', in Elphick and Giliomee, Shaping of South African Society, p. 27.
12 Graham Renshaw, 'The blaauwbok', JSPFE, New Series, I (1921), pp. 24-6. See also R. I. Pocock, 'The extermination of the quagga', JSPFE II (1922), pp. 26-7.
13 Neumark, Economic Influences, pp. 63-4.
14 Thomas Pringle, Narrative of a Residence in South Africa, London, 1835, pp. 177-9.
15 Andrew Steedman, Wanderings and Adventures in the Interior of Southern Africa, London, 1835, Vol. II, pp. 6, 9, 40.
16 J. G. Wood, Through Matabeleland, London, 1893, p. 130.
17 Pringle, Narrative, pp. 38-9.
18 Pringle, Narrative, pp. 41, 65, 66, 79, 81, 97, 145-9.
19 Steedman, Wanderings, Vol.II, pp. 55, 125, 126-9.
20 Neumark, Economic Influences, pp. 64-8.
21 Steedman, Wanderings, Vol.II, pp. 296-8.
22 Tony Kirk, 'The Cape economy and the expropriation of the Kat River settlement, 1846-53', in Shula Marks and Anthony Atmore (eds.), Economy and Society in Pre-industrial South Africa, London, 1980, pp. 226-46.
23 Thunberg was on his way to Japan for his major botanical study, published as Flora Japanica in 1784. In South Africa he was joined on two of his trips by Francis Masson, who had been sent to the Cape by Kew Gardens. Thunberg (1743-1828) was Professor of Botany at Uppsala from 1784. His South African observations were contained in Travels in Europe, Africa, and Asia, performed between 1770 and 1779, London, 1793, and extracted as An Account of the Cape of Good Hope and some Parts of the Interior of South Africa, London, 1814. The Travels had been published in Swedish between 1788 and 1793 and were also translated into French (1794) and German (1792-94) as well as English.
24 Anders Sparrman, A Voyage to the Cape of Good Hope, towards the Antarctic Polar Circle and round the World, but chiefly into the Country of the Hottentots and Caffres from the year 1772 to 1776, London, 1785. There were many subsequent editions.
25 François Le Vaillant, Travels from the Cape of Good Hope into the Interior Parts of Africa, London, 1790. Le Vaillant (1753-1824) was fascinated in his youth by the

cabinets and collections of natural history in Paris. He was the first to bring a specimen of a giraffe to the Jardin des Plantes. His publications included *Histoire naturelle des oiseaux d'Afrique*.

26 John Barrow, *An Account of Travels in the Interior of Southern Africa in the years 1797 and 1798*, London, 1801. Barrow (1764-1848) visited China with Lord Macartney, left South Africa after the Treaty of Amiens of 1802, and subsequently became Secretary to the Admiralty.

27 Martin Heinrich Carl Lichtenstein, *Travels in South Africa in the years 1803, 1804, 1805, and 1806*, London, 1812-15.

28 W. J. Burchell, *Travels in the Interior of Southern Africa*, 2 vols., London, 1822.

29 H. A. Bryden, *Gun and Camera in Southern Africa*, London, 1893, p. 328.

30 Andrew Smith, *Illustrations of the Zoology of South Africa*, 5 vols., London, 1838-47.

31 William Cornwallis Harris, *The Wild Sports of Southern Africa, being the Narrative of a Hunting Expedition from the Cape of Good Hope through the Territories of the Chief Moselikatse to the Tropic of Capricorn*, London, 1852 (fifth edition; first 1839), p. xiii.

32 Harris, *Wild Sports*, pp. xiv – xv, 6, 9-10, 37.

33 Harris, *Wild Sports*, pp. 27, 55, 163, 169, 197, 213, 253-5 and *passim*

34 Roualeyn Gordon Cumming, *Five Years of a Hunter's Life in the far Interior of South Africa*, 2 vols., London, 1850, vol I, pp. vii–viii.

35 Cumming, *Five Years*, Vol. I, pp. 63, 74-7, 106, 260; Vol. II, p. 295, and *passim*.

36 Keith Thomas, *Man and the Natural World*, London, 1983, p. 243.

37 Cumming, *Five Years*, Vol. II, p. 92.

38 Cumming, *Five Years*, Vol. II, p. 63.

39 Cumming, *Five Years*, Vol. I, p. 52; Vol. II, pp. 96, 327, 355 and *passim*.

40 William Cotton Oswell's friend, Frank Vardon, wrote to Oswell on 12 August 1851 with the information that Cumming's exhibition was still going on, and 'Methuen tells me that a black fellow parades up and down in front of it in a leopard skin kaross to attract visitors.' Vardon 'never thought African wanderers would come to this.' W. Edward Oswell, *William Cotton Oswell, Hunter and Explorer*, 2 vols., London, 1900, Vol. I, p. 260. On another occasion Vardon wrote that Andrew Smith had lost money showing his trophies, but 'I cannot fancy Cumming losing by anything, can you?.' Oswell, *Oswell*, Vol. I, p. 193.

41 Cumming, *Five Years*, Vol. II, p. 164.

42 Oswell, *Oswell*, Vol. II, p. 131.

43 Oswell, *Oswell*, Vol. I, p. 83.

44 David Livingstone, *Missionary Travels in South Africa*, London, 1857, p. 76.

45 Oswell, *Oswell*, Vol. II, p. 240.

46 Livingstone, *Missionary Travels*, pp. 152, 161.

47 Livingstone, *Missionary Travels*, p. 166.

48 Livingstone, *Missionary Travels*, pp. 486, 562-3.

49 Oswell, *Oswell*, Vol. II, p. 20.

50 Livingstone, *Missionary Travels*, pp. 76, 580.

51 William Charles Baldwin, *African Hunting and Adventure from Natal to the Zambezi*, London, 1894 (first edition 1863), pp. 4-22 and *passim*.

52 Baldwin, *African Hunting*, p. 209.

53 Baldwin, *African Hunting*, p. 223.

54 Baldwin, *African Hunting*, p. 256.

55 Baldwin, *African Hunting*, p. 336.

56 Baldwin, *African Hunting*, pp. 391-2, 417.

57 Roger Wagner, 'Zoutpansberg: the dynamics of a hunting frontier, 1848-67', in Marks and Atmore, *Economy and Society*, pp. 313-49.

58 Andrew A. Anderson, *Twenty-five Years in a Wagon: Sport and Travel in South Africa*, Cape Town, 1974 (first edition 1887), pp. 1-87 and *passim*.

59 Anderson, *Twenty-five Years*, p. 300.

60 Sir Arthur Thurlow Cunynghame, *My Command in South Africa, 1874-78*, London, 1879, pp. 41, 73.

61 Cunynghame, *Command*, pp. 80-1, 167. Despite his alarm at the destruction of game, Cunynghame offered advice on how to go big-game shooting and described expeditions made by officers under his command, pp. 284-91.

62 Cunynghame, *My Command*, pp. 9, 18.

63 Introduction to Wood, *Through Matabeleland*.

64 Wood, *Through Matabeleland*, pp. 34-5, 128-9.

65 C. H. W. Donovan, *With Wilson in Matabeleland, or, Sport and War in Zambezia*, Bulawayo, 1979 (first edition 1894), pp. 119-21.

66 Bryden, *Gun and Camera*, pp. 187-90. Bryden carried a copy of Cornwallis Harris's book with him (p. 36.)

67 Stanley Trapido, 'Reflections on land, office and wealth in the South African Republic, 1850-1900', in Marks and Atmore, *Economy and Society*, pp. 356, 359.

68 Bryden, *Gun and Camera*, p. 197.

69 Bryden, *Gun and Camera*, pp. 61-2, 268, 272.

70 Bryden, *Gun and Camera*, p. 247.

71 Bryden, *Gun and Camera*, pp. 331-5.

72 Bryden, *Gun and Camera*, p. 488

73 H. A. Bryden, 'The extermination of game in South Africa', *Fortnightly Review*, 62 (1894), pp. 538-51.

74 Steedman, *Wanderings*, Vol. II, p. 93.

75 S. C. Cronwright-Schreiner, *The Migratory Springboks of South Africa (the Trekbokke)*, London, 1925, pp. 11-13, 45-8, 57-8 and *passim*.

76 William Charles Scully, *Further Reminiscences of a South African Pioneer*, London, 1913, and *Lodges in the Wilderness*, London, 1915.

# CHAPTER FIVE

# Game and imperial rule in Central Africa

Many of the characteristics of the southern Africa exploitation of animal resources were transferred to Central Africa. The time scale, however, was compressed, and towards the end of the period there were some significant differences. As always, ivory acted as the first lure to the interior, and elephants began to beat a further retreat to the fastnesses of the continent. Africans had, of course, been exploiting the ivory for some time but, until the nineteenth century, without making serious inroads on the elephant population. The first European exploiters of ivory were individual hunter-traders, some of whom established close relations with African traditional leaders, but who essentially worked for themselves. Later ivory was used as a subsidy to underpin other endeavours: prospecting, missionary activity and commercial expansion. Ivory hunters tended to produce a considerable quantity of meat as a by-product of their activities. They fed not only themselves and their followers but also large numbers of local people, often ensuring safe passage for themselves and a supply of labour for hunting and transport. The meat subsidy became even more significant at the second level of the European advance into the interior of Africa. Missionaries, prospectors, pioneers, administrators and railway builders supplied themselves and their followers with the gun, in many cases offering meat in lieu of payment for services performed by Africans. In the pause before the establishment of more settled forms of European economic activity the supply of hides, trophies and meat formed a useful cushion for many well armed Europeans. Traders and transport riders whose peripatetic work took them into remote areas were notoriously profligate hunters, subsidising their 'legitimate' trades and paying for local services.

Once the transition period in expansion and settlement was over, legislation was introduced to curb hunting. The earliest game laws offered exemptions to travellers, administrators, police, military authorities and landowners. Later legislation, however, began to concern itself with the more extreme forms of asset-stripping and restricted social access to hunting. Not only were Africans excluded by gun laws and various provisions but ordinary Europeans too began to find their access to animals limited. The meat subsidy became an important aspect of the 'pacification' period, feeding officers and troops on campaigns against African resisters. But as time went on hunting generally became a perquisite of the colonial elite, an activity restricted to the larger landowners, senior civilian and military officals, and visiting tourists able to pay the high licence fees. Chapters eight to ten examine the manner in which the eras of primary exploitation (mainly ivory) and secondary subsidy (meat, skins, hides and trophies) gave way to the elite Hunt of the periods of preservation and conservation. This chapter examines the primary and secondary periods in Central Africa, and the ways in which they began to give way to the Hunt. The various phases are reflected in the careers of professional hunters. They began as rugged individualists; with the era of settlement they often worked within the new institutional frameworks of the nascent colonies; by the 1920s and '30s they have become transformed into safari leaders for elite tourist hunters.

It was in fact through contact with European elephant hunters that African rulers first began to ride the tiger of the European advance. White hunters appeared in Central Africa from the 1850s, and by the 1870s and 1880s they had become very nearly a flood.[1] In 1853 the Boers secured a treaty with Mzilikazi for the protection of hunters and traders, and a number of Boer hunters – Piet Jacobs or Jacobus, Jan Abrahams and Franz Joubert – soon headed for the interior. The hunter-traders Samuel H. Edwards and James Chapman accompanied Robert Moffat on a visit to Mazilikazi in 1854. Later Chapman was a frequent visitor to the first Christian mission in Matabeleland in Inyati. As we have seen in the previous chapter, hunters from the south were penetrating regions which are today parts of Angola, Zimbabwe and Mozambique by the 1860s. The Boers of the Zoutpansberg were employing African hunters operating north of the Limpopo and themselves made expeditions to Khama's country, Lake Ngami and the north-west. The Boer hunters of the Merico were also making their annual hunting trips to the north, often skirting Ndebele country to the west to reach the region of the rivers Chobi and Zambezi, still rich in elephants. Some English hunters from Natal, like Baldwin and Anderson, were making the same journey, through with varied success. From the 1860s these hunting explorations were becoming more systematic and hunters were beginning to settle at the courts of African kings, often trading more successfully than they hunted themselves.

Henry Hartley and George McCabe, who both farmed in the northern Transvaal, began to hunt in Matabeleland from 1861. George Phillips was active from 1864 to 1890, in Matabeleland in the 1860s and in Lozi country from the 1870s. In 1865 Hartley, together with the Boer hunters Jan Viljoen and Piet Jacobs, secured permission from Mzilikazi to hunt in Shona country up to the Umfuli river. In his later expeditions, between 1866 and 1868, Hartley teamed up with Karl Mauch, combining ivory hunting with gold prospecting.[2] Adam Render or Renders settled in the area of Great Zimbabwe in 1867 or 1868 as an ivory hunter-trader. Thomas Baines arrived in Matabeleland in 1868 and proceeded to prospect and hunt as well as produce his famous series of water colours.[3] Frederick Selous reached Matabeleland in 1872 as a youth of eighteen, and secured permission from Mzilikazi's successor,

Lobengula, to hunt in both Matabeleland and Mashonaland.[4] Selous was later instrumental in creation of the 'Hunters' Road', a wagon track from Bulawayo to the Hartley Hills, to facilitate the arrival of yet more hunters.

Both Mzilikazi and Lobengula attempted to control the entry of white hunters into their kingdom, but with varying success. We have seen how Baldwin's party was 'humbugged' by Mzilikazi, and in the late 1880s Lobengula was still denying Boer hunters permission to hunt in many areas. In 1870, at the beginning of his reign, Lobengula issued hunting regulations restricting white hunters to enter by a particular route, charging a licence fee of a gun (to a value of £15) and ammunition to hunt.[5] He permitted white men to hunt only in the outer regions of his kingom and tried to ensure that Ndebele hunters did not suffer from unfair competition from the whites. Moreover, Lobengula attempted to use white hunters for his own ends both in diplomacy and commerce, attempting simultaneously to keep enemies at bay and exploit ivory resources. Favoured hunters and traders became convenient conduits for the flow of ivory from the region and a useful source of firearms and ammunition. Thomas Baines, George Phillips and Frederick Selous all, at different times, enjoyed influence at Lobengula's court in exchange for favours of this sort.[6]

North of the Zambezi Sipopa of the Lozi essayed the same objectives, using white hunters in a variety of diplomatic and commercial roles as well as his principal defence against his enemies, the Ndebele.[7] To this end he formed a close relationship with George Westbeech, one of the most successful of the hunter-traders of the period. Westbeech had landed in Natal in 1862, made his first visit to Matabeleland in 1863, was closely associated with Lobengula in the period of the Ndebele succession crisis in 1868-70, and moved into Barotseland in 1871, where he settled until his death in 1888.[8] Sipopa permitted Westbeech to establish his hunting and trading base at Pandamatenga, conveniently at the farthest point wagons could reach before encountering the tsetse, in the no-man's-land between Ndebele and Lozi country. Westbeech was able to survive the upheavals of the Lozi State and maintained his influence under Sipopa's successor, Lewanika. In 1882 Lewanika gave Westbeech a concession to hunt in the Machili Valley and later made him a member of one of the Lozi royal councils.[9]

The figures for the export of ivory and the consequent destruction of elephants are striking. The hunter William Finaughty, who operated between 1864 and 1875, shot ninety-five elephants in 1868 yielding 5,000 lb of ivory.[10] Henry Hartley killed between 1,000 and 1,200 elephants in his career.[11] Boer hunters were even more successful. In 1867 Jan Viljoen shot 210 elephants in one trip, and Petrus (or Piet)

Jacobs was alleged to have achieved yet more prodigious feats with the gun.[12] Karl Mauch's bag for one season in 1867 was ninety-one elephants yielding 4,000 lb of ivory.[13] This rapid destruction of the ivory resource reached a climax in the early 1870s. By the time F. C. Selous arrived in Central Africa in 1872 the elephants, as he later lamented, had been harried out of the fly-free country, where they could be hunted on horseback, and had retreated to the fly country in the river valleys to the north of the Zambezi.[14] Nevertheless, the war against the elephants continued, with African hunters of Lobengula's kingdom as active as their European counterparts. In fact, in the peak years, Europeans were trading more ivory from Africans than they themselves were shooting. In the three years from 1872 to 1874, an estimated total of 100,000 lb of ivory was exported from the area that is now western Zimbabwe. Lobengula traded 60,000 lb to Europeans and 40,000 lb were exported by European hunters on their own account.[15] Selous may have been right in judging later that African hunters slaughtered more elephants than Europeans killed, but they did so to satisfy the demands of European hunter-trader, and were often armed by them to do so.[16] They were merely the agents of the European market.

Meanwhile, in Barotseland, Phillips and Westbeech began to operate a modified version of the Zoutpansberg system. By this system they were able to maximise ivory exports while minimising risks to themselves. They operated as ivory entrepreneurs, employing large numbers of African hunters (as many as fifty at times), supervised by young Boer and mixed-race hunters, to enter fly country on foot to shoot elephants. It was by this technique that Westbeech sent out no fewer than ten to fifteen tons of ivory each year he was trading in Barotseland between 1871 and 1888.[17] Some hunters provide sufficient figures to enable us to work out the mean weight of ivory per animal. Mauch's average was 44 lb per animal, Finaughty's 53 lb. Using the mean of these, Westbeech's annual figure represents the destruction of approximately 460 to 690 elephants each year. Using the same (very approximate) calculation, Selous's 100,000 lb of ivory from Matabeleland between 1872 and 1874 would represent over 2,000 animals. In 1876 40,000 lb (or 825 elephants) were traded on the Zambezi in one season.[18] In the following year the figure declined to 25,000 lb, illustrating the increasing difficulties in finding elephants. By 1886 Lewanika was lamenting that the ivory riches of his kingdom were almost all spent.[19] Selous devoted the later part of his hunting career, in the 1880s, to the largely unsuccessful search for a new elephant-hunting ground.[20] His repeated attempts to penetrate the area which is now eastern Zambia were thwarted by African resistance, and he turned to collecting specimens for museums and leading safari parties of tourist hunters. In fact the resources of eastern Zambia were still being exploited, as they always had been, by African hunters. Montagu Kerr, a traveller on the Zambezi in the 1880s described the manner in which thousands of African hunters left Tete in Portuguese East Africa each year, heading north for Ngoni country or north-west for Lake Bangweulu. 'They are armed with flint locks and Tower muskets, but these antiquated weapons are found destructive enough for the great war of extermination.'[21] Even at this late date Europeans had failed to penetrate the ivory-rich regions of eastern Zambia and northern Malawi.

A number of points can be made about the above, admittedly crude, calculations. In the first place, the average tusk size of 22 lb to 26 lb is relatively low, given that a mature bull could bear tusks at least twice that size, while tusks in the 60 lb to 80 lb range were not uncommon. Tusks over 80 lb were a great prize. Selous later estimated that of all the thousands of elephants shot in South Africa only fifty had borne tusks of 100 lb or more each. The average of the hunters of the period were undoubtedly depressed by many immature bulls and, above all, by cow ivory. This ivory, known as *kalasha* in East Africa, often reached no more than 10-15 lb per tusk. It was particularly valued for billiard balls. The figures for the slaughter of elephants in these key decades seem strikingly high, remembering that large quantities of uncounted ivory also left by a wide range of routes. The geographical range of the elephant was reduced. By 1899 there were only two small herds left in the whole region south of the Limpopo, one in the Addo bush near Port Elizabeth, the other in the Zitzikanna forest near Mossel Bay.[22] There was only one resident herd left in Khama's country, and two small herds in the hinterland of Delagoa Bay. As we have seen, the elephant population had been severely reduced in southern Angola (partly by the Boer trek of 1877-81), in the area between the Limpopo and the Zambezi, and above all on the upper Zambezi. The elephant was never again to recolonize large parts of its former territory, but nonetheless its recuperative powers in the areas where it did survive were extraordinary. By the 1920s and '30s the problem of the elephant in Northern Rhodesia (Zambia) was not its decline but its excessive numbers, causing severe damage to crops and demanding control policies.[23] In Southern Rhodesia, also, the elephant population, though restricted in its incidence, grew to such an extent that large-scale culling was required down to modern times.[24] The picture is a mixed one, of contracting geographical range coupled with population growth once the period of the hunting 'free-for-all' was over, about 1900.

The ivory hunters did a great deal, however, to prepare the way for subsequent imperial advance. Indeed, the decline of ivory resources reduced the black kings' bargaining power. Westbeech succeeded in reorienting the trade of the Lozi country away from the Ovimbundu traders of Angola and therefore away from the Portuguese coastal sphere.[25] Westbeech did much to ensure the acceptance of missionaries like F. S. Arnot and François Coillard at the Lozi court.[26] The group of hunter-traders at Lobengula's court were active in helping concession hunters of the 1880s achieve their ends; the hunters' reconnaissance provided much information about the lie of the land and its possible resources; those who published their experiences offered propaganda for expansion bound up in an attractive adventure format, contributing a great deal to the pioneering myth of Central Africa. Selous, who was both a product and the contemporary personification of that myth, played a crucial role in guiding the British South Africa Company's Pioneer Column into Mashonaland in 1890.

Moreover, ivory acted as an important subsidy to the second level of the imperial advance. If the great hunters and traders were interested only in the personal fortune that could be secured from ivory, others were concerned to use it to finance other objectives. The London Missionary Society (LMS) missionary Thomas Morgan Thomas, who arrived at Inyati in northern Matabeleland in 1859, hunted and traded to finance his mission.[27] In 1870 he was expelled from the LMS for these activities, but he returned to found an independent mission which he subsidised from his hunting exploits between 1874 and 1884. The Moir brothers, who founded an evangelical trading concern, the African Lakes Company (ALC), in 1878 to pursue Livingstone's favoured combination of Christianity and commerce, used ivory as a means of furthering their ambitions. As F. L. M. Moir put it in his memoirs, the large sums realised from ivory kept the company going, 'and so enabled it to carry on the work for which it had been founded'.[28] Soon the missionary Robert Laws was lamenting the fact that the herds of elephant Livingstone had seen in the Shire and Nyasa areas had all disappeared.[29] Both Karl Mauch and Thomas Baines funded their prospecting expeditions on the proceeds of ivory sales.[30] To this end, Baines and Mauch (on different trips) joined forces with the great elephant hunter Henry Hartley, who had first noticed the gold workings while hunting. Those who sought real gold financed their mineralogical expeditions on the basis of 'white gold'. In 1867 Henry Faulkner, a cavalry officer who joined a Royal Geographical Society expedition to find David Livingstone when rumours of his death reached the outside world, did his best to turn the event into a hunting trip, no doubt hoping to recover his expenses on ivory sales.[31] He was outraged when the leader of the expedition, E. D. Young, a mere gunner in the Royal Navy, attempted to frustrate him. Young, wrote Faulkner, was not a sportsman, which neatly reflected the class conflict inherent in their relationship. Faulkner's gunbearer, on the other hand, who looked forward eagerly to the total disappearance of the elephant (as perhaps any peasant might), was a 'thorough sportsman'.

Many publicists for hunting trips into the interior, designed to secure game trophies as well as see famous sights like the Victoria Falls, pointed out that such trips could be financed by shooting a few good elephants. One hunter advertised in *The Field* that he would lead such expeditions into Central Africa.[32] By the late 1880s Selous was leading hunting parties into Mashonaland in anticipation of the systematic white advance on the region. J. G. Wood, a member of the Legislative Council of Cape Colony, encountered Selous so employed when the former was involved in an expedition to Matabeleland and Mashonaland in 1887. Selous 'must have done tremendous execution among the game, judging by the number of bones and heads of animals to be seen at his outspan place'.[33] Wood's own party was followed by a large number of camp followers eager for the venison they could secure. Tourism, and its pickings, arrived in Central Africa before colonial rule.

The exploits of Frederick Lugard illustrate the manner in which hunters, campaigners and administrators fused in the years immediately before and after the establishment of white rule.[34] When Lugard arrived in Africa as a penniless adventurer in 1888 he was taken on by the ALC as an elephant hunter and leader of campaigns against the Arab-Swahili traders on Lake Nyasa. He was later to perform similar functions for the Imperial British East Africa Company (see the next chapter). Sir Alfred Sharpe, an early governor of Nyasaland, had also been an elephant hunter, as had Robert Coryndon, who became the first BSAC administrator in Northern Rhodesia and later Governor of Uganda and Kenya.[35] All the company administrators in North Western Rhodesia were eager hunters who encouraged Lewanika's developing taste for the hunt.[36] During the First World War Sharpe made an extended private journey through Central and East Africa and once more partly financed his expedition by elephant hunting.[37] The dividing line between the freebooters of the open frontier and the administrators of the closed was often very thin.

Because ivory was such an important export from East and Central Africa in the nineteenth century elephant hunting has received some attention from historians. The hunting of rhinoceros, hippopotamus, buffalo and the various forms of antelope has, however, been ignored. Yet they too constituted direct and indirect subsidies to the European advance. As in southern Africa they also formed, at varying speeds and geographical incidence, retreating game frontiers. As the elephant declined in numbers or sought inaccessible regions, other animals were subject to assault by professional hunter, sportsmen, and the pioneers of the new imperialism.

The rhinoceros was vulnerable because it presented, like the elephant, a valuable and easily realised asset, its horn. This was exported to the East in large quantities and the trade experienced something of a boom in the late nineteenth century. Selous provides evidence for the rapid decline of the rhino in Central Africa.[38] When he first arrived in Matabeleland the Ndebele were only just beginning to acquire firearms. In his first years there he encountered large numbers of rhinos, both black and white. In 1878 he saw five white rhinos, already comparatively rare, in one day. But from 1880 the value of rhino horn suddenly increased and this coincided with the increasing scarcity of ivory in the region. From that year European traders in Matabeleland began to employ African hunters to shoot rhinos for the sake of their horns and their hides, which were made into wagon whips and sjamboks. One trader supplied him with information on the quantity of rhino horn exported to Europe in the period, while India and China remained large markets for the horn. Selous claimed that several hundred African hunters, armed with smooth-bore muskets, must have killed at least a thousand rhinos between 1881 and 1886 in the region from the high plateau of Matabeleland to the Zambezi river.

> One trader alone told me that he had supplied four hundred Matabele hunters with guns and ammunition, and between 1880 and 1884 his large store always contained great piles of rhinoceros horns – of all sorts and sizes, often the spoils of over a hundred of these animals at one time, although they were constantly being sold to other traders and carried south to Kimberely on their way to Europe.[39]

The hippopotamus was also vulnerable. It was relatively easy to find in its river habitat. It supplied vast quantities of meat for porters, followers and local Africans; its teeth were saleable; its hide was the most favoured for the manufacture of thongs and whips. Despite its great bulk, when bloated in death it could be easily manhandled to river banks to be skinned and cut up. It had been among the first animals to be endangered in South Africa, and its numbers were soon put at risk in many of the rivers north of the Limpopo.

Selous also lamented the rapid decline of the buffalo throughout southern Africa and noted its continuing retreat in Matabeleland and Mashonaland.[40] The hunters of the early nineteenth century had encountered great herds of buffalo in the northern Cape, in the area that later became southern Botswana, and along the coasts of the eastern Cape and Natal. Wherever the land was reasonably well watered and grass-covered the buffalo survived in profusion. During the era of game destruction in South Africa in the middle decades of the century the buffalo was shot out or retreated to more remote areas. Its attraction lay not only in its hide but in its capacity to supply a great quantity of meat, a full-sized bull offering at least 1,000 lb for conversion to biltong or the feeding of African followers. Increasing desiccation in south-western Africa and elsewhere in the sub-continent had contributed to the flight of the buffalo. In the early '70s Selous encountered large herds in Matabeleland and around the Victoria Falls. Like the elephants and rhinos their numbers rapidly declined over the succeeding two decades. The missionary François Coillard also noted the rapid diminution of game around the Victoria Falls during the years he was working in Lozi country. Selous, in common with other travellers, contributed to the decline of the buffalo, using them as his favoured meat source. In one day he shot six bulls to feed the fifty followers of two other whites who were ill. The disappearance of the buffalo had its positive aspects, for Selous identified a close relationship between it and the tsetse fly, an impression which was confirmed by the observations of Lobengula:

> The last time I saw Lo Bengula alive – early in 1890 – I spent the greater part of two days talking to him on many subjects, especially game, for he loved to talk about wild animals, having been a great hunter in his youth. He told me that there were then no more buffaloes anywhere in the neighbourhood of the Gwaai and Shangani rivers, and that with the buffaloes the 'fly' had gone too, and that as the buffaloes and fly had died out, he had gradually pushed his cattle posts down both the Gwaai and Shangani rivers, and that at that time, 1890, he had actually got a cattle post at the junction of the two rivers, where seventeen years before I had found buffaloes and tsetse flies both very numerous.[41]

The connection between game and the tsetse fly will be examined in greater detail in chapter nine. The buffalo was to decline yet further in the late 1890s because of its susceptibility to rinderpest.

Another vulnerable animal was the giraffe. It had retreated, in the face of much persecution for its meat and hides, to the arid zones of southern Africa, where European hunters found it more difficult to follow.[42] Selous frequently shot giraffe for meat, which seems to have been particularly favoured by his Bushmen followers, and noted that the giraffe population, like those of the more favoured antelopes – oryx or gemsbuck, kudu, roan and eland – were already sharply reduced before the arrival of more systematic colonisation and diseases like rinderpest in the 1890s.

Just as ivory and rhino horn provided a subsidy to other concerns, missionary and commercial, exploratory and administrative, so game constituted a vital support system for the often tenuous survival of European pioneers. All the pre- colonial hunters, prospectors, traders, explorers and missionaries lived off the land. That represented a significant subsidy when large numbers of porters, beaters and servants had to be fed. In June 1886, for example, George Westbeech found himself feeding a party of hunters and carriers numbering eighty-six in all.[43] As we have seen, Selous shot buffalo and giraffe to supply his own and others people's followers. Given the necessity of human transport throughout eastern and central Africa such parties were common as late as the First World War, when Sir Alfred Sharpe's expedition required at least 100 porters.[44] It would be tedious to enumerate more examples of a universal practice. The publications of explorers, pioneers and missionaries repeatedly allude to the insatiable demand of Africans for meat.[45] Every category of traveller testified to it, and it raises the question whether this demonstrates the importance of hunting in the pre-colonial economy and to the African diet or reflects the comparative lack of success of the pre-colonial hunter. Certainly, European success was often based on African tracking expertise and precise knowledge of the environment. White hunters were dependent on trackers, auxiliaries and local people eager to secure meat for themselves. Europeans capitalised on this craving by combining local expertise with European technology. Game meat was the great concealed subsidy of the European advance.

Hunters not only fed their followers; they could 'sweeten' local peoples and pay for labour. David Livingstone[46] had done it and hunters like Westbeech did it on a grand scale.[47] Indeed, missionaries often found that they were welcome less for the gospel than for the gun. T. M. Thomas relates how at the end of a sermon to a large company of Africans in the 1860s his listeners sought the reward of patience by demanding that he shoot some animals for them.[48] On a journey to the Zambezi Thomas was subjected to constant requests from his followers to shoot game.[49] Another missionary reported that the delight of a people on hearing that he was to establish a mission on their territory seemed to be due primarily to the fact that he would hunt for them.[50] François Coillard, according to his biographer, secured a great deal of his prestige from his prowess with a gun.[51] He also travelled with Boer hunters and traded meat with them. F. S. Arnot and George Grenfell, both missionaries to the Congo, rewarded their followers with meat.[52] Livingstone paid for the thatching of his mission church in this way,[53] while Bishop Knight-Bruce secured the labour for the building of his church and kept all his followers happy on the mission lands in Manica by providing plentiful supplies of meat, despite paying them very little for work.[54] Donald Fraser in Nyasaland was under constant pressure to supply his mission with game, and found that he could keep all his followers in food – including a school of some seventy catechists – by trading meat for other foodstuffs with the surrounding populace.[55] Isaac Shimmin, the leading Methodist missionary in Mashonaland in the 1890s, prided himself on his hunting and was prepared to pit himself against local lay hunters.[56] Thus the successful missionary had also to be a successful hunter.

Trading meat for grain was another survival technique of all early travellers. Even the very grand expedition of Lord Randolph Churchill to Mashonaland in 1891 indulged in such trade.[57] The archaeologist J. Theodore Bent subsidised his studies by hunting and trade.[58] When Bent and his wife travelled to Zimbabwe to excavate the ruins of Great Zimbabwe in 1891 they employed a young hunter called Harrington to keep their party supplied with meat. Lord Randolph Churchill also described the manner in which members of the local population tended to follow hunting parties (much as they sometimes used carnivores like lions as auxiliary hunters) to secure meat.[59] Animals were often left in the bush once trophies and choice portions of meat had been removed. These followers of the chase could be induced to provide services – game driving, skinning, transport, and so on – in exchange for the meat. The meat subsidy thus operated on a variety of levels. It kept Europeans and their followers alive; it acted as a 'sweetener' for relations with peoples through whose lands they travelled; it could be traded for grain, beer and other foodstuffs and it could be used as a substitute for wages in the earliest days of employment.

In 1890 the haphazard intrusions of hunters, prospectors, traders and missionaries had been replaced by the systematic invasion of the British South Africa Company. The Chartered Company despatched a Pioneer Column and a protecting police force which was notable for the public school background and superior social class of its members.[60] Many of them were lured northwards by the complex myth of Central Africa, incorporating gold, adventure and the Hunt. Several proclaimed themselves as influenced by the popular literature of the period, the works of Rider Haggard and the hunting books of Cornwallis Harris, Gordon Cumming, W. C. Baldwin and Frederick Selous.[61] When the pioneers fanned out from Fort Salisbury to stake their gold claims in late 1890 few of them wished to be settlers. Their prime desire was to 'get rich quick' on the alleged gold reserves of the new colony and return home as soon as possible. In persuading Africans to take them to the many gold shafts excavated by medieval miners they were free in distributing arms as a reward (arms which were used against them in the 1896-97 revolt). These arms were to be used in a further assault on the game resources of the territory. They also hunted almost daily to feed such labour as they could secure, to trade for grain with the locals, and sometimes to subsidise their prospecting from the sale of skins and trophies. There are again several instances of Africans working solely for meat.[62] Yet another missionary was said to have built his church by this method.[63]

Although the pioneers were also allowed farms, few (except the Boers among them) desired to be farmers. One transport rider remarked that he had yet to meet a Rhodesian farmer who actually grew anything.[64] Nevertheless, they staked out their putative farms, hoping to obtain the labour of the Africans resident upon them, and find profit in plunder combined with the hope that the land would rapidly increase in value. Their asset-stripping involved the removal of all timber for sale to the townships, to such few mines as did develop, and later to the railways.[65] It also involved the shooting-out of all game anywhere near the wagon routes across the country or on alienated land. As the Hudson's Bay Company had discovered in western Canada, hunting and settlement were incompatible. Randolph Churchill, on his famous visit to Mashonaland in 1891, noted that same incompatibility in Central Africa, and he urged that the BSAC's territories should be seen as a happy hunting ground for commercial killer and gentleman sportsman, not as a field for settlement.[66]

The building of the railways further contributed to the assault upon game. There is ample evidence that railway engineers, like missionaries, had to be good shots in order to keep their labourers and staff in meat.[67] Supplying large numbers of labourers was a vital subsidy in both calorific and financial terms to the tight financing of railway lines like the Beira-Mashonaland railway, or its counterpart to the Victoria Falls and beyond into Northern Rhodesia, all of which passed through regions rich in game. James Stevenson-Hamilton described the importance of the meat subsidy in the building of South African railway lines: 'including that of the Selati railway itself . . . the game had as a matter of course always provided free meat, and thus cheapened working expenses'.[68] In 1891 Selous saw the Pungwe area, through which the Beira-Mashonaland railway was later to be driven, as one of the last great game regions of southern Africa, contrasting strikingly with the receding game populations elsewhere.[69] H. F. Varian, one of the most distinguished of the railway engineers, was the son of a hunter (who had helped the Prince of Wales, later Edward VII, to bag his first elephant in Ceylon).[70] Varian was an excellent shot who seems to have kept his men well supplied. On the Beira-Mashonaland route Varian and an Italian inspector of works hunted regularly along the line. The carcasses would be sent back by ganger's trolley and cut up by the white ganger for distribution to the workers. 'In this way sport and utility were combined.'[71] Later, when the route north from Bulawayo was being driven into Northern Rhodesia from the Victoria Falls, Varian used two hunting dogs to help him bring his game to bay. 'Shooting big game for sport at one's leisure is one thing, but having to provide meat for a large and hungry gang in the absence of other food, and when there is a great deal of other work to do, is quite another.'[72] Once the lines were built, they brought in a fresh flood of rather less intrepid hunters, some of whom were known, in the early days of the railway, to shoot at the rich game resources of the Pungwe Flats in Mozambique from the windows of the carriages.[73] The tourist hunter's field of operation was greatly extended by the arrival of regular shipping services, the railway lines and comfortable hotels. The Union Castle Line guides to East and southern Africa from the 1890s devoted a great deal of attention to African fauna, hunting and game laws.[74]

If the rich game resources of Central Africa were to prove a significant subsidy to peaceable occupations like prospecting, missionary work and 'farming', they were also to prove an essential supply element in time of war. In the campaign against the Ndebele in 1893, and in the revolt of the Shona and the Ndebele in 1896-97, the provisioning of troops and settlers was a desperate problem. In 1893 Captain C. H. W. Donovan, who was serving in West Africa, arrived in southern Africa on a hunting trip. With the outbreak of the Ndebele war he immediately volunteered for service. When he wrote the inevitable book about his experiences he divided it into two sections, 'Sport' and 'War'.[75] The practical connection between the two was indeed frequently made by both officers and the gentlemanly troopers of the local forces, who were as proficient in the hunt as they were in the prosecution of war. The two military accounts of the revolt of 1896-97, by Baden-Powell and Lieutenant Colonel Alderson, made it clear that the authors saw little difference between the hunt and African warfare.[76] Hunting stories abound in their books, and hunting metaphors were seldom far from their pens. This led Baden-Powell in particular to elide the hunting of animals with the hunting down of Africans. 'The work,' he wrote, 'involved in the military operations was sufficiently sporting in itself to fill a good measure of enjoyment coupled with the excitement incidental to contending against wild beasts of the human kind.'[77] Elsewhere he remarked that 'The longest march seems short when one is hunting game . . . lion or leopard, boar or buck, nigger or nothing.'[78] Baden-Powell and Alderson encouraged their men and the local volunteers who joined them to see these campaigns as little more than sporting expeditions.[79] However, it was mainly the officers who made sport with the game, which could not shoot back, while troopers took on Africans, who could. Baden-Powell describes several columns as being saved by the shooting of game when other supplies were running short.[80] After the Ndebele revolt had been resolved in 1896, General Sir Frederick Carrington, Baden-Powell and Earl Grey, the new administrator, proceeded to Mashonaland, enjoying a most successful hunting trip *en route*.[81] Shortly after their arrival in the capital, Fort Salisbury, they led the opening meet of the Salisbury hounds.

The supply difficulties of the 1896-97 revolt had been hugely exacerbated by the rinderpest epidemic which broke out in early 1896, destroying hundreds of oxen in transport spans throughout the country, as well as entire cattle herds, before proceeding like a bush fire through Bechuanaland and the South African territories, reaching Cape Town by the end of the year. Rinderpest had been introduced into the Horn of Africa, probably by infected cattle from India, in 1889.[82] From there it had spread, seemingly growing in virulence as it went, throughout East Africa. Lugard encountered it on his way to Uganda in 1890.[83] The Zambezi seems to have briefly held it up, but once across that natural barrier in February or March 1896 its progress south was unimpeded. Studies of rinderpest have generally concentrated on its effects on cattle, but it was no less devastating in its onslaught on the game of the region. Elephant, hippo and rhino were immune, but entire buffalo herds were destroyed. The large antelope like kudu and eland seem to have been particularly susceptible, although none of the buck were free of the scourge. At one stage it was thought that zebra had escaped, but they soon succumbed. As the rinderpest spread southwards hunters, warriors and settlers commented with alarm upon the dramatic destruction of the game. In 1896 Baden-Powell saw the ravages of rinderpest among the oxen of Bechuanaland as making the task of destroying the revolts in Matabeleland and Mashonaland much more difficult that it otherwise would have been.[84] 'The scourge of rinderpest' also reduced the quantities of game available to his troops, and no doubt it was partly for this reason that all game laws were suspended for the duration of the revolts.[85] H. F. Varian noted that in the rinderpest's 'full toll of game throughout South-East Africa, buffalo were especially hard hit'.[86] But for Varian 'the unnecessary and undesirable slaughter' of the game was the main evil, the success of the shooting trip being primarily judged by the numbers of animals killed, bags of 300 being achieved on trips of less than three months. Sir Alfred Sharpe had seen vast herds of buffalo on the Congo-Northern Rhodesia frontier in 1890.[87] After rinderpest had struck the area in 1892 there were none. Selous's biographer, J. G. Millais, claimed that in 1896 nine-tenths of kudu, eland and buffalo were carried off by the rinderpest in the Pungwe district of Mozambique, and similar effects occurred in the British territories.[88]

In Southern Rhodesia the rinderpest accelerated the decline in the game population and greatly helped the process of transformation and redefinition of land use. It also had, as we shall see, a dramatic effect on the distribution of tsetse. In Northern Rhodesia, particularly in the eastern half of the territory, the hunters' assault on game had been less devastating than in the south. In Northern Rhodesia and Nyasaland the rinderpest was seen to have an effect, but the capacity of the game to make a swift recovery was already apparent in the early years of the twentieth century. The game subsidy continued to be important after it had declined in Southern Rhodesia. So far as the fortunes of game are concerned the Zambezi can be seen as a genuine frontier. To the south Europeans had slaughtered and marginalised game, rendering species extinct or endangered. To the north and east of the Zambezi they began to conserve game in such a way as to tip the balance of nature away from human settlement to animal habitat. These themes will be developed in chapters eight to ten, but the continuing role of hunting in the Central African territories north of the Zambezi can perhaps best be identified by examining the careers of three hunters, an adminstrator, a professional hunter and settler, and a soldier tourist.

John 'Chirupula' Stephenson was a striking product of the imperial frontier. In 1896 he migrated from Northumberland to Kimberely, where he worked as a telegraphist. Soon he was lured north, partly by a desire to hunt, and worked for the BSAC in Bulawayo before moving on to Blantyre in British Central Africa (Nyasaland). By the beginning of the twentieth century, still in his mid-twenties, he was helping to establish the company's administration at the Hook of the Kafue in Northern Rhodesia. Later, in 1904, he established the *boma*, or government office, at Ndola. In both these positions he consciously set out to fit himself into the myths of hunting leadership of the local peoples.

Game was plentiful; he kept his followers well supplied with meat; and above all he offered lavish hospitality to the local chiefs, feeding them from the products of his guns.[89] He established his authority through hunting prowess, his prestige through the feast. He had also become a bigamist, having married two African women. When sexual relations with the local population ceased to be countenanced after the colonial authorities had become aware of the frequency of these liaisons he left government service and established himself on an estate in the Irumi Valley.[90] There he became a sort of white chief, surrounded by his extended family and his workers, He fed them by hunting, and, at least in the beginning, subsidised his operations from ivory. He also acted as guide to prestigious hunting expeditions like those of Prince Albert of Belgium and the Duchess of Aosta. The administrator of north-eastern Rhodesia, Robert Codrington, himself a hunter, released Stephenson, at least for a period, from the provisions of the game laws.

Denis Lyell, a Scot by birth, was a tea planter in India who moved to Africa in 1899 because he was disappointed by the hunting opportunities in Assam. He worked for the King's African Rifles for a period, seizing every opportunity of hunting that came his way. Whithin a few years he had become a professional, hunting throughout the protectorate and in the game-rich Luangwa Valley of Northern Rhodesia. He sold ivory, collected specimens for several museums and indulged in the trophy trade. From 1906 he also came to live by his pen, publishing a whole series of books well into his retirement in the inter-war year.[91] He corresponded with famous hunters and published a collection of their letters.[92] In 1912 he brought out a short work entitled *Nyasaland for the Hunter and Settler*[93], in which he lamented that it was no longer possible to live by one's rifle, though quite a good income could still be made from collecting natural history specimens. He advised potential settlers to establish themselves in agriculture, using the dry season for hunting. In the same year he established a permanent hunting camp in central Angoniland and hunted extensively from it during the succeeding twelve months.[94] By that time his reputation was such that large numbers of Africans came in to work for him, recognising that they would acquire considerable quantities of meat from his hunting exploits.

W. T. Shorthose was an officer in the South Staffordshire regiment, then serving in South Africa, who went on a hunting trip from Broken Hill to Lake Bangweulu in Northern Rhodesia in 1910.[95] As a result of that experience he transferred to the KAR in East Africa and combined hunting with warfare in the First World War and the campaign against

the 'Mad Mullah' (Sayyid Mohammed Abdul Hassan) in Somalaliland
that followed it. The South Staffordshire regimental interest in hunting
in Northern Rhodesia arose from a hunting trip undertaken by two
officers in 1908. In 1910 a senior officer invited two subalterns, of
whom Shorthose was one, on a hunting expedition primarily to shoot
elephants. The senior officer, Shorthose wrote, 'was a hero'. In three
days he shot four buffalo, two lions, two black lechwe, one situtunga
and an elephant. The carriers sang his praises into the night. The party
visited a mission, where the Catholic Fathers were keen hunters, before
continuing their daily hunting exploits across the territory. In three
months they shot 126 head of big and 110 of small game.

These three examples illustrate the various functions of hunting in
the territories north of the Zambezi, as a source of prestige and influence to the administrator, a subsidy to the settler, and a violent recreation and training for the soldier. As the hunting frontier receded with
settlement and conquest, animal resources continued to provide the
same underpinning of European expansion as they had done in South
Africa a century earlier. Lyell headed for the north because he judged
that hunting opportunities in Southern Rhodesia were in steep decline.
The South Staffordshire officers serving in South Africa had to reach
beyond the Zambezi, aided by the new railway line, before they could
re-create the conditions of the nineteenth century.

The decline in the numbers of game had already been noted, as we
have seen, in the last decades of the independent Ndebele kingdom.
King Lobengula had indeed attempted to introduce conservationist
measures, forbidding hunters, white or black, to take cow elephants
or ostrich eggs.[96] In 1883 he fined the hunters Selous and Martin and
others for shooting hippo against his wishes.[97] Ndebele hunters found
that they had to move farther and farther from the heartland of their
State in order to secure game of any sort.[98] Traditional African hunting
had been relatively inefficient, but the acquisition of modern guns had
transformed the situation. Lobengula's efforts to control hunting can
well be understood in the light of the scale of the bags of the well
known hunters. In *A Hunter's Wanderings* Selous proudly listed his
kills. Between 1877 and 1880 he shot 548 head, of which only twenty
were elephants.[99] With high-velocity magazine rifles Europeans were
to become even more devastatingly competent. Wherever game was
disturbed it lost its innocence and its curiosity. No longer did the herds
graze near wagon tracks or railway lines. They steadily retreated from
all lines of communication and from all the settlements of the white
invaders.

[ *137* ]

When the Pioneer Column assembled at Macloutsie in British Bechuanaland the presence of so many men soon ensured that no game was to be had anywhere in the vicinity.[100] As Hugh Marshall Hole put it,[101] 'The entry of the Pioneer column with its long train of waggons, its search-light and other military paraphernalia, probably gave the big game animals of Mashonaland a scare from which they never fully recovered.' Once the column arrived at Fort Salisbury, the professional hunter and natural history collector William Harvey Brown was sent out to secure meat for the new settlement. He described his wonder at finding great herds of game on the Gwibi Flats little more than ten miles from Salisbury.[102] The following year Lord Randolph Churchill's party proceeded to exactly the same area and found no game at all.[103] Churchill travelled with a famous hunter, Hans Lee (who was aided, as several other hunters had been, by a Bushman tracker), and it is clear that the expedition, which was supposed to be primarily an investigation of the economic potential of Rhodesia, was in fact almost entirely taken up with virtually daily hunting exploits. Churchill's book on his journey certainly spends more time on hunting than on economics. He describes the manner in which, when an area rich in game was found, the party would settle for several days until the game had been driven off by the daily depredations of the hunt.[104] As we have seen, Africans emerged to take advantage of the meat abandoned in trophy hunting. Churchill's party followed the traditions of Selous and others in indulging in a veritable orgy of killing, as the size of their daily bags frequently illustrated. As they travelled they often heard the shots of other hunting parties near. It is not surprising that others should soon be lamenting the lack of game on all the main routes.

The BSAC introduced game laws at an early date. But they followed the pattern of the Cape Colony, where laws were passed only when very little game survived, and all observers testify that in the years before the First World War the game laws were almost impossible to enforce. As in the case of the revolts, they were promptly suspended in times of difficulty. Even the animals which were proclaimed royal game continued to be hunted vigorously. In 1899-1900 the transport rider Stanley Portal Hyatt shot hippos because they produced the best leather for reins, thongs, whips and other items associated with transport riding.[105] He manufactured these items on the road, and did a very profitable business in them in Bulawayo. When questioned about the hippos, he always asserted that they had been shot in Portuguese territory, where there were no game laws. Hyatt suggested that one or two of the Native Commissioners did attempt to enforce the game laws – while entirely ignoring them themselves.[106] The Union Castle guides to South and East Africa annually encouraged hunters with the remark that game laws were very difficult to enforce, particularly in the remoter districts.[107] Some sectors of the Rhodesian pioneer community refused to observe them. When a herd of elephants (by that time, like the hippo, royal game) appeared in the Lomagundi District in 1908 the local Afrikaans farmers shot them all out, and little could be done about it.[108] In any case the concept of 'vermin' ensured extensive slaughter. The hunter Marcus Daly described in his memoirs the manner in which he had added to his income by shooting lions for the BSAC (he was also able to make money from sales of the much-prized lion fat). He frequently shot entire herds of buffalo when they appeared a danger to travellers or settlers.[109]

If game laws did little to hinder the white onslaught they were largely irrelevant to Africans. Africans were denied access to game primarily through the operation of gun laws.[110] Large numbers of antiquated guns had always circulated in Africa, but African ownership of guns grew enormously in the years immediately preceding and just after the imposition of white rule. Martini-Henry rifles were traded for ivory; rifles were also given in exchange for concessions. Europeans gave out rifles, including advanced designs like the Lee-Metford, for being shown old gold working.[111] The Ndebele were not disarmed after the war of 1893, and in the revolts of 1896-97 Europeans were constantly surprised by the number and quality of the arms used against them. Until the revolts these arms were, of course, used primarily for hunting. In 1893 one pioneer on a journey from the Tokwe to Bulawayo met at nearly every river 'either a party of Matabele hunters with guns who were returning with hides or meat or I found their lately deserted camps'.[112] When the revolts were crushed the military and civilian authorities were determined to flush out African arms, and the first duty of the Native Commissioners throughout the country was to take in an extensive arsenal. In the future a few chiefs would be permitted to keep old Tower muskets as symbols of status and as a means of protecting their gardens.[113] It was only for this 'defensive' purpose that Africans were ever again permitted to bear arms, except when enlisted to fight in European wars. As part of the same regulations, spears, assegais and bows and arrows were also handed in, and the tradional iron-smelting industry collapsed.[114]

When Africans were resettled on reserves in the remoter areas of the country it was the administrators who became the greatest and indeed often the sole hunters. They protected Africans gardens, were called upon by villagers to shoot man-eating animals like crocodiles and lions, and continued to hunt whenever they could to supply their followers with meat and themselves with trophies and yarns with which to regale their guests and the readers of their memoirs. The connection between the prestige of the ruler and his prowess in the hunt had now been firmly transferred to the white administrators. Earl Grey hunted his way into Rhodesia in 1896 despite the scourges of war, rinderpest, failed rains and famine which afflicted the country. His predecessor, Dr Jameson, frequently indicated that he was more interested in hunting than in administration. On a visit to Fontesvilla on the Beira-Mashonaland railway, the railway engineer found himself being questioned much more closely about the local hunting prospects than about the railway.[115] Similarly, on a trip to the Victoria Falls in 1904, when he was premier of the Cape, Jameson delayed his train at the Falls to indulge in some sight-seeing and to hunt, and cut short his visit to the Wankie Colliery, which apparently bored him.[116]

All the early native commissioners were hunters, and the first Chief Native Commissioner, Brabant, seems to have been appointed largely on his hunting and veld craft ability, since he was subsequently discovered to be barely literate.[117] In later years the Native Commissioner H. N. Hemans refused promotion and always insisted on being sent to the remote Gokwe District because it was one of the few areas where the hunting remained good.[118] It was a special treat for one of his assistants to be sent on a tax-gathering safari because of the hunting which could be enjoyed *en route*. By that time, indeed, hunting was largely restricted to government officials, landowners, and tourist hunters, often in marginal areas of the country.[119] Writing in 1907, Selous remarked that the journey from Bulawayo to the Victoria Falls had become monotonous and uninteresting, passing through endless wastes of low forest and scrubby bush.[120] Thirty years earlier, the land had been filled with game – elephants, black and white rhinos, giraffes, buffaloes, zebras and varieties of antelope. It had also supported a considerable human population.

The decline of game had a much more serious import, however, than the removal of a tourist spectacle or a hunters' paradise. In exploiting the game resource as a crucial underpinning of the imperial advance, Europeans removed an important source of protein from the African diet. When famine struck Southern Rhodesia in 1922 game meat was no longer available as a hedge against starvation. In this and other years of failed rains Africans had lost the opportunity to turn to the protein bounty with which Africa had endowed their forefathers. One rare

African source, the history of Manyika, written by an employee of the Methodist Episcopal Mission press in Umtali, Jason Machiwayika (undated; he died in 1922) lamented the loss of meat from the African diet: 'Europeans took all guns from Africans and refused to let them shoot game. But Europeans shoot game. If an African shoots an animal with a gun, the African is arrested and the gun is confiscated.'[121] When elderly Africans were asked (in an oral research project) about the changes to the landscape in the previous seventy years, many reflected on the compression of African peoples upon the land, the removal of trees and the disappeance of the animals with which they had formely contested control of the environment.[122] It is true that those animals had ravaged crops, but they had at least offered meat in compensation.

Hunting had been for Africans a route into the international economy through ivory, even if the terms of trade had invariably been loaded against them. It had been a source of meat, at the very least a valuable addition to diet, particularly in times of famine. Skins, tails, plumage and teeth had provided covering, raiment and ornament, while horns often made valuable receptacles and tools. For whites hunting provided an irresistable lure to the interior and a vital support system in the early years of European encroachment. Ivory profits subsidised the activities of imperial companies, wars of conquest, individual salaries and colonial revenues. Meat provided a not inconsiderable concealed subsidy to exploration, military campaigns, missionary activity, prospecting, farming, railway contracts and administration costs. By the First World War hunting for sport had become virtually the norm. The economic enterprise of hunting had become the symbolic activity of the Hunt. Access to animal resources had become a source of pride, power, prestige and popularity to administrators, and finally a revenue-earning rich man's diversion in the remoter corners of Africa. Much the same progression can be identified in East Africa, although game populations there were never placed under threat to the extent that they were south of the Zambezi.

## Notes

1 An incomplete and sometimes inaccurate survey of this period can be found in A. J. Wills, *An Introduction to the History of Central Africa*, London, 1973, pp. 114-18, and Lewis Gann, *A History of Southern Rhodesia*, London, 1965, pp. 38-50.
2 F. O. Bernhard (ed.), *Karl Mauch, African Explorer*, Cape Town, 1971, E. E. Burke (ed.), *The Journals of Karl Mauch, 1869-72*, Salisbury, Rhodesia, 1969.
3 Thomas Baines, *Explorations in South West Africa*, Salisbury, Rhodesia, 1973 (first edition 1864); J. P. R. Wallis (ed.), *The Northern Goldfields Diaries of Thomas Baines*, 3 vols., London, 1964.
4 F. C. Selous, *A Hunter's Wanderings in Africa*, Bulawayo, 1970 (first edition 1881).

5 Wallis, *Thomas Baines*, Vol. II, pp. 325, 805.
6 Wallis, *Thomas Baines, passim.* Other hunters, like John Lee, were also active there. F. C. Selous, *Travel and Adventure in South East Africa*, London, 1893, *passim.* Phillips introduced Selous to Lobengula in 1872, by which time Phillips had already been hunting and trading in Matabeleland for eight years. Selous, *Hunter's Wanderings*, p. 29. Not all elephant-hunter diplomacy was successful. Lobengula refused to accept Henry Hartley as an emissary of the Transvaal Boers, and when Sir Bartle Frere sent the elephant hunter Patterson to Lobengula's capital in 1878 Patterson was murdered after receiving permission to hunt in the north.
7 When Norman MacLeod visited Lozi country Sipopa used him and his party for the king's own ends, directing them where to hunt, confiscating their ivory, and so on. E. C. Tabler, *Trade and Travel in Early Barotseland*, London, 1963, p. 43. Sipopa even moved his capital to Sesheke on the advice of Westbeech in order to be near the elephant-hunting grounds. Lewis Gann, *A History of Northern Rhodesia*, London, 1964, p. 44. See also François Coillard, *On the Threshold of Central Africa*, London 1897, pp. 365, 591, 598, 600, and Gervas Clay, *Your Friend Lewanika*, London, 1968, p. 22.
8 Tabler, *Table and Travel*, pp. 5-7.
9 Andrew Roberts, *A History of Zambia*, London, 1976, pp. 133-4.
10 William Finaughty, *The Recollections of William Finaughty*, Philadelphia, Pa., 1916. In one five-month period Finaughty shot fifty-three elephants, yielding 3,000 lb of ivory, an average of fifty-six. In 1868 Finaughty received 6s 10d per lb for ivory.
11 Selous, *Hunter's Wanderings*, publisher's introduction to the new edition, Bulawayo, 1970.
12 J. G. Millais, *The Life of Frederick Courtenay Selous*, London, 1918, pp. 74-5.
13 Bernhard, *Mauch*, p. 24.
14 Millais, *Selous*, pp. 113-15.
15 These figures come from an article on elephants by Selous in H. A. Bryden (ed.), *Great and Small Game of Africa*, London 1899, pp. 5-7.
16 See Chapter eight for a discussion of the controversy as to the relative destructiveness of European and African hunters.
17 Gann, *Northern Rhodesia*, pp. 41-2. Westbeech realised £12,000 for the ivory he collected and received from Sipopa between 1872 and 1874. Clay, *Lewanika*, p. 16. An illustration of Westbeech's trading establishment at Pandamatenga can be found in C. W. Mackintosh, *Coillard of the Zambezi*, London, 1908, p. 264.
18 Millais, *Selous*, p. 112.
19 Coillard, *Central Africa*, p. 222.
20 Millais, *Selous*, pp. 120, 130, 158.
21 W. Montagu Kerr, 'The Upper Zambezi zone', *Scottish Geographical Magazine*, 2 (1886), pp. 385-402, particularly p. 395.
22 Bryden, *Great and Small Game*, pp. 2-3.
23 See Chapter nine.
24 In 1983, for example, 6,000 of Zimbabwe's stocks of 49,000 elephants had to be shot. *The Observer*, 26 June, 1983, p. 6
25 Gann, *Northern Rhodesia*, p. 41.
26 Tabler, *Trade and Travel*, p. 7. Roberts, *Zambia*, p. 155.
27 Thomas Morgan Thomas, *Eleven Years in Central South Africa*,London, 1873. See also publisher's introduction to new edition Bulawayo, 1970.
28 F. L. M. Moir, *After Livingstone: an African Trade Romance*, London n.d., pp. 90, 110.
29 R. Laws, *Reminiscences of Livingstone*, London, 1934, p. 212.
30 Thomas Baines, *The Gold Regions of Central Africa*, London, 1877, p. 41; Wallis, *Thomas Baines, passim.* Bernhard, *Mauch, passim.*
31 Henry Faulkner, *Elephant Haunts: being a Sportsman's Narrative of the Search for Dr. Livingstone*, London, 1868.
32 The hunter was Harry Ware, who led parties north in the late 1880s. Tabler, *Trade and Travel*, p. 29.
33 J. G. Wood, *Through Matabeleland*, Bulawayo, 1974, (first edition 1893), p. 23.

**34** F. D. Lugard, *The Rise of our East Africa Empire*, London, 1893, 2 vols., Vol. I, p. 2. Margery Perham, *Lugard: the Years of Adventure*, London, 1956, p. 70. Lugard had learned his hunting skills in India. Perham, *Lugard*, pp. 47-8.

**35** Christopher P. Youé, *Robert Thorne Coryndon: Proconsular Imperialism in Southern and Eastern Africa, 1897-1925*, Waterloo, Ont., 1986. Both Coryndon and Robert Codrington, the administrator of north-eastern Rhodesia, had been members of the Bechuanaland Border Police and were keen hunters.

**36** Colin Harding, *Far Bugles*, London, 1933.

**37** Sir Alfred Sharpe, *The Backbone of Africa*, London, 1921, p. 198.

**38** F. C. Selous, *African Nature Notes and Reminiscences*, London, 1908, pp. 187-9; Bryden, *Large and Small Game*, pp. 54- 6. In 1886 two Boer hunters, Karl Weyand and Jan Engelbrecht, shot ten white rhinos, already very rare, west of the Umfuli. Selous and Coryndon spent some time pursuing white rhinos, eager to secure specimens for museums before they became extinct in the regions.

**39** Selous, *African Nature Notes*, pp. 188-9.

**40** Selous, *African Nature Notes*, pp. 143-56.

**41** Selous, *African Nature Notes*, p. 163.

**42** Selous, *African Nature Notes*, pp. 206-14.

**43** Tabler, *Trade and Travel*, pp. 56-7.

**44** Sharpe, *Backbone*, pp. 33-4.

**45** G. W. H. Knight-Bruce, *Memories of Mashonaland*, London, 1895, p. 41; Thomas, *Eleven Years*, pp. 386-7; H. N. Hemans, *The Log of a Native Commissioner*, London, 1935, p. 40; S. P. Hyatt, *The Old Transport Road*, London, 1914, pp. 176-7; J. T. Bent, *The Ruined Cities of Mashonaland*, London, 1892, pp. 33-4, and many other references. F. L. M. Moir also commented on the meat subsidy supplied by game, *After Livingstone*, pp. 116-18.

**46** Horace Waller (ed.), *The Last Journals of David Livingstone*, London, 1880, Vol. I, p. 145.

**47** Tabler, *Trade and Travel*, pp. 57, 81.

**48** Thomas, *Eleven Years*, p. 104.

**49** Thomas, *Eleven Years*, p. 365.

**50** *Central Africa: Monthly Record of the Work of the Universities' Mission to Central Africa*, XXIV (1915), p. 147.

**51** Mackintosh, *Coillard*, p. 325.

**52** F. S. Arnot, *Missionary Travels in Central Africa*, London, 1914, p. 64. F. S. Arnot, *Garenganze: Mission Work in Central Africa*, London, 1889, p. 188. Arnot shot zebras to pay his porters. Shirley J. Dickens, *Grenfell of the Congo*, London, n.d., p. 69.

**53** R. Gordon Cumming, *A Hunter's Life in South Africa*, London, 1850, Vol. II, p. 63.

**54** R. Blennerhasset and L. Sleeman, *Adventures in Mashonaland*, London, 1893, p. 180.

**55** Agnes Fraser, *Donald Fraser*, London, 1934, p. 239. Donald Fraser, *Winning a Primitive People*, London, 1914.

**56** W. H. Brown, *On the South African Frontier*, London, 1889, p. 223. Shimmin was a close friend and admirer of Selous. See Shimmin's tribute in Millais, *Selous*, pp. 369-73.

**57** Lord Randolph Churchill, *Men, Mines, and Animals in South Africa*, London, 1893, p. 254.

**58** Bent, *Ruined Cities*, p. 33. Bent employed large numbers of Africans on the excavation of Great Zimbabwe, presenting considerable commissariat problems.

**59** National Archives of Zimbabwe Historical Manuscripts Collection (NAZ Hist. MSS Coll.), the papers of Hubert Tyler Harrington, HA5/1/1. See also the reminiscences of L. C. Meredith (uncatalogued), who thought little of Harrington's hunting capacities.

**60** C. E. Finlason, *A Nobody in Mashonaland*, London, 1893, pp. 99-100. Correspondence of Henry John Borrow, Borrow to his mother, 26 May 1871, NAZ Hist. MSS Coll BO11/1/1.

**61** Papers of W. I. S. Driver, NAZ Hist MSS Coll, Misc. DR2. Also Borrow to father, 24

September 1891, BO11/1/1.

62 Papers of J. J. F. Darling, NAZ Hist MSS Coll, DA 6/3/2/. Brown, *South African Frontier*, pp. 128, 147, 279.

63 Reminiscences of William Edward, NAZ Hist MSS Coll ED6/1/1.

64 Hyatt, *Transport Road*, p. 173.

65 Brown, *South African Frontier*, pp. 304-7. W. I. S. Driver, who was the Native Commissioner in Selukwe, also made money out of timber-cutting contracts. NAZ Hist MSS Coll Misc DR 2.

66 Churchill, *Men, Mines*, pp. 199, 212, 330.

67 H. F. Varian, *Some African Milestones*, London, 1953, pp. 80-3, 120-3, 166. George Pauling, *Chronicles of a Contractor*, London, 1926, pp. 135, 207.

68 J. Stevenson-Hamilton, *South African Eden*, London, 1937, p. 126.

69 Selous, *African Nature Notes*, p. 88.

70 Varian, *African Milestones*, pp. 283-6. Varian's father was a forest officer in Ceylon who shot 101 elephants before his death at the age of thirty-four.

71 Varian, *African Milestones*, p. 80.

72 Varian, *African Milestones*, p. 120.

73 E. A. H. Alderson, *With the Mounted Infantry and the Mashonaland Field Force*, London, 1898, p. 52.

74 *The Guide to South Africa for the Use of Tourists, Sportsmen, Ivalids, and Settlers*, Castle Mail Packets Company, first edition, 1892-93. Over thirty pages were devoted to game, hunting and game laws, material which remained largely unchanged in successive editions until the 1930s.

75 C. H. W. Donovan, *With Wilson in Matabeleland, or, Sport and War in Zambezia*, Bulawayo, 1978 (first edition 1894).

76 R. S. S. Baden-Powell, *The Matabeleland Campaign*, London, 1898, and Alderson, *Mounted Infantry*.

77 R. S. S. Baden-Powell, *Sport in War*, London, 1900, pp. 17-18.

78 Baden-Powell, *Matabeleland Campaign*, p. 417.

79 Alderson maintained the metaphor of the fox hunt throughout his account of the Mashonaland campaign. *Mounted Infantry*, pp. 45, 56. At different times he compared hunting the Shona with rabbiting from bolt holes (p. 93), shooting snipe (p. 114), and scaring rooks (p. 114). On one occasion he told his men to treat an attack as an August bank holiday outing (p. 83). When the Acting Administrator of Mashonaland, Judge Vintcent, joined Alderson's column, he behaved, Alderson wrote, 'like a schoolboy out hunting in the holidays at the idea of having a go at the Mashonas'.

80 Baden-Powell, *Matabeleland Campaign*, pp. 308, 338, 403-4. The white laager at Enkeldoorn survived on game shot every day by the (mainly Boer) menfolk. *Matabeleland Campaign*, p. 420.

81 Baden-Powell, *Matabeleland Campaign*, pp. 436, 445.

82 Charles van Onselen, 'Reactions to rinderpest in South Africa 1896-7', *JAH*, XIII, 3 (1972), p. 473. Helge Kjekshus, *Ecology Control and Economic Development in East African History*, London, 1977, pp. 126-32.

83 Lugard, *East African Empire*, Vol. 1, p. 356.

84 Baden-Powell, *Matabeleland Campaign*, p. 15. In one area he despaired of shooting game for his men when he found carcasses of kudu which had died of rinderpest, p. 327.

85 Baden-Powell, *Matabeleland Campaign*, p. 22.

86 Varian, *African Milestones*, p. 77.

87 Sharpe, *Backbone*, p. 74. Elsewhere Sharpe estimated that the mortality among game at the north end of Nyasa was 90 per cent. At the south end of Lake Mweru 'enormous quantities of game have died'. On the Luapula he counted forty dead puku around his camp. *Geographical Journal*, Vol. I, p. 530.

88 Millais, *Selous*, pp. 183-4, 209.

89 Kathaleen Stevens Rukavina, *Jungle Pathfinder: the Biography of Chirupula Stephenson*, London, 1951, pp. 73, 90 and *passim*. Stephenson's first wife, Loti, was

apparently an eager huntress.

90 Ronald Hyam, 'Concubinage and the colonial service: the Crewe circular (1909)', *JICH*, XIV, 3 (1986), pp. 170-86. See also Ronald Hyam, 'Empire and sexual opportunity', *JICH*, XIV, 2 (1986), pp. 34-89.

91 Denis D. Lyell (and C. H. Stigand), *Central African Game and its Spoor*, London, 1906. Denis D. Lyell, *Hunting Trips in Northern Rhodesia, with Accounts of Sport and Travel in Nyasaland and Portuguese East Africa*, London 1910, *Memories of an African Hunter*, London, 1923, *The African Elephant and its Hunters*, London, 1924, *The Hunting and Spoor of Central African Game*, London, 1929. More detail on Lyell can be found in John M. MacKenzie, introduction to a new edition of *Hunting and Spoor*, forthcoming.

92 Denis D. Lyell, *African Adventure: Letters from Famous Big Game Hunters*, London, 1935.

93 Denis D. Lyell, *Nyasaland for the Hunter and Settler*, London, 1912.

94 Denis D. Lyell, *Wild Life in Central Africa*, London, 1913.

95 W. T. Shorthose, *Sport and Adventure in Africa*, London, 1923, pp. 19-33.

96 Edward C. Tabler, *The Far Interior*, Cape Town, 1955, p. 159.

97 Selous was fined £60 and always regarded the imposition as unjust. Fifty hippos had been shot because the trader Martin wished to send sjamboks to Cape Colony, where they were much in demand. Selous, *Travel and Adventure*, pp. 135-8.

98 J. R. D. Cobbing, 'The Ndebele under the Khumalos, 1820-1896' unpublished PhD thesis, University of Lancaster, 1976, p. 175.

99 Selous, *Hunter's Wanderings*, pp. 444-8.

100 A. G. Leonard, *How we made Rhodesia*, London, 1896, p. 25.

101 Hugh Marshall Hole, *Old Rhodesian Days*, London, 1928, p. 82.

102 Brown, *South African Frontier*, pp. 113-19.

103 Churchill, *Men, Mines*, p. 211.

104 Churchill, *Men, Mines*, pp. 170-3.

105 Hyatt, *Transport Road*, pp. 182-3 and 271-4.

106 Hyatt, *Transport Road*, pp. 174-5.

107 *Castle Guide to South Africa* (1899-1900 edition), p. 218.

108 Hole, *Old Rhodesia Days*, p. 84.

109 Marcus Daly, *Big Game Hunting and Adventure, 1897-1936*, London, 1937, pp. 6, 10-16, and 205-6.

110 Possession of Arms by Natives and Asiatics Restricting Regulations, 1897, Delivery of Arms to Natives and Asiatics Restricting Regulations, 1897, Rifle and Ball Ammunition Ordinance, 1902.

111 The African police also took Lee-Metfords with them when they deserted, Baden-Powell, *Matabeleland Campaign*, p. 35.

112 Vavasseur to Colenbrander, 6 May, 1893, NAZ His, MSS Coll. Correspondence and other papers of J. W. Colenbrander, 1881-1917, quoted in Cobbing, 'The Ndebele', p. 175.

113 In 1974 I was shown Chief Vhondo of Gutu's Tower musket and was told that it had been used the week before to chase baboons from growing crops. By the Possession of Arms by Natives for Self-protection Act, 1932, Native Commissioners were permitted to issue a rifle and not more than ten rounds of ammunition for the purpose of protecting crops from wild animals.

114 John M. MacKenzie, 'A pre-colonial industry; the Njanja and the iron trade', *NADA*, XI, 2 (1975).

115 Varian, *African Milestones*, p. 66.

116 Papers of Herbert Percy Hale, NAZ Hist. MSS Coll. HA4/1/1.

117 Papers of Mansel Edge Weale, NAZ Hist. MSS Coll. WE 3/2/5.

118 Hemans, *Log*, p. 5.

119 Hemans, *Log*, pp. 48, and 153. Hemans emphasised the importance of hunting to the administrator's prestige, p. 83. Lugard also wrote that hunting was a vital part of his expeditions to keep his men happy and enhance his prestige. Lugard, *East African Empire*, Vol. I, p. 279.

120 Selous, *African Nature Notes*, p. 271.
121 Jason Machiwanyika, NAZ Hist. MSS Coll. MA 4/1/2.
122 I collected some eighty interviews, which included questions on hunting in the Chibi, Gutu, Wedza, Mrewa, Mtoko, Godhljwayo and Matobo districts of Zimbabwe in 1973-74. They are deposited in the oral evidence collections of the Department of History of the University of Zimbabwe.

# CHAPTER SIX

# Exploration, conquest and game in East Africa

The ivory trade of East Africa was of long standing. There are references to it in the earliest sources on East African history, like the Periplus of the Erythraean Sea, compiled nearly 2,000 years ago. Since the Middle Ages a complex network of African hunters and traders, Muslim middlemen and shippers, and Indian capitalists had supplied the Asian and later the European markets. The Portuguese attempted to divert this trade into their own hands, but without notable sucess. By the mid-nineteenth century Muslim caravan leaders and slavers were themselves penetrating East Africa, trading ivory, attempting to outwit African middlemen, and establishing hunting and trading 'colonies' in the interior. By the later nineteenth century European hunters, traders and shipowners were in their turn subverting the Swahili ivory network, using the attack on the slave trade to commercial advantage.[1]

American and European demand expanded rapidly in the nineteenth century with the dramatic growth in the manufacture of cutlery, pianos, billiard balls, combs and ornaments. The British imported more ivory than any other power, though the principal use in Britain was for cutlery handles, which required 'hard' ivory of the forest regions, much of it imported from West Africa. Exports of East African 'soft' ivory increased in this period, possibly reaching a peak between 1879 and 1883, while the West African trade seems to have reached its zenith at a somewhat later date. It has been estimated that 12,000 elephants were being killed each year during those years, though alarmist contemporaries put the figure even higher. Ivory figures and their relation to elephant deaths are, however, notoriously difficult to handle, and it may be that the increase in demand was satisfied to a certain extent from African ivory hoards that had been in existence for some time. The growth in demand is well illustrated by the expansion in the output of pianos in the United States from approximately 10,000 instruments in 1850 to 370,000 in 1910 and in Britain from approximately 23,000 in 1850 to 75,000 in 1910.[2] Throughout this period the world market price of ivory remained buoyant, although there were some short-term fluctuations, at a time when other commodity prices were often undergoing severe depression.

East Africa was the world's greatest source of ivory, and exports exceeded those of any other part of the continent. This was because the catchment area of the East African trade was so large. It tapped not only the vast elephant resources of Somaliland, the southern Sudan, Kenya, Uganda and Tanganyika , but also the equatorial regions of the Congo (Zaire), the territories to the south of the Sahara as far west as Lake Chad and at times the Central African regions that are now Zambia, Malawi and Mozambique. Throughout East Africa, as in Central Africa, ivory was the vital constituent of pre-colonial white freebooting. It later became an important subsidy to initial imperial endeavour, and later still moved on into a third phase when it became a significant source of revenue to several poverty-sticken East African administrations. As we shall see, the 'offtake' of elephants was considerable, but in East Africa there was nothing like the devastation of the elephant population or the severe contraction of its geographical incidence that took place south of the Zambezi. Elephants retreated from coastal areas and their immediate hinterland in Somaliland to remote regions on the Abyssinian border. The most accesssible herds of the Kenyan and Tanganyikan coasts were similarly depleted and dispersed. But destruction on the southern African scale was averted because of the smaller size of the white population, the later arrival of European hunting operations, and the development of exaggerated ideas of conservation in the late 1890s. The scale of ivory exports and the depletion of the most visible elephant stocks led to a conviction that the experience of southern Africa was about to be repeated. In fact elephant populatons were considerably underestimated, as were the recuperative powers of the herds reduced by hunting. By the 1920s, as we shall see in chapter nine, the problem had become one of elephant control and crop protection, and by the 1940s elephants had even recolonised the coastal areas of Kenya.

The meat, hide and trophy subsidy was also important in East Africa. Settlers indulged in asset-stripping, and military campaigns used game as a vital part of the commissariat. Disease took its toll, but conservation policies were more extreme than in southern Africa and faunal population recovery was more dramatic. The settlers were, in many cases, of higher social standing than in the south, and consequently more interested in preservation for purposes of the Hunt. Many, but not all, of the governors came from the British (or German) hunting elite and in some cases had been professional hunters themselves. Above all, East Africa became the paradise of the rich tourist hunter, an important source of income to struggling colonial revenues such that preservation policies were geared to their requirements. Thus East Africa followed, or appeared to follow, the southern and Central African pattern until the late 1890s. The region then became the setting for the more extreme forms of game preservation and the prime example of the third level of imperial hunting, the elite Hunt. The inevitable concomitant of these two linked developments was that attempts would be made to enforce prohibitions on African hunting.

European ivory hunters did not penetrate East Africa until the last years of the nineteenth century. The ivory trade remained in African and Swahili hands until then, and Swahili caravans continued to bring ivory to the East African coast during the early years of the European protectorate. Indeed, the regulations relating to game, arms and the organisation of caravans seem to have been partly designed to frustrate them. There were a number of reasons for the late arrival of Europeans. The Africa–Swahili trade had already reduced the elephant population in the more accessible regions. The horse could not be used in the areas there elephants were most plentiful, and there were no pliant African kings, as in Central Africa, with whom an ivory hunting and trading relationship could be established. European hunters were fully occupied elsewhere, and the first thrust of the European approach to East African ivory was to secure the marketing and shipping sectors from Zanzibar and the rest of the coast. The Americans, swiftly followed by the British, the north Germans and the French, were active in this from the 1840s.[3]

Fears of the decline and extinction of the East African ivory trade were firmly planted in the European mind by the writings of Joseph Thomson. After the death of its original leader, Thomson led the Royal Geographical Society's expedition to East and Central Africa in 1878-80. This took him to the northern shores of Lake Nyasa, Lake Tanganyika and the caravan routes of what is now Tanzania. In his account of the journey, he described the disappearance of the elephant populations and the consequent decline of the ivory trade:

> The fact that the trade in ivory and slaves now almost entirely depends on the distant countries to which these routes lead, suggests a woeful tale of destruction. Twenty years ago countries between Tanganyika and the coast were rich in ivory. Trade routes ramified through every part. Caravans came laden from Mambwe, Ulungu, Urori, Ubena, Ugogo, and Unyantambe, and the more distant regions were scarcely known. Now these countries are completely despoiled. Over that vast region hardly a tusk of ivory is to be got.[4]

The traders, he went on, have to push farther and farther inland each year, and only the most remote and central parts of Africa yield ivory. The ramifications of the ivory trade were enormous and no one country could adequately supply the demand. The ruthless destruction of elephants could not continue for long. 'An iron band of ruthless destroyers is drawing round it; and it may be safely predicted that in twenty years, the noble African elephant will be a rare animal.' Although he estimated that 30,000-40,000 lb of ivory per annum were still passing through Iendwe, he thought the rapid decline and disappearance of the trade were at hand. He underlined this by asserting that in fourteen months in the Great Lakes region he never saw a single elephant. Twenty years before they had roamed unmolested, but now they were 'almost utterly exterminated'. Only ten years before, David

Livingstone had written of the abundance of elephants at the southern end of Lake Tanganyika. They had entered Livingstone's camp and African villages with impunity. 'Not one is now to be found.' There are, he asserted, few corners of Africa where they have not been harried out.[5]

Thomson was unaware of the vast elephant herds still to be found in many parts of the Congo, in Uganda, the southern Sudan, northern Kenya and Somaliland. His forebodings were to be repeated by other travellers and were prominent in the anxieties of the preservationist movement active from the last years of the century. In fewer than fifty years the elephant populations of both Tanganyika and North Eastern Rhodesia were almost out of contol, and massive culls, sometimes over 3,000 a year, were the order of the day. Thomson's apocalypatic version of the fate of the East African elephant merely illustates the lack of opportunities for adequate observation available to the nineteenth-century travellers on foot and an unawareness of the recuperative powers of animal populations. The rapidity of population growth from small stocks of even the elephant had, after all, been noted by Darwin. Faced with persecution, the elephants merely retreated to more inaccessible regions.

In fact ivory was to prove an even more important subsidy to European imperial activities in East Africa than it had been in Central Africa. Lugard, who had begun his career in Africa as an elephant hunter for the African Lakes Company, transferred his skills to the Imperial British East Africa Company. In the early 1890s he mixed a series of campaigns in Uganda with elephant hunting, the former partly financed by the latter. The value of ivory he sent to the coast averaged £5,300 per annum. Emin Pasha had been able to collect enough ivory to pay the costs of his administration in the equatorial provinces of the Sudan.[6] Indeed, he was none too happy about being 'rescued' by H. M. Stanley in 1887-88, because of the hoard of ivory he had amassed.[7] One of Lugard's fellow employees of the IBEAC, Frederick Jackson, was also an eager hunter. He arrived in East Africa in 1884 with the intention of hunting and paying his expenses from ivory sales. He joined the IBEAC in 1888, led a number of expeditions on its behalf and finished his career as Lieutenant Governor of Kenya and, in 1911, Governor of Uganda. In 1890 King Mwanga of Buganda offered him 3,500 lbs of ivory if Jackson would help to restore him to his throne.[8]

Jackson's nephew, Sir Geoffrey Archer, who later became Governor of Somaliland, Uganda and the Sudan, similarly arrived in East Africa as an adventurer and hunter. He met the celebrated elephant hunter

Arthur Neumann, and was nearly influenced by him to join the ranks of professional hunters. Instead he became District Commissioner of Kenya's northern frontier district and there augmented his salary by annual elephant hunting.[9] This form of subsidy, to the personal salaries of imperial administrators, was appropriated by many of the officials and was pursued both legally and illegally.[10] In the East Africa Protectorate they had preferential hunting rights under the game legislation for a number of years. In Uganda the right to augment official salaries from the two elephants (whose tusks, if large bulls, could be worth several hundred pounds) permitted under licence was jealously guarded for several decades. There was even an attempt to use the arrangement as a means of elephant control in the 1920s, an attempt which failed since the hunters inevitably looked for large bulls who were not necessarily the same beasts as the crop destroyers.[11] By that time the sale of ivory by the East African administrations had become a not inconsiderable part of their often exiguous income. In the 1930s, when culling had become necessary, ivory sales helped to tide colonial revenues, particularly those of Uganda and Tanganyika, through the difficulties of the depression period. Thus the ivory subsidy was important to chartered companies, the campaigns of 'pacification', the personal finances of the *conquistadores* who became imperial officials, and the revenues of relatively impecunious colonies.

In the final years before game legislation was introduced and colonial administrations set about appropriating the full benefit of ivory income, European hunters operating on their own private account became active in East Africa. Arthur Neumann had arrived in Durban in 1869 only to find that the great days of hunting in southern Africa were over. He lamented the time, little more than three decades earlier, when elephants could be found on the Berea just outside the port. By 1871 the last buffaloes in Natal, following the fate of the elephants, had been shot. In 1888 he moved to East Africa. In 1890 he took service with the IBEAC and secured an official appointment in Zululand the following year. In 1893, well blooded on hunting in southern Africa, he achieved his ambition of becoming a professional elephant hunter in East Africa, setting out from Mombasa with an expedition of fifty porters and twenty donkeys financed from his savings. He made two hunting trips to northern Kenya, reaching Lake Rudolf on his second journey. He had nothing like the success of the great hunters of southern Africa and was frequently frustrated in his attempts to find elephants, but the high prices obtainable for ivory in the 1890s seem to have provided him with a handsome profit, although he offers no details. Like so many other 'hunters' he traded as much ivory as he shot himself, and encountered the last of the Swahili caravans trading in northern Kenya. He shot only twenty-five elephants on his first expedition, though his killing of thirteen in one day helped to ensure his place in hunting lore. His book *Elephant Hunting in East Equatorial Africa*, published in 1898, and his continued presence in East Africa as a hunter and safari guide, made him a celebrated figure.[12] But he was a morose man who shunned human company and eventually took his own life.

Another famous elephant hunter of East Africa was W. D. M. 'Karamojo' Bell, who similarly hunted in the last years before the introduction of the licence system. Bell was a classic late nineteenth-century adventurer. He had sailed on windjammers, lived in New Zealand, and landed in East Africa in 1897 when still in his teens. He was employed as a lion-killer on the construction works for the Uganda Railway. After a spell in the Yukon gold rush, where he shot game to supply Dawson City with meat, and service with the Canadian Mounted Rifles in the Boer War, he returned to East Africa in 1902 and became a professional elephant hunter for over twenty years. To operate successfully at such a late date he had to devote himself to the avoidance of areas where game regulations were in force. This led him to Karamoja, a largely unknown and uncontrolled no-man's-land between Abyssinia, the Sudan, Uganda and Kenya. As his nickname implies, he spent much time there, though he also moved into the Lado enclave of the Congo during the interregnum after the death of King Leopold of the Belgians in 1909, before its administration was fully taken over by the Sudan in a transfer arranged some years earlier. Bell had been influenced, like so many other hunters, by reading Gordon Cumming's account of hunting in southern Africa, and he seems to have been as financially successful as Cumming. He kept a cattle ranch in Nandi country in Kenya and mounted his expeditions from there, rather like the practice of the Boers of the Merico of the western Transvaal. On one trip he shot nine bulls in one day, yielding 1,463 lb of ivory (one bull had only one tusk, though an exceptionally large one) worth £877 on the London market. He returned from a hunting expedition with 14,000 lb of ivory, worth, by the same computation, over £23,000. He also traded and described the manner in which in his earliest days a tusk worth £50 to £60 could be acquired from Africans for the equivalent of two or three shillings, although prices were later forced up by competition among Swahili traders. In the Lado, Bell shot 210 elephants in nine months and brought out over five tons (11,200 lb) of ivory, a quarter of his lifetime total. Bell was but one of several hunters who assaulted the Lado elephant herds in the years before the First World War, several of whom, including John Boyes, another well known hunter, made considerable fortunes. The main problem faced by these hunters was the difficulty of transport, the removal of large quantities of heavy ivory from such a remote region solely by human porterage. In 1911, still looking for fresh hunting grounds, Bell went to Liberia in West Africa, where there was no game legislation, but he was disappointed by the small size of the West African elephant. The exploits in the Lado were, in fact, the swan song of the professional European ivory hunter.[13] Many turned themselves into safari leaders, made what they could under licence, or indulged in poaching. Cross-border poaching into the territory of rival colonial powers was often regarded as 'fair game', adding to the swashbuckling image of the hunter. It continued until at least the 1930s. Bell was sufficiently successful as an ivory hunter to take up ocean yacht racing and retired to a 1,000 acre Highland estate at Garve in Ross-shire, where he lived into the 1950s.[14]

After the First World War many ivory hunters operated in the Belgian Congo and French Equatorial Africa. Until the late 1920s the game regulations there were more liberal than in British territories, while vast remote areas offered opportunities for infringements of such regulations as did exist and cross-border smuggling facilitated the disposal of ivory. Moreover large numbers of African hunters continued to operate either on their own account or at the behest of Europeans. The hunter Dugald Campbell continued to take ivory in both Belgian and French territory until the 1920s. In French Equatorial Africa a 500 franc (£5) licence permitted the killing of three elephants, while that at 3,000 francs (£30) offered unlimited shooting of elephants and other game. A fortune could be secured from the latter licence. Despite Belgian claims to be leaders of the national park movement (see chapter ten), the Congo continued to offer opportunities akin to those of the late nineteenth century. The river Congo provided ready access to vast game regions for the big-game hunter. Campbell observed the assault of traders upon the rare gorilla population of the north-eastern equatorial forests and published a photograph of nine gorilla heads laid out on a hunter's table. A Belgian newspaper printed a photograph of a big-game hunter proudly displaying twenty-one hippo heads.[15] Both Campbell and Marcus Daly observed the activities of Muslim hunters and traders in the western Sudan. Under-weight tusks which infringed British regulations were smuggled out of the Sudan into French territory while large tusks passed the other way because of the higher prices obtainable in the Sudan.

Daly, who started hunting in Matabeleland in 1897 after the deaths of his father and brother in the Ndebele revolt, hunted throughout central, eastern and equatorial Africa for a period of nearly forty years. After the First World War he hunted illegally in Tanaland, on the borders of Kenya and Italian Somaliland. There he encountered a great deal of ivory raiding and poaching by British and Italian hunters. On one occasion he 'stampeded' a group of raiders and 'acquired' their tusks, thirty in all. These, and others he had shot himself, made up a dhow-load for India. Once, when he encountered a District Officer, he regaled him with whisky while his carriers took a load of ivory across the river a mile away. Imperial freebooting continued well into the period of supposedly settled colonial rule. In French Equatorial Africa Daly hunted from three large camps, 150 miles apart. He moved from camp to camp, spending betweeen one and three months at each, and employing 100 carriers. Many of the European ivory traders were operating on the 'powder and cap' method, purchasing ivory for the powder and caps required for the African hunters' muzzle-loaders. In the Belgian Congo hunters took out licences for two elephants, repeatedly shooting two and selling the tusks across the French border. When the system of unlimited licences came under threat, Daly was arrested by a French *chef de circonscription*, and had 10,000 lb of ivory and his rifles and ammunition confiscated. He was fined 2,000 francs and his licence was revoked. Daly laid a claim against the French authorities for £25,000 compensation, but he continued to hunt and at a later date based himself in the Sudan, 'raiding' French territory for ivory. By the later 1920s Daly was leading American hunting parties and scientific expeditions. He was guide to the Harvard trans-Africa Scientific Expedition, which was eager to secure a specimen of the mountain gorilla.[16]

These hunters were, of course, dependent on the meat subsidy when feeding their porters on the journeys to and from elephant country. That same meat subsidy had been of varying significance in the financing of expeditions of explorers, missionaries and treaty hunters in the years leading up to the establishment of imperial rule. Obviously a good deal did depend on the country through which expeditions passed and on the skill of their leaders with the rifle. There are as many tales of frustration and of failure in efforts to supply meat as there are of success. Joseph Thomson, for example, seems to have done very little shooting on his 1878-80 expedition. When he recounted the system of

[ 155 ]

rationing used for caravans he referred only to methods of exchanging cloth for food.[17] In his later journey, described in *Through Masailand* (1887), he seems to have frequently shot buffalo 'to replenish the larder'.[18] Lugard saw the shooting of meat as vital to the prestige of the leader and to the happiness of the men.[19] His account of operations in East Africa abounds in descriptions of maintaining meat supplies for large parties of porters and askaris. Jackson was more explicit in noting the significance of meat as a subsidy. On one of his earliest hunting trips, in 1886-87, he discovered the great savings he had made by living on the game resource:

> When it came to packing I was amazed to find that there still remained a large quantity of trade goods on hand. This was due to my having insisted on the meat of everything I shot, not excepting warthogs, being brought into camp, and there divided up. In Taveta the men bought flour, or anything they cared for, with biltong, or half-cooked meat. In other words, I had had a splendid time for ten months, on less than three months' supplies.[20]

Later, when Jackson was the IBEAC representative at Eldoma Ravine, he described the immense slaughter of game by the road-making party under Captain Bernard Slater. His NCOs, Sergeant Ellison and Corporals Brodie and Simmons,

> were all first-rate shots, and they were all mounted, their combined bag of game, if a record had been kept, would have been little less than staggering; their slaughter of rhinoceroses alone in the open thorn-bush country between Sultan Hamud and Machakos Road was only equalled by that of a man named Gardner Muir and his Scots ghillie, who between them killed over eighty round about Machakos in 1893 in less than three months.[21]

Gardner Muir, incidentally, so incensed the company by advertising his feats against the rhino that it led to the introduction of the first game regulations. The above sounds as though the main objective was 'sport', but the meat by-product must have been considerable.

Arthur Neumann was so assiduous in shooting meat for his men that they nicknamed him 'Nyama Yangu', or 'My Meat'. Among other animals he shot rhinos, oryx and giraffe for this purpose.[22] Dugald Campbell supplied his men with monkey meat in the Congo and delighted them with the occasional chimpanzee.[23] Marcus Daly kept up a constant flow of meat throughout his extensive hunting travels.[24] When ex-President Roosevelt visited Kenya on a massive specimen-collecting expedition in 1909 his party was supported by 200 porters.[25] The game regulations were suspended for his benefit and he described the manner in which the porters were dependent for their meat supply on the guns of the leadership. Such a system neatly emphasised the dependence of Africans on the superior technology of their European masters.

Rinderpest, despite its great virulence, presented only a temporary hitch to the meat bonanza. Lugard recounts daily hunting on his journey to Uganda in 1890. For example, on the Njams plains in November that year game abounded and he was forced to let wounded animals escape. He confided in his diary:

> It is miserable work wounding game and leaving it; but we are butchers now, not sportsmen, shooting for so many pounds of meat, and weighing and issuing it. My consolation is that the game is so plentiful that a few more or less make no difference. . .

A few days later, in the Kamazia range, he began to find carcases of buffalo, 'recently dead of the plague',

> and, as we passed onwards, they daily became more numerous, and we found that this dreadful epidemic had swept off all the cattle and the wild buffalo, and much of the other game beside. The vultures and hyenas were too surfeited to devour the putrid carcases which lay under almost every tree near water.

The same was true of the Kavirondo:

> Through all this great plain we passed carcases of buffalo; and the vast herds of which I had heard, and which I hoped would feed my hungry men, were gone! The breath of the pestilence had destroyed them as utterly as the Westerners of Buffalo Bill and his crew and the corned-beef factories of Chicago have destroyed the bison of America.

But because the rinderpest affected some species much more than others, herds survived to provide meat. In Nandi he encountered a herd of hartebeest and shot four. He used the meat as part of a system of rewards and punishment, providing an interesting additional twist to the meat subsidy.

> I used the meat proportionately; those who had marched most willingly, carrying the heaviest loads, and giving no trouble, received the largest share, while some, who had been laggards and grumblers, got none. Such a division, of course, takes much time; but I found that there is no more effective way of maintaining a good spirit in the caravan, and of saving the necessity of flogging and such like punishments. The common custom, I believe, is for the meat to be thrown, as it were, to the dogs – either scrambled for or left to the head-man to divide with what favouritism or carelessness they like – and hence it becomes a source rather of discontent and quarrels than of reward and incentive.[26]

[ *157* ]

Lugard believed, in fact, that the rinderpest helped rather than hindered the white advance. In an oft-quoted passage he judged the effects of the rinderpest:

> In some respects it has favoured our enterprise. Powerful and warlike as the pastoral tribes are, their pride has been humbled and our progresss facilitated by this awful visitation. The advent of the white man had else not been so peaceful. The Masai would undoubtedly have opposed us, and either by force of arms or by protracted methods of conciliation (whose results would have been doubtful), we should have had to win our way to the promising highlands beyond their country. . . Never before in the memory of man, or by the voice of tradition, have the cattle died in such vast numbers; never before has the wild game suffered.[27]

But while cattle had almost no immunity, devastating the pastoral economies, the effect on game was selective. Buffalo, eland, giraffe, bushbuck, reedbuck and warthog nearly all died in the most affected areas, but the nsunu or kobus kob was affected only partially, and the elephant, hippo, rhino, hartebeest, wildebeest and water buck seemed to be exempt.

Within a few years the game had made a remarkable recovery. The diaries of Richard Meinertzhagen illustrate the significance of the meat subsidy in the 'pacification' period after the turn of the century. Meinertzhagen transferred from the Indian Army (after a hunting slight in Burma) to East Africa in 1902. He had read Cornwallis Harris and Gordon Cumming and, fired by the southern African myth, was enthralled at the prospect of combining hunting with fighting. He was shocked to be told by his commanding officer in Nairobi that he should train his men by using game for target practice, but the scruples of the sportsman seemed to wear thin once the opportunities for the slaughter of game as well as humans became apparent. He was involved in a series of expeditions against the Irryeni, the Embo, the Sotik and the Nandi, killing hundreds of Africans as well as burning their villages and granaries. He shot some of his own men when they killed women and children. On one occasion he killed twenty-five baboons in reprisal for one killing his dog while being tormented by it.[28] He shot game daily and later wrote in a commentary on his diaries:

> For the amount of big game I shot during my first tour in Kenya I have no excuse. I am not proud of it, neither am I ashamed of it. When I arrived in the country I was obsessed by an unashamed blood-lust. Hunting is man's primitive instinct, and I indulged it and enjoyed it to the full. In Kenya's early days fresh meat was not easy to obtain. The African was loath to part with his stock and there was no European settler in the

country who could provide meat. Also, when travelling with from 20 to 200 healthy Africans, all doing hard work, meat becomes almost an essential, and more than three-quarters of the animals I shot went to provide meat for hungry and deserving mouths.[29]

As he himself indicates, not all his shooting was for utilitarian purposes. On one occasion he obtained a record day's'sport', killing more animals than his party could eat. He had no excuse, he wrote, other than a the hunter's love of the chase. There is, moreover, a discrepancy in Meinertzhagen's account of his financial success in East Africa. In the four years he was a King's African Rifles subaltern he earned £400 a year, but left the protectorate having saved £4,000.[30] It must be presumed that much of this nest egg came from the sale of ivory.

Meinertzhagen's diaries are exceptionally honest. They even recount, unusually for that period, the sexual exploitation of the African population by European officers, missionaries and settlers. They demonstrate the amount of violence inherent in the colonial situation and the manner in which the killing of game prepared Europeans for and inured them to the killing of Africans. In Nairobi Meinertzhagen teamed up with Sir Claude Champion de Crespigny. They enjoyed hog-sticking together and imported pig-sticking lances from India. They also attempted to stick lions, but after their first alarming experiences Meinertzhagen's commanding officer forbade him to be involved any further.[31] De Crespigny had served in the army in Ireland and India. In 1870-71 he fought as a mercenery in the Franco-Prussian War on the Prussian side. He was a passionate fox-hunting man who attributed the lack of French military skill to their incompetence in hunting. He took up hawking and was proud of having destroyed 576 head of prey in 1887. He organised pugilists to beat up radicals in an election campaign and on one occasion travelled to Carlisle to witness the hanging of three murderers lest, as sheriff of his county, he might have to conduct executions himself. He attempted to join every African expedition and campaign of the 1880s and 1890s and participated in the Boer War. He arrived in East Africa in 1905 to indulge in big-game shooting, but was swept up in the punitive campaigns of the period.[32]

As de Crespigny put it, he 'had the good luck to arrive just in time to join the Sotik punitive expedition, so that I was able to combine a certain amount of fighting with some excellent sport'. He was disappointed that he would be leaving the country before he could participate in a 'far bigger job. . . with the Nandi tribe'. On 26 June 1905 he laconically noted in his diary that he had been involved in removing 1,500 cattle and 4,000 goats and sheep from the Sotiks. 'Sotiks killed,

50. The latter we had hoped to make 500.' Later he helped Major Pope Hennessy, KAR, the leader of the expedition, to raise the cattle figure to 2,400 and the Sotik fatalities to nearly 100, 'including one biggish chief'.[33] Meinertzhagen also had a tendency to elide human with animal bags, and it earned him a rebuke from the Commissioner of the East Africa Protectorate, Sir Charles Eliot.[34]

Meinertzhagen was related to Eliot, met him socially, and attempted to convince him of the need for a full-blown game preservation policy in Kenya. Eliot was unconvinced. He was in fact an unusual figure to be a colonial governor, or its equivalent, and this brought him into conflict with his deputy, Frederick Jackson. Eliot was a scholar and linguist, an intellectual who had a passing interest in aquatic wildlife. Meinertzhagen remarked that he 'studies sea slugs and looks like one, invertebrate, icy cold, unsympathetic', a man 'more like a university don or a priest'.[35] Eliot believed wholeheartedly in a settler policy, the restriction of Africans to 'native reserves' from where they could supply the cheap-labour needs of the European economy. If this was the 'radical' and capitalist approach, that of Jackson and Meinertzhagen was romantic and conservative. They disapproved of settlers and seemed to believe that the British should rule the territory as preservationists, maintaining humans and wildlife alike in what was supposed to be their natural condition. Eliot disliked hunting and opposed what he regarded as a sentimental approach to animals. He was an interventionist administrator who resigned when he appeared not to get his way on the opening of the Masai reserve to white settlement, although it was, in effect, his policies that were to be pursued in the future. He later became Vice-chancellor of the Universities of Sheffield and Hong Kong, and British ambassador to Japan. An orientalist, he settled in Japan when he retired.[36] Jackson was a man of action, a hunter and campaigner who greatly disliked administration. Many, including another Governor of Kenya, Sir Percy Girouard, doubted his capacity for the high offices he reached.[37]

Nevertheless, Jackson was influential in the development of game preservationist policies and the foundation of a game department to administer them in Kenya.[38] His mistrust of non-sporting settlers seemed to be confirmed when landowners in the Rift Valley and elsewhere asset-stripped all the game while waiting for their land to increase in value.[39] But the manner in which Kenya became the prime happy hunting ground of the international elite also alarmed him. By 1906 the game warden, Blayney Percival, was reporting that several dozen European hunting parties were to be seen within sight of each other on the Athi plains.[40] Rich and titled hunters from France, Germany, Austria and the United States as well as Britain, had indeed been active in Kenya since the 1890s. The German Count Teleki, one of the earliest, who claimed the discovery of Lake Rudolf, emerged from the interior boasting that he had 'shot 35 elephants and 300 niggers'.[41] He had become embroiled in altercations with local peoples and had also seen many of his porters die of starvation. Nevertheless the game regulations were, in effect, designed to encourage elite hunting, which was soon contributing a significant proportion of the revenue of the protectorate.

In consequence a whole hunting and safari industry grew up in Nairobi. The firms of R. J. Cunninghame and A. C. Hoey were the most celebrated and the most respectable. Other safari hunters included Will Judd, who always sported an immaculate hunting kit (he was later killed by an elephant) and an Austrian named Fritz who encouraged his clients to commit breaches of the regulations. A number were genuine hunters, but a few were imposters who decked themselves out in ludicrous garments to appear to play the part. Some had 'very little experience' while others were 'fond of shooting and out to have good time' at the 'patron's expense'.[42] But all, regardless of qualifications or reputation, drew the same rate of salary. Indeed, the overheated state of the Nairobi safari market is well represented by the assessment of the professional ivory hunter, Marcus Daly. He claimed that in Rhodesia hunters charged £50 per month to lead six-to-twelve-month safaris, while in East Africa "white hunters" not fit to be gun bearers' extorted £200-£300 per month to secure trophies a good Rhodesian hunter could get in quarter of the time at a fraction of the cost.[43] It was, of course, much cheaper to reach Kenya. A Tanganyika guidebook of 1948 advised that a white hunter's salary would cost from £50-£200 per month to lead a safari.[44] Jackson considered that many dubious visitors broke the game laws, took immature trophies or shot females, left meat rotting in the bush, or tried to pull bogus scientific purposes or rank in order to shoot many more 'specimens' than was permitted.[45]

Some hunters of rank were, however, permitted to do just that. When Winston Churchill, as Parliamentary Under-secretary for the Colonies, visited East Africa to inspect the newly completed Uganda Railway in 1907 he seems, like his father, to have spent more time on sport than on business. His private carriage was repeatedly detached and left in sidings at railway stations across Kenya. His was a particularly sybaritic form of the chase, sometimes hunting from a railway trolley, which also carried victuals, champagne and ice to refresh the distinguished Nimrod during the day. Great was his delight when he received a telegram announcing that the sitting of Parliament had been postponed two weeks, enabling him to indulge himself further. Churchill hunted, as his father had done, for sport and prestige rather than for economic benefit. He was permittd to secure as many trophies as he pleased to symbolise his physical as well as political dominance of the imperial environment.[46] Members of the royal family arrived too, the Duke of Connaught before the Great War and the Duke and Duchess of York (the future George VI and Queen Elizabeth) on their honeymoon in 1924.[47]

Two years after Churchill, Theodore Roosevelt, a mythical figure for all the hunter-naturalists of the period, arrived. He had just relinquished the American presidency and travelled under the auspices of the Smithsonian Institution in Washington and the National Museum in New York, charged with collecting specimens for them. These partly spurious scientific credentials induced Jackson to waive the game regulations in his case. Roosevelt was an anglophile who wrote lyrically of the effect of the British in East Africa, of the contrast between advanced civilisation and 'primeval' life. The frontier spirit reminded him of Wyoming thirty years earlier, and he adjudged Africans a less formidable foe than Red Indians. During his trip Roosevelt's party shot 512 head of big game – many more, he admitted then were required as specimens.[48] Jackson later recanted his opinion of Roosevelt. The ex-President was overweight and suffering from poor eyesight. He was a bad shot who permitted many wounded animals to escape, particularly when shooting from horseback at long range. His principal companion, his son Kermit, was inexperienced. It was, wrote Jackson,

a matter of great regret to learn from Colonel Roosevelt's own showing and from others that he was so utterly reckless in the expenditure of ammunition, and what it entailed in the matter of disturbing the country; and that he so unduly exceeded reasonable limits, in certain species, and particularly the white rhinoceros, of which he and Kermit killed nine.[49]

Despite Jackson's scruples about Roosevelt, officers of the East African administrations and of the King's African Rifles continued to enjoy privileged access to the Hunt. Captain Shorthose, whom we have already encountered hunting in Northern Rhodesia in 1910, secured ten days' leave for hunting soon after joining the KAR in 1912, an indulgence resulting from the fact that the adjutant was himself a keen sportsman. Leaves and weekends were devoted to the chase, elephants with fine tusks falling to the officers' rifles. Shorthose recounted his success in securing in the months before the First World War tusks weighing (individually) 90 lb, 65 lb and 50 lb. It was, he wrote, 'most exciting and remunerative'. In the East African campaigns of the war, campaigning was combined with hunting and once again leave was devoted to the chase. The officers were often 'out shooting' while the askaris marched. In German East Africa Shorthose was intrigued to discover that the German settlers had attempted to exterminate or at least drive out the wildebeest from Ngorongoro. They had made 'a roaring trade' of canning the tongues. Sport and war were again combined in the campaign against the so-called 'Mad Mullah' in Somaliland in 1919-20. The officers were given permission to shoot game and their exploits were often 'not of the gentlemanly sort'. Wounded animals were allowed to get away, breaking the 'first rule of shikar'. Elsewhere the men were often used as beaters in buffalo hunts. On one occasion Shorthose secured a rhino, offering meat for his men and a lucrative 21 in. horn for himself.[50]

The transformation of hunting into the elite Hunt, the 'all-red route to slaughter' as one ivory poacher called it with commendable irony, was effected by the exclusion of Africans from access to the chase.[51] The legislative and administrative means by which this was effected will be examined in subsequent chapters, but as ritual and symbolic dominance took over as the primary aspects of the exploitation of animals, Africans were denied the resort to game meat as a hedge against famine. The Kamba of Kenya had been avid hunters who became particularly active when crops failed. When famine struck the Kamba in 1899 they had already been cut off from their old hunting grounds. Jackson indeed argued that the worst effects of the famine could have been alleviated by the supply of meat to the victims by the administration. A few hundred of the 'countless hartebeest and zebras in the near vicinity' could have been shot, and 'properly organised so that the same ground was not shot over two days running, and each "gun" knowing his beat, it would not have been costly and would certainly have helped greatly to reduce the mortality and dreadful sufferings.'[52]

In fact the administration set about excluding Kamba hunters from all access to game. It was believed that the Kamba were 'destructive', that they were not dependent on game, and that it was illegitimate of them to hunt because they hunted outside their own territory, in the adjacent Athi plains. Famine struck again several other years before the First World War and the Kamba attempted to renew their hunting, but the game department under Blayney Percival set itself the task of keeping them away from areas in which game preservation for licensed sport had become the norm.[53] Farther west the game regulations bore down on other peoples who had been accustomed to hunt to supplement their diet. Even the Masai, generally thought not to hunt (except to defend their stock) had, according to Jackson, partaken of game meat in times of difficulty, for example during the rinderpest.[54] The colonial administration, obsessed with notions of economic evolution, drew a sharp distinction between hunter-gatherers who were dependent on game and peoples with mixed economies who ought not to be. Indeed, they went further. It was thought regressive if pastoralists and agriculturalists were permitted to hunt.[55]

Thus hunting, the earliest phase of man's struggle for survival, had become the prerogative of the bearers of industrial civilisation. The Victorians were so convinced of the validity of economic evolution that they believed that subsistence hunting should fall away as the pastoral and agricultural stages were reached. The true marker of advanced culture was the final transformation of subsistence hunting into the elite sporting Hunt. Although hunting had been crucial for survival, as subsistence and financial subsidy, to Europeans in the recent past, it had become primarily a source of sport with its own elaborate code. In the space of a few decades it had made the transition from economic necessity to ethical luxury. Nowhere was this truer than in East Africa. The development of European sensibilities towards animals has to be seen in this light. So has the development of conservationist policies in the twentieth century.[56]

## Notes

1 E. A. Alpers, *Ivory and Slaves in East Africa*, London, 1975. C. A. Spinage, 'A review of ivory exploitation and elephant trends in Africa', *East African Wildlife Journal*, Nairobi, Vol. 11 (1973). p. 281, J. Forbes Munro, *African and the International Economy*, London, 1976, R. W. Beachey, 'The East African ivory trade in the nineteenth century, *JAH*, 8 (1967), pp. 269-90, E. D. Moore, *Ivory, Scourge of Africa*, London, 1931, Roy Bridges is currently preparing a fuller history of the trade.

2 Cyril Ehrlich, *The Piano; a History*, London, 1976, p. 221.

3 N. R. Bennett, *A History of the Arab State of Zanzibar*, London, 1978.

4 Joseph Thomson, *To the Central African Lakes and Back* (2 vols.), London, 1881, Vol. II, pp. 17-18.

5 Thomson, *Central African Lakes*, Vol.II, p. 285.

6 F. D. Lugard, *The Rise of our East African Empire*, (2 vols.), London, 1893, Vol. I, p. 428. By the time Lugard was active, ivory imports to London had declined from an average of 580 tons per annum in the 1860s and early 1870s to 484 tons. Lugard, *East Afican Empire*, Vol I, p. 505.

7 Geoffrey Archer, *Personal and Historical Memoirs of an East African Administrator*, Edinburgh, 1963, p. 14.

8 Frederick Jackson, *Early Days in East Africa*, London, 1969 (first edition 1930),

222, 251.

9 Archer, *Memoirs*, pp. 10, 15-17. C. H. Stigand attempted to combine hunting with survey work in East Africa, but found that work interfered with hunting. C. H. Stigand, *Hunting the Elephant in Africa*, London, 1913, p. 17.

10 One company official, Martin, who later became a District Commissioner despite being illiterate, was alleged to have traded £12,000 to £15,000 worth of ivory in a six-year period on his own account. Jackson, *Early Days*, p. 70.

11 See chapter nine.

12 Arthur Neumann, *Elephant Hunting in East Equatorial Africa*, London, 1898.

13 W. D. M. Bell, *The Wanderings of an Elephant Hunter*, London, 1958 (first edition 1923). Stigand, *Hunting the Elephant*, p. 46. See also Valerie Pakenham, *The Noonday Sun*, London, 1985, pp. 141-66.

14 Bruce Kinloch, *The Shamba Raiders*, London, 1972, pp. 265-70.

15 Dugald Campbell, *Wanderings in Central Africa*, London, 1929.

16 Marcus Daly, *Big Game Hunting and Adventure, 1897-1936*, London, 1937, pp. 67, 73, 116, 121-9, 214.

17 Thomson, *Central African Lakes*, Vol. I, pp. 295-6.

18 Joseph Thomson, *Through Masailand*, London, 1887, pp. 304-7.

19 Lugard, *East African Empire*, Vol. I, p. 279.

20 Jackson, *Early Days*, p. 136.

21 Jackson, *Early Days*, p. 288.

22 Neumann, *Elephant Hunting*, pp. 6, 83, 93.

23 Campbell, *Wanderings*, pp. 127-8.

24 Daly, *Big Game Hunting*, pp. 22-3, and *passim*.

25 Theodore Roosevelt, *African Game Trails*, London, 1910, pp. 17, 53.

26 Lugard, *East African Empire*, Vol. I, pp. 352, 356, 359.

27 Lugard, *East African Empire*, Vol. I, pp. 527-8.

28 Richard Meinertzhagen, *Kenya Diary, 1902-6*, Edinburgh, 1957, pp. 11, 40, 147-8, 152, 172-3, 242.

29 Meinertzhagen, *Diary*, p. 178.

30 Meinertzhagen, *Diary*, pp. 21, 317.

31 Meinertzhagen, *Diary*, pp. 84-5, 96-7.

32 Sir Claude Champion de Crespigny, *Forty Years of a Sportsman's Life*, London, 1925.

33 De Crespigny, *Forty Years*, pp. 248-9, 255-8.

34 Meinertzhagen, *Diary*, p. 158.

35 Meinertzhagen, *Diary*, pp. 31, 59.

36 Sir Charles Eliot, *The East Africa Protectorate*, London, 1905. See also *DNB*.

37 Introduction by H. B. Thomas to new edition of Jackson, *Early Days*, p. ix.

38 See chapter nine for a discussion of Jackson's role in conservation policies.

39 Memorandum by Jackson on game in East Africa, enclosed in Hayes Sadler to Elgin, 28 September 1906, in Further Correspondence relating to the Preservation of Wild Animals in Africa, Cd 4472, lix, p. 635.

40 Report by Blayney Percival, enclosed in Sadler to Elgin, 28 September 1906, Cd 4472, as above.

41 Jackson, *Early Days*, pp. 126-7.

42 Jackson, *Early Days*, pp. 368-70.

43 Daly, *Big Game Hunting*, p. 160.

44 *The Tanganyika Guide*, 1948, p. 67.

45 Jackson, *Early Days*, pp. 371-9.

46 W. S. Churchill, *My African Journey*, London, 1908.

47 Bruce Kinloch, *The Shamba Raiders*, London, 1972, p. 112.

48 Roosevelt, *African Game Trails*, pp. vii, 30-8, and appendix.

49 Jackson, *Early Days*, p. 381.

50 W. T. Shorthose, *Sport and Adventure in Africa*, London, 1923, pp. 34, 41, 57-76, 173-5, 216-19, 259, 279.

51 Derek Temple, *Ivory Poacher*, London, n.d. (1930s), p. 5.

52 Jackson, *Early Days*, pp. 299-300.

53 Memo on game laws in Ukamba province by John Ainsworth, 6 June 1900, in Correspondence relating to the Preservation of Wild Animals in Africa, Cd 3189, 1906, lxxix, p. 25. Report by Jackson and Notes on Game by Blayney Percival, enclosed in Sadler to Elgin, 12 March 1906, also in Cd 3189.

54 Jackson, *Early Days*, p. 131; Lugard, *East African Empire*, Vol. I, p. 340.

55 This point was made several times in reports by Percival and Jackson, and most explicitly in *JSPFE* XXVII (1936), p. 36, commenting on the game reports of Kenya an Tanganyika for 1935. In 1934 drought and locusts had caused crop failure and famine in East Africa. Many 'distressed natives' had turned to hunting, and since the animals were lethargic and concentrated at water holes the hunter's lot had been easy. Africans had to be prevented from hunting for their own sake – 'for the hunting life once adopted is hardly relinquished and it spells retrogression'.

56 Unfortunately, this book went to the press before the publication of Thomas P. Ofcansky's *A History of Game Preservation in British East Africa, 1895-1963* (West Virginia University Press, 1987) but it is clear from Ofcansky's PhD thesis of the same title (University of Wisconsin, 1981) that the approach is somewhat different from that of this chapter.

# CHAPTER SEVEN

# The imperial hunt in India

Sport was an obsession in British India. And among sports those relating to hunting were the most highly regarded. Various forms of hunting were the standard recreation of officers of the civilian, military and forestry establishments. In the military almost everyone, from high-ranking officers to white troopers, participated, in their respective places, in some form of the chase. Indian troops often acted as auxiliaries or spectators and the Gurkhas were given a special dispensation to hunt in the areas around their cantonments.[1] As we have seen in chapter four, British Indian officers frequently attempted to recover their health, or simply seek an adventurous leave, in southern and later East Africa. Within India short leaves were often devoted to hunting trips and every opportunity was taken to combine military activities with the hunt. The civilian administrator developed a patriarchal approach to hunting in many parts of India, seeing it as an obligation, a source of prestige, a route to understanding his district and people, as well as a means of recreation. Among Europeans, forest officers had the best opportunities for hunting and regarded it almost as a professional requirement. Even the commercial elite of the port cities regarded it as a useful means of making social contacts.

The obsessive character of Indian 'sport' is well reflected in the publications of British India, for the sources on hunting are very numerous. As one author (A. I. R. Glasfurd) put it, 'Few subjects of such comparatively circumscribed bounds have elicited more literature than has Indian sport.'[2] A 'steady succession' of publications in the nineteenth century had produced a vast 'accumulation of works'. Many officials cast their accounts of their time in India in the form of sporting memoirs, relegating work to the sidelines, as a disagreeable duty to be fitted in among hunting experiences. The engineer W. Hogarth Todd kept the work to a minimum and ensured that the sport predominated in his book *Work, Sport, and Play*.[3] W. O. Horne had little to say about his administrative duties in *Work and Sport in the old ICS*,[4] while the distinguished forest officers, E. P. Stebbing[5] and Sir Sainthill Eardley-Wilmot,[6] concentrated almost entirely on hunting in their memoirs. This was also true of military men who, perhaps inevitably, contributed most of the corpus of hunting literature. Moreover, judging by reprints and new editions, this hunting literature sold well. It fed a market for the combination of natural history and tales of hunting exploits that were the accomplishments, real and imagined, of talented imperial amateurs and their readership.

The British in India fused two hunting traditions. They adapted some of the spectacular forms of the Mughal Empire and of its inheritor princely States, many of which were preserved after 1858. They also adopted the more humble practices of low-caste Indian hunters and in the course of the nineteenth century appropriated the words *shikar* (hunting) and *shikari* (hunter) from them.[7] To these they added classic British activities like fox hunting, angling and a form of the *battue*. In the realm of technology they were entirely schizophrenic. They enthusiastically adopted the atavistic use of spear and knife, but they also applied the rapidly developing precision of nineteenth-century firearms, culminating in the high-velocity cordite rifle at the end of the century. Thus hunting represented a historic cultural interaction which the British were able to use to build social bridges with Indians, particularly the Indian aristocracy. They consciously sought to inherit the mantle of the Mughals through an opulent and highly visible command of the environment, as well as to establish relations with the princely States through an apparently shared enthusiasm. The more distinctively British hunting sports were in turn taken over by Indians, and the heirs and wards of the Indian elite were encouraged to adopt the combined tradition at the English-style public schools where they were educated.[8]

There are a number of ways of classifying British hunting activities in India. First, they can be categorised according to geographical region and terrain.[9] Different forms of hunting were appropriate to the cultivated plains of India, the great dry sal forests of the Central Provinces, the Doars or deciduous forests of northern India, Bengal, and Assam, the coniferous regions in the foothills of the Himalayas, and the broken wooded terrain of the Nilgiris in the south. Various types of deer and the blue bull or nilgai [10] (the only Indian antelope) were to be found in the cultivated plains, along with wild pig and many types of wildfowl. Wild buffalo and bison or gaur, together with species of deer and the carnivora, were to be found in the forest regions. The forests of the northern Terai were so dense that they could be hunted only with the use of elephants. The Himalayas offered a completely different group of species as hunting quarry, while the mountainous and wooded regions of south India offered a great range of rough shooting, but no pig-sticking. Tigers were widely distributed, elephants restricted to a few though well scattered habitats, while lions and rhinoceros were increasingly rare. The princely states were celebrated for hunting specialisms, some in the north containing opportunities for shooting waterfowl in vast numbers.

Second, the chase can be divided according to method. There were many forms of shooting, with muzzle-loader, rifle and shotgun. Various quarry were pursued with auxiliary animals, whether hounds, scratch or 'bobbery' packs of assorted dogs or, in the Indian States, cheetahs. Sometimes the auxiliaries effected the kill themselves, but dogs might also be used to bring the quarry to bay, holding them until the human

Nimrod could despatch them with spear, knife or gun. A variety of creatures — bear, deer, even carnivora, but above all wild pig — could be ridden down and speared. Pig-sticking became the supremely popular sport of the military, though it was only appropriate in certain forms of terrain, in eastern Bengal and some parts of the Central and United Provinces.

Third, the chase might be classified according to object and function. In some forms of hunting the recreational purpose predominated, although there could be associated social and political considerations. In others defence was the prime object, defence of stock against carnivora, of humans and their habitations against maneaters, of crops against antelope (the nilgai), deer, buffalo or wild elephants. Other hunting was utilitarian, supplying flesh for the subsistence of troops, the local subordinates of European enterprise and for varying the diet of the European officers themselves. These categories are not, of course, exclusive. The defence of Indians provided recreations for Europeans as well as supporting an extensive symbolic superstructure. Defence might yield a lot of meat as a by-product. Supplying subsistence requirements could also act as recreation, the scale of the enjoyment probably depending on the extent of the real subsistence need.

Finally, the British experience of hunting in India can be divided chronologically. Until the early nineteenth century the British were often spectators at or participants in the sport of Indians. With the extension of military activity and administrative power in the late eighteenth and early nineteenth centuries they began to take over and adapt Indian hunting practices as well as introducing their own. Up to the 'Mutiny' British and Indian hunting co-existed. The British themselves indulged in a relative 'free-for-all' with very little regulation, codification of specific sports and of 'sportsmanship' or institutionalisation of team activities. It is alleged that with the disarming of Indians in north central India, after the Mutiny and the preoccupation of the British with reconstruction and the re-establishment of control, the faunal population of that area greatly increased.[11] From the 1870s British rule moved into the era of imperial bombast; the viceroys became more political and aristocratic than practical; the feudal relationship with the princely States became an important prop of their power; administrative and military practice came to be regularised and more uniform systems were established; the State proclamation and control of the vast forest areas proceeded rapidly; and as the social distance between Britons and Indians increased, British recreational institutions were regularised and hedged about with codes and rules.

It is in this period that British hunting in its turn tended towards extravagance. The more opulent forms of Mughal hunting were

[ *170* ]

enthusiastically taken over; the British no longer spectated or participated as guests; the elephant-borne tiger-shoot had become their own.
The visit of the Prince of Wales, the future Edward VII, in 1875-76
inaugurated a succession of royal journeys in which hunting took more
time than any other activity. The viceroys seemed to be chosen as
much for their distinction in the field as for their political reputation
or aristocratic pretensions. Ripon, Dufferin, Curzon, Minto, Irwin, Willingdon and Linlithgow were all well known figures in the hunting
and shooting world and embraced the opportunities presented to them
in India with real enthusiasm. The same was largely true of the governors, lieutenant governors and commissioners of presidencies and provinces. The residents in the Indian States invariably cleaved to their
hunting duties as part of their romantic attachment to the 'traditions'
of their State.[12] It was perhaps inevitable that an activity so sanctified
by the leaders of British India should be seen as an important criterion
of acceptability for most administrative, forestry and military person-
nel in the imperial establishment. The great hunts became, in effect,
annual durbars; the little ones, a prime ceremonial for each petty
potentate in his own locality.

This apotheosis of the hunting mentality survived at least into the
inter-war years and was indeed inherited by the Indianised ICS and
army in the years leading up to independence.[13] The period was charac-
terised by a wave of books and memoirs on shikar, handbooks for the
intending shikari, codes and regulations for particular sports and provinces, and prescriptive works on the necessity of various forms of the
chase to imperial rulers. Accounts of royal tours also emphasised the
hunting activities of the distinguished visitors as well as the interests
of their princely hosts. Careful game records were kept and entered
the muniments and memorabilia of viceregal families. Thus while the
height of the hunting craze coincided with exploration, expansion and
exploitation in Africa, the cult was in some ways emblematic of the
developing weakness of the Indian empire. Like most of the invented
traditions of the later nineteenth century, hunting represented an
increasing concern with the external appearance of authority, the fascination with the outward symbols serving to conceal inner weakness.

This final period in the chronological division of the hunting ethos
can be subdivided. From about the turn of the century there was an
increasing concern with game preservation. This was particularly true
of some of the Indian States and of the Indian forest service. In Kashmir,
for example, the maharajah developed a vigorous approach to preservation, and, as one observer put it, this helped to ensure that hunting in
the State was open only to the elite.[14] By the 1920s and '30s many
thought that the decline of the Indian fauna had reached crisis propor-

tions. The buffalo had disappeared from the Central Provinces in the late nineteenth century and the *Rhinoceros unicornus* had become extinct in India. Both buffalo and bison had been seriously depleted in the rinderpest epidemics of 1896-97. The shift from preservation for sport to genuine conservation, however, arrived late in India. If anything, anxieties about the decline of game ensured that access to it would be progressively restricted to the elite, heightening the appearance of the Hunt as the perquisite of the powerful and the rich – royal visitor and viceroy, senior administrator and army officer, wealthy tourist and Indian prince. In fact the locus of power was moving towards the intellectuals and lawyers of the Indian National Congress, most of whom did not hunt and who, ironically, were to be involved in the conservation movement after independence.

There were two notable works on hunting in India in the early nineteenth century, those of Thomas Williamson and Daniel Johnson. Williamson, whose *Oriental Field Sports* was published in 1808, described India as providing 'for Nimrods new and arduous species of the chase'.[15] East India Company service opened the door to an immense range of hunting unencumbered by rules or laws. Some of the practices described by Williamson, illustrative of the free-and-easy approach of the late eighteenth and early nineteenth centuries, would soon be regarded as unsporting – for example, hog hunting with greyhounds or riding down peafowl and other birds on horseback. Interestingly, Williamson sometimes saw 'sport' as leading to ill health, whereas the opposite connection was often made in the late nineteenth century.[16] Moreover, it is noticeable that in this period there was as much interest in Indian hunting as in European. By the end of the century Indian hunting was seen as auxiliary to that of the British masters, or, in the princely States, as the joint hunting of an elite; or, most commonly, as 'poaching'. While Williamson saw the British as introducing 'sporting' characteristics (essentially the elements of exertion and difficulty) he described many Indian practices – from the activities of local shikaris to the great hunts and staged animal fights of the Indian aristocracy – without any note of disapproval. Only in his preface did he suggest that the great Indian hunts with hundreds of elephants and thousands of horse and foot soldiers were not 'sport'.[17]

Daniel Johnson published an account of Indian hunting in 1822 and dedicated it to the Court of Directors of the East India Company. He noted the existence of many professional hunters in India, skilled men who pursued a hereditary occupation.[18] Their main functions were to protect villagers, stock and travellers from carnivores and crops from herbivores. When guarding those passing through dangerous country

[ *172* ]

they often wore the skin of a tiger or leopard, and carried bows and arrows, a large ornamental shield, or sometimes a spear, a matchlock gun or a sword. They received land or an allowance from rajah or landowner and presents from travellers for this service. Johnson wryly commented that they gave the travellers more confidence than protection.

These hunters, usually Hindus of low caste, often had specialised functions, some catching birds and hares, others being concerned with the destruction of tigers. A whole variety of techniques were used, involving nets, bamboo frames, nooses, birdlime and camouflage (particularly to catch waterfowl). The products of this hunting were sold in markets and villages to Muslims and low-caste Hindus prepared to eat the meat. The European market in Calcutta was kept well supplied with duck, wigeon, teal and hare. Significantly, Johnson himself and another 'gentleman' hired two shikaris for three rupees per month to kill game and keep their table supplied daily.[19] Johnson and his companion frequently accompanied their shikaris to watch their techniques and were astonished at the quantities of game they were capable of flushing out of cover. In the hunting of larger animals both 'defensive' and subsistence hunters used *machans* (tree platforms), pits, elaborate traps and apparatus for the release of poisoned arrows (which Johnson described as 'complicated and ingenious', the Indian equivalent of the spring gun). Later in the century Europeans appropriated both the name and the functions of shikar. Aided by the much developed, and exclusive, technology, they did their own hunting. In the twentieth century the forest officer and hunter E. P. Stebbing described in detail many of the individual Indian hunting techniques surviving in much the same form as in Johnson's day, but whereas Johnson saw them as legitimate activities worthy of his attention as an observer of the Indian scene, Stebbing dubbed them all 'poaching', illicit acts requiring to be stamped out.[20] Stebbing went further, and saw them as putting the Indian fauna at risk.

In addition to the traditional 'individualist' hunting there were great communal hunts. Landowners and potentates often commanded the services of hundreds or even thousands of beaters, including men, women and children, to beat whole areas of territory. Using drums, other noisy instrumentrs, fireworks and their own voices they created a hideous noise to drive the animals towards nets or to huntsmen in machans or pits. Sometimes fire was used in connection with these great hunts, which were known as *hunquahs*. This technique was used both for elite sport and as a communal exercise for defence and subsistence. Johnson himself attended one of these beats but was so overcome with the heat, noise and danger from flying missiles that he acquired a severe headache and resolved not to participate again.[21] The great drive was taken over by Europeans, who laid down standards of organisation, rules for the marshalling of beaters, and positions for themselves on elephant and machan which helped to alleviate the problems Johnson encountered.

Europeans seem to have been less eager to take up some of the other elite sports of India; hawking, the use of fierce greyhounds, or of captive cheetah to secure quarry. The latter sport, which is described without comment in many nineteenth-century works (though Johnson found it distressing) seems to have been frowned upon in the twentieth century. On his visit to India in 1921-22 the Prince of Wales (the future Edward VIII) was treated to such a spectacle, but he and his entourage seem to have found it cruel and un-British; the experiment was not repeated.[22] George Stubbs painted a cheetah with two Indian attendants facing a stag in Windsor Great Park about 1765. The cheetah had been sent from India as a present to George III. In the 1880s the stag, interestingly, was painted out – it is usually thought because its proximity to the cheetah was inauthentic, but it may be that the scene offended late Victorian sensitivities. In the early nineteenth century Europeans watched the great staged combats between elephants (which in the Mughal period had been seen as representative of dynastic conflict for the succession) and tigers and buffaloes. Harriet Tytler witnessed animal fights at the court of the king of Oudh in 1847. The fights, involving tigers and buffalo, bears and tigers, elephants, rams, and a donkey and a ḥyena, were arranged in honour of the Governor General, Lord Hardinge, and the Resident, Colonel Richmond. Harriet Tytler described the encounters in graphic and harrowing detail. Her own reactions seem to have been a mixture of horror and amusement, the latter experienced both when the elephants scattered a crowd of watching Indians and when the donkey succeeded in killing the hyena. Cock-fighting, quail-fighting and confrontrations between snakes and mongooses were also enjoyed by many observers. All these, like bear-baiting and cock-fighting at home, passed out of favour in the course of the century.[23]

But the British enthusiastically adopted, in modified and more controlled form, the great elephant-borne hunts of the northern aristocracy. Johnson vividly describes such a hunt by the king of Oudh. This ruler generally took the field in March, April and May, when the cover was thin, after months of preparations. 'All the court, great part of his army, and seraglio, accompanied him; a guard only being left for the protection of his capital. About ten thousand cavalry, nearly the same number of infantry, thirty or forty pieces of Artillery, and from seven to eight hundred elephants attended', the whole being accompanied by a considerable travelling market.

Early in the morning his Highness left his Palace at *Lucknow*, with a number of noisy instruments playing before him; as soon as he was clear of the city and suburbs, a line was formed with the *Nawaub Vizier* in the centre, generally on an elephant elegantly caparisoned, with two spare elephants, one on each side of him. The one on his left bore his state *howdah* empty; the other on his right, carried his spare guns and ammunition also in a *howdah*, in which two men were placed to load the guns, and give them to his Highness when required, and to take back others that had been discharged. Several guns were kept ready loaded with ball and shot, on each side of the two elephants. I believe that I am within bounds, when I say that he took with him from forty to fifty double barrel guns, besides a number of single barrel long guns, rifles, and pistols. Behind him were several beautiful led horses handsomely caparisoned.[24]

On the journey to the main ground all forms of hunting were indulged in. Hawks were released, greyhounds slipped, guns fired – 'resembling a feu de joie' – and rewards doled out to keepers and others. Dancing girls and musicians provided entertainment. After a journey of ten to fifteen days the main camp was established and the pursuit of tigers, lions (at that time more widespread), leopards and buffaloes commenced. There they remained three weeks or a month, the 'cavalcade . . . presenting the appearance of a large army going to a field of battle, rather than that of a hunting party', a war 'not against men, but against the destroyers of men.' Having assailed the animals in one neighbourhood they might change ground and begin another campaign before returning to Lucknow 'in the same manner and style as they left it, but by a different route.'

The functions of such a Hunt are readily apparent. The monarch was displayed to his people in the grandest and most powerful manner imaginable. He exercised his obligation to offer protection in a very tangible way. The army was taken on a form of manoeuvres, provisioning itself as it went. Tribute was exacted and rewards were distributed. The chroniclers of the Mughal court in the sixteenth and seventeenth century had stressed the practical aspects of the Hunt.[25] The monarch was able to examine matters of taxation and discover intelligence about developments in his kingdom. He was rendered more accessible, at least to his aristocracy, who in turn were able to catch the ruler's eye by deeds of valour or hunting expertise. The formality of the court was broken down. The British annexation of Oudh helped to precipitate the Mutiny of 1857, but the great Oudh hunt was to some extent taken over by the British. Viceroys, governors and visiting royalty displayed themselves in the same way. These Hunts invariably took place in the now preserved princely States and performed a significant role in the feudal relationship between the viceroy and the princes, but officers of the ICS, the Indian Army and the forestry service developed, on a smaller scale, similar tastes wherever elephants were available. And their hunts performed many of the same functions as those of the Mughals and their satraps.

On ordinary shooting trips British officials were able to appear in remote areas, check on subordinates, and gather intelligence. ICS and forestry men were both encouraged to use hunting for precisely this purpose.[26] Hunting could therefore be highly public or almost furtive. It also played an important role in the interaction of the imperial elite. As at the Mughal court junior officers were able to meet their seniors in a more relaxed atmosphere and, perhaps, catch their eye with deeds of hunting prowess. Younger officers were eager to impress the visiting high-ranking administrator by offering him good sport.[27] Thus hunting had a propitiatory function, a mediatory role in easing tension within the British hierarchy. There were, however, social dangers. The peppery senior officer could be infuriated by a breach of etiquette or by greater success than his own. Many writers testified that shikari stories became the prime preoccupation of male conversation in club, mess and dinner party. Evidence of this comes from the works of hunters – a biased sample – but there can be no doubt that in the second half of the nineteenth century the obsession with trophies reached India. Conversation, whether obsessively on hunting or not, certainly took place surrounded by trophies, horns and skins of all sorts. Judging by contemporary photographs, no club or mess was without them, as were few of the residences of officials or army officers. The Indian princes enthusiastically adopted the fashion, and trophies hang on their walls to this day.

Major Shakespear, writing in the middle of the century, neatly represents the transition point in the British cleaving to the Hunt. With the Mutiny fresh in mind, he suggested that the insurrection might have been better handled had more officers been trained in hunting, since it offered knowledge of weapons and the ability to manage horses at speed oblivious of danger.[28] England's sons had to be 'roused from their beds of luxury and ease'; shikari in India would keep them from a 'thousand temptations', 'injurious pursuits' and 'effeminate pleasures'. If the urge for excitement was not satisfied in an 'innocent, manly and useful' way in hunting, then they might take 'to the gaming table, or to an excess of feasting, rioting, or debauchery'. All boys should be taught to shoot, starting on sparrows and working up. On the other hand, the 'sporting code' does not seem to have been particularly important to Shakespear. He cheerfully describes digging pits at water holes for night shooting or blazing away into a herd of sambur, both practices which were disapproved of by the end of the century. The severely practical aspects of hunting were represented by constant shooting for the pot on the march, securing venison and other game for troops and people.

Shakespear's advocacy may have worked. A supplement of *The Times* in 1930 asserted that it was 'sport' which had attracted bright and able administrators to India.[29] This seems to be borne out by any number of memoirs of Indian service, and was of course related to contemporary obsessions in Britain. The Indian Army and the ICS recruited from public schools whose magazines published accounts of big-game shooting throughout the world.[30] The class background of most recruits would have ensured experience of shooting in Britain before travelling to India. The developing obsession in the sub-continent reflected the elevation of the hunting and shooting craze into a cult by the end of the century. A police officer in India, Gouldsbury, announced in his memoirs that he despised those who did not hunt.[31] For many imperial officers hunting alleviated boredom as well as adding to the variety of the table. Several sources indicate that certain postings would have been the dullest days of their lives but for the sporting opportunities.[32] One ICS man described the disappointments of his first posting in the Madras presidency.[33] There was no sport; it was therefore bad for vice; and the Collector had a distressingly keen interest in music. The writer ensured that the whole of his subsequent career was undertaken in hunting areas. Some ascribed to hunting an almost religious significance. It involved considerable ceremony and ritual, and where live baits were used there was also the element of sacrifice. Some military men seem to have enjoyed hunting over historical sites and battlefields of the past, trying to fit their own activities into a historical context and remembering the manner in which Arthur Wellesley (later Duke of Wellington) combined war and hunting in his Indian campaigns (as he subsequently did in the Peninsular War).[34]

The British transferred a version of the fox hunt to India, attempting to hunt in this manner from the late eighteenth century. Although foxes do exist in India, they are found in restricted localities, so the creature that was hunted was generally the jackal. Williamson described its wiles and sporting characteristics and the efforts to acclimatise foxhounds and train Indian dog handlers.[35] Over much of India the heat was too great and the ground too hard for the working

[ *177* ]

of dogs, but in some hill stations and provincial cities there were celebrated hunts on the English model.[36] There was a famous one in Ootacamund, founded in 1844,[37] that of Madras was extremely active and brought together the civilian, military and commercial elite. Lord Connemara, Governor of Madras 1887-91, hunted regularly with the Madras hunt, which even had a master of foxhounds from the commercial community in the twentieth centrury.[38] There were well known hunts in Lahore and Peshawar. Like their English counterparts they constituted important social gatherings, proving opportunities for contact and competition among the elite as well as a source of employment to Indians as dog handlers, grooms, and the like. Foxhounds were imported from England and also bred locally.[39] In other cantonments where climate and terrain were suitable, officers frequently assembled 'bobbery' packs, composed of various breeds and sizes of dog, some designed to hunt by sight, some by scent.[40] These were used for a variety of hunting and coursing activities.

Dogs were also used in large numbers in hunting in Ceylon, an activity which took place primarily in the highlands. During the middle decades of the nineteenth century, indeed, Ceylon was known as one of the prime sporting paradises. Its assumption of that status had, however, to await the British penetration of the highlands. It is interesting that in *The Wanderer in Ceylon* (1817) Captain T. A. Anderson made no mention of hunting.[41] Certainly by the time Samuel Baker arrived in 1845 the island was celebrated for its hunting. He was indeed lured there from Mauritius by tales of sport and in his two books, *The Rifle and the Hound in Ceylon* of 1854 and *Eight Years' Wanderings in Ceylon* of 1855, he described almost daily hunting exploits. He settled on a large estate at Nuwara Elia, where he established a settlement of emigrant workers from England in an 'English village'.[42] There he indulged his 'infatuation for sport' to the full, owning scores of dogs, a formidable battery, and often leading aristocratic and military parties on hunting trips. The island, he wrote, was full of first-rate sportsmen, producing 'whole hecatombs of slaughter'.[43] He himself seems to have shot hundreds of elephants and buffaloes. On one occasion he 'bagged 31 elephants in a few days' shooting'; on another twenty-one fell to his gun on a three-week trip.[44] It was not uncommon for hunting parties regularly to shoot twenty in a month. He hunted 'elk' (sambur deer) on foot with packs of dogs that were a cross between foxhound and bloodhound, and coursed spotted deer on horseback with packs of greyhounds. He also pursued wild boars, bears and leopards. These exploits helped to establish his fame before his African explorations.

The two Ceylon books, the first of his many publications, went through several editions and made him a great deal of money, much in the manner of the contemporary work of Roualeyn Gordon Cumming. So intensive was the hunting exploitation in Baker's day that animal resources were swiftly depleted. He described the manner in which the island was 'spoiled' by an excess of European and 'native' hunters. By the 1870s, in the preface to a new edition of 'The Rifle and the Hound, he was noting 'the great diminution in the wild animals', the clearance of the forests for plantations, and the advance of civilization into 'the domains of wild beasts'.[45] Just as Gordon Cumming's tales encouraged a great range of southern African hunters in the late nineteenth century, so Baker's books encouraged the placing of Ceylon on the hunter's Grand Tour. Significantly, in 1875, his friend the Prince of Wales shot elephants in the highlands at just the time when it was becoming necessary to protect them.[46]

There were three animals in India with which the British had a special hunting relationship, the tiger, the elephant and the pig. The tiger possesssed a compelling fascination, inspiring a great range of both negative and positive responses. From the earliest years of British rule its danger had been apparent. Travellers' accounts and memoirs abound in tales of European deaths when tigers seized people on journeys, on picnics, or out hunting, as many graves in European cemeteries testify. The most famous such incident was the death of the son of Sir Hector Munro on Saugor Island, near Calcutta, in 1792. Munro's seizure by a tiger was commemorated in Staffordshire ornaments and may well have inspired the remarkable mechanical toy 'Tippoo's tiger', taken at the capture of Seringapatam in 1799 and displayed in turn at the East India Company's offices in Leadenhall Street, the India Office, the Indian Museum and, since 1879, at the Victoria and Albert Museum.[47] This model of a tiger devouring an Englishman, with sound effects provided by an organ and other contrivances, was built to amuse Tipu Sultan (whose name means 'tiger') and fascinated the British public in the nineteenth century. It perfectly symbolised the frisson of fear which mention of the animal has always induced. Keats incorporated a reference to it in his satire on the Prince Regent, The Cap and Bells, and both he and his contemporaries could see the real thing at the zoos at the Tower and the Exeter 'Change or in Mr Pidcock's travelling menagerie (although Thomas Williamson considered the captive tigers much inferior to their counterparts in the wild).[48] Blake's 'Tiger! Tiger! burning bright in the forests of the night', with its repeated use of the word 'dread', was known to most nineteenth-century schoolchildren. The limerick 'There was a young lady of Riga' succeeds in making fun of the tradition while still conveying the combination of cruelty, furtiveness and treacherous elegance that are the essential elements of the tiger's image. In the 1930s Churchill played upon the sense of voracious inevitability it induced in his remark 'Dictators ride to and fro upon tigers which they dare not dismount. And the tigers are getting hungry.'

As British power extended its grip the full toll of tigers on the indigenous population of the sub-continent became known. By the second half of the nineteenth century it was estimated that 1,600 people were killed by tigers each year.[49] It was thought that each tiger was capable of killing cattle worth between £300 and £600 in a single year,[50] though another authority considered £70 nearer the truth.[51] On the other hand, tigers kept down animals that attacked crops. The British saw the tiger as a magnificent beast, revelling in its 'grim joy of overlordship of the jungle', but also defined it as vermin.[52] This status, shared with the other big cats, was emphasised by the fact that they were such successful and prolific animals, inhabiting a great variety of habitats, from the deep south to the mountains of the north. Tigers, leopards and panthers had been much more successful than the Indian lion. The latter had never been able to survive in such a variety of ecologies, and its population had declined drastically in the face of hunting, increasing desiccation in the north-west, and probably even competition with the tiger. The fecundity of the latter ensured that every man's hand was against it, and every right-thinking Englishman wished to possess a tiger skin.

The British and the tiger seemed in some ways to be locked in conflict for command of the Indian environment. News of the appearance of a man-eater had a powerful impact on any district. Stories developed into myths and legends of startling proportions. Superstitions were rife among Indians and Europeans alike, and the maneating tiger often approached the status of the werewolf of European lore. The hunting books starting with Williamson are full of stories of beasts with over a hundred human victims to their credit, some of which were never destroyed, while others inspired startling deeds of avenging heroism on the part of the bereaved relatives.[53] Whereas in the past threatened villagers would have turned to the professional shikari with his muzzle-loader, traps or spring poisoned arrows, they increasingly looked to the British official for protection. Every ICS man, army officer or policeman was expected to be a tiger-slayer (though in reality many, of course, spent their entire career in India without ever encountering a tiger). This protective function was even more significant in the case

[ *180* ]

of the many more tigers that took to killing domestic stock. This protection service was normally performed from the machan over tethered live bait (goat or young buffalo, usually) or the tiger's recent kill, even if it were human remains (though the relatives often protested). The more intrepid tiger hunters shot on foot, having the tigers beaten to them by the massed forces of the local villagers. It was alleged that great celebrations could break out after the killing of a man-eater, and thousands of villagers would congregate to exult over the carcase. The noblest European shikari would divide the reward among his followers.

Tiger shikar for sport rather than protection was normally conducted from elephant-back, again with the aid of a large army of beaters. It was the sport of the most senior officials, and women could participate either as spectators or as shots. In its 'bread and butter' form, as pursued, for example, by forestry officers, the hunters would ride on the back of the 'pad' elephant, the riders perched on the pad – an arrangement of heavy materials like a flexible mattress over the elephant's back – and the elephant often moved in search of the quarry. Deer, antelope and buffalo were often shot in this way, too, since the animals were usually unaware of the humans on the elephant's back. The 'state' version saw the hunters seated in howdahs on backs of elephants, and the tigers were always driven towards them. There were rules about the order in which the guns on a line of elephants were permitted to fire, about the positioning of the elephants according to the status of the occupants, and the right of the 'first shot' to acquire the skin. Each viceroy had to indulge in the obligatory tiger shoot and often secured 'record' tigers because the method of measuring them was more favourable in the case of the viceroy.[54]

Although advantages were built in for the highest echelons of the elite, the British expected the true sportsman to be unselfish. The tiger's status as vermin was not a licence to unlimited killing by the officer afflicted with hunting mania. A hunter who claimed to have shot 100 tigers was considered a 'selfish old swine' by a rival.[55] Sir John Hewett was held up for emulation. Although he was described as being keen on the preservation of game, it was said that 250 tigers had been shot in his presence, only forty to his own rifle.[56] He liked to see to it that subalterns being trained in the Hunt had their proper opportunity. Sir Bindon Blood, GOC Northern Command, had been present at the killing of 150 tigers, fifty-two to his own rifle, a somewhat less meritorious proportion, it would seem, commensurate perhaps with his name. There was, however, sneaking admiration for the sportsman who lost his arm to a tiger and sought retribution by killing 100 in his subsequent career.[57] Officials also liked to use the tiger hunt to put more mundane business into perspective. Sir Henry Ramsay, known as the 'king of Kumaon' was enraged at having to deal with urgent business on a tiger shoot.[58]

The craze for the tiger skin spread far beyond India. In the twentieth century taxidermists and dealers employed Indian shikaris to satisfy the extensive tourist demand in port cities. There was also a considerable demand for them in the United States. The Inspector General of the Indian Forest Service, writing before the First World War, saw the disappearance of the tiger as inevitable.[59] No government would dare to conserve such a dangerous animal. Indeed, the rewards for killing tigers, first introduced by the East India Company, in the eighteenth century and continued into the twentieth, were exceptionally high, reflecting perceptions of the creature's destructive powers. In the late eighteenth and early nineteenth centuries the reward was ten rupees, which Williamson translated as 25s.[60] The amount could be augmented by the sale of the talons and other products, such that an Indian shikari who killed a tiger and two cubs made 100 rupees for his day's work, which, according to Williamson, kept him for a year. Later it was possible to receive from fifty to 200 rupees, depending on the locality and the danger.[61] There were also rewards for killing panthers and leopards, these cats fetching, as an example, twenty-five rupees in Mysore in the 1870s.[62] There are stories in the early days of Indians carrying rotting corpses into the offices of the administration after several days' march, so it became necessary to offer the reward for a part of the animal, such as the tail. No doubt Indian hunters benefited from the reward system in the early days, but gradually the killing of tigers was largely taken over as a European prerogative.

While these policies certainly sent the tiger population into decline, it nonetheless remained viable until the 1930s. By that time the tiger was becoming an endangered species, and it was then that the celebrated Jim Corbett worked both to eliminate man-eaters and to develop the conservation movement.[63] Full conservation measures were not, however, introduced until after independence, by which time the population had collapsed under the weight of its reputation as public enemy number one.

The status of the tiger and the ludicrous efforts to which the British would go to acquire its skin are conveyed in the Saki story 'Mrs Packletide's tiger.'[64] Interestingly, Saki (Hector Hugh Munro) was a member of the same family as the victim of 1792, and in many of his other stories he appears fascinated by the idea of animals wreaking revenge on their human tormentors. The obsession with the tiger gave rise to much big-game hunting satire and remains a source of inventive television advertisements.

The relationship with the elephant was somewhat different.

Although it was a crop destroyer on a grand scale and could also pose a danger to human life, its incidence was much more restricted, and it became a legitimate prey of the gun for only a few decades of the nineteenth century. Williamson indeed doubted whether it was possible to shoot elephants at all, even asserting that it was hard to believe Vaillant's stories of having actually done so in southern Africa.[65] But within a decade or two it was regarded as the peak of courageous hunting in the sub-continent. Since elephant were invariably shot in a jungle environment it was necessary to stalk the animal with great care and reach a much closer range than in the more open country of southern Africa. They were shot in Ceylon, South India, the western Ghats, Chittagong and Assam, largely under the guise of crop protection, since the Indian elephant seldom affords commercial ivory. But the elephant was apparently saved by its capacity to be domesticated. Alarm was already growing about its diminishing population, and therefore of stock for domestication, by the 1870s, and it was protected from the end of that decade. In fact the use of domesticated elephants began to decline from this period. It was, however, the first instance of animal conservation in India (see chapter 10).

The close relationship with tame elephants was developed from the days of the East India Company. The company allocated an elephant and a camel to each battalion in the army, and each European officer was allowed an elephant or two camels to convey his personal effects. The allowance for elephant purchase was 500 rupees, or sixty guineas. Elephants were captured by driving them into a *kheddah*, a large enclosure surrounded by a ditch and a paling of timbers, with a long funnel leading to its entrance. The drive itself could last several days and, according to Williamson, often involved 6,000–8,000 persons using firearms, drums, trumpets and fireworks to force the herd towards the *kheddah*.[66] Once enclosed, they were starved into submission and then controlled by other elephants already tamed. It was soon discovered, however, that starvation made them more difficult to control, and the opposite technique was employed: they were fed their favourite foods to console them and accustom them to the presence of humans and the attentions of the tame animals. The word 'kheddah' also came to mean the government establishment in which the elephants were kept. Another technique involved the use of a tame female decoy elephant, or *koomkjie*, to capture a lone male outside the herd. The female, ridden by a *mahout* or elephant handler, used sexual wiles to lure the male into a position where he could be secured. Williamson claimed that it was the only instance in which an animal enslaved a fellow member of its species and was fully aware of its function.

The stock of tame beasts was maintained mostly by imports from

Ceylon, Burma and Siam, but the capture of elephants in *kheddahs* was still being practised in Bengal and Mysore in the 1870s. The government *kheddah* at Dacca had been capturing elephants for a number of decades. In the seven years up to 1875 it caught an average of fifty nine each year. After training at Dacca they were despatched to Barrackpur and from there allocated to different government stations. The government also bought elephants from the great annual elephant fair at Sonepur on the Ganges, where dealers had traditionally bought and sold elephants since Mughal times, trading mainly with the Indian aristocracy. The animals were graded according to their value for pageantry or as working beasts, the former type being known as *koomeriah*.

Most of our information for this period comes from the hunter and elephant catcher G. P. Sanderson. Sanderson arrived at Mysore in 1864 as a coffee planter. When the coffee was destroyed by borer he joined the irrigation department of the government of Mysore. In both capacities he secured a great deal of hunting, including the shooting of elephants (and tigers) that were causing the peasantry serious problems. Villagers used a range of techniques to scare them off, and watchers' platforms could be seen in the trees throughout the cultivated areas. In some districts they employed Shologas, hill tribesmen, for the purpose (in exchange for grain or rice). These people used large bamboo torches, 8 ft long and 8 in. in diameter, to drive off elephants at night. Many villages had become deserted in the wars of 1780-1800 and the presence of elephants as well as tigers was a barrier to reoccupation. Intensive hunting by Europeans, Sanderson claimed, helped to release more land for cultivation. He was himself an avid hunter of elephants, although he deprecated the local method, pitfalls, which had been used to kill and capture them by the rulers of Mysore until 1868.[67]

In 1874 Sanderson turned his hand to the capture of elephants. He built a *kheddah* near a village in Mysore and, using 500 beaters, captured a herd of fifty-five elephants (which were sold for £3,754 after an expenditure of £1,556).[68] In 1876 he moved his operations to the Chittagong hill tracts and captured eighty-five elephants for supply to the government establishments at Dacca and Barrackpur.

Sanderson was opposed to the conservation policies of the later 1870s, believing that the elephant (unlike 'the sad fate that is pursuing his African congenor') was not endangered in India, though its numbers were declining in Ceylon, where it was 'the peculiar object of pursuit by European sportsmen and paid native hunters.' The government of Ceylon offered a reward of 10s for the tail of each elephant shot. This was later reduced to 7s since the numbers killed were so great that the government could scarcely afford the rewards. According to Baker,

[ *184* ]

three first-rate shots bagged 104 in three days, and native hunters swiftly acquired guns to participate in the profits.[69] By the 1870s these efforts at crop protection had proved so successful that the government deemed it necessary to conserve the species. The policy of the Presidency of Madras also oscillated between treating elephants as vermin and as a protected creature. Rewards for their destruction had been offered to Indian hunters but were later withdrawn. For Sanderson elephant shooting was the supremely exciting sport, demanding perseverence, endurance and nerve in the face of great danger.[70] 'To stand up to within ten paces and drop an elephant dead before he is aware of danger is the poetry of the sport; to kill him by body shots the prose.'

With the promulgation of the Madras regulations on elephant conservation in 1873, extended to the whole of India in 1879, elephant hunting ceased to be significant 'sport' of British India. Officials continued to shoot for crop protection, and occasionally rogue elephants attacking villagers had to be destroyed. At the same time the use of tame elephants began to decline, partly as a result of their cost. In the course of the century prices rose steeply, from an average of £45 per head in 1835 to £75 in 1855 and £150 by the late 1870s.[71] Good working females could fetch £200-£300, males sometimes £800 to £1,500, while the finest *koomeriah* could be worth £2,000. Elephants did not breed in captivity and their death rates, particularly in the period soon after their capture, were high. They were imported into Madras from Burma and an attempt to catch them in the presidency between 1874 and '77 had to be abandoned because the costs and the death rate were both unacceptable. Moreover, elephants were expensive to keep, requiring from 400 to 800 lb of green fodder per day. A full-size female (including her *mahout* and grass cutter) cost twenty-four rupees per month in Bengal and forty-eight in Madras. By the end of the century the government elephant establishments had been wound up. Only the Forestry Department continued to provide beasts for its officials, since they remained the best means of locomotion in forest areas. Although one of the enduring images of the British in India in the twentieth century is of state processions and tiger hunts on elephant-back, in fact by that time the British seldom owned elephants themselves. Civilian and military officers requiring them for pageantry and sport tended to borrow them from the Indian princes. Sir Edward Braddon described the intricacies of borrowing elephants. They were recruited from the stables of the nawabs and rajahs, and the process involved eleborate diplomacy. The lenders evaluated the importance of the borrowers and doled out the number and quality of elephants accordingly. When Braddon was revenue secretary of Oudh he was valued as a first-grade borrower but later sank to the second grade and was lucky to secure one lame elephant.[72]

Of all the hunting sports of India, pig-sticking had the best press. Even W. O. Horne, who spent his entire hunting and administrative career in South India, where it was almost unknown, declared it the finest of Indian sports after only one brief experience in the north of the Madras presidency.[73] The military revered it as the perfect 'image of war without its guilt', though the danger might often have been put at more than 'five and twenty per cent.'[74] It was therefore the classic sport of the military cantonment, where the terrain was suitable. Horsemanship was, of course, vitally important to an officer class, and pig-sticking was an even greater test of equestrianism than polo. It took place over broken ground against a foe all too willing to turn, charge and injure the hunter's mount. It was capable of evincing an ecstatic bloodlust that was a useful attribute in any campaign. Its exponents would have agreed with the Mughal court chronicler, Abul Fazl, when he wrote of Akbar's fascination with polo that it was more than amusement or mere play: 'men of more exalted views see in it a means of learning promptitude and decision. It tests the value of a man, and strengthens the bonds of friendship'. While strong men learnt the art of riding, 'the animals learn to perform feats of agility and to obey the reins'.[75]

Pig-sticking seems to have developed in Bengal in the late eighteenth century from bear-sticking; as bears became less numerous the hunters turned to pigs. At first the spear was thrown, but once it was attached to a longer lance the custom developed of impaling the pig direct. Williamson described the varieties of hog hunting in detail, the different sorts of crops in which the quarry was found, and the manner in which the chase often scattered the stock and villagers of the settlements where it was conducted.[76] The villagers were willing to help in the hunt when their crops were standing, but lost interest when they were safely reaped. In Williamson's day there were still many varieties of length, shape and weight of spear, and his contemporaries also speared porcupines and even tried the technique on buffaloes and tigers. In 1822 Daniel Johnson contrasted European hog-hunting on horseback and with spears, 'a noble and manly sport', with the Indian killing of hogs from platforms or in nets in defence of their crops.[77] For the British pig-sticking had the added attraction of creating a link with the medieval boar hunt.

Major Henry Shakespear described hog-hunting as the best sport in the world, particularly in the hilly regions of the Deccan and Nagpur.[78] He seems to have participated from his arrival in India in 1834. By the 1850s three types of pig-sticking had emerged, in Bengal, the Deccan, and the Bombay presidency. In Bengal a short spear, not more than 7 ft long was used, not as as a lance but in such a way that a charging boar ran against it. The Bombay pig-sticker, operating in the area of Poona and Ahmednagar, used a longer and lighter spear from 8 ft to 9 ft long, while in the Deccan a middling sized spear of 8 ft was the norm. Each was supposedly appropriate to the terrain. At a later date the United Provinces became celebrated pig-sticking country and Meerut one of its most important centres. For Shakespear, the hog was 'the most courageous animal in the jungle' and its pursuit offered the opportunity for European and 'native officers' to come together.[79]

That was, perhaps, a distinctly pre-Mutiny sentiment. After the Mutiny Indians were much more likely to find themselves performing the menial tasks, acting as beaters to flush the pigs from their coverts, looking after horses and equipment, or even acting as spectators, since, as one source put it, it did Indian troops good to be able to cheer their sahibs on when playing polo or sticking pigs. It was also in the post-Mutiny era that the sport came to be more highly regularised and institutionalised. The Prince of Wales gave it royal respectability in 1875. Beaters and elephants had to be withdrawn from elephant catching operations in Bengal to assist in the flushing of pig coverts for him.[80] The notion that pig-sticking was valuable to the peasant population in keeping down crop destroyers was somewhat subverted by the development of preservation policies. The pig had made the same transition as the fox in England, from vermin to protected species for sport. Coverts were preserved in the Central Provinces, and action was taken to discourage poaching by 'professional hunters of the criminal tribes'. To prevent it, the author of one shikar guide suggested, the Deputy Commissioner or District Superintendant of Police should be asked for help. A special shikari could also be retained to watch the coverts. In the Wardha district of Nagpur, excellent pig country, it was necessary to send a shikar into the area two or three weeks before it was intended to hunt in order to mark down and protect the quarry, for:

> Of late years the cultivators have devoted a good deal of attention to the destruction of pig, in order to protect their crops, and a good many of the wandering tribe of Pardhis, who are noted pig killers, have been employed for the purpose. It is useless going down to the Wardha Country and endeavouring to hunt places which have been visited at all recently by the Pardhis.[81]

In this period pig-sticking was organised into hunts or tent clubs. The Nagpur hunt, for example, was founded in 1863.[82] It had two cups, one presented by Colonel MacMaster in 1869, the other subscribed by members in 1893, to be awarded to the member who obtained the largest number of 'first spears' (i.e. the first, but not necessarily fatal, spear driven into the pig) in the course of the year. Between 1863 and 1892 it was customary in the Nagpur hunt to stick sows as well as boars, but from 1893 a fine was imposed for sticking a sow or an unridable boar.[83] Tent clubs were also founded at Saugor, Delhi, Agra and Meerut and many other places. Meerut became the centre of the sport, where General Wardrop, one of its authorities, officiated as secretary. The hunts and tent clubs laid down the rules, and, in contrast to the free arrangements of the first half of the century, no one could hunt in their areas without the permission of the captain or secretary. Like the vulpicide in England, the man who shot pigs was considered distinctly unsporting.[84]

General Wardrop's son, Major A. E. Wardrop, wrote one of the classic works on pig-sticking, a manual offering advice on the training of horses, equipment, styles of lance, the organisation of tent clubs, the preservation of pig, the thwarting of poachers, the keeping of logs and the organisation of the annual meet. He himself was secretary of the Meerut Tent Club, which hunted over 200-300 square miles of *kadir*, or river bed, around Meerut. His book reflected the renaissance in pig-sticking that took place just before the First World War, when the tent clubs became more highly organised and preservation policies paid off. In Delhi, for example, average bags of fifty-six boar had been recorded early in the twentieth century, but after their posting to Delhi the 18th Lancers set about codification and preservation. By 1911 and 1912 they were recording bags of 257 and 385 boar respectively. Muttra returned a record bag of 400 in 1911, and the sport seems to have been pursued with greater assiduity than at any other time. Like so many other pursuits, pig-sticking had its Edwardian final fling. Thus Wardrop and his associates maintained and developed a tradition described by Sir Edward Braddon. In pre-Mutiny days Henry Torrens, the Resident of Murshidabad, had held a pig-sticking meet at which 100 elephants had flushed out pigs and ninety-nine boars were killed in twelve days. Sir George Yule, Resident at Hyderabad and Chief Commissioner of Oudh, was described as 'the emperor of spears', who had killed his hecatombs of boars. The boar, wrote Braddon, 'is like an Englishman in that it does not know when it is beaten'.[85]

This was a sentiment to which R. S. S. Baden-Powell would have fervently adhered. He produced the most influential work on pig-sticking which was re-issued after the First World War, in an attempt to maintain the popularity of the sport. Baden-Powell, the hero of the Mafeking siege and founder of the Boy Scouts, revered pig-sticking as an ancient sport and admired the pig-sticker as 'a man who goes straight to his point, plays fair, rides with courage and judgment to help to kill the pig, and not to win the suffrages of the gallery'. Earlier in the nineteenth century, he claimed, the death of the pig was not an important consideration – securing the first spear was the main object – but by B.-P.'s day killing had become the whole 'object of the hunt'. Thus it was the 'brutal and most primitive of all hunts', in which, 'blind to all else but the strong and angered foe before you, with your good spear in your hand, you rush for blood with all the ecstasy of a fight to the death'. It was both individualist and communal, health-giving ('hundreds of lives and thousands of livers are saved every year by the exercise and outdoor life of pig-sticking'), and an excellent pre-paration for battle, developing 'an eye for the country, horsemanship, endurance, quick decision, and determined attack'. When a revised and enlarged edition was produced in 1924 B.-P. expressed anxiety that neither the Indian Army nor the ICS was attracting the same quality of young men. To improve their prospects, health, energy and spirit they should be given time off to hunt. It would also offer opportunities for closer contact with Indian officers and with ordinary Indians and troops employed as beaters.[86]

Pig-sticking, in short, represented the anachronistic survival of the cavalry mentality. Indeed, B.-P. invoked the pervasive imperial icon of St George as the patron saint of both the cavalry and the pig-sticker.[87] St George could, after all, have killed the dragon with a piece of poisoned pork, but instead he chose a hand-to-hand weapon in face-to-face combat and had to cope with a frightened horse into the bargain. In drawing this connection with St George B.-P. implied that pig-stick-ing was not merely a training in horsemanship, courage and attack but also an emblem of the moral force of imperialism, vanquishing the darker forces of an outer world, as well as representing an act of protec-tion by the rulers on behalf of the ruled. It is not surprising that when the Prince of Wales visited India in 1921-22 he participated in pig-stick-ing. He took part in a boar hunt at Jodhpur in November 1921 and a meet in Patiala in February 1922, effecting kills on each occasion. His pig-sticking activities culminated in a hunt at Meerut in competition for the Kadir Cup, which, of course, he won. In this he was following in the hoof-prints of his uncle, the Duke of Connaught, who had regularly hunted with the Delhi Tent Club.

The British liked to portray hunting as conciliatory between Briton and Indian. This was clearly true of the princes, the administrative elite and, if Shakespear and Baden-Powell are to be believed, of Indian army officers, but hunting authorities also suggested that shikar offered opportunities for the British to encounter ordinary Indians, bringing subaltern and peasant together, as one described it.[88] Another suggested that in responding to the 'inherited memory . . . of primitive hunting-man' imperial ruler found common cause with the ruled.[89] One stated baldly that villagers liked to see the sahib shooting. There is, however, a good deal of evidence to suggest that hunting was a source of strain rather than of conciliation. Perplexed hunters often reported that villagers had declined to give information about game, even man-eating tigers.[90] This they attributed to the superstition that the hunted animal, if missed, would return to plague the village all the more, but the villagers' unwillingness to co-operate may well have been a more positive act of social resistance. Judging by the cases that came before administrators, and occasionally before the courts in the cultivated areas of northern India, such rebuffs are not surprising. Villagers often resisted hunters who came on to their lands to shoot peafowl and blue bulls, both of which were venerated by the Hindus. Other animals came into this category. Worse, groups of white troopers out shooting in the fields sometimes wounded or killed local cultivators and, not surprisingly, became involved in affrays with them.

British administrators were frequently exercised by such accidents, affrays and murders.[91] In 1898, for example, a Private Piper of Poona, who had fatally shot an Indian while hunting, was acquitted. An official minuted that 'nothing can be a greater misfortune than that rude and irritable British soldiers should be allowed to sport at their pleasure with dangerous weapons to the detriment of poor weaponless rustics, and that Government . . . should silently connive at such incidents'. 'The majority of soldiers,' he went on, 'are illiterate and hot-blooded and hold the life of a native very cheap.' That view seemed to be confirmed by another incident in 1900. Four soldiers of the 16th Lancers shot sacred pigeons and peafowl in an Indian garden near Umballa. The villagers pursued them, and when one of the soldiers shot and killed his pursuer the four were captured, tied up and beaten. Two of the solders went before a court-martial and were given terms of imprisonment, but the two prime culprits were charged in the criminal court and acquitted. The case seemed to confirm the unsuitability of jury trial (where the juries were all white) in cases involving European murder of Indians. These examples could be multiplied and had indeed been reported for several decades. An attempt in one district to limit hunting exploits by a pass system, restricted to trustworthy men – one of whom had to speak the vernacular – and who were equipped with a list of sacred birds and animals, seems to have failed.

The hunting cult emphasised other inter-religious and inter-caste distinctions. The activities of the European hunter pointed up the different relationship to the chase of Muslims, lower and upper-caste Hindus, and aboriginal 'animists'. In employing the various groups as auxiliaries in a variety of roles, in supplying them with meat, in usurping the functions of the indigenous hunter, and in hunting across cultivated land or through villages, Europeans cannot have failed to stimulate tensions out of this blend of clientage and religious disaffection. While the lower castes ate meat, pious Hindus were known to move around releasing live baits.[92] E. P. Stebbing had to instruct his Muslim followers in the precise place where they could 'hal-lal' (the Islamic ritual blood-letting to make the meat acceptable) his kills so that the skin or head would still be suitable as a trophy.[93]

On the other hand, the trophy craze served to stimulate the activities of the Indian professional hunter, who by the twentieth century was regarded as a poacher. A complex network of hunters, middlemen, taxidermists and dealers supplied trophies of all sorts to eager tourist consumers. Dealers who had access to firearms and ammunition supplied the hunters in a 'putting out' system familiar in the African context. This trade was to continue into the early years of independence. It was much deplored by elite shikaris, yet it was of course merely the imitative consequence of the interest which they themselved fostered, a downward filtration from the walls and floors of the genuine hunter to the indoor decoration of the armchair traveller. Indians could make a few rupees by picking up horns that had been shed and selling them in the local bazaar.[94] Glasfurd discovered a hunters' network leading to a taxidermist known as Ishnaag and set out to discover his trophy prices, which ranged from 300 rupees for a tiger skin to sixty five for an indifferent sambur head.[95] Eardley-Wilmot described the joy of trophies and skins and revealed that the British also contributed to the trade:

> America takes many to decorate the rooms of the wealthy, in spite of the enormous duty levied by customs officials, and the young and needy sportsman will have the less chagrin in parting with one or two of his trophies if their proceeds provide him with a trusty rifle with which others can be obtained.[96]

Most of the writers of hunting memoirs noted that the results of memorable hunts looked down upon them as they wrote.

Other elements had entered the Anglo-Indian fascination with hunting by the late nineteenth century. These concerned the irrisistible attraction for the British of forests and above all mountains. Romantic shikaris thought that the forests evoked a distant era of human history. In them it was possible to commune with a somewhat nebulous past through their 'glorious solitudes', inspiring a sense of disquietude bordering on fatalism. The works of hunters and forest officers abound with orotund descriptions of the atmosphere, flora and fauna of the forests, 'the Empire of Nature' as one put it, an *imperium in imperio*, a vast natural world that lay in some respects beyond the full grasp of British power. It was only the hunter and forest officer who maintained a tenuous grip on 250,000 square miles of forest, a quarter of the land area of British India.[97] One administrator described the forests as 'a foretaste of Paradise'.[98] Another saw the forest officer as 'working in the van of civilisation', in a magical world in which hunting constituted the essential charm of forest life.[99]

These officers also came into contact with the aboriginal inhabitants of the forests and hills, for example the Gonds of the south and the Korkus and Kols of central India. These people maintained a precarious existence cultivating clearings, keeping a few stock, and hunting for both defence and subsistence. Like the Bushmen of southern Africa some of them were regarded as providing the best trackers and auxiliaries for the European hunter. Stebbing enthused about the expertise of his Kol trackers in Chota Nagpur, pursuing a trail 'at a smart walk over hard trap rock where, to the ininitiated and untrained eye, it appears to be an impossibility to say that an animal has passed by'.[100] The 'jungle eye,' he went on, 'is not born with the man of the higher civilisation.'

This sense of uncertain hold combined with respect for hill men was even truer of the great mountain regions to the north and north-west, many of them just beyond the reach of British power, harbouring both mythic beasts and human enemies, a source of danger yet also of purity and mystical power. In the northern hill stations the British sought to regenerate themselves and recover their health in sight of those very mountains. There were hunting opportunities around the hill stations, though they declined rapidly in the twentieth century. But for many the hunting of the Himalayan regions remained the summit of shikar.

Kashmir constituted, perhaps, the tamed and half-familiar part of this region. The mountains remained wild and remote enough, but by the end of the centrury they had inspired another hunting cult, the stalking and long-range shooting of ibex, black bear, gural stags, markhor, ammon and red bear on steep mountainsides, creating a combination of trekking, mountaineering and shooting which proved irresistible to officials, army and forestry officers enjoying shooting leave. As Sir Francis Younghusband put it, the hunters descended (or perhaps ascended) on Kashmir like swallows in the appropriate season.[101] One regimental journal described the manner in which every one of the officers from the regiment's station had gone hunting in the course of the year, several of them to Kashmir. One party had driven themselves into forced night marches in order to overtake other groups and secure the best valleys, since etiquette demanded that hunters should not encroach on each other's territory.[102] E. P. Stebbing, a senior forest officer who was later Professor of Forestry at Edinburgh University, spent all his leaves in Kashmir and elsewhere in the Himalayes, contrasting their shikar with his normal forest experiences, seeking relief from one terrain in the most highly contrasting environment that India could offer.[103] Although the Maharajah of Kashmir introduced game preservationist policies before the First World War army officers continued to make the pilgrimage in the 1920s, sometimes commemorating their journeys in meticulously kept diaries and scrapbooks containing maps and photographs, accounts of the chase and kills, as well as other daily occurrences.[104] A number of firms flourished in Srinagar to equip such expeditions and supply them with guides, trackers and gun bearers.[105]

Kashmir had its fair share of royal and viceregal visitors and it was indeed at this end of the social scale that the hunting cult was carefully nurtured into the twentieth century.[106] In the hierarchical hunting scheme it was essential that the most notable hunting feats were performed by those at the apex of the social order. The visit of the Prince of Wales to India and Ceylon in 1875-76, in which hunting played a prominent part, was a relatively isolated event in the nineteenth century, but such tours were more frequent in the twentieth . The future George V hunted in India in 1905, and when he returned for his coronation durbar in 1911 he proved sufficiently adept with a rifle to be proclaimed a great shikari in the dedication of one hunting book, a 'Bayard in the Realm of Sport'.[107] The future Edward VIII hunted frequently on his visit to India in 1921-22. Sixty 'loyal duck' (as the Maharajah put it in an after-dinner speech) fell to his gun at Bikaner.[108] His first tiger was shot in Nepal to earn him the plaudits of notable tiger hunters, while Baden-Powell proclaimed in a dedication that he had 'in the pig-sticking field proved himself in the fuller sense of the word a Prince among Sportsmen.'[109] He had shown his 'pluck' in 'ding-dong horsemanship'.[110] One account of the Prince's tours took care to justify pig-sticking: it was a 'wild, exhilarating sport' in which 'the pig has a better chance than in any other form of big-game chase' and those who took part ran 'considerable risk'.[111] The prince lectured Indian students on the importance of sport and games and was welcomed in Nepal by a banner proclaiming the ultimate accolade: 'Hearty welcome to Britain's sporting prince'. All these exploits were lovingly retold in popular works for adults and children which described his world tours.

In the absence of royalty ministers and viceroys had to display similar prowess in the Hunt. When the Secretary of State, Edwin Montagu, visited India during the First World War he relaxed on a weekend shoot, and noted, 'I am never so happy as when shooting.'[112] Sir David Waley, who wrote a memoir of Montagu's visits to India, wrote, 'It seems incredible that the kindest of men could so have enjoyed mass murder.' There the twentieth-century note of doubt creeps in. No such doubt afflicted the Viceroy Irwin. In a shoot in Bikaner in February 1929 he participated in the destruction of 10,000 imperial sandgrouse.[113] The viceroy stood for the King in this as in other respects, and his feats with the gun had to be unmatched in his hunting party. The Viceroy Linlithgow made frequent visits to the princely States to shoot, and printed records of each day's activity indicate the social etiquette powerfully at work.[114] The viceroy, with very rare exceptions, always secured the largest bag, followed by the maharajah, then by the vicereine (if shooting) and the maharajah's heir apparent. On one occasion, again in the State of Bikaner, the heir apparent got so far above himself as to shoot more duck than the viceroy, a social solecism no doubt attended by a combination of family recrimination and wry comment on the part of the British. It was as though there had to be a repeated statistical underpinning of the social hierarchy. It is clear that hunts of all sorts had to be carefully stage-managed events in which it was the mythic figure rather than the corporeal presence that achieved the outstanding successes chronicled in accounts of royal journeys and viceregal progresses. The viceroy had to shoot a record tiger; the Prince of Wales had to win the Kadir Cup. The Hunt was a ritual of quasi-feudal authority.

Never had this been more true than during Edwards VII's visit as Prince of Wales, which prepared the way for the proclamation of Victoria as Empress of India. Edward's passion for big game 'enhanced his standing in the eyes of princes and chiefs', while, according to Sir Bartle Frere, his 'wonderful sport' made 'an impression of manly vigour and power of endurance which pleased everyone, Europeans and natives alike', proving that he possessed 'Royal qualities of courage, energy and physical power', which helped to display him as 'the incarnation of the British Raj'. Significantly Frere wrote that it was as though he had won a battle.[115] British hunting in India constituted a repeated winning of battles in maintaining a hold upon the sub-continent. As in Africa, sport and war were easily elided. When Sir Edward Braddon was involved in putting down the Santral rebellion in 1855 he regarded it as a 'splendid substitute for tiger-shooting'.[116] In placing 'sport' above administration British hunters implicitly acknowledged that their rule was maintained more successfully by the power of the gun, even in symbolic action in the natural world, than by bureaucracy alone. Wardrop recounted how, when news of a panther came in, he hastily consigned accounts and the pay-sergeant to the devil and set off after it. Braddon similarly described how, whenever news was brought in of a tiger, panther or bear anywhere within twenty miles his court was 'closed *instanter*'. His predecessor, he went on, had not shot, predators had increased, and British rule had suffered as a result.[117]

As well as being a vital element in relations with the princes, hunting took the British to the very frontiers of their empire, where they were able to gather intelligence and offer a display of power. This was true of their trips to the Himalayas, the Nepal Terai or their hunting activities in Burma and Malaya (on which there is also a considerable literature). Between 1863 and 1876 Braddon hunted every year in the Nepal Terai, as did many senior administrators before and after him. So detailed and extensive were the preparations that 'it might have been supposed our object was to wage war against the people, not merely the tigers, of Nepal'.[118] In this they cheerfully flouted the king of Nepal's conservation measures and his requirement that they should enter only with permits. Yet the British saw themselves as unique, 'the only true sportsmen in the world', and this not only inflated their self-confidence but enabled them to portray Indian hunting as 'poaching', 'cruel and unmanly sport', 'in which no true hunter could take pleasure'.[119]

While the upper reaches of British society in India maintained these hunting rituals until the Second World War, there is some evidence that hunting and shooting declined as imperial power waned. A number of writers in the inter-war years lamented the fact that young recruits to India were no longer taking up some at least of these sports. There are a number of reasons. To a certain extent the hunting ethos was itself in decline. Paradoxically, the technical precision and killing potential of modern firearms led not only to the hunting heyday of the Edwardian period but also to new sensibilities about the humane 'clean kill' and the recognition that some species were at risk. By the inter-war years some animal stocks had become seriously depleted and it was no longer easy to find certain quarry. Famous hunters like Jim Corbett were beginning to turn their energies towards conservation. Moreover the civil unrest and relative administrative chaos of the period made it much more difficult for officers to indulge themselves in the nineteenth-century manner. Nevertheless, oral evidence suggests that some forms of shooting remained popular until the end of British rule, and, as the ICS became progressively Indianised, some Indian officers took over the interests of their predecessors.[120] But conservation was in the air, and many found it difficult to secure the unalloyed satisfaction in killing that was so often the mark of the nineteenth-century hunter.

## Notes

1 E.P. Stebbing, *The Diary of a Sporting Naturalist in India*, London, 1920, p. 190.
2 A. I. R. Glasfurd, *Rifle and Romance in the Indian Jungle*, London, 1921 (first edition 1905), p. v.
3 W. Hogarth Todd, *Work, Sport, and Play* London, 1928. 'But I have said enough about work,' p. 27.
4 W. O. Horne, *Work and Sport in the old ICS*, Edinburgh, 1928.
5 E. P. Stebbing, *Jungle By-ways in India*, London, 1911, and Stebbing, *Sporting Naturalist*.
6 Sir Sainthill Eardley-Wilmot, *Forest Life and Sport in India*, London, 1910.
7 'Shikar' is a Persian word.
8 See, for example, Horne, *Work and Sport*, pp. 270-2.
9 The different types of terrain are discussed in Eardley-Wilmot, *Forest Life*, and A. A. Dunbar-Brander, 'Game preservation in India', *JSPFE* (XIV), 1931, pp. 23-35.
10 The nilgai was painted by Stubbs for Sir William Hunter in 1765.
11 Glasfurd, *Rifle and Romance*, p. 298.
12 See, for example, Mark Bence-Jones, *Palaces of the Raj*, London, 1973, p. 107.
13 Roland Hunt and John Harrison, *The District Officer in India*, 1930-47, London, 1980, pp. 130-5; Charles Allen, *Plain Tales from the Raj*, London, 1976, pp. 129-39.
14 E. Molyneux and Sir Francis Younghusband, *Kashmir*, London, 1924 (first edition 1909), p. 40. The number of visitors to Kashmir was restricted to 100 (for hunting purposes). See also Eardley-Wilmot, *Forest Life*, p. 273.
15 Thomas Williamson, *Oriental Field Sports*, London, 1808, Vol. 1, p. v.
16 Williamson, *Field Sports*, Vol II, pp 64, 72, 74, 276-80 and *passim*.
17 Williamson, *Field Sports* Vol I, p. xii.
18 Daniel Johnson, *Sketches of Field Sports as followed by the Natives of India*, London, 1822, pp. 1-35.
19 Johnson, *Sketches*, pp. 36, 39-40.
20 Stebbing, *Sporting Naturalist*, pp. 241-567.
21 Johnson, *Sketches*, pp. 13-23.
22 Charles Turley, *With the Prince round the Empire*, London, 1926, p. 71.
23 The Stubbs can be seen in Manchester City Art Gallery. Anthony Sattin (ed.), *An Englishwoman in India: the Memoirs of Harriet Tytler, 1828-58*, Oxford, 1986, pp. 66-8.
24 Johnson, *Sketches*, pp. 169-79; the quotation is on pp. 172-3.
25 M. N. Pearson, 'Recreation in Mughal India', *BJSH*, 1, 3 (1984), pp. 342-4.
26 Evan Maconochie, *Life in the ICS*, London, 1926, p. 83. Stebbing, *Sporting Naturalist*, and Eardley-Wilmot, *Forest Life*.
27 Glasfurd, *Rifle and Romance*, p. 318; p. 70 for obsessive conversations.

28 Henry Shakespear, *The Wild Sports of India*, London, 1862 (first edition 1859), pp. xi-x, 2-3, 8, 223-4 and *passim*.
29 J. C. Faunthorpe, 'Shikar', from *India*, a reprint of a special India number of *The Times*. 18 February 1930, London, 1930, pp. 271-7.
30 J. A. Mangan, *Athleticism in the Victorian and Edwardian Public School*, Cambridge, 1981, p. 137.
31 C. E. Gouldsbury, *Life in the Indian Police*, London, 1912.
32 Glasfurd, *Rifle and Romance*, pp. 202 and 243; Horne, *Work and Sport*, p. 37 and *passim*.
33 Horne, *Work and Sport*, pp. 25-6.
34 R. G. Burton, *Sport and Wild Life in the Deccan*, London, 1828, pp. 19, 52-60. Burton also saw the system of hunting drives as akin to the techniques of war, p. 119.
35 Williamson, *Field Sports*, Vol. II, pp. 121-2, 194.
36 Allen, *Plain Tales*, p. 132.
37 Mollie Panter-Downes, *Ooty Preserved: a Victorian Hill Station in India*, London, 1967, pp. 68-71. Horne, *Work and Sport*, p. 56.
38 Horne, *Work and Sport*, pp. 16, 55-6, 106 and *passim*.
39 Williamson, *Field Sports*, pp. 121 and 194, Allen, *Plain Tales*, p. 132. Sir Samuel Baker (see references below) described in detail the importation and use of hounds in Ceylon.
40 J. W. Best, Indian Shikar Notes, Lahore, 1931 (first edition 1920), pp. 147-57.
41 T. A. Anderson, *The Wanderer in Ceylon*, London, 1817.
42 Samuel W. Baker, *Eight Years' Wanderings in Ceylon*, London, 1855, p. 16.
43 Baker, *Eight Years*, p. 15.
44 Samuel W. Baker, *The Rifle and the Hound in Ceylon*, London, 1890 (first edition 1854), p. xvi.
45 Baker *The Rifle*, pp. 13-15, 204, 251 and *passim*.
46 'India and the Prince of Wales', *Illustrated London News* supplement, 1876.
47 Mildred Archer, *Tippoo's Tiger*, London, 1959.
48 Williamson, *Field Sports*, Vol. I, pp. 136, 205.
49 Burton, *Sport and Wild Life*, p. 89.
50 James Forsyth, *The Highlands of Central India*, London, 1871.
51 G. P. Sanderson, *Thirteen Years among the Wild Beasts of India*, London, 1878, pp. 266-7.
52 Glasfurd, *Rifle and Romance*, p. 23.
53 Descriptions of tiger shooting are legion, but see particularly W. Hogarth Todd, *Tiger, Tiger!* London, 1927; Nigel Woodyatt, *My Sporting Memories*, London, 1923; Burton, *Sport and Wild Life*; Eardley-Wilmot, *Forest Life*.
54 Allen, *Plain Tales*, p. 139.
55 Woodyatt, *Sporting Memories*, p. 12.
56 Woodyatt, *Sporting Memories*, pp. 18-19.
57 Burton, *Sport and Wild Life*, p. 203.
58 Woodyatt, *Sporting Memories*, p. 16.
59 Eardley-Wilmot, *Forest Life*, p. 89.
60 Williamson, *Field Sports*, Vol.I, p. 211.
61 Sometimes rewards for notorious man-eaters went as high as 500 rupees. Information on rewards can be found in Johnson, Sanderson, Eardley-Wilmot, Stebbing and many other sources.
62 Sanderson, *Thirteen Years*, p. 360.
63 R. E. Hawkins (ed.), *Jim Corbett's India*, Oxford, 1986. Jim Corbett, *Man-eaters of Kumaon* , London 1946; *My India*, London, 1952.
64 *The Best of Saki* (H. H. Munro), introduced by Tom Sharpe, London, 1976, pp. 36-39.
65 Williamson, *Field Sports*, Vol. I, p. 141.
66 Williamson, *Field Sports*, Vol. I. pp. 56, 108-35.
67 Sanderson, *Thirteen Years*, pp. 1-3, 53-5 and *passim*.
68 Sanderson, *Thirteen Years*, pp. 68, 101-19.
69 Baker, *Eight Years*, p. 127.

70 Sanderson, *Thirteen Years*, pp. 188, 226. See also Shakespear, *Wild Sports*, pp. 28, and 191-207.
71 Sanderson, *Thirteen Years*, pp. 91-2, 99-100, 119, 226 and *passim*.
72 Sir Edward Braddon, *Thirty Years of Shikar*, Edinburgh, 1895, pp. 227-8.
73 Horne, *Work and Sport*, p. 125.
74 R. S. Surtees, *Handley Cross*, London, 1843, chapter 7.
75 Quoted in Pearson, 'Recreation in Mughal India', p. 340.
76 Williamson, *Field Sports*, pp. 15-31.
77 Johnson, *Sketches*, p. 48.
78 Shakespear, *Wild Sports*, p. 29.
79 Shakespear, *Wild Sports*, pp. 41, 50.
80 Sanderson, *Thirteen Years*, p. 133.
81 Best, *Shikar Notes*, pp. 186-7.
82 Best, *Shikar Notes*, p. 199.
83 Best, *Shikar Notes*, pp. 198, 202-3.
84 Stebbing, *Sporting Naturalist*, p. 158.
85 A. E. Wardrop, *Modern Pig Sticking*, London, 1914 (second edition 1939): Braddon, *Thirty Years*, pp. 14, 24, 101.
86 Robert Baden-Powell, *Pig Sticking or Hog Hunting*, London, 1924 (first edition 1889), pp. 20, 22, 27, 34 and *passim*.
87 Baden-Powell, *Pig Sticking*, p. 21.
88 Sir Reginald Craddock, in the introduction to Todd, *Work, Sport*, p. 5. Baden-Powell, *Pig Sticking*, pp. 38, 46. Horne, *Work and Sport*, p. 121.
89 Burton, *Sport and Wild life*, p. 48.
90 Burton, *Sport and Wild Life*, pp. 182, 187. Stebbing, *Jungle By-ways*, pp. 212, 238.
91 I am indebted for the references that follow to David Arnold. They come from the *India, Public Proceedings*, India Office Library and Records.
92 Best, *Shikar Notes*, p. 39.
93 Stebbing, *Sporting Naturalist*, pp. 109, 160.
94 Stebbing, *Jungle By-ways*, xviii.
95 Glasfurd, *Rifle and Romance*, pp. 299-305.
96 Eardley-Wilmot, *Forest Life*, p. 129.
97 Eardley-Wilmot, *Forest Life*, p. 3.
98 Stebbing, *Sporting Naturalist*, p. vii.
99 Eardley-Wilmot, *Forest Life*, p. 43.
100 Stebbing *Sporting Naturalist*, pp. 5, 204.
101 Molyneux and Younghusband, *Kashmir*, p. 102.
102 Anon, 'Ibex shooting', *Kings Royal Rifle Corps Chronicle* (1913), p. 35.
103 E. P. Stebbing, *Stalks in the Himalayas*, London, 1912.
104 Gardner-Waterman Kashmir Collection, RCS Library MSS 22V.
105 Molyneux and Younghusband, *Kashmir*, pp. 44-6.
106 Minto, for example, paid visits to Kashmir in 1906 and 1908. Molyneux and Younghusband, *Kashmir*, pp. 35 and 105.
107 Woodyatt, *Sporting Memories*.
108 Turley, *With the Prince*, p. 76.
109 Baden-Powell, *Pig Sticking*, dedication.
110 Baden-Powell, *Pig Sticking*, pp. 47-9.
111 Turley, *With the Prince*, pp. 74 and 78.
112 S. D. Waley, *Edwin Montagu: a memoir and an Account of his Visits to India*, Bombay, 1964, p. 149.
113 *India, The Times*, p. 276.
114 These albums and accounts of bags can be seen in the Library of Hopetoun House. There are similar materials in the Minto papers in the National Library of Scotland.
115 Philip Magnus, *King Edward the Seventh*, London 1976, pp. 176, 183.
116 Braddon, *Thirty Years*, p. 84.
117 Wardrop, *Pig Sticking*, p. 19. Braddon, *Thirty Years*, p. 157.
118 Braddon, *Thirty Years*, pp. 275, 306-13.

119 R. H. W. Dunlop, *Hunting in the Himalayas*, London, 1860, p. 2. Robert Armitage Sterndale, *Seonee, or Camp Life in the Satpura Range: a Tale of Indian Adventure*, Calcutta, 1887, p. 322. Both quoted in Scott Bennett, 'Shikar and the Raj', *South Asia*, VII (1984), pp. 72-88.
120 Hunt and Harrison, *District Officer*, pp. 130-3.

# CHAPTER EIGHT

# From preservation to conservation: legislation and the international dimension

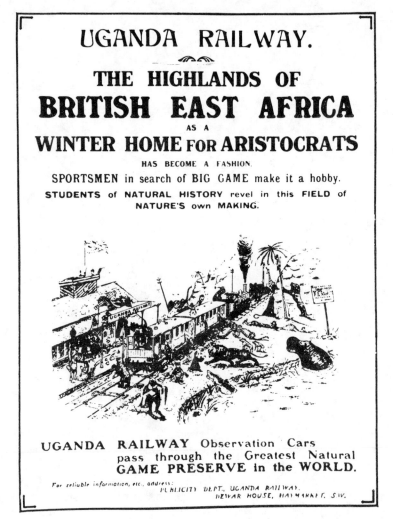

UGANDA RAILWAY.

## THE HIGHLANDS OF
# BRITISH EAST AFRICA
### AS A
## WINTER HOME FOR ARISTOCRATS
HAS BECOME A FASHION.
SPORTSMEN in search of BIG GAME make it a hobby.
STUDENTS of NATURAL HISTORY revel in this FIELD of NATURE'S own MAKING.

UGANDA RAILWAY Observation Cars pass through the Greatest Natural GAME PRESERVE in the WORLD.

For reliable information, etc., address:
PUBLICITY DEPT., UGANDA RAILWAY.
DEWAR HOUSE, HAYMARKET. S.W.

By the end of the century the hunting and natural history elites were beginning to sound a note of alarm. The combined ravages of over-hunting and rinderpest had produced such a marked diminution of game that conservation measures seemed necessary. Pressure groups became active in promoting legislation, the creation of reserves, and the funding of societies dedicated to the protection of game. Since these pressure groups included many governors and other senior colonial offi-cials, aristocratic and 'sporting' hunters, and leading landowners in col-onies of settlement, suggestions for preservation were swiftly trans-lated into practice. Inevitably, the form that preservation took was shaped by the social and economic realities of Empire. It also bore a marked resemblance, now worked out in detailed and sophisticated legislation, to the historic themes surveyed in chapters one and two. Access to animals was to be progressively restricted to the elite; animals were to be categorised according to sporting rather than utilita-rian characteristics; some were to be specially protected for their rarity, others shot indiscriminately as vermin; separation was to be attempted between areas of human settlement and those appropriate to animal occupation. The first phase of the new movement was to be game pre-servation for sport rather than true conservation.

This and the next two chapters will examine the manner in which an attempt was made to curb the game destruction that had been a necesary part of the conquest and initial settlement of Africa. The attempt was based on the transfer to Africa of property rights in game, the vesting of those rights either in white settlers or in a colonial administration, the exclusion of Africans from hunting, and the pro-gressive conversion of the game from a direct economic resource in ivory, meat, hides and skins into an indirect one, a means of raising revenue from 'sport' and tourism. New colonial officers, game wardens and rangers were appointed with wide administrative and judicial powers not only over game reserves – often vast tracts of territory – but also over the Africans who lived within their borders or around their fringes. These officials often spearheaded the next phase, which was the conversion of the reserves into national parks. Reserves had been created for the protection and management of game, combined with some controlled hunting, in often inaccessible regions. The prin-ciple was to separate human and animal living space, encouraging the latter by the exclusion of the former. National parks permitted the return of the humans – as visitors, onlookers and photographers rather than as hunters. Live animals became a tourist resource, a vast outdoor zoo, their haunts made accessible by the building of roads, hotels and rest camps. The national park was rendered possible by the develop-ment of the internal combustion engine and involved vital changes in legal status for the territory concerned. The parks were develped in the years before and immediately following the Second World War. Outside the reserves and parks, hunting went on in private and Crown lands subject to the repeated fine-tuning of game legislation, which reached a peak of intensity in the 1920s and especially the '30s. Seldom can legislation have performed such a continuing role in the management of a resource.

In this chapter the main concern will be with international action, intense colonial legislative activity, and the development of a pressure group, the Society for the Preservation of the Fauna of the Empire (SPFE). Chapter nine will survey the appearance of reserves as the second part of the preservationist programme. When human sleeping-sickness broke out in various areas of East and Central Africa the creation of separate animal habitats together with legislative protection helped to fuel the controversy regarding the relationship between the tsetse fly and game. Although imperial enthusiasm was checked for a period, reserves continued to be created and game departments were founded to administer game policies and attempt to accomplish the separation of human settlement and animal habitat. Chapter ten will consider the expansion and freezing of these reserves into national parks, both in Africa and in Asia. The gradual transition between preservation and conservation will be charted through the three chapters. The first proponents of game protection were preservationists, as their language indicates. Gradually conservation took over (involving, for example, a shift in the status of vermin, and the eventual exclusion of even elite hunting in the reserves). With the appearance of national parks, conservation on more modern lines was fully in place.

Much of the legislative activity to protect game in Africa can be seen as a response to two international agreements on game protection, the Convention for the Preservation of Wild Animals, Birds and Fish in Africa, signed in London on 19 May 1900, and the Agreement for the Protection of the Fauna and Flora of Africa, of November 1933.[1] To a certain extent the first can be seen as a preservationist document, the second as conservationist. The first addressed itself to the question of legislation and that of reserves, particularly emphasising the former. The legislative action of the new imperial powers was seen as the distinctive quality of European empires, a panacea for a range of ills in the colonial world.

Yet some at least of the legislative provisions that were to be developed in the twentieth century had been in existence for a long time. The first game legislation had been introduced to the Cape by the Dutch East India Company as early as 1657 and '58, and a significant law was passed in 1684.[2] The first major piece of colonial legislation on game was Lord Charles Somerset's proclamation of 12 July 1822 in the Cape Colony.[3] The preamble lamented the fact that the 'rapidly increasing population' rendered it 'daily more necessary to guard against the total destruction of game in this colony'. It introduced the notion of the closed season (from 1 July to 30 November) and the need to take out a licence (at a cost of five rixdollars) to kill game in the open season. Game was, in effect, divided into three categories. Some large game – elephant, hippopotamus and bontebok – could be shot only under a special licence from the Governor, while other animals were categorised as vermin and their killers could receive rewards ranging from twenty five rixdollars for a 'tiger' (presumably a leopard), five rixdollars for a wild hog, down to four skellings for a hawk. It was the extensive category between the 'royal' game (not yet described as such) and the vermin which was subject to the licensing system. Heavy penalties were introduced for infringement of the regulations, but some very interesting exceptions were made. Slaves were not permitted to hunt, while 'Hottentots and other servants' might shoot only for their master on their employers' land and not elsewhere. Travellers were allowed to shoot game at any time for 'actual consumption on the road', provided it was in the region beyond the Hottentots' Holland Kloof and on the other side of the Great Berg river. Most interestingly of all, property rights to game on private lands were established (some years before the same principle was introduced into the United Kingdom) and proprietors and occupiers of land were given the absolute right to 'kill, destroy, and drive forth' all game out of cultivated land. Hunting with hounds had already become a significant sport of the whites in the colony and it was specifically excluded from the provisions of the proclamation 'as in no wise tending to the destruction of game . . . provided it be conducted by hunting clubs established under the sanction of his Excellency the Governor'.

The provisions on vermin were subsequently repealed. Elephants were removed from the category of royal game within a matter of months when it was discovered that the inhabitants of the Under Bosjeman's River division were subject to harassment by 'numerous elephants'.[4] On the other hand the 'beautiful and scarce species of Deer [sic] called Eland' were added to the category in March 1823. This seems to have been a response to a specific event: land proprietors in the Attaquas Kloof had been attempting to protect eland, but the animals had 'lately been wantonly dispersed and destroyed by some evil-disposed persons'.[5] The Orange Free State and the South African Republic introduced game laws in 1858, but there seems to have been little further activity in game protection in the Cape Colony for some sixty years. When an Act for the Better Preservation of Game was promulgated in July 1886 it had become clear that many more species were at risk of extinction from the colony's fauna.[6] The list of specially protected game was extended to include elephant, bontebok, gemsbok, rietbok, zebra, quagga, Burchell's zebra or any gnu or wildebeest of either variety. In fact by 1886 little hunting was to be found in Cape Colony. The quagga was already extinct throughout the whole of southern Africa, and few of the specially protected species remained in the colony. The migrating springbok were specifically excluded from the provisions of the Act and were subject neither to close seasons nor to licences. Yet the extraordinary migrations of springbok were almost at an end, the last recorded taking place in 1896. But the rights of land-owners were made even more explicit in this Act – 'No landowner shall require a game licence for the purpose of shooting game on his own land.'

Despite the fact that much of the game had been destroyed or had bolted to remote regions or beyond the frontiers of the colony by the last years of the century, the 1886 Act heralded a flurry of legislative activity. Its provisions were extended to the Transkei and Griqualand East in 1887 and to Tembuland in 1893. There were new Acts in 1890, 1891, 1894, 1899 and 1908, all consolidated into a new game law of November 1909. By this time the category of 'royal game' (now described as such) had been extended yet again. Nevertheless royal game could be shot under a special licence, and the horns, hides and skins of royal game were subjected to a 20 per cent export duty (so dealing in them was not banned). No tusk under 11 lb weight could be traded (one of the provisions of the 1900 Convention). Licences had to be taken out for the hawking and selling of game, an activity that could be entirely prohibited in any division of the Colony if three-quarters of the Divisional Council desired it. Hunting game by night could be prohibited, again if local government desired it, while African hunting was effectively banned by a clause which decreed that game could be hunted and killed only by shooting. A tax was placed on greyhounds except those registered by members of recognised coursing clubs. Finally, the Governor was empowered to establish 'game preserves' by proclamation.

From the 1890s many of these Cape principles were extended to other colonies. Game laws were introduced into Natal in 1890, 1891 and 1906.[7] African hunting techniques, the use of nets, springs, gins, traps, snares and sticks were prohibited in 1891. The rights of land-owners were affirmed, a close season was established, and provision was made for special permission to attack game destroying crops. Animals were divided into three schedules, the third being protected. In 1897 reserves were established in Zululand – well away from white settlement – by proclamation of the Governor. They were confirmed under the Act of 1906, and the special consent of the Minister was required to allow Africans to defend their crops in Zululand, such permission not extending to elephants, white rhinos, eland, roan antelope, buffalo cow, koodoo (kudu) cow or springbok. No person was permitted to employ a native to hunt game, effectively ending the system of 'subcontracted' hunting that had been in use in Natal for several decades.

It is a curious fact that although there was already a tradition of game legislation and preservation in British territories, the British chose to be influenced by the Germans in the acceleration of conservation measures in the 1890s. The Cape Colony and other British African possessions had concentrated on close seasons, licences and the scheduling of animals. Some private 'preserves' had been established, but it was the concept of the game reserve that the Germans were to promote most strenuously. In 1896 the Marquess of Salisbury, Foreign Secretary and Prime Minister, wrote to Messrs Hardinge and Berkeley, respectively the Commissioners for the East Africa Protectorate and Uganda, about game policy. Salisbury's attention had been drawn to the excessive destruction of big game. 'There is reason to fear that unless some check is imposed upon the indiscriminate slaughter of these animals, they will, in the course of a few years, disappear from the British Protectorates.'[8] He asked how the game regulations imposed by the Imperial British East Africa Company had operated, called for a full report on game, and suggested improvements including 'reserved districts' and an increase in the licence fee to the British Central Africa level of £25. In fact the IBEA fee had indeed been £25 for one year's shooting, although no limit seems to have been imposed on the numbers that could be shot under such a licence. Licensees had to deposit £100 surety and pay 15 per cent duty on ivory and 10 per cent on rhino horn.

Salisbury's enquiry produced a flurry of imperial correspondence. Salisbury also received information from Berlin on the measures taken by Hermann von Wissmann in German East Africa.[9] Game regulations had been introduced into the Moshi and Kilimanjaro districts in 1891. In 1896 they were extended to the entire territory. Wissmann had introduced licences which were available to Africans as well as Europeans, but had prohibited the use of nets, fire and other forms of driving game. In 1896 he asked his officials to nominate areas suitable as reserves, and declared two, one on the Rufiji river and another to the west of Kilimanjaro. These regulations, crudely drafted though they were, were promptly sent to all British territories and to India for comment. Sir Graham Bower, the Imperial Secretary in Cape Town, reacted unfavourably to the idea of reserves.[10] They were, he said, no good without gamekeepers, and the cost of a proper policing system would be prohibitive. He argued that African chiefs should be encouraged to take an interest in game preservation, and, significantly, suggested that the buffalo should not receive special protection, as it was known that they encouraged tsetse fly. Bower's scepticism about reserves was confirmed by the Government Secretary of Zululand, although several small reserves had already been established there in 'unhealthy and uninhabited parts of the country'.[11] Sir John Kirk, the former Consul General at Zanzibar, whose views were also canvassed, was equally doubtful, agreeing that they would not work without 'rangers and park keepers'.[12] European hunters, he suggested, could simply be banned from entering certain districts.

Of all the colonials responses the most substantial came from Alfred Sharpe, the Acting Commissioner of the British Central Africa Protectorate.[13] He concerned himself principally with elephants and suggested that the only way to save them was to place a minimum 15 lb limit on tusks that could be taken. He too opposed sanctuaries on the German East Africa model. Small ones would be ineffective and large ones hard to police. Sharpe opened up another controversy. He pinned the blame for game destruction firmly on African hunters. Frederick Selous agreed that African hunters were exterminating the game in Central Africa. Of every 1,000 elephants, he suggested, 997 were killed by Africans.[14] Sharpe's views were sent to Wissmann, who denied the fault lay with Africans, pointing instead to the profligacy of Europeans with guns, and repeated his arguments for reserves.[15] Sir John Kirk was characteristically candid in his apportionment of blame. 'It is wonderful how little effect natives with spears, traps and arrows have on game in a country, and how suddenly it disappears before the gun and the rifle.'

Nevertheless, new game regulations introduced to German East Africa in 1898 began the process of excluding the African hunter, while Lord Delamere, the premier Kenyan settler, pressed upon the Foreign Office the need to prohibit African hunting. 'There seems to me excellent reasons for preventing natives killing game. It is easy enough to say natives have been centuries in Africa and have not exterminated the game, but that was under different conditions.'[16] John Ainsworth, a celebrated district official in the East Africa Protectorate, reporting on the operation of the game laws in Ukamba Province in 1900, observed that although the 'Wakamba, Wataveta, and Wanderobo' hunted, they killed few animals.[17] Hunting became particularly important in time of famine, but now that the recent famine was over, he argued, native hunting should be stopped.

Regardless of the identitiy of the prime enemies of game, Hermann von Wissmann proposed that an international conference should be convened to discuss the whole question of game preservation. This conference was three years in the making, but the idea was promoted strenuously by the British. The extent of the Government's interest and the scale of the correspondence is indicated by the fact that the exchanges quoted above, colonial game regulations, and a large number of reports and many other materials were gathered together and published in a parliamentary command paper, running to 391 pages in 1906. Further extensive Blue books followed, in 1909, 1910, 1911 and 1913.[18] British concern was presumably grounded in the fascination of its elite with hunting. Sir Clement Hill (head of the African Protectorates Department at the Foreign Office) had spent a great deal of his time hunting on a visit to East Africa. Hunting figured prominently in the aristocratic cults of both the Germans and the British. Moreover, travellers and hunters like H. A. Bryden were predicting the total extermination of all the great pachyderms within a few decades.

The alarm of the official conservationists is well illustrated by the reports the Foreign Office elicited from the British Museum (Natural History) on the extermination of species. In one of these the Director of the Museum referred to the extinction of the blaubok and the quagga in southern Africa, the survival of only a handful of white rhinos in Mashonaland, and the fact that the bontebok and white-tailed gnu survived on a few scattered farms in the Cape Colony and the Orange Free State.[19] He drew on other examples from Kashmir (the hangal stag), the Gold Coast (the colobus monkey, much in demand for its skin), the USA (the bison) and the Shetland Islands (the great skua). Another report charted the demise of millions of American bison in detail, and provided tables of kills for the destruction of fur seals, sea otters, beavers, Gold Coast monkeys, the quagga and the mountain zebra.[20] Examples were given of the scale of destruction of elephants, particularly in the Congo. The recent outlawing of the destruction of millions of birds, like the osprey, for their plumage to satisfy the dictates of fashion was used as a precedent to emphasise the need for international legislative action.

These examples fuelled British alarm. Some African species were certainly in danger, but, as was soon apparent, the threat to African wildlife was generally exaggerated. Alarmed, however, by the gloomier prognostications the government took the initiative in establishing the first conference on African wildlife, organised by Sir Clement Hill at the Foreign Office in 1900.[21] Although attended by all European powers with African possessions, it was clearly the British and the Germans who predominated. The British were represented by the Earl of Hopetoun (later Marquess of Linlithgow) and Sir Clement Hill, the Germans by Baron von Lindenfels and Hermann von Wissmann. The Convention which emerged from the conference suggested that all colonial powers should introduce game regulations, that the killing of young females should be banned, that there should be close seasons and hunting only by licence, and that the use of nets, pitfalls, poison and dynamite should be prohibited. The regulations on guns and ammunition recommended at the Brussels conference of 1889-90 (particularly keeping firearms out of the hands of Africans) should be strictly enforced. No tusks should be taken under 5 kg, export duties should be placed on hides and skins, and measures should be adopted to prevent the spread of contagious diseases from cattle and game. Animals were divided into five schedules, ranging from those that should be preserved because of their usefulness or rarity to those which were harmful, could be treated as vermin, and shot at will. These included the big cats, hyenas, hunting dogs, otters, baboons, crocodiles and poisonous snakes. The principle was reaffirmed in articles that distinguished between the ostrich egg, to which every protection should be given, and the eggs of crocodiles, pythons and poisonous snakes, which could be destroyed at will. Finally, the need for reserves was clearly laid out, and it was asserted that they should be 'sufficiently large tracts of land', to facilitate large-scale animal migrations.

Most of the parties to the Convention failed to ratify it, but the British and the Germans eagerly set about establishing its principles in colonial legislation. Arthur Hardinge in the East Africa Protectorate was even charged with attempting to harmonise the game regulations of German East Africa and Italian East Africa with those of the British territories.[22] Over the succeeding years the British repeatedly prodded the Liberian, Congolese, Abyssinian, Italian, Portuguese and German authorities to tighten up game regulations. They received little response from Liberia or Abyssinia, although the government of the latter was prepared to attempt to control the flow of immature ivory through its territory. The Italians eventually produced game regulations for Eritrea; the Portuguese issued game laws for some of the territory directly administered by the Portuguese government and persuaded the Nyassa and Mozambique chartered companies, which controlled vast tracts of Mozambique, to introduce game regulations of their own; the government of the Congo declined to act until the other powers had ratified the Convention; the Germans repeatedly insisted that their arrangements were adequate.

The legislation of British colonies in East and Central Africa broadly followed the principles of the Cape Acts, but was often a great deal more complex, and – vitally – incorporated the notion of reserves that had been resisted at the Cape.[23] A stream of game regulations appeared around the turn of the century, influenced by Colonial Office and

Foreign Office interest and the 1900 Convention; a set of consolidating ordinances, partly responding to the initial experiences and partly to the pressures of the Society for the Preservation of the Wild Fauna of the Empire, were enacted in the years before the First World War; new legislation in the 1920s set out to cope with what were perceived as the ravages of the First World War; and yet more in the 1930s was designed to include the provisions of the 1933 International Agreement (see below). Another body of legislation starting from this period set up the national parks. It would be tedious to survey all this colonial legislation, some of which can be found listed in appendix I, but a number of themes emerge strongly from it.

In most British colonies Africans were excluded from hunting. The process was begun by stringent gun laws, introduced in Kenya and Southern Rhodesia, for example, in the late 1890s. In some colonies African licences could be taken out, but since most African techniques were banned few actually did so. As the game legislation was developed the contrast between humane and cruel killing was often explicitly introduced, as in the 1928 Game Amendment Ordinance in Kenya. Humane killing could be effected only by modern firearms; pitfalls, snares, traps, nets and drives were prohibited. In Kenya the sale of snares, gins and traps was forbidden in 1937, while in Southern Rhodesia the possession of snares was made illegal in 1938. Sometimes it was specifically enacted that no 'native' could hunt except as an assistant to a European, in which case he could not bear firearms. In Kenya a 'resident' for the purposes of a resident's licence was defined in such a way as to exclude Africans. In one or two cases an exception was made for Africans who were said to subsist solely on the flesh of hunted animals, but the notion that pastoralists or cultivators might also hunt was rejected. It was even suggested that such hunting was regresssive. In other words the legislation had the effect of emphasising economic specialisation and limiting dietary choice. The role of the 'defensive' hunter to protect crops was usually vested in the local colonial officials or the police. In Uganda chiefs were permitted, within careful limits, to shoot for crop protection.

Europeans were divided into different categories for the issue of licences. Officials and the police often had special status, being empowered to shoot for their men and themselves, as well as being able to secure a cheaper licence for sport and shooting for profit. Residents had certain privileges, while 'sportsmen' or 'visitors' had to take out a special licence. The complexities of licensing reached a peak in the Kenyan ordinance of 1937, which specified no fewer than twelve different licenses available to Europeans. The special privileges granted to travellers and police officers to provision their men were eventually dropped, but the rights of landowners were protected throughout.

Before the First World War dealing in game meat, hides, skins and trophies was normally permitted under licence, but in the 1920s such dealing was generally banned. In some colonies a distinction was drawn between domestic trading and export, the latter being prohibited. In other words, shooting was being restricted to personal consumption, and the acquisition of trophies and skins was limited to the people who actually shot them. As animals retreated from the vicinity of townships, from cultivated land, and from African reserves, access to them became increasingly restricted to more senior officials, the larger landowners, and wealthy visiting sportsmen. Specialisation in land use, separation in settlement patterns, and the removal of hunting opportunities to remoter regions, had the effect of emphasising the shift towards the third level of imperial hunting, the Hunt.

The scheduling of animals became as complex as the licensing of hunting. Game was divided into categories, ranging from three to five at different times and in different colonies, according to rarity and degree of protection. The concept of vermin appeared early in the century, but had tended to disappear by the Second World War as more extensive notions of the protection of fauna developed. The Germans stressed the status of vermin in the German East Africa game regulations of 1898, which offered a bounty of thirty rupees for each lion killed. (The British, it will be remembered, offered fifty to 200 rupees for each tiger destroyed in India). Mozambique regulations of 1906 offered a reward 'for the purpose of promoting the extinction of those wild and harmful animals' defined in an accompanying list. The management of game and predators was achieved in two ways. From the beginning of the century the schedules laid out the numbers of each animal that could be shot per annum under licence. In successive pieces of legislation these numbers could be varied, usually from two up to an unlimited figure. Licence holders had to keep a record of game shot which had to be signed and returned to the appropriate authority at the expiry of the licence. Thus the game book, in miniature form, was given official recognition. Both the East and Central African Protectorates found it necessary to issue additional regulations, emphasising the need to keep such records. To add to the complexities, specific species might be moved by repeated amendments from one schedule to another, shifting in status from what might be described as 'fair game' to 'royal game'. A certain species might have a 'low' status in one district and a 'high' one in another (low here reflecting availability to be shot). It is noticeable that repeated tinkering of this sort, occurring on an annual basis, took place in territories like Kenya and Southern Rhodesia, which had considerable settler population as well as popularity (especially Kenya) among tourists hunting for sport. Territories with fewer settlers that were less open to hunting tourism, like Uganda and Northern Rhodesia, amended their legislation much less frequently. Finally, in prohibiting the killing of young and females (particularly when accompanied by young) of many species legislation sanctioned the 'sporting code' in the name of conservation. A fairly typical example of a colonial game law can be founded in appendix II.

The conservationists had intended that the 1900 conference should be the first of a series, and the publication of Parliamentary Papers between 1906 and 1913 was a response to the growing power of the lobby, particularly as represented by the Society for the Preservation of the Fauna of the Empire (which before the First World War sometimes added the word 'Wild' before Fauna to its title). The society was foremost among the pressure groups campaigning for game preservation and prompting the government to publish these extensive materials. It was founded in 1903 because, it claimed, 'the destruction of wild animals throughout the British Empire, more especially in Africa, had become . . . appalling.'[24] It had its origins in a meeting of a few interested parties in the home of Edward North Buxon, a prominent hunter. It soon had its own rooms, was holding public meetings, and issued a journal. Its objects were to collect information as to the number of wild animals killed each year, chart the gradual disappearance of species, create 'a sound public opinion' and 'further the formation of game reserves and sanctuaries, the selection of the most suitable places for these sanctuaries, and the enforcing of suitable game laws and regulations'. Its members included almost all the great African hunters of the day, several of them members of the House of Lords, and it proudly announced that 'the principal officials in charge of the various sections of British Africa are impressed with the importance of immediate steps being taken for the preservation of African game, and have, without exception, consented to become Vice-Presidents or Honorary Members of the Society'. Indeed, the fact that the most avid hunters were also the keenest conservationists led to its membership becoming known as 'the penitent butchers'.

It also formed close connections with the British Museum (Natural History) and published the *Journal of the Society for the Preservation of the Wild Fauna of the Empire*. This was filled with articles by hunters and conservationists on the decline of game, disease, the tsetse fly controversy, the foundation of reserves, natural history observation, the characteristics of individual species and also, significantly, accounts of hunting trips. The journal reached volume 12 in 1914, was stopped by the war, but was restarted (with *Wild* dropped from the title) in 1921. It continued until 1950, when it became the magazine

[ *211* ]

*Oryx.* The society was, however, more than just another imperial pressure group. Many such groups are noted for their failure to achieve their objectives – from imperial federation to tariff reform – but the society contained a winning combination of aristocrats, hunter-naturalists and officials. As its journal reveals, it was a pseudo-scientific body which set out to make many of its objectives hard to argue with. It was clearly received with sympathy in the Colonial Office and the Foreign Office; it prompted official publications and legislation, pressing for the issue of annual Blue books (although the momentum was already there); and, as we shall see, it had a powerful effect on the 1933 Agreement on the Protection for the Fauna and Flora of Africa.

The society's considerable influence emerges very clearly from the Blue books. Deputations from the society were received by successive Secretaries of State for the Colonies. Alfred Lyttelton received its representatives in February 1905.[25] They included the Marquess of Hamilton, Sir Henry Seton Kerr, Sir Harry Johnston and F. C. Selous. The chairman of the society, Edward North Buxton, did most of the talking. Buxton was himself a fervent hunter who travelled throughout Europe, Asia Minor and Africa in pursuit of game and trophies. Sir Alfred Pease, another passionate hunter and a Member of Parliament, who sometimes complained that his 'parliamentary duties interfered with hunting', wrote:

> Buxton firmly held the view that one, and not the least, of the purposes for which the British Diplomatic and Consular Services and Colonial and Military Governors existed was to assist him personally to obtain any coveted trophy or curious animal upon which he had set his heart. Some were charmed, some amazed at his presumption, but I am bound to say he invariably convinced them that his view of their functions should be acted upon.[26]

Buxton used the same principles in his approaches to the Colonial Office and was no less successful in achieving his objectives.

The first deputation urged upon Lyttelton the need for large reserves, the reclassification of more game as 'royal', the appointment of game officers and increased expenditure on preservation and a prohibition on the export of hides and undersize ivory. They expressed concern about the lack of action on game in northern Nigeria and the British South Africa Company territories and also about Boer hunting in East Africa. The notion that game harboured tsetse was attacked, and there was a demand fom one member that the minimum tusk size should be raised to 40 lb. These issues were to recur, in increasingly detailed form, in the subsequent delegations to the Colonial Office. The second deputation waited upon the Earl of Elgin, the Liberal Colonial Secretary, in June 1906.[27] It was again led by Buxton; Selous and Seton Kerr were members once more; and aristocratic ballast was provided by the Duchess of Bedford and the ex-viceroy Curzon. On this occasion Buxton opened the meeting by pointing out that the attraction of game to young officials 'is a very important thing'. 'Your services . . . are better and more efficient because of that attraction . . . to those young men who live in unhealthy climates it is an element of health that they should have that means of recreation.' The connection between preservation and the Hunt as an elite imperial privilege is made explicit. Curzon professed himself a keen sportsman, but took his usual high-minded approach. 'We are the owners of the greatest Empire in the Universe' and are 'trustees for posterity of the natural contents of that Empire', including its 'rare and interesting animal life'. The society was particularly concerned that reserves should be sacrosanct. Elgin expressed a great interest in the subject and promised his sympathy, consideration and assistance 'so far as it is in my power'.

Elgin's successor, the Earl of Crewe, received an even more heavyweight deputation in 1909.[28] It comprised the Marquess of Hamilton, Viscounts Newport and Valentia, Lords Aberdare, Cranworth, Elphinstone and Monk Bretton, Sir Clement Hill (now retired), Sir Harry Johnston, H. A. Bryden, Buxton and fourteen others. Curzon was unable to attend through illness. Buxton renewed the attack on the Chartered Company, which had permitted the shooting of an entire herd of eighty-one elephants in the Lomagundi District of Southern Rhodesia, and had suspended the game regulations because of tsetse. Again the society insisted that reserves should be sacrosanct, asked for a 25-30 lb minimum tusk limit to be uniform throughout British territories, and requested that the ban on the sale of hides and skins should be tightened up. Cranworth gave an eye-witness account of the wholesale slaughter of game in Southern Rhodesia, and Johnston and Hill offered evidence on the tsetse and indiscriminate Boer shooting in East Africa. The secretary of the society provided detailed figures on the ivory trade. Crewe honoured the society as a scientific body and treated most of its suggestions sympathetically, though he did point out that elephants caused serious destruction of crops, particularly in Uganda.

There can be little doubt that the Secretaries of State shared the interests and perceptions of the society. Lyttelton actually became a member and undertook a shooting trip in East Africa after he left office. They offered more than sympathetic words. They drove the Colonial Office into practical reactions to the society's recommendations. The minutes of the meeting with the first deputation were sent to every African colony for comment.[29] The governors' and commissioners' responses were sent to the society for discussion at their meetings, and in June 1906 the society submitted comments on specific colonies and issues as well as offering a series of general recommendations to the Colonial Office.[30] They asked for the printing of annual returns of game killed in each colony, the compilation of a map of game reserves in Africa, stricter prohibitions on the sale of hides, a minimum tusk limit of 25 lb, an absolute prohibition on shooting in reserves, and the enforcement of the recording of kills by licence holders. A number of colonies duly amended their game regulations in line with the suggestions.

A few colonies attempted to resist the making of imperial policy by a private pressure group. In West Africa, where African hunting was permitted and European hunting parties were virtually unknown, the conditions were somewhat different from those obtaining in the east and south. Nevertheless, the Governor of Lagos reported on the serious diminution of game and several colonies adopted measures derived from the society's ideas.[31] Only the Governor of the Gambia, Sir George Denton, put up any resistance.[32] Hippos, monkeys and baboons caused serious crop damage, and he saw no point in driving the skin and ivory trades to French West African ports. The Gambia was, of course, a tiny colony where the whole land area was under cultivation. More significant was the resistance offered by Uganda. In late 1905 Commissioner Sadler asserted that game was greatly on the increase, that the reserves (particularly Toro, at 1,300 square miles) were too large, and that the preservation of the elephant was causing hardship through crop destruction in Ankole and Toro.[33] Acting Commissioner Wilson was even more forceful in his representations to the Colonial Office in 1906.[34] He counselled against 'the absolute preservation of game', which was causing devastation of villages and crops. Elephants, hippos, buffaloes and pigs were particularly destructive, and the reserves had to be reduced to practical dimensions. It was in his view impossible for Uganda to follow the East African Protectorate in introducing a 30 lb minimum tusk size. In 1908 the Governor of Uganda, Sir Hesketh Bell, removed buffalo from the list of protected game, not only because hundreds of acres of gardens had been destroyed, but also because of loss of human life.[35] Fourteen people had been killed by buffaloes in the kingdom of Buganda, and no fewer than eighty-seven in Toro. By 1909 the Governor was protesting that in Toro, where the game reserves still constituted half the kingdom and the whole area was thickly populated, Africans were being driven out.[36] Nevertheless the society continued its pressure for the raising of the 11 lb tusk limit in Uganda and supported protests, made in an anonymous article in *The Times*, that Ugandan chiefs should not be granted licences to shoot game.[37]

If the society was anxious to promote a policy of preservation for elite access, it was prepared to be sympathetic towards the demands of white settlers, although distinctions were drawn between different types of settler. The Colonial Office had been alive to the needs of settlers since at least 1903. Despite his alleged uninterest in game, Sir Charles Eliot had noticed that settlers could shoot large numbers of antelope under licence. He decided to restrict them to a maximum of ten of each species per annum.[38] Lansdowne, the Foreign Secretay, refused to allow this on the grounds that it would 'press heavily on particular settlers' who had a 'need to shoot game for food'. In 1906 Arthur Blayney Percival, the game ranger, noted that most settlers were 'of a good class' and that they wanted to found a game preservation society of their own. 'Only settlers from South Africa' shoot everything.[39] The hunter and deputy commissioner Frederick Jackson reported that the settlers in the Nyando Valley were shooting indiscriminately. 'These people are simply squatting on their land with no intention of attempting to improve it.'[40] They were, in short, assetstripping before seeking an opportunity to sell at an enhanced price. Boer immigrants were 'promiscuous hunters' and needed to be restrained, particularly those who entered the southern reserve from German territory.

In July 1908 Jackson met representatives of the Kenya Colonists' Association and came to an agreement with them about access to game.[41] There was to be more equality in hunting privileges between officials and settlers. The northern reserve was to be reduced to a reasonable size, and the game reserves were to be recognised as sanctuaries in exchange for the principle that 'outside the reserve the presence of game cannot be allowed to interfere with the economic development of the country'. This 'concordat' with the settlers was welcomed by the society. The settler policy contrasts with the approach of Percival and Jackson to African hunting.[42] It was agreed that the Ndorobo had to hunt while their subsistence depended on it, but that they could be gradually persuaded to become herders for others. The Kamba, on the other hand, had no need to hunt and should be prohibited from using their former hunting grounds on the Athi Plains. Farther west, Kavirondo hunting was being eliminated by the

arrival of settlers in the hunting areas. The society's avowed policy
was to eliminate African hunting.

By the First World War the tsetse debate had to a certain extent
checked the influence of the society, and the war itself put an end to
its lobbying and to international collaboration. It is noticeable that
after the war less deference was shown to the society in the Colonial
Office, where deputations tended to be received by under-secretaries.[43]
Moreover, by that time the society's interests had been extended to
Asia, and many new issues were raised, removing some of the attention
from Africa. The society found itself lobbying the India Office and,
later, the new Dominions Office, where it could easily be fobbed off
with the demands of dominion nationalism. Nevertheless the membership of the society grew immensely in the post-war period and it maintained its close connections with the hunting aristocratic elite.
Moreover it played a central role in the reappearance of the international conservation movement. It was not until 1931 that an International Conference for the Protection of Nature was held in Paris.
The British delegation introduced a draft Convention for the Protection
of African Fauna and Flora and invited the colonial powers to another
London conference. It was held at the House of Lords between 31
October and 8 November 1933.[44] It was a much larger conference than
that of 1900, with representatives from the Union of South Africa,
Belgium, Egypt, Spain, Abyssinia, France, Italy, Portugal, the Anglo-
Egyptian Sudan and the United Kingdom, as well as observers from
the USA and India. The British delegation of five was headed by the
Earl of Onslow, president of the society, and included a former Governor of Uganda, the Governor of Sierra Leone, and representatives of
the Colonial Office and of Southern Rhodesia. It was supported by no
fewer than fourteen advisers, including a game ranger from Uganda,
an honorary game warden from Kenya, and others with a technical
interest in game. Yet again it appears that the conservation lobby was
making policy.

The Convention reaffirmed the provisions of 1900, but introduced
some important new principles and suggested regulations. Notice was
taken of new technology. It was proposed that the hunting of animals
from motor cars, motor boats and aircraft should be banned. The exclusion of trains from the list is perhaps an indication of the extent to
which game, frequently persecuted by rail travellers, had retreated
from lines of rail. (In fact a specific prohibition of shooting from trains
and railway stations had been introduced in Kenya in 1902.) Night
shooting (rendered easy by the use of flares, electric torches and lamps

which attracted game) ought to be banned, as were poison, explosives, gins, traps, snares, set guns and missiles containing explosives. This suggested a much more comprehensive banning of African techniques than in 1900. The export and sale of all trophies, tusks and rhino horns should be controlled and regulated. The 1933 Convention greatly reduced the complexities of scheduling animals. In place of five categories in 1900 there were only two – class A, which required special protection, and class B, which needed some protection. The concept of vermin and its concomitant, the killing of 'harmful' or unattractive animals at will, was removed.

But by far the most important development of the 1933 document was the provisions for the establishment of national parks. It called upon governments to explore the possibility of establishing such parks or at least setting aside areas for future conversion into full park status. They should be under public control, with boundaries that could be changed only by legislative action. All white and African settlements within them should be regulated so as to give rise to minimum disturbance to animals; they should be areas large enough to permit migration; and they should be surrounded by natural reserves or intermediate zones as a buffer between them and territory occupied by humans. The signatories of the Convention also agreed that all game regulations and provisions for the estblishment of national parks should be communicated to the British government, which in turn would inform all the other parties. For the first time suggestions were also made about the preservation of flora. Finally it was agreed that there should be periodic conferences, the next to be held in four years' time. Again it would be organised by the British, and it was suggested that topics for discussion might include the treatment of persistent offenders against the game laws and the problems of contagious diseases. Another conference was in fact held in 1938, but the conservation movement was about to be overwhelmed by another international crisis.

The international agreement of 1933, like that of 1900, was ratified by very few of the attending parties, but its provisions were incorporated into legislation in British colonial territories. Complex and lengthy Acts were framed in the 1930s to bring together the growing corpus of conservationist ideas. Many of the old provisions were extended to include the prohibitions on hunting from motor vehicles, launches and planes. Dealing in trophies and skins was banned in most colonies, as was night shooting, with or without lights. The sale of dried meat, or biltong, was declared illegal in some places, and increasing restrictions were placed on the use of dogs, although, as always,

[ 217 ]

private land was exempt. Some laws prohibited 'unnecessary or undue suffering' and wasteful killing. The unrestricted shooting of vermin was no longer permitted and some at least of the 'harmful' animals, like lions, appeared on the lists of species which could be shot only in limited numbers. Hyenas and hunting dogs, however, often remained beyond the pale. The ban on all African hunting methods was tightened up. It is clear from several of these provisions that the legislation had taken on a 'prevention of cruelty' aspect as well as the purpose of game preservation. C. R. S. Pitman, the Uganda game warden and one of the observers at the conference, referred in his books to the 'wickedly cruel' character of African hunting methods.[45] Another sign of the times was the introduction of a 'photographic permit', authorising the holder to 'hunt' animals for photographic purposes provided no molestation occurred. All the legislation ended with the scheduling, by complex boundary descriptions, of game reserves.

How effective was all this activity? The answer needs to be divided into two parts: effectiveness in curbing white hunting and in controlling African 'poaching'. The legislation was exceptionally complex, which cannot have facilitated its enforcement. Summaries of the game laws were invariably issued with licences, but once the hunter reached a relatively remote area he could easily become a law unto himself. Moreover, impecunious colonial administrations could not afford adequate numbers of enforcement officers. The full panoply of wardens, rangers and game police began to appear only in the 1920s, and their work was of course primarily restricted to the reserves. Elsewhere hard-pressed district administrations and police were expected to enforce game laws which they often broke themselves. The despatches of commissioners and governors often complained of the impossibility of enforcing regulations without adequate game departments. It was, for example, exceptionally difficult in Somaliland, where the commissioner proposed an expenditure of £500 on a game department in 1905.[46] The detailed numbers of each species permitted under the regulations and the requirement to keep a record of kills placed a premium on the 'sportsmanship' of hunters. While it was possible to check the number of trophies exported, that was of course no true indication of the number of animals that might have been shot for meat or rejected as inadequate, their remains left in the wild.

Moreover, officials and governors granted exemptions from game laws to distinguished visiting parties, which hardly set a good example to the rest. As we have seen, one such exemption was given to the party of Theodore Roosevelt by the Acting Governor of Kenya,

Frederick Jackson, when the ex-president visited the colony in 1909. News of the destructive activities of the party soon reached Jackson (and were confirmed by Roosevelt's staggering figures of his kills offered in his book *African Game Trails*, published in 1910). Jackson subsequently repudiated Roosevelt's activities, but it was but the most notable example of the waiving of the game laws.[47] Jackson gave other examples of aristocrats and army officers who tried to secure concessions for themselves; when refused they made every effort to conceal breaches of regulations and export illicit trophies for their collections. This is indicative of the pressures set up by the hunting and collecting cult.

There are other indicators. Prosecutions of Europeans for infringements were rare, despite the fact that the legislation often enacted that one witness was enough and that half the fine should be paid to the informer. A number of secondary sources indicate that breaking the laws was widespread and guidebooks encouraged intending visitors by suggesting that game laws were difficult to enforce, particularly in remote districts. When annual returns of licences and game killed were submitted to the Colonial Office from 1905, very few convictions for infringements were recorded, seldom more than six or seven in most colonies, and fewer still led to fines. Only Kenya, by a long way the most popular hunting territory, produced a significant revenue from fines. There were forty-five convictions in 1905, and similar figures were returned for ensuing years.[48] A fair proportion were of Africans, and it is also clear that tourists were prosecuted more readily than public officers or settlers.

It is doubtful if close seasons were particularly effective in protecting game. Close seasons generaly coincided with wet seasons, when it was difficult for hunters to move about and when the animals would be widely dispersed. In any case landowners and other settler occupiers of land had comprehensive powers over game that entered their lands. The repeated tightening of the game laws is to some extent an indication of the difficulty of enforcing them. Moreover the legislation was applied to very different situations. In many parts of East and Central Africa it turned relative abundance into over-abundance, while in southern Africa the laws were the proverbial 'too little too late'. The quagga was protected in the Cape Colony and other southern African territories when it was already extinct. Indeed, the flurry of legislation in both British colonies and Boer republics in the late nineteenth century came when little game was left except in the remoter fastnesses of the low-veld. As we have seen, migrating springbok were specifically

[ *219* ]

excluded from the Cape Colony game law of 1886, no doubt to assuage the fears of farmers. They were subjected to massive depredations in the ensuing years. It is ironic that the animal which became the emblem of the Union of South Africa was in fact so little protected.

African hunting was inhibited in a number of ways. The removal of African guns and other weapons, particularly in the aftermath of revolt or 'pacification' campaigns, was more effective than game legislation. The general retreat of game reduced access, since Africans lacked the mobility of Europeans. As the district officials were primarily concerned with the administration of Africans, and as they generally accepted the distinctions drawn by the game laws between 'cruel' African hunting methods and the allegedly clean kills of European rifles, they devoted a great deal more attention to African 'poaching' than to European offences against the game laws. In remote areas and on the edges of game reserves, however, African hunting continued on a relatively large scale. Game laws were often no more effective in stamping out subsistence hunting than they had been in Britain over many centuries. The possession or sale of traps and snares was illegal in many colonies, but they were relatively easy to make and easier to hide. More visible techniques like game pits could be stamped out more readily.[49] Muskets and other weapons remained in African hands and were hidden in hollow trees or in caves. So long as villagers were careful to leave incriminating horns and skins in the bush, meat could still be procured where game survived. In the low-veld of the Transvaal a seasonal system had established itself by the late nineteenth century and survived into the early decades of the game reserve era.[50] Boer farmers took their flocks down to low-veld grazing in the dry and healthy winter season. They hunted at will while they were there. In the wet and malarial season they retreated to the high-veld and their place was taken by African hunters who moved in from adjacent lands or from Portuguese East Africa. In many places, as this indicates, precautions against poaching were only as effective as border control. The northern areas of Kenya and Uganda were essentially hunting frontiers, and administrations often failed to control the incursions of ivory poachers and raiders.[51] In the 1930s, for example, thirty-five game scouts patrolled 80,000 square miles of the Kenyan frontier, including the Northern Reserve. A complex network of hunters and traders continued to exist, and the Somali who made incursions across the border may well have seen hunting as an act of resistance to colonial rule. It was this activity, together with the work of highly armed gangs after the Second World War, that helped to give poaching its evil connotations.[52]

There is a good deal of evidence to suggest that Africans in many places succeeded in avoiding game legislation. In the early years of the century Blayney Percival saw the Kamba using bows and arrows, and creating a hedged game drive, between the Tsavo river and the Serengeti plains.[53] The Kenyan game department may have frustrated African hunting in the more frequented areas but it was powerless in remoter regions. The Kamba of Kitui, for example, continued to hunt throughout the colonial period, and Europeans officials and their African auxiliaries could do little about it.[54] The Kitui District covered 18,281 square miles and was administered by no more than three Europeans and a body of African police ranging from fifteen to forty-six at different times. In addition, some of the game department's scouts, who were very unpopular with the local people and were often themselves implicated in poaching, were deployed in the area from time time. When rains failed, inducing famine, as in 1934-35 and 1940, the number of poison dealers in the area grew and the Kamba stepped up their hunting. They were principally concerned to secure saleable products like ivory and rhino horn, but such hunting would also have produced large quantities of meat.

In Tanzania the Nyamwezi were still hunting very effectively, as we saw in chapter three, as late as the 1920s, and the 1934 crop failure drove Africans in many parts of East Africa back to the game.[55] Among the Kimbu in central Tanzania the positioning of villages became partly conditioned by the attentions of the game department. The Kimbu also developed a number of techniques, including a modification of the layout of their roadside villages, in order to be able to slip into the forest to hunt and outwit the authorities. A few Kimbu took out licences to hunt elephant, but most continued to hunt illicitly.[56]

The picture is, therefore, a complex one. It is clear that game legislation did little to restrain the depredations of well armed white hunters. Anxieties arising from the experience of southern Africa were translated to other territories where the situation was different and the dangers to game stocks were greatly exaggerated. African 'poaching' continued where it could, but in some places, notably Nyasaland, the game laws were credited with inhibiting traditional hunting thus leading to an increase in the game population. Clearly there are three variables: the continuing existence of game in close proximity to human settlement, the effectiveness of white administration in specific areas, and the changes in game distribution as the period of colonial rule advanced. The locality of game stocks, for example, might be closely related to the level of white settlement and the degree to which land apportionment among whites, blacks and animals was developed and effectively administered. Generally the greater the extent of white settlement the more complete would be the frustration of African hunting.

Game legislation was, however, seldom as effective as its framers hoped it would be. Its objectives were often thwarted by its very complexity, and there were never sufficient resources to fund adequate policing. Nevertheless the progressive separation of human and animal settlement did take place in most colonies. Barbed wire around farms in settler colonies and the war waged by white farmers upon carnivores which attacked their stock and herbivores that caused havoc among their crops helped to drive animals to remoter regions. The developing over population and over stocking of the reserves set aside for African settlement had the same effect. The establishment of game reserves and later national parks confirmed this separation of human and animal zones by the creation of internal frontiers. This was the second and more effective level of game preservation and it is to this that we must now turn.

## Notes

1 Convention for the Preservation of Wild Animals, Birds and Fish in Africa, signed in London, 19 May 1900, Cd 101, lvi, 825. Agreement for the Protection of the Fauna and Flora of Africa (November 1933) 1932-33, Cmd 4453, xxxviii, 1.

2 Dutch regulations distinguished between protected animals and vermin. Hippos were protected within twenty-five years of the establishment of the Dutch settlement, while a high bounty (the equivalent of £5.4s 2d) was offered for lions, which were causing excessive cattle deaths. There were several efforts in the eighteenth century to introduce a close season, but they generally failed.

3 Cape of Good Hope, Proclamation by His Excellency General the Right Honourable Lord Charles Somerset, 21 March 1822.

4 Government advertisement on elephants, 23 August 1822.

5 Cape of Good Hope, Proclamation by HE General the Rt Hon. Lord Charles Somerset, 14 March 1823.

6 Cape of Good Hope, Act for the Better Preservation of Game, No. 36, 6 July 1886.

7 Natal, No. 28, 1890; No. 16, 1891; No. 8, 1906.

8 Marquess of Salisbury to Mr A. Hardinge (East Africa Protectorate) and Mr Berkeley (Uganda), 27 May 1896. Correspondence relating to the Preservation of Wild Animals in Africa, Cd 3189 (1906), lxxix, p. 25. Subsequent references (except where otherwise specified) are to this Blue Book.

9 Mr Gosselin (Berlin) to the Marquess of Salisbury, 29 June 1896.

10 Joseph Chamberlain to Marquess of Salisbury, 15 August 1896.

11 Memorandum on the Game Laws of Zululand, 29 August 1896.

12 Memorandum by Sir John Kirk, 31 July 1897.

13 Acting Commissioner Sharpe to Marquess of Salisbury, 9 September 1896.

14 F. C. Selous to Foreign Office, 15 August 1897.

15 Major von Wissmann to Baron Richthofen, 2 April 1897.

16 Lord Delamere to Sir Clement Hill, 13 August 1900.

17 Memorandum on the game laws of Ukamba Province, 6 June 1900.

18 Correspondence relating to the Preservation of Wild Animals in Africa, Cd 4472 (1909), lix, 635. Further Correspondence relating to the Preservation of Wild Animals in Africa, Cd 5136 (1910), lxvi, 253; Cd 5775 (1911), lii, 521; Cd 6671 (1913), xlv, 759.
19 E. Ray Lankaster to Sir Clement Hill, 11 January 1900.
20 Memorandum on the extermination of American bison, n.d. and no provenance.
21 See note 11.
22 Hardinge wrote to all his opposite numbers in August 1900. Their responses and further monitoring of game laws and their effects appear in successive Command Papers.
23 Many of the draft game laws were printed in the Command Papers and were sent to interested parties like the Society for the Preservation of the Wild Fauna of the Empire, the British Museum (Natural History) and the Zoological Society of London. I am grateful to the Bodleian Law Library, Oxford, for help in surveying the statute laws of almost all the British African colonies.
24 Details on the foundation of the society can be found in the early issues of the *Journal of the Society for the Preservation of the Wild Fauna of the Empire*. Since 'Wild' was subsequently dropped, the abbreviations SPFE and *JSPFE* will be used.
25 Minutes of a deputation from the SPFE to Lyttelton, 2 February 1905.
26 Sir Alfred Pease, *Half a Century of Sport*, London, 1932, pp. 163-4.
27 Minutes of a deputation from the SPFE to the Earl of Elgin, 15 June 1906.
28 Minutes of a deputation from the SPFE to the Earl of Crewe, 26 February 1909, Cd 4472.
29 Lyttelton wrote to all the High Commissioners and Governors of the West African, East African and southern African colonies in the months following the visit of the society's deputation to the Colonial Office. The Governors' despatches in reply to Lyttelton's requests for information were sent to the SPFE, the British Museum (Natural History) and the Zoological Society of London in February 1906.
30 SPFE to CO, 9 June 1906.
31 Acting Governor Thorburn to Lyttelton, 30 November 1905.
32 Sir G. C. Denton to Lyttelton, 22 June 1905.
33 Commissioner J. Hayes Sadler to Lyttelton, 11 November 1905.
34 Acting Commissioner Wilson to Elgin, 4 April 1906.
35 Bell to Elgin, 21 January 1908, Cd 4472.
36 Bell to Crewe, 22 April 1909. Sir Alfred Sharpe of Nyasaland also commented on excessive numbers of elephants in the central Angoniland district. He himself had beeen trying to control numbers by killing a few. Sharpe to Crewe, 30 April 1909, Cd 4472.
37 SPFE to CO, 30 December 1910, Cd 5775.
38 Eliot to Lansdowne, 7 May 1903. Lansdowne to Eliot, 11 June 1903.
39 Report by Percival, enclosed in Sadler to Elgin, 28 September 1906.
40 Memorandum by Jackson on Percival's report.
41 Memorandum by Jackson, 11 August 1908, enclosed in Sadler to Crewe, 29 August 1908, Cd 4472.
42 Memorandum by Jackson and Percival on natives and game, enclosed in Sadler to Elgin, 6 March 1906.
43 Deputations visited and papers were submitted to the Colonial, Foreign and India Offices in 1919-21, *JSPFE*, New Series, 1 (1921), pp. 25-8.
44 See note 1.
45 C. R. S. Pitman, *A Game Warden among his Charges*, London, 1931, p. xv.
46 Commissioneer E. J. E. Swayne to Lyttelton, 221 November 1905.
47 Frederick Jackson, *Early Days in East Africa*, London, 1969, p. 381.
48 Jackson to Lyttelton, 25 August 1905. There were only four convictions in Uganda that year. Wilson to Elgin, 4 April 1906.
49 F. H. Melland suggested that in over thirty years' experience in Central Africa from 1901 he never saw a freshly dug game pit. Quoted in Stuart A. Marks, *Large Mammals and a Brave People*, Seattle, Wash., 1976, p. 73.
50 J. Stevenson-Hamilton, *South African Eden*, London, 1937, pp. 44-8, 134.

51 P. J. Dalleo, 'The Somali role in organised ivory poaching in north-eastern Kenya, *c.* 1909-39', *Int. J. Af. Hist Studs.*, 12 (1979), pp. 472-83.
52 For an organised poaching ring of the 1950s see Anthony Cullen and Sydney Downey, *Saving the Game*, London, 1960.
53 Memorandum on natives and game by A. Blayney Percival, enclosed in Sadler to Elgin, 12 March 1906, Cd 3189.
54 M. L. Stone, 'Organised poaching in Kitui district: a failure in district authority, 1900-60', *Int. J. Af. Hist. Studs.*, 5 (1972), pp. 436-52.
55 *JSPFE* XI (1930), pp. 50-1. *JSPFE*, XXVII (1936), p. 36.
56 Aylward Shorter, *Chiefship in Western Tanzania*, Oxford, 1972, pp. 56-8, 63.

# CHAPTER NINE

# Reserves and the tsetse controversy

It was the realisation that game legislation was at most only a partial success that led the conservation lobby to demand the accelerated demarcation of game reserves and tighter restrictions on hunting within them. If close seasons and limits upon numbers of kills did not work, then closed lands might. It was easier to police specific tracts of territory if specialised staffs could be appointed to manage the game and control access to it. These objectives were enshrined in the international agreement of 1933 and appeared in the colonial legislation of the later 1930s. Although pressure was now mounting to give reserves statutory protection, to tranform them from proclaimed territory to national parks in perpetuity, the reserves themselves were not a new policy. They had constituted the second great thrust of the preservation programme from the turn of the century, even though their establishment had been more half-hearted than the enactment of game legislation.

Reserves had, however, emerged out of that very legislation. The right of governors to proclaim them was established in colonial legislation from 1900 onwards (although some reserves had been proclaimed earlier), and it is also from that date that we encounter official recognition of the office of game ranger. As it happens, many of the early wardens, who were generally military men, often ex-hunters, and amateur natural history enthusiasts, were reasonably literate individuals. They were eager to record their experiences in establishing the new game reserves, create some propaganda for them, or alternatively publish their natural history observations arising out of their duties. James Stevenson-Hamilton, the first warden of the Sabi game reserve – later the Kruger National Park – in the Transvaal, offers us the most complete and intelligent account of the development of a reserve.[1] One of his original staff, Harry Wolhuter, wrote some rambling reminiscences of his experiences in the park.[2] In East Africa, Arthur Blayney Percival, the first game ranger appointed by the East Africa Protectorate (later Kenya) published two volumes on the natural history of the reserves that contain some information on their administrative history.[3] Charles Pitman, the first game warden in Uganda, produced two books of reminiscences, although in them the natural history predominates.[4] His successor, Bruce Kinloch, also wrote a work on the national parks.[5] An attempt was later made to write a history of the Ugandan national parks.[6] This was commissioned by their director in the late 1960s and was to have been published by, or with a subsidy from, the Uganda government. The *coup* of Idi Amin intervened, and though the book was written and submitted to the Government Printer, it was never published. The author was Rennie Bere, an ex-provincial commissioner in Uganda who was a trustee of the newly created national parks in the 1950s, and fortunately he deposited a typescript in the Royal Commonwealth Society Library. Ian Parker, a member of the Kenya game department for some years after 1956, published a work on ivory which contains interesting information on the history of Kenya's game policy.[7]

It is possible to reconstruct the history of many of Africa's game reserves from these books, together with official sources and the legislation by which they were established. A great deal more work remains to be done in this area, but what follows is offered as a preliminary survey of the reserves and (in the next chapter) of the national parks that emerged out of them.

The reserves did not enjoy such a secure history as game legislation. The conservationist lobby was committed to them, as were many of the early naturalist and hunting governors, but, as we have seen, some British officials were sceptical about their cost and effectiveness. Both the Convention of 1900 and the agreement of 1933 recommended their adoption, but they faced two great hazards – first, the opposition of settlers, who saw them as taking up usable land, harbouring predators and encouraging the spread of diseases from wild to domestic stock; second, the combination of missionaries (influenced by medical men) and the scientific lobby in settler territories which saw the reserves and protection of wild animals as a barrier to tsetse control. The first 'wave' of reserves was attacked by both these pressure groups, and their opposition occasionally found parliamentary expression in Britain. The reserves were constitutionally highly vulnerable, since they were established by governor's proclamation or ministerial decree delegated under the game legislation. They could be revoked, and sometimes were, equally easily. It is notable, however, that neither metropolitan scientists nor colonial researchers in non-settler territories subscribed to the anti-reserve standpoint.

*Reserves in Southern Africa.* It is one of the great ironies of the white exploitation of animals in Africa that the first moves towards formal preservation through reserves came from a Boer republic. The Boers have frequently been depicted as the main destroyers of game in the period before 1880. There can be no doubt that they shot game relatively indiscriminately or that it constituted a vital resource and a prime survival system in their expansion in the conquest of the region. Perhaps it was precisely this close relationship that led President Paul Kruger, himself a fervent hunter in his youth, to suggest to the Volksraad in 1884 that if the children of his generation were to see and hunt game some kind of sanctuary was required to protect it.[8] Kruger received no support that year, but in 1889 he caused another resolution to be submitted to the Volksraad proposing that hunting should be

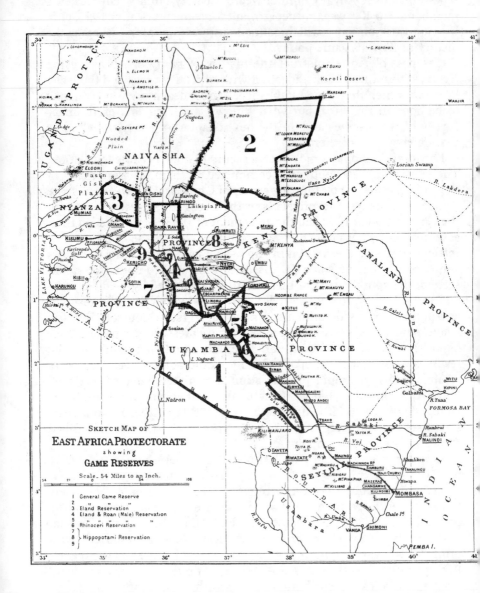

The East Africa Protectorate, showing game reserves

prohibited on some portions of government land to prevent the total extermination of game in the South African Republic. He suggested two areas suitable as reserves, one on the Pongolo river just north of the Zululand border and another between the Zoutpansberg and the Portuguese boundary. This resolution was passed with only two dissenters and was translated into legislation the following year. In 1894 the Pongolo game reserve was proclaimed, followed by two very small reserves near Pretoria in 1895. A ranger, H. F. van Oordt, was appointed, and he devoted his time to destroying domestic dogs and eliminating poachers.[9]

The Sabi reserve, which was to become South Africa's most celebrated wildlife sanctuary, was proclaimed in 1898. These early efforts at conservation were, however, overtaken by the Boer War. Apart from the activities of van Oordt the reserves existed only on paper. During the war, game was killed indiscriminately to feed the troops. An irregular force known as Steinacker's Horse operated in the Sabi area, its eponymous commandant, an eccentric Austrian self-styled baron, acting as a despot over a wide region. Boer commandos also invaded the region, and under the combined ministrations of Steinacker's men, the Boers and African hunters the vast region of the low-veld was virtually denuded of its game. The reserve was reproclaimed in 1902 and James Stevenson-Hamilton was appointed its warden. Interestingly, the reserve was initially established under the authority of the Native Affairs Department and its Secretary, Sir Godfrey Lagden, who was himself a keen big-game hunter. At first Stevenson-Hamilton found very little game to protect. He and his first assistants, notably Harry Wolhuter, decided on a number of policies to help the relict population to recover and to induce animals to cross the border from Portuguese East Africa. They were operating in a relatively barren, poorly watered area covering 1,800 square miles.

There had been a fairly considerable African population in the region, a mixture of Tonga, Venda, and Swazi peoples, but the conditions of the 1890s had caused this population to decline. The successive droughts of that decade had driven people into better-watered areas. Nonetheless Africans remained and had subsisted on game meat. Stevenson-Hamilton estimated at a later date that there were some 450 able-bodied men in the reserve, of whom 150-200 went to work on the mines and elsewhere in white employment, while 150 found work on his reserve staff. He and Wolhuter set out to ensure that, whatever their employment, they would not be hunters.[10] Firearms, assegais, snares and traps were confiscated. Wolhuter describes anti-poaching campaigns, many of them violent and some leading to fatalities. As a result the rangers had to take over all crop protection.

Bushpigs were particularly troublesome, and Wolhuter took to hunting them down with a pack of twenty-five dogs. Stevenson-Hamilton and his staff set out to frustrate animal predators as well as human ones. They believed that lions, leopards and wild dogs had to be reduced before the game could recover. They set about extensive shooting of these animals, wild dogs offering, as Wolhuter put it, particularly good sport.[11] Subsequently a form of distemper – noted also in East Africa – acted as a natural check to the wild dog population, and it must be said that by the 1930s Stevenson-Hamilton had repudiated his policy of culling predators. At the time, however, if fitted perfectly the concept of vermin enshrined in so much game legislation.

Dramatic changes took place in the Sabi game reserve in the years before the First World War. The bush cover returned and the animal population recovered with great vigour. Species that had become rare in the region reappeared, many of them crossing from Portuguese territory. Stevenson-Hamilton even attempted to improve eland stocks by relocating tame eland from Mozambique. Moreover, he progressively increased his own powers.[12] He became a Justice of the Peace in order to administer the game regulations. He acquired from the Native Department the right to act as Native Commissioner for the Africans in the reserve. In the 1920s he even established his authority over Africans in an adjacent native reserve where Africans hunted game that had passed over from the game reserve but was still regarded as part of the protected stock of game.

Nevertheless a number of obstacles stood in the way of the firm establishment of the reserve in perpetuity. In the late nineteenth century the government of the South African Republic had alienated land to settlers, who had soon sold out to Johannesburg mining and land companies. Since these companies had done little to exploit the land, they had acquiesced in its inclusion in the reserve, expecting that its value would increase if game returned and that the reserve would be a purely temporary affair. There were some efforts to begin ranching on some parts of this privately owned land just before the First World War, and it was apparent that this would constitute a serious legal obstacle to the continuation of the reserve. Stevenson-Hamilton discovered that much public opinion saw the reserve as just such a temporary expedient, a means of permitting the game to recover before it could be exploited once more. The scientific lobby, including the Veterinary Department in Pretoria, viewed the recovery of the game with alarm, particularly as it was able to roam freely from Portuguese territory. The game might transmit East Coast fever and rinderpest from East Africa. Even more seriously, it would, in their view, harbour the tsetse fly, encourage its spread, and place domestic stock at risk from nagana (tsetse-transmitted cattle sickness) in all the adjacent areas. Before these risks had been evaluated, however, European graziers prevailed upon the Transvaal to reintroduce the pre-war system whereby they drove their stock to graze on the low-veld in the winter season. In 1910 stockholders were permitted to do this on payment of a £5 grazing fee. These stockholders were difficult to control. They burned the veld, as they had been accustomed to do in the past, to encourage the growth of new grasses, and they hunted at will. There was little that Stevenson-Hamilton or his staff could do about it. A further hazard to the reserve seemed to be the failure to place it under Union jurisdiction in 1910. Stevenson-Hamilton lobbied Smuts, but by an oversight it was omitted from the Union agreement and in consequence remained under Transvaal provincial control.[13]

With the First World War the cause of the reserve seemed to be put back yet further. Half the European staff, including Stevenson-Hamilton himself, left to enlist. Half the African staff were laid off to save money. The administration largely broke down, and both white and African hunting resumed. As demands for grazing and land in the low-veld increased, the Transvaal government appointed a Commission of Enquiry to consider the future of the reserve. The commission sat in 1916- 17 and issued its report in 1918. In the course of its hearings it appears to have been converted to the idea of the reserve, and somewhat unexpectedly recommended that the land should continue to be devoted to the preservation of game. In the years following the war the administration was re-created, again under Stevenson-Hamilton, boundaries were adjusted, and the government took over land which was later to prove useful in an exchange arrangement with the companies that owned land within the reserve. Nevertheless, demands for deproclamation built up in the 1920s. The scientific and farming lobbies ranged themselves against the conservationists, who organised themselves into the Transvaal Game Protection Society and later into the Wild Life Protection Society of South Africa, while members of the Transvaal establishment, attempting to maintain elite 'preservation', tried to secure shooting rights in the reserve. But the reserve had won friends in high places, particularly successive Ministers of Lands, Deneys Reitz and Piet Grobler. The latter, Kruger's great-nephew, was eager to ensure that the former President should be commemorated when the idea was put to him that the Sabi reserve should be converted into the Kruger National Park. The move from reserves to national parks is considered below.

The Cape Colony's hostility to reserves was gradually abandoned. In 1898 Milner reported that proposals to create reserves on the Cape flats and on 200,000 *morgen* (424,000 acres, or 662·5 square miles) of land in Zandveld, Bushmanland, had been abandoned.[14] The same year the Cape government indicated that while in theory it wished to preserve elephants it put the problems of human habitation first. At the time it was estimated that only 175 elephants survived in the Cape, twenty-five in Knysna and 150 in the Addo bush. In 1905 the SPFE protested at a rumour that the Knysna elephants were to be shot out[15], while in 1919 complaints of crop damage led the Cape to decide to exterminate the elephants in the Addo, and 120 were killed before shooting was stopped.[16] Sixteen survived and the area later became a national park. The Cape government continued to believe that game preservation could best be effected by appealing to the sporting instincts of landowners, and reserves continued to enjoy rather chequered fortunes. A game reserve was created in Namaqualand in 1903; the Gordonia game reserve was established in 1907, but was halved in area the following year.[17] Further north, in 1909, the Rustenberg game reserve was founded to protect hartebeest. Stevenson-Hamilton noted its existence (covering a large area) in *Animal Life in Africa* (1912), but it was deproclaimed in 1914 after, it is alleged, the warden had shot most of the animals.[18] The Rustenberg and Addo incidents should not, however, be seen as representing a real check to the idea of reserves. They merely demonstrate the power of white farmers and of hunting rangers to overturn preservation ideas.

From the late 1890s game reserves began to appear in many other parts of Africa, although some British colonial administrations were tardy in establishing them and subsequently hesitan' 'n confirming their continuing existence. A game protection association, the first in Africa, had been founded in Natal in 1883, and it soon pressed for the establishment of reserves. The brief Natal game law of 1891 made no mention of reserves, but four small ones were established in 1897 in a critical year for the fortunes of game. In 1896 rinderpest had ravaged the game population and the reserves had the effect of protecting small surviving herds. These reserves were confirmed under the Natal Act of 1906; the Umfolosi reserve was extended that year and the Giant's Castle, Estcourt, reserve was established in 1907. These reserves were to be at the centre of the tsetse controversy until the elimination of tsetse in the early 1950s. It was in Zululand that Dr (later Sir) David Bruce, an army doctor who subsequently became Surgeon General of the British Army, proved the connection between game animals and tsetse flies in 1894, and the belief that the preservation of game encouraged the survival and spread of tsetse was to inhibit the establishment of reserves elsewhere in southern Africa for several years. It is significant that this connection between the proclamation of game reserves and the expansion of the tsetse was never fully accepted in the East

African colonies. In 1905 the Hlabisa game reserve was proclaimed in Zululand, but abolished only two years later. Hunting regulations were lifted between 1913 and 1916 and large quantities of game were destroyed. The pressures of the SPFE in London, which did not accept the game/tsetse theory, ensured the continuing creation of reserves. The Hlatikulu reserve in southern Swaziland was proclaimed in 1905, while a second was declared in the north of that territory. The latter was on the borders of Mozambique, and it was hoped that animals would populate it from Portuguese territory. In South West Africa the Germans created two reserves in 1907, the Etosha and Namib desert reserves, in areas that had been closed to hunting for some years.

*Reserves in Central Africa.* The British South Africa Company was anxious to raise revenue from hunting tourism and, faced with a relative abundance of game at least in the low-veld areas of Southern Rhodesia and in many parts of Northern Rhodesia, was reluctant to declare reserves. Various suggestions were made by conservationists for establishing protected areas. Some preservationists had a plan to buy land near Salisbury (Harare) in the 1890s to create a private reserve, but they failed to secure the support either of the BSAC or of financial backers.[19] The first reserves in Southern Rhodesia were not to appear until the 1920s and are examined later in the chapter.

The first plan for a reserve in the Victoria Falls area (presumably on the Northern Rhodesian side) was also privately mooted. We know of it from the missionary François Coillard, who expressed concern about the rapid decline of game in a region where Livingstone had seen vast herds. By 1895 the game had almost entirely disappeared from the vicinity of the falls and Coillard blamed African hunters 'who, totally destitute of conscience in this respect, are hastening the extermination of certain species'. In consequence he gave his blessing to game legislation and a reserve:

> It is high time that strict and intelligent laws should protect what survives; and one cannot too highly applaud the project Captain Gibbons is promoting – namely, to convert the neighbourhood of the Victoria Falls into an immense park for the African fauna.[20]

Gibbons had set out to map the entire course of the Zambezi in 1895, but he suffered much from fever and his planned 'park' never materialised.[21]

Nevertheless, game reserves were to appear much earlier in Northern than in Southern Rhodesia. The Mweru Marsh reserve was created in 1899 and gazetted in 1900, the Luangwa appeared in 1904, a small reserve (not quite an 'immense park') on the Victoria Falls in 1907, and the large Kafue in 1908.[22] In 1901, in a rare instance of concern for

[ 233 ]

the effects of a reserve on the African population, Robert Codrington, the administrator of North Eastern Rhodesia, reduced the size of the Mweru Marsh reserve by excluding the populated area on the eastern boundary of Lake Mweru because lions, leopards and hyenas were causing loss of life.[23] These three reserves were confirmed in the Northern Rhodesia game legislation of 1925.

In the adjacent territory, the British Central Africa Protectorate (later Nyasaland), the founding of reserves was greatly encouraged by naturalist governors. Commissioner Harry Johnston proclaimed the Elephant Marsh and Chilwa game reserves as early as 1896, proudly referring to them in his annual reports to the Foreign Office.[24] His successor Alfred Sharpe, a noted hunter, did his best to maintain them, but the Chilwa reserve was abolished in 1902 when it was discovered to contain no game, and the Elephant Marsh suffered the same fate in 1911 under pressure from missionaries and medical men concerned about the spread of tsetse and of sleeping sickness within the territory. However, the much larger Central Angoniland reserve, proclaimed in 1904, survived.

*Tsetse control.* The fate of Elephant Marsh was indicative of the alarm raised by the spread of sleeping sickness and the development of tsetse studies. Since the fate of the tsetse is closely interwoven with conservationist policies, it is necessary to examine the tsetse controversy. The connection between tsetse and game had long been observed. Livingstone, Stanley, Baines and Selous had all noted the conjunction of the two. Livingstone had suggested as early as 1865 that the tsetse would disappear only with the destruction of game. Sir Bartle Frere read a paper on the subject to the Royal Geographical Society in 1880 and on that occasion Sir Thomas Fowell Buxton had similarly argued that tsetse could be driven out only with the departure of big game.[25]

The expansion of the incidence of the fly had been occurring in some areas during the nineteenth century, but it was tremendously accelerated by the sequence of disasters attendant upon the imposition of European rule. In his work on the trypanosomiases in African ecology John Ford argued that the tsetse had long inhabited the no-man's-lands between African States and regions of African settlement.[26] These focal points of infection had been known and avoided; the tsetse had not been permitted to expand because of the density of cultivation, and therefore of bush clearance, the capacity of large herds of cattle to keep bush cover down through grazing, and African hunting practices. Over a period of 2,000 years Africans had thus achieved 'a mobile ecological equilibrium with the wildlife ecostystems and their associated diseases'.[27] But between 1830 and 1870 the expansion of the Ngoni people in the Mfecane had helped to depopulate certain areas of Central and Eastern Africa, thereby encouraging the spread of tsetse. The kings of the Nguni States, notably Lobengula of the Ndebele and Mzila of the Gaza, were, however, well aware of the tsetse fly problem and took steps to counteract it. With the arrival of Europeans a whole series of disasters – rinderpest, smallpox, the plague of jigger fleas, drought, the wars of 'pacification' and finally the First World War – led to the destruction of stock, the failure of harvests, and population collapse on a large scale. Depopulation set in train a disastrous cyclical process, facilitating bush regeneration, which encouraged the spread of the tsetse, which in turn forced more depopulation. The establishment of game reserves particularly in East Africa (detailed below), in areas thus released from human occupation helped to convert grazing grasslands and cultivated areas into regions of untidy thicket, the ideal habitat of the tsetse. As we shall see, the initial colonial response to the crisis exacerbated rather than alleviated the problem.

At first the concern about tsetse and game related entirely to nagana, itself a Zulu word for cattle sickness. The Zulu themselves had no illusions about the relationship between game, tsetse and nagana. In 1892 the magistrate at Mtonjaneni reported that 'the natives attribute the increase of nagana to the increase of large game under the protection afforded by the government'. Nagana had appeared in areas where it had formerly been unknown. In the past the Zulu kings had organised large hunting parties to clear game so that cattle could be introduced. The disease had 'disappeared with the game, but made its appearance again on the return of the game'. By the 1890s concern about the presence of tsetse was growing, because it was a serious impediment to white settlement, inhibiting movement by horses or ox wagons and, of course, preventing stock rearing. In 1894 David Bruce, experimenting in Natal, proved conclusively that the trypanosome of nagana was borne in the blood of certain big-game animals, particularly the larger ungulata. They usually remained uninfected, but acted as a reservoir from which the tsetse could transmit the infection to stock. The human disease, sleeping-sickness, or trypanosomiasis, had been known since the days of the transatlantic slave trade, when it was often called the negro lethargy, but it was not until 1901, when an epidemic broke out in Uganda, that serious notice was taken of it.[28] In 1903 it was discovered that sleeping-sickness, like nagana, was caused by the tsetse. In East Africa the carrier was *Tsetse palpalis*, which injected the *Trypanosoma gambiense*, first identified in West Africa. In 1910 Bruce established in Uganda that antelopes could carry *Trypanosoma gambiense*, but despite this discovery a number of misconceptions about tsetse and sleeping-sickness were to survive for several years. It was thought that man was the principal reservoir of sleeping-sickness and that infection took place by a mechanical process, that is, direct from man to tsetse to man.

Sleeping-sickness broke out in Central Africa, principally in Northern Rhodesia and Nyasaland, between 1908 and 1910.[29] In the latter year two researchers from the Liverpool School of Tropical Medicine, Stephens and Fantham, identified a new trypanosoma, which they named *rhodesiense*, and which was transmitted by the tsetse *Glossina morsitans*. The British South Africa Company appointed two entomologists, Kinghorn and Yorke, to a sleeping sickness commission to investigate the problem in Northern Rhodesia. It reported in 1912 and confirmed that game blood was the principal reservoir of *T. rhodesiense*, that tsetse was primarily dependent on certain types of game, and suggested that only a policy of culling could drive the tsetse back and prevent sleeping sickness. In 1911 the Colonial Office appointed a commission, headed by Sir David Bruce and supervised by the Royal Society, to study tsetse and sleeping-sickness in Nyasaland.[30] It was given three years to report and a budget of £3,000 per year. Bruce confirmed his previous results and took them a stage further. He suggested that *T. brucei*, which produced nagana, and *T. rhodesiense* were one and the same. He also supported a policy of culling and identified game preservation as a reason for the spread of tsetse and sleeping-sickness. Moreover, by this time it had been established that trypanosomes were transmitted biologically, that is, they had to multiply and develop within the body of the tsetse before they could be passed into the blood of a new victim. It was also discovered that the tsetse remained infected throughout its entire life span of several months rather than for a few days, as previously thought.

Scholarship, however, remained divided. German scholars disputed Bruce's findings, denying that *T. brucei* and *T. rhodesiense* were related, and persisted in identifying man as a more important reservoir than game. E. A. Minchin, Professor of Protozoology in the University of London, denied any connection between sleeping-sickness and big game.[31] Dr May, the Medical Officer of Northern Rhodesia, continued to insist, despite the findings of Kingman and Yorke, that even in Central Africa man was the principal reservior, a view long held in East Africa.[32] E. E. Austen of the Natural History Museum (Keeper of Entomology from 1927) denied that the tsetse followed game:[33] In his view tsetse was restricted to particular habitats, outside which they could not survive, and these could in consequence be denuded of human population and left to the game. Austen's arguments seemed to deny the possibility of the ebb and flow of tsetse and were a support to both the notion of game reserves in uninhabited areas and the policy of clearance of the human population. Moreover, he and several other scholars perpetuated the idea that there was a real distinction between the East and Central African situations. It comes as no surprise to find that Austen was a member of the SPFE, was described as a passable shot and was also a member of the Museum Rifle Club.

In fact the policy of human evacuation was pursued with disastrous consequences in Uganda. From 1907 24,000 peoples were moved from the shores of Lake Victoria and thousands more were cleared out of the Budonga game reserve on the Nile.[34] It was thought that the infection would be eradicated by removing the human reservoir and permitting the repopulation of the areas at some future date. In fact the absence of cultivation encouraged bush cover, the growth of animal numbers and a tremendous increase in the fly. Moreover, it soon became apparent that East Africa was afflicted with the *Glossina morsitans*. Two colonial authorities, that of Natal and the BSAC administration in Southern Rhodesia, pursued the opposite policy, the extermination of game in infected areas. Both were prompted by an expanding and land-hungry settler population eager to invade tsetse-infected areas. In each case the policy was designed to eradicate nagana rather than human sleeping-sickness. Rigorous game control was begun in Southern Rhodesia in 1901, when free shooting was permitted in the Hartley district for three months.[35] The game laws were suspended for large areas between 1905 and 1908 and again between 1910 and 1915.

Many hunters and conservationists, including those in the SPFE (aided by members of the staff of the Natural History Museum) kept up a constant campaign against this tsetse policy. The society held public meetings and memorialised on the subject. Its journal repeatedly attacked the notion of tsetse control by game extermination, and its representatives protested to the Colonial Office. These protests began in 1907, when the society attacked the BSAC's 'unscientific decision' to suspend the game regulations in an area 'twice as big as Wales', thereby unjustly condemning game because of tsetse.[36] Harry Johnston, Alfred Sharpe and E. E. Austen of the Natural History Museum continued to question tsetse control by game culling over the succeeding years. The BSAC responded vigorously to this attack, citing all the known authorities on the tsetse and renewing its adherence to the 'avowed policy' of the government (of Southern Rhodesia) 'to allow no sentimental considerations with regard to big game preservation to interfere unduly with the crusade to which it is committed against the tsetse fly'.[37]

Soon the company had some unexpected allies. The various missionary societies in Nyasaland became alarmed at the spread of the tsetse and the increased incidence of sleeping-sickness. They pinned the blame firmly on the colonial policies of game preservation. A medical missionary, Dr George Prentice, sent a series of memoranda to the Governor of Nyasaland and the Colonial Office, pillorying the game regulations:

> In all my travels in North Eastern Rhodesia and in Nyasaland I have never seen tsetse whose presence could not be accounted for by the presence of game . . . Further, though I need not now state all the arguments for and against my view, my honest conviction is that the presence and increase of game is entirely responsible for the presence and increase of tsetse, and that our game regulations are mainly, if not wholly, responsible for the increase of game. I hold that those who are responsible for the game laws are responsible for the presence of tsetse, and that the victims of trypanosomiasis are martyrs to the foolish policy of game protection. Any official, high or low, or any member of the Society for the Preservation of the Fauna of the Empire, who, in the face of the known facts, asserts the contrary, may prove the sincerity of his assertion by allowing us to experiment upon him with our local forms of tsetse.[38]

Later the same year eight missions operating in Nyasaland submitted a paper to the Colonial Office, and on 23 November 1911 a sizeable deputation met the Secretary of State, Lewis Harcourt.[39] Prentice was one of the representatives of the United Free Church of Scotland Livingstonia mission on the delegation, which included several of the great names of mission work in Nyasaland. It is quite clear that in their eyes the prime demon was game. The Rev. Dr Alexander Hetherwick, for example, argued that in the past, when he had first entered the country, Africans had kept the vicinity of their villages clear by destroying game. Then they were prevented from doing so by the colonial authorities. The realisation was only dawning of 'the enormity of what we have done'. Reserves had been established in populous districts and 'the balance of nature has been upset'. The government would not be justified in continuing its present policy on game. The Rev. Dr Emslie took up the cry. He had been in Nyasaland for twenty-seven years and also remembered the days before the balance of nature was upset. The missionaries proposed that Africans should be permitted to bear arms and that 'their ancient hunting rights' should be restored.

Missionary views were soon under attack. Arthur Bagshawe of the Sleeping Sickness Bureau opposed the arming of Africans and the concept of 'ancient hunting rights', while Governor Manning of Nyasaland saw the missionaries' suggestion as an 'absurdity'.[40] Still, the SPFE seems to have been less welcome at the Colonial Office and ceased to have such ready access to Colonial Secretary. The command papers have a curious symmetry about them – at first entirely about preservation, punctuated by deputations from the SPFE, later mainly about tsetse, with many representations against game protection.

Bowing to this missionary pressure, the Colonial Office established an interdepartmental committee on sleeping-sickness which took evidence from a large number of witnesses, including colonial governors, big-game hunters, as well as medical and scientific authorities, and reported in 1914.[41] It heard Bruce's evidence, although he had not yet finally published the results of his Nyasaland research. The report of the committee was to add to the confusion and disarray in tsetse studies and nagana and sleeping-sickness control. Four of the members of the committee belonged to the SPFE, one of them being Edward North Buxton, the chairman of the society. It sought refuge in the scholarly disagreements and declined to come to any firm conclusions. It refused to sanction a game clearance experiment on the grounds that there were too many variables in the proposed locations. It recommended that game reserves should be protected and concluded that the shooting of game was not justified. There was, moreover, one large inconsistency in its conclusions. It was confident of only one thing, that the advance of cultivation killed the fly. Yet it suggested that the movement of people from infected zones was preferable to the culling of game. It is significant that two MPs who were members of the committee, J. Duncan Miller and W. A. Chapple, issued a minority report asserting in forceful language dissent from the main conclusions of the game lobby and arguing for suspensions of the game laws, 'preventive operations' (presumably shooting) and the removal of restrictions on native hunting.

Before the committee reported, the Southern Rhodesian government's entomologist, Rupert Jack, published a justification of game destruction in tsetse-infected regions. He presented four pieces of evidence 'in favour of the necessity of big game to the tsetse in Southern Rhodesia and adjacent territory':

1. Tsetse retired before the advance of civilisation in the Transvaal, the only known modification of conditions being the destruction of the game.

2. Tsetse disappeared from large tracts of country immediately after the rinderpest epizootic in 1896.

3. Tsetse had increased and spread since the rinderpest only in those parts of Southern Rhodesia where big game had increased.

4. Tsetse had greatly decreased of late years in the Hartley district in those parts where the big game had been most effectively destroyed or driven away.[42]

Sir David Bruce was as uncompromising as Jack. In 1915 he argued that the extermination of wild game should be vigorously undertaken in endemic areas. 'It would be as reasonable,' he wrote 'to allow mad dogs to live and be protected by law in our English towns and villages. Not only should all game laws restricting their destruction on fly country be removed, but active measures should, if feasible, be taken for their early and complete blotting out.'[43] Bruce's achievements in tsetse research were remarkable and have largely withstood the test of time. Above all, he recognised the trap into which many of his scientific contemporaries fell, namely an excessive desire, born of the current obsession with classification, to subdivide tsetse and trypanosomes and identify different diseases and types of transmisison, distinctions which were often illusory and caused much confusion to tsetse research and policies adopted to deal with outbreaks of nagana and sleeping-sickness. But Bruce's research and his uncompromising views on game were at odds with the conservationist lobby and the report of the 1914 committee. Despite his distinction, his advice was ignored and colonial policies remained confused. There can be few better illustrations of the power of the SPFE.

Southern Rhodesia was, however, a different case. The Colonial Office maintained only indirect control over it, and the SPFE, despite much agitation, failed to influence its settler-dominated policies. Jack's interpretation of the historical evidence and his estimation of the initial success of the game elimination programme inflenced policy in Southern Rhodesia until the 1960s.[44] However much the conservationists railed at game destruction, the territory pursued a consistent and generally effective policy, eliminating tsetse from a larger area and at a faster rate than any other colony. Moreover, game stocks are more secure in Zimbabwe today than in many other African countries. But it should not be forgotten that it was nagana in settler cattle that prompted more vigorous action than sleeping-sickness in humans when those humans were generally Africans. It should also be remembered that the expansion of tsetse in Southern Rhodesia had been helped by the maintenance of large tracts of empty land in the hands of absentee landowners, companies and individuals, and Europeans were often able to use African lands as a peripheral buffer against tsetse encroachment.

In 1925 22,000 square miles of Southern Rhodesia were 'fly'- infested. As game increased from the late nineteenth century, so the tsetse had spread, converting isolated focal points of fly into one large belt. In 1919 shooting operations in the Winkie district succeeded in driving the fly back across the Shangani river, and nagana was stamped out on the Gwaai river, so that cattle could be introduced. The operation ended in 1922. In 1924 the fly was found to be expanding into the Lomagundi district. Fences were established ten miles apart, and all game within the fences was destroyed. Again the measure was said to have been successful and cattle were reintroduced. Similar fencing was erected in the Hartley district in 1926, and the fly was eradicated over a wide area. In 1929 a conference in Salisbury decided to extend these policies. Ten European rangers supervising 400 armed Africans eliminated game in 6,000 square miles of fly country, leaving 16,000 square miles of fly country undisturbed where game increased naturally. Twenty-five thousand head of game were destroyed annually under this policy. A trypanosomiasis bureau was established and the policies were continued until 1961. There was more shooting between 1962 and 1967. There were many complaints from the SPFE about this policy. In 1950, the President of the Society, the Duke of Devonshire, sent a vigorous protest to the Prime Minister of Southern Rhodesia, Godfrey Huggins, which was equally vigorously rebuffed.[45] In fact in 1951 987 African hunters were employed, and between 1948 and 1951 102,025 head of game were killed.[46] It was estimated that over 750,000 animals were destroyed in the course of these tsetse operations. Between 1930 and 1950 10,000 square miles of the Zambezi Valley were freed of tsetse. The policy can be deemed a success, although in the early stages the shooting of animals was unnecessarily indiscriminate. In the 1960s tsetse control concentrated on the elimination of warthog, bush pig, kudu, and bushbuck, known since the late 1940s to be the principal hosts of the trypanosomes and the favoured source of meals for the tsetse.

In Natal game elimination started in 1917. In 1920 a large game drive was held to appease the settlers, and pressures for the abolition of the reserves built up.[47] As farmers settled in the Ntabanani Valley, extending towards the southern boundary of the Umfolosi reserves, they found that nagana was destroying stock in what was regarded as magnificent cattle country. The fly belt had extended south as game had moved out of the reserve in search of water. R. H. Harris, an entomologist employed by the Natal authorities, was by this time beginning to have some success in trapping tsetse with the 'Harris fly trap'. In the late '20s, after a fresh outbreak of nagana, Harris worked on a Government Advisory Committee and it was decided to set up a large buffer area between the reserve and the settled region. Game elimination took place within this area, only the rare white rhino being spared. In the end tsetse was cleared from Natal with the use of insecticides.[48] The three Natal reserves, covering 200 square miles, were treated with insecticide in 1952 at a cost of £2·5 million, or £20 per acre. Policies of game shooting were also adopted in Bechuanaland and Nothern Rhodesia.

Such policies were rarely pursued in East Africa, where the tsetse affected mainly African areas. Tsetse research stations were established at Entebbe in Uganda and Tinde in Tanganyika. In the 1920s and early '30s C. F. M. Swynnerton, the dominant figure in tsetse research in Tanganyika, faced a fly belt 500 miles by 300 miles in extent.[49] He experimented with fly trapping, bush clearance, and also the opposite, 'densification', a policy where the avoidance of grass fires caused the bush to become so dense that the fly deserted it. He attempted to control the advance of the fly by creating either cleared or 'densified' barriers, in each case a habitat which the tsetse would dislike. Swynnerton has been much criticised as representing the game lobby (he was the Game Warden of Tanganyika until 1929 and Director of Tsetse Research thereafter until his death in an air crash when surveying game in a tsetse region) and therefore avoiding game elimination.[50] It is true that Swynnerton was over-anxious to exonerate game, but he was a much more able tsetse researcher than some historians have noticed. He published a number of papers on the tsetse and had one strain, *Glossina swynnertoni*, called after him.[51] He studied, using oral evidence, traditional methods of tsetse control, particularly those of Mzila, king of the Ngoni Gaza kingdom on the borders of Zimbabwe and Mozambique in the 1860s and '70s. Mzila discovered that tsetse had spread as a result of the initial depopulation of the area in the Mfecane of the 1830s. The fly was beaten back by a combination of bush clearance by human settlement and large-scale hunting, although 'reserves' were left where animals were permitted to survive. Swynnerton succeeded in clearing over 800 square miles in Sukumaland (Tanzania) by his techniques, though tsetse withdrew from 2,400 square miles purely because of the growth of the human population and the expansion of cultivated land as a result. Numbers of stock also increased in the same period, before and after the Second World War.

A number of conferences were held on the tsetse problem, though each merely highlighted the continuing disparity between opposing views, both on the scientific character of tsetse and trypanosome-related disease and on methods of controlling fly infestation. There were international conferences in 1907 and 1925. In 1933 a conference was held at Entebbe and in 1935 a tsetse fly committee, appointed under the East African sub- committee of the Economic Advisory Committee, reported to Parliament.[52] One of its members was Sir Arthur Bagshawe, Director of the Sleeping Sickness Bureau in London, who had also been a member of the 1914 committee. The 1935 body acknowledged that the evacuation of humans had been a mistake. 'Bush, game, and fly represent a hostile coalition before which retreat is unavailing and the best form of defence is attack.' Instead it recommended the amalgamation of scattered human settlements into concentrated 'villages' of 3,000 to 4,000 people. Only by such concentration could sufficient labour be provided to clear bush and take the necessary precautions against the fly. The Swynnerton methods received the approval of the committee, which also urged that the tsetse research programme in Uganda and Tanganyika should be continued despite financial retrenchment. In fact village concentration was another mistaken policy. The abandonment of dispersed village settlements in some areas allowed the fly to advance. Theory and practice were again at odds, and, as Ford has shown, the retreat of the tsetse eventually occurred fortuitously. More land was freed of the fly by the increase in population and the extension of settlement from the 1930s to the 1950s than any amount of scientific effort. Interestingly, when the Shinyanga tsetse research laboratory and its associated controlled game reserve, established by Swynnerton, were abandoned and the game was destroyed by advancing human settlement, tsetse promptly disappeared from that area.[53]

The 1935 committee had little to say about either game or reserves – beyond noting that the dispute about the precise role of game continued. It would indeed be wrong to see tsetse control as causing a severe check to the reserve movement. Throughout the tsetse control period reserves continued to be established. Some of the great African reserves were entirely free of tsetse and were not therefore under threat, but there were tsetse-infested reserves which remained sacrosanct. In fact by the 1920s and '30s the protagonists of game elimination were beginning to have second thoughts. One student of the tsetse problem, Colonel Hamerton, an associate of Bruce, recanted the evidence he had given on game shooting to the 1914 committee.[54] In South Africa the Veterinary Department and government entomologists, who had opposed the creation of the Sabi reserve, were converted to support for it as it developed towards national park status.[55]

Farther north the '20s and '30s were indeed to be important in the spread of reserves. The Gorongoza reserve was founded in an area of Mozambique where tsetse was present in 1921. Next door, in Southern

Rhodesia, where the company's policies had held up the creation of reserves for so long, the settler government established after 1923 embarked on a preservation policy. The first reserve was a private one. H. G. Robins established a 25,000 acre game sanctuary forty miles west of Wankie in 1925. When he died in 1939 this was bequeathed to the country. In 1927 a member of the Southern Rhodesia Legislative Assembly, Major W. J. Boggie, took up the issue of game preservation and won the support of the Minister of Agriculture; as a result the Wankie reserve was declared in 1928. Ted Davison became its first warden, with a budget of £500 per annum. Davison concentrated on improving the water supply and encouraging the recuperation of game. He ejected Bushman 'poachers' and reduced the lion population. As the game population increased, African poachers, interestingly, arrived to supply meat to locations and mine compounds.[56] Wankie was eventually to form the basis of a 5,271 square mile national park which boasted 25,000 visitors in 1965.

In Northern Rhodesia land demarcation policies between the wars encouraged the growth of game populations. Large tracts of the territory on the line of rail and in the north-east were allocated to European occupation, and Africans were moved into reserves. A great deal of the 'white' land was not taken up and game swiftly reoccuppied it.[57] By 1950 the original three reserves had become twelve, occupying 18,435 square miles of the territory. The Luangwa North and South reserves, respectively 1,890 and 3,200 square miles, were declared in 1938, and the others included the Kafue (8,650 square miles), Lavushi-Manda (800), Lukusuzi (1,050), Lunga (600), Mweru Marsh (1,210), Sumbu (550) and Fort Rosebery (750). The appearance of national parks in both Southern and Northern Rhodesia after the Second World War will be examined in the next chapter.

*Game departments and reserves in East Africa.* Although reserves were in existence in almost all colonies by the 1920s there were often no separate departments to protect them. In Nyasaland the reserves were placed under the Forestry Department in 1926, as was the Wankie Reserve in Southern Rhodesia in 1928. Game departments were, however, established in East Africa. The first such department in the British African territories was founded in Kenya in 1900. As officer of the protectorate administration, Richard Crawshay, was seconded to enforce the game laws. The first permanent game ranger, Arthur Blayney Percival, was appointed the following year. Percival was born in 1875, described himself as a 'naturalist and ornitholigist', and had led a British Museum expedition to Arabia to collect mammals in 1899.[58]

In 1900 he joined the East African administration as an assistant collector, moving in 1901 to the new Game Department, which he dominated for over twenty years.[59] When he retired he became a farmer and died in Nairobi in 1961 on the eve of independence. He was the sole ranger until 1907, when Colonel J. H. Patterson, of Tsavo lions fame, was appointed head of the department. Percival was acting head between 1908 and 1910, when he again took second place to a veterinarian, R. B. Woosnam. In 1919 Percival at last became head of the Game Department with the title of Game Warden. He was succeeded in 1923 by A. T. A. Ritchie, an Oxford graduate in zoology, who was the chief game ranger of Kenya until 1950. He was assisted by Captain Keith Caldwell, as active propagandist for game preservation, who contributed articles to the *JSPFE*, was an assiduous lecturer on the subject, and later became active in international wildlife concerns. From 1907 there were four European officers and thirty African game scouts in the departments; from 1912 the white establishment was increased to five and remained at that strength, except during the First World War, until 1939, although the number of African scouts was raised to seventy. This tiny staff, which attempted to enforce game regulations in an area of nearly 220,000 square miles, was supplemented by honorary game wardens. From the late 1930s to the 1950s one of these was Jim Corbett, the celebrated Anglo-Indian hunter and conservationist, who spent part of each year in Kenya and eventually retired there.

The Athi game reserve seems to have been first proclaimed in 1897. In 1899 Sir Harry Johnston sent an ecstatic account of a train journey through it to the Foreign Office. It was, he wrote, 'a wonderful zoological garden, a sportsman's dream'.[60] After two years of strictly enforced regulations the animals had become confident and displayed themselves to the rail passengers. The game regulations of 1900 greatly increased the size of this reserve. It now consisted of a vast area from Tsavo along the Athi river to Donyo Sapuk, north-east of Nairobi, thence to the frontier of the Uganda Protectorate, bounded on the west and south by Uganda and German East Africa. Such an enormous region was entirely unpractical. It contained a large African population, a considerable proportion of Kamba territory, almost the whole of Masailand, the densely populated lake-shore regions, and some Kikuyu land. It cannot have been particularly well publicised, as it is clear that hunting continued throughout the area. Moreover, a notable hunter like Richard Meinertzhagen seemed unaware of its existence. In April 1904 he noted in his diary:

I have made great friends with Blaney [sic] Percival, the game ranger. He

[ 245 ]

is not only very knowledgeable about big game but is madly keen on birds and has a large collection. I like him. In view of the likelihood of a vast invasion by European settlers it seems that the larger game must disappear. One cannot have farms and game, and I have suggested to Blaney that he puts up a scheme for a very large area in country unsuitable for white settlement where game can remain for ever. This area would need to be vested in trustees based in London and be completely divorced from the local government, the trustees being responsible only to the British Parliament. There must be no risk of interference from an East African administration which cares nothing for game. I think the area might be some three or four thousand square miles and possibly in Masai country. The Masai are good game preservers but are very wasteful of grazing land. Moreover, both game and Masai cattle can co-exist. Blaney has promised to formulate a scheme.[61]

Meinertzhagen enjoyed portraying himself as the instigator of such plans, but although his notion of imperial trustees was a new one, the reserve idea was already established in Kenyan legislation. In any case, judging by the repeated hunting exploits described in his diaries, he must have been one of the prime infringers of game regulations, even if officers of the King's African Rifles were granted an exemption.

Meinertzhagen's conviction that the East African administration would do nothing for game was based largely on information derived from his family connection with the commissioner, Sir Charles Eliot. Eliot disliked hunting, favoured a settler policy, and believed that sentiment about animals should not be allowed to stand in the way of 'progress'.[62] Meinertzhagen pressed game preservation on him, but received little reponse. Indeed, in 1901 Eliot had already complained to the Foreign Office that the game regulations were unnecessarily severe, particularly the ban on the sale of the heads, horns, skins, feathers and flesh of animals in the schedules. The prohibition was unreasonable since 'the Protectorate is positively swarming with game'.[63] The Foreign Secretary, Lansdowne, replied with a mild reprimand. It was, he pointed out, essential to stick to the provisions of the international Convention, although Eliot had the power to move specific animals out of the schedules if he wished to. In fact Eliot was unrepresentative of African administrators, and soon after the encounter with Meinertzhagen he resigned.

In the game ordinances of 1906 and 1909 the unwieldy reserve of 1900 was cut down. The remnant, less than half the original, still took up much Masai and Kamba land, but its north-eastern border ran along the railway line whereas formerly the reserve had covered both sides of the line for more than 150 miles. It was now known as the southern reserve, and a second, the northern, was established between the Uaso Nyiro river and a line from Mount Marsabit to Mount Nyiro. The idea of this reserve had been pressed upon the Foreign Office by Lord Delamere, Kenya's most notable settler, in 1900.[64] It was, he pointed out, too hot for European settlement, and there were only a few Ndorobo hunters in it. There should be a complete rather than a partial ban on hunting. As it turned out, Sir Clement Hill, the responsible officials in the Colonial Office, and Eliot's successor, Sir Charles Stewart, required little persuasion. Special reserves were also established to protect eland, roan, rhinoceros and hippopotamus. The main outlines of these reserves were maintained and confirmed in the 1937 Kenyan game law, the largest and most complex piece of legislation on game to be enacted in any British Afican territory to that date.

Arthur Blayney Percival was, at least in part, the architect of these policies. He was active in pointing out to the Kenyan government the economic significance of game to the colonial economy. Kenya was the most popular big-game hunting country of the period. It was easily accessible from Europe and India. Its terrain was open and largely fly-free, so that horses could be used. The Uganda railway provided comfortable access to many game-rich areas. Equipment, porters and hunting guides were readily available. Nairobi indeed became the great centre of African elite hunting activity, with many professional hunters and safari companies plying for hire. The territory was reasonably healthy and scenically attractive, great open plains offering a different hunting experience from the forest and woodland savannahs with quite dense bush cover elsewhere. In 1899 licence fees and the duty on trophies of visiting 'sportsmen' – particularly ivory – raised 9 per cent of the revenue of the protectorate. An indication of the rapid increase in the popularity of Kenya for the tourist hunter can be derived from figures given by Frederick Jackson in 1905 and 1906.[65] The licence revenue increased from £1,600 in 1901-02 to £5,900 in 1904-05. By 1906 it had reached £9,000. In 1904-05 £1,050 was taken in fines and £100 was raised from the sale of confiscated ivory (a noticeably low sum). The expenditure on the Game Department in the same period rose from £250 to £354. In 1909 Jackson suggested that the existing department, consisting of Percival and six Africans, was a farce.[66] He proposed the expenditure of just over £2,000 on four European officers and a larger contingent of African scouts. The expansion of the department was approved later that year. In 1910 Percival argued that between £50,000 and £100,000 per annum was spent by visitors on their safari equipment and staffs in addition to the license fees and duties.[67] The significance of hunting to the Kenyan economy was indeed much envied by other territories, particularly those of the BSAC in Central Africa.

Hunting was a good deal less important in adjacent Uganda, although that colony enjoyed some income from ivory. Some of the grandest parties hunted in the Sudan and crossed the northern territory of Uganda before reaching the main goal in Kenya. Uganda's reserves policy was founded on human tragedy attendant upon ecological disaster and was promoted by one of the great naturalist administrators, later active in the SPFE. The western region of Uganda around Lake George in the fertile foothills of the Ruwenzori mountains, on the borders of the Belgian Congo, was particularly hard hit by rinderpest. The disease arrived in the Ruwenzori early in 1891, with devastating effects on both cattle and ungulates.[68] The pastoral people of the region saw whole herds destroyed and many of them migrated eastwards out of the stricken area. With the destruction of the game and the departure of the humans the bush encroached once more and was soon harbouring tsetse fly. The land was then considered unfit for human habitation. When Frederick Lugard visited the area in 1891 he found that the elephants had gone and that all the buffalo were dead.[69] All other game was scarce, only a few waterbuck and kob surviving. Sir Harry Johnston, the Commissioner of the Uganda Protectorate in 1899-1901. was a naturalist and artist who produced the first significant works on Uganda mammalia and East African birds, and he set about establishing reserves in the affected areas. These were intended to be remote reservations where the game could recover entirely unmolested by an indigenous human presence or by visitors. No game department was established and there was no intention of managing the area.[70] By 1906 these reserves had been consolidated into the Toro reserve, which became the Lake George reserve (226 square miles) in 1925. The Lake Edward reserve followed in 1930. Both were later greatly enlarged.

In 1899 Johnston proclaimed the vast Sugota reserve in the north-east of Uganda in territory that later became part of Kenya when he heard that a shooting party led by a Frenchman called Sporck was heading for the region.[71] He also created small reserves around government stations in which only officials of the administration could shoot.[72] He tried to stop elephant hunting, particularly by Somali caravans, but asserted that Africans were not very destructive of game. He believed they should be allowed to kill hippos, since the beasts destroyed crops, were a danger to humans and offered a great deal of meat. The largest reserve declared in the early days of the territory was the Budonga, in the northern Nile regions. The protection of game there considerably increased the incidence of tsetse fly, and between 1907 and 1912 the region was depopulated as part of the policy of separating people from the fly after it had been declared a sleeping-sickness restricted area. By 1910 the depopulated area covered no fewer than 5,000 square miles and the Uganda administration was undecided as to whether it should greatly increase the size of the reserve or considerably reduce it.[73] In the end the Budonga reserve was renamed the Bunyoro reserve to mark its expansion. In 1928 the Bunyoro reserve was extended yet further, this time to the north of the Victoria Nile, with the addition of the Gulu reserve. Although sleeping-sickness had been eliminated by the 1930s the reserves were confirmed and enlarged.

Thus tsetse could have entirely opposite effects in the balance between humans and game in different parts of the continent. In areas of white settlement with large and influential farming communities and well established veterinary departments – as in South Africa and Southern Rhodesia – game was seen to harbour tsetse and threaten domestic stocks. Tsetse control was game control, and to the rage of the preservationist hunters extensive culling programmes were developed. In Uganda, however, the combined ravages of rinderpest and sleeping-sickness cleared human populations, leaving remote areas free for game protection and recovery policies.

Uganda, in fact, acted as a laboratory in which the recuperative powers of animals could receive conclusive proof. There was an explosion of both the elephant and the buffalo populations in the first twenty years of the century. By the early '20s it was apparent that the balance of nature had indeed been tipped in favour of animals and that their depredations on crops had reached alarming proportions. Offering licences to chiefs was inadequate and the arming of peasant farmers was considered dangerous and ineffectual, so the colonial administration attempted to used European professional ivory hunters. They were given bulk permits to kill elephants, one tusk of each to be levied by the government. This method also proved a failure, since the hunters' criterion was size and value of ivory rather than potential as a crop destroyer. In 1924 Keith Caldwell was seconded from Kenya to organise a game department, three ivory hunters having already been appointed game rangers.[74] Caldwell was swiftly recalled to Kenya to organise a four-month safari for the Duke and Duchess of York, the future George VI and Queen Elizabeth, who were on their honeymoon. In 1925 the Uganda Elephant Control Department was at last firmly established, with Charles Pitman as Game Warden.

As its title implied, the department was designed to enforce the separation between human habitation and the officially sanctioned habitat of wildlife. It was, however, a battle in which the line was scarcely held over the succeeding decades. It has been estimated that the Uganda Elephant Control Department shot 1,000 elephants per annum between the 1920s and the 1950s, yet when Pitman retired in 1950 there were as many elephants as there had been when he was appointed in 1925.[75] The bias towards control was still apparent in 1949, when the department consisted of two European game rangers, forty-four African game guards (who were the main foot soldiers in the war against elephants), eight game scouts and seven gun bearers.[76] For the rest, the game staff, together with District Commissioners and police, were concerned to prevent hunting in the game reserves, keep those parts of the country undisturbed for game, and prevent their repopulation by African pastoralists and cultivators. Small populations of fishermen and salt workers were allowed to visit or inhabit the western lakes reserves to exploit fish and salt resources, but they were not permitted to hunt. The police periodically patrolled the northern reserve to ensure that the villages were not reoccupied.[77]

The third East African territory, Tanganyika, under German rule until the First World War, became a British mandated territory under the League of Nations from 1919. As we have seen, the Germans were avid hunters, and some conservationists in the SPFE were anxious about the survival of the rarer species in the German empire.[78] Nevertheless, the Germans were active conservationists. Game legislation and reserves were introduced into South West Africa in the first decade of the twentieth century, and one of the leaders of the conservationist movement (a prime mover behind the 1900 London conference) was Hermann von Wissmann, imperial commissioner and Governor of German East Africa in the 1890s.[79] The German colonial administration in Tanganyika introduced game and hunting ordinances in 1896, 1898 and 1908. Two game reserves were established in 1896, one on the Rufiji river and the other west of Mount Kilimanjaro. At the same time Hermann von Wissmann asked his officials to demarcate other tracts of land suitable for reserves. In the 1908 shooting regulations of the colony no fewer than eight reserves were defined. At first the German game regulations made no distinction between Europeans and Africans in the issue of licences, but from 1898 they were more concerned, like the British, to prohibit African hunting. As the fortunes of the tsetse indicate, it may well be that as a result of the ecological disasters that hit German East Africa in the 1890s, and the 'pacification' campaigns of the Germans, the balance was tipped in favour of animal as against human life. In the aftermath of the Maji Maji revolt of 1905-06, for example, game began to recolonise areas formerly under human habitation.[80] During the First World War, however, game regulations were entirely abandoned and, as in previous wars, the game resource became a vital means of provisioning troops. The Germans employed specially selected hunters to supply meat, particularly elephant meat, to the troops in the southern part of the territory. Game meat was equally important to the campaigns on the railway line and on the northern border.[81]

At the end of the war there were eleven game reserves in Tanganyika. The British confirmed and extended them, and by 1933 there were thirteen, totalling 16,300 square miles in area.[82] In 1921 they introduced a Game Preservation Ordinance which extended to Tanganyika the game regulations and reserves provisions prevalent in other territories.[83] A stream of amendments and regulations followed in the 1920s and 1930s. The Selous, Ntetesi, Ngorongoro and Serengeti reserves were confirmed under this legislation. The latter two were extended in size in 1936, and further regulations relating to their management were issued in 1937. In 1929 the posts of game warden and game ranger were defined in an amendment. The Lake Rukwa and Northern Railway Usambara reserves were proclaimed in 1933; preservation orders relating to the Southern Highlands, Idodi, Iringa, Usagara, Tabora and elsewhere were issued in 1938; and further reserves were demarcated in 1939. Efforts were also made to indulge in detailed management of specific species through legislation. For example, zebra and hippo were declared vermin in certain districts in various years.

As was the case elsewhere, these reserves were often built on human tragedy. The Ngorongoro Crater had been thickly populated by Masai, but rinderpest destroyed their herds and drove them out.[84] A German settler took over half the crater, and after the war Sir Charles Ross established a hunting lodge and hunting estate there. The Masai attempted to return, but they were frustrated by the creation of the reserve in 1928. The Masai suffered a similar fate in the Serengeti and were reduced to less than one-sixth of their former land area. The Lake Rukwa region was subjected to a prolonged drought between 1905 and 1929. The lake contracted and the people retreated. Game returned, and a game reserve was proclaimed in the early 1930s. When it was extended to the west in 1937, 10,000 people were incorporated in it. When the British created the Selous reserve (which contained the grave of the famous hunter) they moved out 40,000 Ngindo people in the mistaken belief that they frequently migrated in any case and would therefore not suffer any inconvenience. As we have seen, the game warden, C. F. M. Swynnerton, did his best to protect game by arguing that they did not pose a serious threat of infection and that tsetse could be contained by other means. One historian of Tanzania has seen the game policy as 'weakening man's mastery of the land',[85] another as permitting nature, against which Africans had waged a long battle, to reconquer the land.[86]

Yet this policy cannot be seen as uniquely British. When they created the Selous reserve, in the angle of the Ruaha and Rufiji rivers, it covered 2,600 square miles. It was extended several times between 1931 and 1940, grew dramatically between 1945 and 1951 (with some small deletions of land between 1951 and 1953) and expanded again between 1960 and 1967, reaching its fullest extent in 1975. As it spread, humans were denied rights of occupancy and the government of independent Tanzania, as part of its policy of collectivisation, was as intent on the elimination of isolated villages as the British had been. By 1975 the Selous covered 55,000 square kilometres or 21,230 square miles.[87]

Moreover, as elsewhere in East Africa, the British were extraordinarily schizophrenic about these policies. The Tanganyikan game department started from very meagre beginnings, but it was soon clear that its role was as much to protect humans as game. The department was founded in 1919 with Swynnerton as its first ranger, and its patterns of expenditure indicate the diversity of its functions. It was concerned with vermin control, tsetse control and elephant control as well as the upkeep of reserves. Annual expenditure grew from 4,840 East African shillings in 1919-20 to 628,160 shillings in 1926-27, through the figure fell back when a separate tsetse department was founded in 1929. In 1925-26 the breakdown in expenditure was as follows (the 1926-27 figures are given in brackets): vermin control, 42,900 sh. (36,560 sh.); tsetse control, 123,860 sh. (264,200 sh.); elephant control 111,400 sh. (75,500 sh.). In the latter year 1,500 sh. was distributed to villagers as rewards for vermin destruction. In 1923-24 the department consisted of one director, one senior ranger, four rangers, eighty-four game scouts and thirty-four trappers and between them they 'accounted four 259 lions, 659 leopard, 70 crocodile and innumerable elephant'. In 1924-25 one ranger, Captain Fairweather, shot 394 elephants in south-east Tanzania. More rangers, game scouts and 'cultivation protectors' were added to the strength later.[88]

Although Swynnerton was determined to control tsetse without large-scale game destruction, by the 1930s culling was being stepped up. Under the administration of Swynnerton's successor as Game Warden, Philip Teare, formely of the British South Africa Police, the rangers became hunters rather than keepers. As in Uganda, the Tanganyika department found itself trying to counteract the effects of the early preservationist policies. In 1932 604 elephant were shot by the department. In the following year the figure reached nearly 2,000 and maintained that average throughout the later 1930s. Yet an article in the *JSPFE* in 1927 had argued that the elephant population was under threat, 'the utter destruction of such fine animals' being affected by a combination of Germans, professional hunters and African poachers. 'Had a stong policy towards game preservation been adopted by the authorities such an *impasse* could never have occurred.' [89] Even the Game Department's own census was wildly out. In 1933 it estimated that there were 5,424 elephants in the Southern Province of Tanzania, but more than that number, 5,580, were killed under control policies between 1933 and 1936.[90] Nothing could better represent the manner in which colonial authorities were pulled two ways and in which policies were based largely on ignorance.

So far as elephants were concerned, the same was true of other colonies. The figures for elephant culling in four African territories in 1935 were as follows: Uganda, 1,546; Kenya, 450; Tanganyika, 2,594; Northern Rhodesia, 4,600 (plus 573 killed on licence). The ivory resulting from these kills produced a great deal of revenue. Between 1926 and 1935 government sales of ivory in the three East African colonies (Uganda, Kenya and Tanganyika) raised £665,400, while expenditure on game departments totalled £292,290.[91] The surplus of £373,000 was no mean sum for struggling colonial economies. In 1936 Pitman described Uganda as overrun by elephants, and 2,300 were killed. It was he who had identified the main problem in Northern Rhodesia in his study of 1931-32: it was one of control rather than of preservation.[92]

We are therefore confronted with the apparent paradox that in Uganda, Tanganyika and Northern Rhodesia at least the game departments (that in the last-named colony was founded only in 1940) were designed to restore some sort of balance to an excess of preservation, particularly in the case of elephants (which, as it happens, did not harbour tsetse). But reserves continued to be confirmed and extended. The paradox is resolved when it is realised that the object of the culling was to emphasise the habitat separation policy. An attempt was being made to control a growing game population in human areas while more extensive living space was created in those demarcated for wildlife. The two policies were the twin motors of the colonial ecological engine. If at times they appeared to work in opposition, they were nonetheless designed to produce the desired separation effect. The apparently contradictory activities of Pitman, Swynnerton and others can by understood only in this light.

*Other reserves.* Reserves were created in several other territories in East and West Africa.

Somaliland, where there was a tradition of indigenous hunting by Somali horsemen and aboriginal Midgans, presents an interesting case of destruction through over-hunting followed by over-protectiveness in reserves of excessive size. A large reserve was created in Somaliland in 1899. Even then Consul General Sadler considered it too large, but he still considered that game was becoming scarce in the protectorate and suggested that the main problem was controlling the Midgan hunters, who had no other source of livelihood.[93] He implied that some other form of employment would have to be found for them. Within a few years the official administering Somaliland was expressing very different views. In 1905 the commissioner E. J. E. Swayne noted a drastic decline in the game population even since the promulgation of the game regulations in 1901.[94] This could not be attributed, he suggested, to disease or native hunting. It was entirely due to the importation of modern rifles, almost all of which were in the hands of European sportsmen and military officers. In the several Somali campaigns 500-600 Europeans officers had been shooting game and they had often permitted Sepoys to kill as many animals as they wished for meat. They had paid little attention to woodcraft and had often shot at a range of up to 500 yards. Two reserves had been established, one on the Damal plain and the other, rather smaller, in hill country in the Golis range. The former, the Hargeisa reserve, was 1,500 square miles in extent and he proposed extending it to 5,000 square miles. This was duly done, and maps demarcating these large tracts, a high proportion of the total land area of the colony, were submitted to the Colonial Office.

In 1908 the Sudan possessed a large reserve to the south of the Blue Nile and a sanctuary to the north.[95] There was special protection for the Nubian ibex, and three districts were closed 'to people travelling for sport and pleasure' to allow the game to recover. These reserves were confirmed and extended under the 1922 game ordinance. From that date there were four reserves covering 5,515 square miles plus the 400 square mile sanctuary for ibex. Farther west Lugard proclaimed the whole of the British portion of the shores of Lake Chad as a reserve in 1905, while by 1907 there were three reserves in southern Nigeria, the Gilli-Gilli, one between the Niger and the Orle rivers and another between the Niger and the Anambra.[96] The Lake Chad reserve was subsequently deproclaimed, and by the 1930s there were four reserves in Nigeria (Bedde, Gilli-Gilli, Orle River and Anambra), covering 1,935 square miles.[97]

*Conclusion.* Throughout a great belt of imperial territory reserves had been demarcated by the First World War and extended and confirmed by the Second. Despite tsetse and sleeping-sickness scares, despite the attacks of white settlers in some colonies and the anxieties of scientists, mainly in southern Africa, despite the complexities of legislation and the half-hearted or non-existent character of the early game administrations, the reserves had become established as accepted policy. Although a few were abolished and one or two became a dead letter because the game departed or was destroyed, the overall pattern was of survival and growth. The international conferences from which conventions and agreements emerged were often an apparent failure, because they were not ratified (and have often been depicted as such), but the game preservationist lobby was an exceptionally powerful one. The list of members of the SPFE (appendix III) makes that clear, as does the consistent interest (with very few exceptions) of colonial governors, members of the royal family (like Prince Arthur of Connaught, who was Governor General of South Africa after the First World War), many aristocrats, and the natural history establishment. The fact that preservationists were almost always distinguished hunters reflects the manner in which the first phase at least of the conservationist movement marked the shift from practical hunting to the Hunt, essentially a perquisite of the elite. The exigencies of war reintroduced the need for practical hunting and marked the major check – more significant than ideas about the tsetse – to the conservation movement, but the evidence of destruction presented by war, particularly the Great War, gave fresh impetus to game preservation in the 1920s. Indeed, the powerful pressure for tsetse control in the early years of that decade had led some scholars into thinking that it was a hesitant period for conservation. In fact, as the Uganda experience demonstrates, the spread of the tsetse was more likely to facilitate rather than inhibit the establishment of reserves.

It is also clear that ideas derived from one part of the continent, the south, where game had been subject to serious depletion, to the point of extinction in some cases, were applied to others, like East Africa, where game was not threatened to the same extent, if at all. Imperial expansion helped to produce the disasters of the 1890s that appeared to put game under real threat, but the conservationists overestimated the scale of destruction and underestimated the power of the survivors to recuperate. The vigour of that recuperation was already apparent within a few years of the opening of the twentieth century, but by then the conservationist movement was firmly entrenched. The spread of the tsetse, the incidence of sleeping-sickness and the evidence of destruction to African crops and to life itself raised some doubts and resulted in some counter-conservation claims from missionaries and a few, but by no means all, medical men and scientists. But that controversy was engulfed by the First World War, and in its aftermath conservation remained the dominant creed.

The first decades of European rule had facilitated the expansion of the tsetse, and, for all the scientific expertise brought to bear on the problem, the early attempts at controlling sleeping-sickness epidemics were disastrously wrongheaded. Pre-colonial African cultivators had kept the tsetse at bay more effectively than the battery of committees and research stations. The conservationists meddled and the scientists disagreed. Only in Southern Rhodesia was a consistent, effective though unnecessarily indiscriminate policy pursued, and that was to protect settler cattle rather than human lives. In East Africa culling as an antidote to excessive preservation became a necessity for crop protection rather than tsetse control, and was pursued in order to achieve effective separation of human and animal habitats, the latter in reserves much bloated by human disaster and successful conservationist pressure. The separation of human and animal living room was effected largely to the detriment of human needs.

Even after the Second World War some game rangers saw the tsetse as a providential game preserver. Bruce Kinloch, in turn chief game ranger of Uganda, Tanzania and Malawi (the latter two after independence) argued that tsetse had 'long discouraged the often destructive and frequently wasteful use by humans of extensive regions of scenically beautiful, unspoilt wilderness, the natural home of the great game herds'.[98] Referring to policies of game elimination, Kinloch went on to suggest that tsetse had led to the 'senseless mass destruction of countless numbers of magnificent wild animals'. There were two flaws in his argument. In the first place, as we have seen, the reserves were not always the 'natural home of the great game herds'. Colonial policies had made them so. Second, the 'senseless mass destruction' in favour of 'often destructive and frequently wasteful use by humans of extensive regions' had taken place in favour of the settlement of whites and not of blacks.

# Notes

1 James Stevenson-Hamilton, *Animal Life in Africa*, London, 1912; *The Kruger National Park* Pretoria, 1928; *The Low Veld: its Wildlife and its Peoples*, London, 1929; *South African Eden*, London, 1937; *Our South African National Parks*, Cape Town, 1940.
2 Harry Wolhuter, *Memories of a Game Ranger*, Johannesburg, 1948.
3 A. Blayney Percival, *A Game Ranger's Notebook*, London, 1924; *A Game Ranger on Safari*, London, 1928.
4 C. R. S. Pitman, *A Game Warden among his Charges*, London, 1931; *A Game Warden takes Stock*, London, 1942.
5 Bruce Kinloch, *The Shamba Raiders: Memories of a Game Warden*, London, 1972.
6 Rennie Bere, 'The Story of the Uganda National Parks', unpublished typescript (completed in 1974), deposited in RCS Library.
7 Ian Parker and Mohamed Amin, *Ivory Crisis*, London, 1983.
8 Stevenson-Hamilton, *South African Eden*, pp. xvii-xviii.
9 John A. Pringle, *The Conservationists and the Killers*, Cape Town, 1982, p. 51-2.
10 Stevenson-Hamilton, *South African Eden*, p. 294: *JSPFE*, VI (1913), p. 12, indicated that there were 4,100 Africans living in Sabi game reserve; for anti-poaching operations see Wolhuter, *Memories*, pp. 115, 513-60.
11 Wolhuter, *Memories*, pp. 124-5, 128-30.
12 Stevenson-Hamilton, *South African Eden*, pp. 52, 103-4, 132.
13 Stevenson-Hamilton, *South African Eden*, pp. 124-5.
14 Milner to Chamberlain, 7 May 1898, Cd 3189.
15 SPFE deputation to Alfred Lyttelton, 2 February 1905, Cd 3189.
16 'Sabi', 'Empire fauna in 1922', *JSPFE*, II (1922), pp. 41-2. Thomas Barbour and Margaret D. Porter, 'Notes on South African Wildlife Conservation', special publication of the American Committee for Internaitonal Wildlife Protection, 1935.
17 The establishment of reserves can be reconstructed from references in the Parliamentary Papers and in the game laws.
18 Stevenson-Hamilton, *Animal Life in Africa*, p. 28.
19 H. A. Bryden, 'The extermination of great game in South Africa', *Fortnightly Review*, 63 (1894), p. 551.
20 François Coillard, *On the Threshold of Central Africa*, London, 1897, p. 638.
21 Coillard, *Threshold*, p. 622.
22 Cd 3189. Appendix to Cd 5136. Ordinances of Northern Rhodesia, game laws.
23 Robert Codrington to Acting Commissioner Manning, 23 February 1901, Cd 3189.
24 Report by Commissioner Sir Harry Johnston on the Trade and General Condition of the British Central Africa Protectorate, 1895-96, appendix 1, pp. 18-20, C. 8254. Report by Acting Commissioner Sharpe on the Trade and General Condition of the British Central Africa Protectorate, 1896-97, C. 8438, p. 9. Annual Report of the British Central Africa Protectorate, 1897-98, C. 9048. See also Cd 3189 and the Nyasaland Ordinances, game laws.
25 This event was called in evidence by the British South Africa Company to defend its game extermination policies. BSAC to CO, 22 November 1909, Cd 5136.
26 John Ford, *The Role of Trypanosomiases in African Ecology: a Study of the Tsetse Fly Problem*, Oxford, 1971.
27 Ford, *Trypanosomiases*, p. 145.
28 Ford, *Trypanosomiases*, pp. 170-6, 181; Report of the Interdepartmental Committee on Sleeping Sickness, Cd 7349, 1914, xlviii, 1. Evidence printed in Cd 7350. But for his death, Alfred Lyttelton was to have been chairman of this sleeping-sickness committee, an appointment eminently acceptable to the SPFE. See also Pringle, *Conservationists*, pp. 110-14.
29 Cd 7349 and Cd 7350.

30  Material on the setting up of the Bruce Commission can be found in Cd 5775 and Cd 6671.
31  E. A. Minchin to Rhys Williams, Secretary of the SPFE, 13 December 1906, *JSPFE*, II (1907), pp. 47-9.
32  In evidence to the Interdepartmental committee, Cd 7349 and Cd 7350. The *JSPFE* devoted a large proportion of its space to sleeping-sickness and the views of many of the authorities appeared in its pages. *JSPFE*, VI (1913), pp. 76-104.
33  Ernest E. Austen, 'The present position of the problem of big game, tsetse flies, and sleeping sickness', *JSPFE*, VI (1913), pp. 57-71.
34  Ford, *Trypanosomiases, passim*. Stanley Tomkins, Acting Governor of Uganda, to Earl of Crewe 18 April and 30 September 1910, Cd 5775; Economic Advisory Council, East African Sub-committee, *Report of the Tsetse Fly Committee, July 1935*, Cmd 4951, 1934-35, vii, 297. For Belgian approaches to sleeping- sickness see Maryinez Lyons, 'From "death camps" to *cordon sanitaire*: the development of sleeping-sickness policy in the Uele District of the Belgian Congo, 1903-14', *JAH* 26 (1985), pp. 69-91.
35  J. K. Chorley, 'The tsetse fly campaign in Southern Rhodesia', *JSPFE*, xxvii (1936), pp. 15-19 Ford, *Trypanosomiases*, chapter 19, 20.
36  Minutes of Deputation from SPFE to CO, 26 February 1909, Cd 5136.
37  BSAC to CO, 22 November 1909, Cd 5136.
38  Memorandum from Dr George Prentice, enclosed in Acting Governor, Nyasaland, to CO, 21 January 1911, Cd 5775. See also Livingstonia Mission to CO, 18 January 1911, Cd 5775.
39  Deputation of missionaries from the United Free Church of Scotland, Church of Scotland, London Missionary Society, Universities' Mission to Central Africa, Zambesi Industrial Mission, Scotch Baptist Mission, Baptist Missionary Society, South African General Mission to Lewis Harcourt, 23 November 1911, Cd 6671. See also another memo from Prentice, 19 February 1912; Livingstonia Mission to CO, 2 May 1912; Memo by Mr Freshwater, LMS, 31 January 1912.
40  Bagshawe to CO, 14 May 1912; Manning to Harcourt, 13 July 1912, Cd 6671.
41  Cd 7349.
42  Rupert W. Jack, 'Tsetse fly and big game in Southern Rhodesia', *Bulletin of Entomological Research*, I (1914), pp. 97-110.
43  David Bruce, Report of the Sleeping Sickness Commission (1915), Royal Society, No. 16, p. 18.
44  The details of the Southern Rhodesian campaign are contained in Ford, Chorley and Jack (notes 35 and 42 above).
45  *Oryx*, I (1950), pp. 352-4.
46  I.D.M., 'The wildlife situation in Southern Rhodesia, 1952', *Oryx*, I (1952), pp. 352-4.
47  *JSPFE*, New Series I (1921), p. 16. *JSPFE*, New Series II (1922), pp. 41-2. Barbour and Porter, 'Notes on South African wildlife conservation', 1935, p. 9.
48  Ford, *Trypanosomiases*, p. 203.
49  Ford, *Trypanosomiases*, pp. 194-219.
50  John Iliffe, *A Modern History of Tanganyika*, Cambridge, 1979, p. 271.
51  Swynnerton's papers were published in the *Bulletin of Entomological Research* and the *Transactions of the Royal Entomological Society* between 1921 and 1936. For his study of Mzila's techiques see Ford, *Trypanosomiases*, p. 334.
52  Tsetse Fly Committee, 1935, Cmd 4951.
53  Ford, *Trypanosomiases*, pp. 229-33 and 235.
54  A. E. Hamerton, 'Remarks on trypoanosomiasis in relation to man and beast in Africa', *JSPFE*, XIII (1931), pp. 20-6.
55  Stevenson-Hamilton, *South African Eden*, pp. 211-13, 165.
56  *JSPFE*, XXII (1934), p. 10. *JSPFE*, XXVI (1935), pp. 57-8. Ted Davison, *Wankie*, Cape Town, 1961, pp. 20-1, 31, 80-3, 120.

57 Andrew Roberts, *A History of Zambia*, London, 1976, p. 185.
58 See the introduction by John M. MacKenzie to a new edition of A. Blayney Percival, *A Game Ranger's Notebook*, Camden, S. C. 1988.
59 This account of the establishment of the Kenya Game Department is based on Percival's two books, Parker's *Ivory Crisis*, and material in the Parliamentary Papers.
60 Notes by Johnston on game seen from the Uganda Railway, 10 October 1899, Cd 3189.
61 Richard Meinertzhagen, *Kenya Diary, 1902-6*, Edinburgh, 1957, pp. 156-7.
62 Meinertzhagen, *Diary*, pp. 59-60, 157-8.
63 Eliot to Lansdowne, 16 April 1901; Lansdowne to Eliot, 15 May 1901; and Eliot to Lansdowne 12 June 1901, Cd 3189.
64 Delamere to FO, 17 July 1900, Cd 3189.
65 Jackson to Lyttelton, 25 August 1905, Cd 3189.
66 Report by Jackson, 16 February 1906 enclosed in Sadler to Elgin, 12 March 1906, Cd 3189.
67 Parker, *Ivory Crisis*, p. 125.
68 Bere, 'Uganda National Parks' chapter 3; Ford, *passim*.
69 Frederick Lugard, *The Rise of our East African Empire*, Edinburgh, 1893, Vol. II. pp. 159 and 211.
70 Bere, 'Uganda National Parks', chapter 3.
71 SPFE Deputation to Lyttelton, 1905 and Jackson's report, 16 February 1906, enclosed in Sadler to Elgin, 12 March 1906, Cd 3189.
72 Johnston to Salisbury, 21 November 1899, and other communications in Cd 3189.
73 Bere, 'Uganda National Parks', chapter 4, pp. 15-16. Acting Governor Stanley Tomkins to Crewe, 18 April and 30 September 1910, Cd 5775.
74 This account of the creation of the Uganda Game Department is based on the books of Pitman and Kinloch, and *JSPFE*, New Series VII (1927), pp. 23-50.
75 Kinloch, *Shamba Raiders*, pp. 202, 233. 1,446 elephants were killed in Uganda in 1932, *JSPFE* XVII (1932), p. 24.
76 Kinloch, *Shamba Raiders* p. 104.
77 Bere, 'Uganda National Parks', chapter 3, p. 19, and chapter 4, p. 17.
78 *JSPFE*, III (1907), pp. 76-7; New Series, I (1921), p. 16; VII (1927), pp. 51-3.
79 The German regulations and details on the establishment of reserves can be found in various documents in Cd 3189.
80 Iliffe, *Tanganyika*, p. 201.
81 For the effects of the war on game see the two books of Blayney Percival: *JSPFE*, vii (1927) p. 51.
82 *JSPFE*, XX (1933), p. 36.
83 Ordinances of Tanganyika, game laws.
84 Helge Kjekshus, *Ecology Control and Economic Development in East African History: the Case of Tanganyika*, London, 1977, pp. 72-5.
85 Kjekshus, *Ecology Control*, p. 170.
86 Iliffe, *Tanganyika*, p. 163.
87 Gordon Matzke, 'The development of the Selous Game Reserve', *Tanzania Notes and Records*, No. 79 and 80 (1970), pp. 37-48.
88 W. A. Rogers and J. D. Lobo, 'Elephant control and legal ivory exploition, 1920-1976', *Tanzania Notes and Records*, Nos. 84 and 85 (1980), pp. 25-54.
89 T. H. Henfrey, 'The menace to the elephant in Tanganyika Territory', *JSPFE*, VII (1927), p. 52.
90 Rogers and Lobo, 'Elephant control', p. 36.
91 These figures are compiled from data given in successive issues of *JSPFE*; elephant kills are in *JSPFE*, XXXIII (1938), pp. 44.
92 Address by Pitman to SPFE, *JSPFE* XIX (1933), pp. 9-10; See also Pitman on the Northern Rhodesian faunal survey, *JSPFE* XXVIII (1936), pp. 24-30.

**93** Sadler to Salisbury, 5 December 1899, Cd 3189.
**94** Swayne to Lyttelton, 21 November 1905, Cd 3189.
**95** For both northern Nigeria and the Sudan see the appendix to Cd 5136.
**96** Acting Governor Thorburn to Elgin, 14 September 1907, Cd 4472.
**97** C. W. Hobley, 'The London Convention of 1900', *JSPFE*, XX (1933), pp. 40 and 44-5.
**98** Kinloch, *Shamba Raiders*, p. 27.

# CHAPTER TEN

# National parks in Africa and Asia

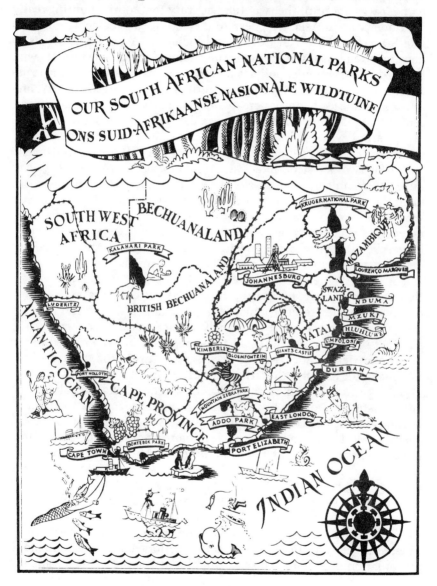

The international agreement of 1933 marked an important stage in the transformation of reserves into national parks. It was also a marker for the translation of African policies into Asia. The conservation movement gathered pace at a rather later date in Asia, for a number of reasons. The animal habitats of that continent were a great deal less publicised than those of Africa. They were less widespread, in some ways less spectacular, and more remote than their African counterparts. It was not until the twentieth century that tourist hunting really got under way in Asia, and, despite the activities of celebrated figures like Sir Samuel Baker in Ceylon and India, the Asian fauna seems to have inspired less interest among the aristocratic hunting tourists who fostered preservationist policies in Africa. There was some game legislation in Asian imperial territories in the late nineteenth century, and a few sanctuaries had been created, particularly in Ceylon, but generally the development of reserves was delayed, and in some cases the direct jump was made to national parks. In India the creation of sanctuaries was placed on a secure footing only after independence.

One or two activists, like Theodore Hubback in Malaya, began to raise the Asian consciousness of the SPFE in the 1920s, but it was not until the 1930s, particularly after the 1933 conference, that the conservation lobby resolved to press for measures of the African type to be taken in Asian territories.[1] There was to have been a conference in November 1939 to discuss the situation in Asia and Australasia, but it was overwhelmed by the war. Given this time lag between African and Asian development, it is perhaps appropriate to consider Asia in this chapter, which surveys the third phase of conservation developments when the preservationist ideas of game legislation and reserves moved towards the more genuinely conservationist concept of the national park. In many ways all three phases were compressed in the Asian experience. But first it is necessary to survey the transfer of the national park idea from North America to Africa.

Just as southern Africa was used as a model, and not always an appropriate one, for the rest of Africa in prognostications about game decline and the need for legislation and reserve provision, so was North America used as a model for the development of national parks. To a large extent the very different conditions of Africa – the problems of human settlement, the presence of the tsetse fly in all its varieties, the diseases to which both wild and domestic animals as well as people were prone – were all overridden in favour of a concept which seemed to represent a North American success story, an example of what conscience could do to redress the destructiveness of America's nineteenth-century frontier and make her flora and fauna available to a population increasingly discovering that it had the affluence and the

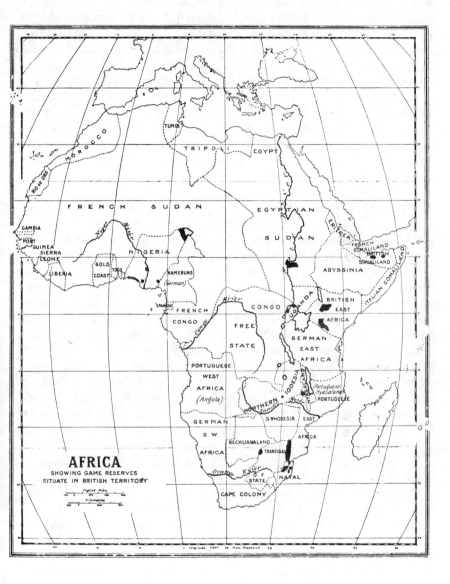

Africa, showing game reserves situated in British Territory

mobility to develop an interest. The American precedent received a great deal of attention from the proponents of African national parks and was the subject of pamphlets, tours, and much discussion in the journals of the preservation societies.[2] The first American national park, Yellowstone, was established in 1872, followed by the Sequoia, General Grant and Yosemite parks. Despite the establishment of the parks, however, early settlers had continued to hunt in them until effective legislation was introduced in 1894 and the ranger service was strengthened. By that time the bison in Yellowstone had been reduced to twenty-two head. To save them animals had to be introduced from two private captive herds, but by the 1930s a viable herd of 1,000 had been built up. In 1906 the United States introduced legislation to establish 'national monuments', and by 1929 the parks covered 12,118 square miles, the monuments 3,728 square miles, and the parks attracted 2,680,597 visitors.

The national park was distinguished from the reserve in a number of ways. Whereas the reserve was established by proclamation or ministerial decree and could be deproclaimed at will, the national park was to be established in perpetuity, requiring legislation to undermine its existence. The corollary was that its management should be largely separated from direct government control. It would be removed from the jurisdiction of any individual Ministry or department and established under a board of trustees who would formulate policy and employ staff. While government might make initial capital grants and perhaps pay the staff, at least for a period, the ultimate objective was that the parks should be self-financing. And to achieve that they would necessarily have to be accessible. Whereas reserves were designed for the recuperation and management of game stocks, often on a temporary basis and sometimes in remote and inaccessible regions, national parks would be concerned with the twin, and in some ways contradictory, aims of preserving all flora and fauna and simultaneously making them available for public recreation. Thus the national parks represented, at least in theory, an entirely new phase in conservationism. Reserves were the policy of the hunter-naturalists, a by-product of game legislation designed to limit social access to hunting. They promoted extreme notions of management such as protecting favoured animals by attacking 'vermin' like lions and wild dogs. National parks, despite their early start in the United States, were designed for an age of tourism, the era of the motor car and the camera. The environment and its inhabitants would still be managed, with all that that implied for potential mistakes in policy, but the criteria of management would be less closely related to the objectives of a hunting elite. On the other hand, national parks need not run counter to the interests of the Hunt. They could co-exist with reserves and with controlled hunting areas often stocked from adjacent parks and reserves.

The National parks were dependent on a chain of conditions. To achieve their stated objectives they had to be removed from the fickleness of government control, be run by supposedly independent agencies, and be dependent on popular support that could be stimulated only by public accessibility. When Stevenson-Hamilton came to survey the South African national parks on the eve of the Second World War he divided conservation into three levels.[3] First he identified private preserves, where specific game was conserved by landowners – sometimes for private hunting – and its natural enemies were exterminated as vermin. Second came the reserves, government sanctuaries designed to build up stocks but now hallowed by permanency. The national park was the final stage, designed – as he put it in a somewhat utopian and unpractical form – to show the public what that particular portion of the earth's surface looked like before the arrival of human influence. This idealistic objective demanded that no species should be introduced that was not indigenous. The national park was also portrayed as a vital corrective to industrialisation and urbanisation. Whereas indigenous and pioneering settler populations had lived in nature, understanding and exploiting it, whole new city populations were emerging in the twentieth century that knew little about the life of the wilds. The parks would be designed to keep them in touch with nature and by implication preserve the national health in an individual and a collective sense. Stevenson-Hamilton went further, seeing national parks as a powerful civilising influence that would remove the hunting 'instinct'. They were 'the best weapon whereby Man's impulse to destroy the beasts of the forest for his own pleasure and profit can be fought and conquered.'[4]

The national park represented a further extension of the concept of separate living spaces. Reserves demarcated land use between human cultivators and fauna. They were designed to avoid rather than promote interaction between them, each being subject to the control of an alien elite. National parks were designed for an urban society so that the denizens of the one could use their industrial technology to visit the inhabitants of the other. The visitors to national parks might come from adjacent urban areas within the same territories or from urban societies overseas, middle-class national and international tourism promoted by comfortable steamships, railways, motor vehicles and hotels in newly opened regions of the globe.

It is not surprising therefore that the first African national parks should have been in South Africa. By the 1920s an urban population suitably endowed with motor vehicles existed there to support such parks, and the country was also on an international tourist trail. The Sabi reserve and its associated extensions appeared to be under threat in the early 1920s. Those elements of the scientific community concerned with tsetse control, as well as the land-hungry farming community, were demanding its deproclamation.[5] But the Sabi reserve was saved for a number of reasons. Despite the ravages of the First World War it had continued to be restocked from Portuguese territory. The Transvaal Game Protection Society and the Wild Life Protection Society of South Africa fought for its preservation. Above all, it had the good fortune to have a railway line running through it. The line had been started before the Boer War, to connect the Lourenço Marques line to Messina on the northern border. It had yet to cross the Sabi river when the money ran out. On the eve of union the Transvaal government had discovered itself to possess surpluses of £2 million and the Selati Railway had been one of the schemes promoted to dispose of the surplus before it could be engrossed into the coffers of the Union.[6] In the early 1920s the South African Railways began to take tourist trains into the park. At first they simply passed through overnight, but they were soon stopping to give travellers a glimpse of the reserve. Almost unwittingly the railways began to demonstrate that there was a market – potentially a very large one – for viewing as well as for hunting.

Ministers of Lands in both Smuts's and Hertzog's administrations, Deneys Reitz and Piet Grobler, were converted to the concept of the national park.[7] Stevenson-Hamilton hit upon the idea of naming the Sabi after Kruger, the founder of the reserve and a great-uncle of Grobler. Landowners were bought out or received land in exchange for their holdings in the reserve, and in 1926 the legislation was passed which created a park 200 miles long by forty miles wide, covering an area of 8,000 square miles – larger than Wales. The government offered an initial capital grant of £8,000 in 1927, and by May 1928 200 miles of road had been constructed and a start made on the creation of rest camps. In succeeding years the roads were extended and improved and pontoons were established on several rivers. In 1928 240 cars containing 800 people at an entrance fee of £1 per car entered the park. By 1938 the park was receiving 38,000 visitors in 10,000 cars. By that year 1,200 miles of motor road, six entrance gates, fourteen rest camps, and low-level concrete bridges on major rivers, were in use.[8]

Earlier scepticism had proved unfounded: there was a considerable market for viewing animals. There were a number of entirely unexpected results of this contact between humans and animals. Animals did not shun the roads but were attracted to them. While earlier visitors all brought guns, the practice was soon abandoned when it was discovered that there was little call for self-defence.[9] Third, the visitors became particularly interested in lions, which Stevenson-Hamilton and his staff had regarded as vermin a short while before.[10] Indeed, the place of lions in the spectatorial passions of park visitors was described in one source as 'leontophilia' and a complete guidebook with many illustrations was issued to celebrate it.[11] The hunting elite had been expanded into a tourist elite, and the criteria of animal attractiveness had changed once more. Edibility had given way to sporting characteristics, which now gave way, at least in the parks, to viewability. By the Second World War the concept of national parks had been greatly extended in South Africa.[12] The Kalahari national park in Bechuanaland, covering 3,600 square miles, had been created to preserve game but remained unopened to the public. The Addo thickets, where the last elephant herd in the Cape had been shot to near extinction in a notorious incident in 1919, was declared a national park and restocked. The bontebuck was saved from extermination in the Bredasdorp national park, a small area of 850 morgen (1,802 acres), while the Mountain Zebra national park was created to save the Cape mountain zebra. In the 1930s there was considerable interaction between South Africa and American national parks and wildlife preservation groups. R. H. Compton, Professor of Botany at the University of Cape Town and Director of the National Botanic Gardens of South Africa, toured American national parks in 1930 and published a report which attacked 'mistaken theories of nagana', 'perverse ideas of sport' and the wanton squandering of game wealth.[13] He argued for the extension of the idea in South Africa, particularly in the Cape and Natal, following American conservation and administrative practices. In 1935 the American Committee for International Wildlife Protection published a pamphlet on South African wildlife conservation by two American zoologists, Thomas Barbour and Margaret Porter.[14] They extolled the work of the Kruger Park, attacked the Addo policy of elephant extermination, and argued that the three Natal reserves, Umfolozi, Hluhluwe and Mkuzi, should be extended and combined into a national park. (The fourth Natal reserve, Nduna, was separated from the others in the north of the province.)

*National park proposals of the 1930s.* Although the Kruger was the first in anglophone Africa, a national park had been founded in the Belgian Congo a year earlier. It was, however, more in the nature of a reserve than a park. The Albert National Park (later renamed Virunga) was created in 1925 under the influence of the American naturalist Carl Akeley.[15] It covered seventy-eight square miles, was not open to visitors, and was designed specifically to protect the mountain gorillas. It was extended in 1929 and 1935 to incorporate the Semliki plains

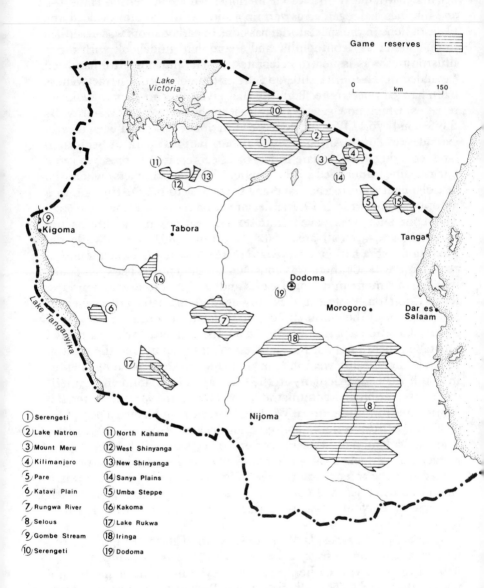

Game reserves in Tanganyika, 1947

and the western slopes of the Ruwenzori, sharing a considerable border with the colony of Uganda. The existence of this reserve gave the Belgians a significant place in the international conservation movement.

They pressed the national park idea upon the British, particularly with regard to the region of Uganda backing on to the Congo.[16] The Belgian scientist van Straelen played a prominent role in the international conferences of 1933 and 1938. Charles Pitman, the Game Warden of Uganda, formed a close connection with the conservationists M. van Tienhoven and Baron Cartier de Marchienne (who later wrote an introduction to one of Pitman's books) and they all heard the King of the Belgians address the Royal Africa Society in November 1933 on Belgium's 'great work' in conservation and the national park movement. This group hoped that the idea would soon gain ground in Asia, though the Second World War held up the plans of the pressure groups.[17] The Belgians had taken over from the Germans in prodding the British conservationist conscience. Nevertheless, the British considered national parks to be premature in British colonies. It is indeed true that the conditions that had so rapidly made the Kruger National Park such a public success did not exist. The reserves were still remote; there was only a small urban population, with few private motor vehicles; international tourism was as yet limited.

Pressures for the creation of national parks in East Africa had, however, been building up for some time. In 1930 the SPFE commissioned Major R. W. G. Hingston to visit the British colonies in East and Central Africa to report on game reserves and the potential for the creation of national parks. [18] Hingston had been a medical officer in India, the Middle East and East Africa, and had held the post of naturalist in the Indian Marine. He was the surgeon and naturalist to the Mount Everest expedition of 1924 and leader of the Oxford University expedition to British Guiana. His African tour was sanctioned by the Secretary of State for the Colonies, and he undertook to discuss game policy with governors and game wardens in Northern Rhodesia, Nyasaland, Tanganyika, Kenya and Uganda. He returned with an apocalyptic vision of the destruction of wildlife, which he saw as being in a retreat leading to annihilation. The white rhino, the gorilla, the nyala and Grevy's zebra were, in his view, on the verge of extinction. He doubted whether 'the three great pachyderms the elephant, the rhinoceros, the hippopotamus will, if present conditions continue, survive beyond the next fifty years'. The forces 'causing this annihilation' were fourfold – the spread of cultivation, the demands of trade, the activities of sportsmen (in fact he exonerated European sportsmen and attacked what he saw as the indiscriminate methods of Africans) and the menace of disease.

His solution was the creation of national parks, and in proposing them he put forward the most uncompromising argument for total segregation of human and animal life. The national park, he argued, must be formed behind inviolate frontiers, a State within a State, a sanctuary for all time. There would be 'no permanent solution' to problems of crops and stock, of disease and the hunting instinct, until 'the human life and the wild life are separated into two completely distinct compartments'. The ideal national park had to be large (he specified 2,000 to 8,000 square miles); it should have few if any inhabitants; it should contain scenic attractions like Ngorongoro Crater, Mount Kilimanjaro and the Murchison Falls, to attract tourists; and it should be made readily accessible and comfortable for them. He proposed nine national parks in the five colonies, involving extensions to and combinations of existing reserves. Three of them were to be small ones to protect specific species (the nyala in Nyasaland, the bongo in Kenya, the gorilla in Uganda), but the other six were to be vast tracts of territory based on the Kruger model. One would straddle the border of Northern Rhodesia and Nyasaland, incorporating the Kasungu and Luangwa Valley reserves, three (the Selous, the Serengeti and the Kilimanjaro) for Tanganyika, one (the northern reserve somewhat extended) for Kenya, and one (the Bunyoro-Gulu reserve on the Nile) for Uganda. His proposals were favourably received by the Royal Geographical Society and the SPFE, but the colonial administration was not yet ready to move.

The 1930s were indeed a decade of intensive activity in reporting upon colonial preservation policies, the creation of game departments, and the transformation of reserves into national parks. Charles Pitman was seconded from Uganda to Northern Rhodesia for two years to examine the reserves, Kafue, Mweru Marsh and the recently created David Livingstone to the south-east of Lake Bangweulu.[19] He made aerial surveys of Northern Rhodesia and saw the havoc wrought upon African cultivation by elephants and other game, despite African efforts to build game fences and watch towers.[20] Nevertheless, some African chiefs were known to favour game preservation, one even creating his own game reserve, which continued to be publicised in *Northern Rhodesian Handbooks* into the 1950s.[21] Pitman saw the need for an Elephant Control Department on the Uganda model. In fact a game department was not created in Northern Rhodesia until 1940.

In 1931 the SPFE sent Colonel A. H. Haywood, formerly inspector-general of the West African Field Force and an ardent hunter, to report on game preservation in the four West African colonies.[22] He made a series of recommendations on the creation of new game reserves in place of older, unsatisfactory ones. He proposed the abolition of the Gilli Gilli and Gorgoram reserves in Nigeria (the latter being in the heart of a sleeping-sickness area), the retention of the Orle and Anambra reserves, one in Borgu to be a national park. The reserve around Lake Chad had already been abolished after the First World War, partly because of an excessive population of elephants, partly to increase the cultivated area. He believed that a game warden and sixty-four native guards could be provided out of licence revenue. So far as the Gold Coast was concerned, he proposed the abolition of the existing reserves at Kwahu, Obusum Sene and Onyim Sene, and the creation of national parks in the Prah-Anum Forest Reserve and either in North Kwachi or north-east Kintampo. As there were no reserves in the Gambia or Sierra Leone, he contented himself with suggesting modifications of the game legislation, as he had already done for Nigeria and the Gold Coast. But there were severe impediments to the development of national parks in West Africa. Just as visiting elite hunting did not take place there, because of its reputation as an unhealthy region, so was it very unlikely that tourists would be attracted to national parks. There was only a small European population in each territory, there were no white settlers, and there was a dense African population which, unlike the colonial territories of eastern and southern Africa, retained traditional hunting rights. Little was done to adopt Haywood's suggestions.

*National parks after the Second World War.* The national park phase of the conservation movement was held up by the Second World War, but with the end of hostilities Clement Attlee's government was anxious to promote the national parks idea.[23] The National Parks Act, providing for the creation of conservation areas in Britain, became law in 1949, but as with so many State initiatives the empire had led the way. The first plans for parks in East Africa had been laid down before the war, and some of these were put into effect imediately after its conclusion. The Kenya National Parks Ordinance was gazetted in 1945, and in the succeeding years there was a great deal of discussion of the extension of the parks in Africa.[24] Pressure groups ranging from the SPFE (later renamed the Fauna Protection Society) to the Zoological Society of London and the British Museum (Natural History) took up the cause, and there was a good deal of press interest in what seemed to be a positive element in a brighter post-war prospect. In 1948 the Colonial Office circularised East African governors on their plans for game conservation, and colonial committees were established. The foundation of national parks followed in rapid succession. In this survey the usual geographical order, moving from Central to East Africa, will be followed, although to a certain extent it conflicts with the chronological progression.

*Central Africa.* In Southern Rhodesia national parks originated in the preservation of areas of natural beauty hallowed by the preference of Cecil Rhodes. Rhodes left land in the Matopo hills and the Inyanga mountains to be developed as public 'parks'. The Rhodes estate, much enlarged, was declared a national park, covering 224,000 acres, by an act of the Rhodesian Assembly in 1926. The creation of parks thus preceded the emergence of game reserves and had only an indirect connection with game. In fact, as parks were enlarged, Africans were dispossessed and animal populations grew. Other national parks associated with gardens were created in the Vumba and at Ewanrigg, north of Salisbury. Parks devoted specifically to game on the Kruger model appeared only after the Second World War.

A Natural Resources Board was established in Southern Rhodesia in 1942 and a commission under the High Court judge Sir Robert McIlwaine proposed the extension of game preservation policies.[25] After the war a Department of National Parks was founded in 1949. Originally it had jurisdiction over the Wankie game reserve shortly converted into a national park, the Robins Sanctuary, Gazuma Pan (seventy-six square miles), the Chimanimani mountains and portions of the Rhodes Inyanga estate. By the time of Rhodesia's unilateral declaration of independence in 1965 reserves and national parks had appeared in the Victoria Falls area (210 square miles); on the southern shores of Lake Kariba (the Chete and Matusadona reserves, the latter 502 square miles); a vast area on the Zambezi stretching from the eastern borders of Kariba to the Dande tribal trust lands bordering on Mozambique, including the Mana Pools reserve (894 square miles), and the Chiriza and Dande game reserves, both on African Parks and Wild Life land; the Rhodes Inyanga and Rhodes Matopos estates; Gona-re-Zhou on the Limpopo; the Malapati game reserve on African land in the south-eastern low-veld; and smaller parks at Sebakwe and around Lakes Kyle, McIlwaine and Ngezi. By that time the national parks and wildlife land (the vast majority of which was devoted to game) covered 12 per cent of the total area of the country, 18,244 square miles (47,264 square kilometres). Most of this land was on the fringes of the territory usually well away from white settlement, with the land demarcated for African use acting as buffer territory between the game and the whites. Thus the establishment of reserves and national parks did not mark a reversal of the shooting policies of the past but the final working out of the tripartite division of land use, whites, blacks and game. Though not planned from the start, the two policies became one, the first eliminating game and tsetse from white and some black land, pressing forward land separation which would be consummated in the Land Apportionment Act of 1931 and the National Parks Department from 1949.

In order to continue policies of encouraging tourist hunting, controlled hunting areas were established around the edges of the Wankie park, along the Zambezi (Urungwe, Nyakasanga, Rekomitche and Sapi), and in the south (Tuli). Large tracts of land were also turned over to game-ranching in the low-veld and to the north and east of Bulawayo.

Policies in Northern Rhodesia were not dissimilar. As we have seen, land segregation on the line of rail and in the north-east of the country had encouraged the recovery of game. The Kafue reserve was transformed into a national park, covering 8,650 square miles, in 1950.[26] By that time it was almost entirely free of African population except for a few small settlements under Chief Kayingu. For five years only the southern portion of the park was open to visitors while roads and rest camps were built. The northern sector was kept closed to permit the game to increase. The parks became more accessible only from 1956. By 1950 the combined area of reserves and national parks, 18,435 square miles, constituted 6.5 per cent of the country. Interestingly, Africans attempted to participate in the income available from game viewing. Chief Nsefu established a game camp in a seventy square-mile reserve on the east bank of the Luangwa.[27] A charge of 10s per night was made for simple accommodation, and African game guards escorted visitors to see the game on foot. It was sufficiently successful for a neighbouring chief to be said in 1953 to be considering the idea.

*East Africa.* In East Africa Kenya led the way, as it had done in the 1890s. National parks were established under the National Parks Ordinance of 1945. The Nairobi national park, forty-four square miles on the edge of the capital itself, was proclaimed in December 1946. The much vaster Tsavo national park, 8,069 square miles athwart the Nairobi–Mobasa road and railway line, much as the original reserve had done, followed in 1948. By the 1950s it had 800 miles of roads and tracks and three safari lodges. The vast northern and southern reserves established under the game legislation of 1906 and 1909 were converted into the Marsabit national park (10,000 square miles) and the Mara, Ngong and West Chyula national reserves respectively. The Amboseli national reserve, on the northern slopes of Mount Kilimanjaro, was converted into a national park and others were established for historical and archaeological purposes, as at Gedi and Olorgesailie, or for scenic and botanical reasons, as in the mountain parks of Mount Kenya and the Aberdares.[28] The latter were closed for the duration of the Mau Mau emergency and the game parks were soon embroiled in problems of drought, overstocking, culling and poaching, but that forms part of a different story. By the 1950s the dreams of Frederick Jackson, Richard

Meinertzhagen and Blayney Percival – the conversion of a large proportion of the land area of Kenya into game sanctuaries – had been achieved.

In Tanganyika the Serengeti national park (including the Ngorongoro Crater) was already being planned by 1947 and was announced in the colony's *Handbook*. However, its boundaries were not agreed and it was officially gazetted only in 1950. By that year there were also eighteen game reserves and controlled areas, and as we have seen the vast Selous had continued to grow dramatically. In 1951 a new Fauna Preservation Ordinance was passed, although the colony's tourist publicity stressed that relatively unfettered game hunting as well as viewing were on offer. The Serengeti remained the only national park for some time, but by 1960 game reserves and controlled areas covered 70,000 square miles, 19.6 per cent of Tanzania's total land areas of 357,000 square miles.[29]

The creation of the Ugandan national parks makes an interesting case study because we have two, in some respects conflicting, accounts of their formation, one by Bruce Kinloch, Chief Game Warden from 1949, and the other by Rennie Bere, Director of the Ugandan national parks from 1954.[30] The Ugandan National Parks Committee was set up in 1948 but did not report until 1950. It recommended the creation of parks in Uganda, but took the small Nairobi park as its model. It therefore proposed that only 10 per cent of Uganda's reserves should be accorded park status. Kinloch set out to rebut the suggestion. He pointed out that the Nairobi park was dependent on the much larger Kitengela conservation area and the Ngong reserve for its restocking and argued, calling the 1933 Convention as evidence, that to be effective national parks had to be large. He faced the opposition of the Department of Agriculture, which was anxious to develop the potential cotton-growing land in the regions of Lakes Edward and George. In 1951 Kinloch successfully lobbied the new Governor of Uganda, Sir Andrew Cohen, before he left London to take up his appointment.[31] Cohen was one of the more imaginative gubernatorial appointments of the twentieth century. He had energy and vision, coupled with an outstanding intellect and radical inclinations. He neatly demonstrates the manner in which the post-war conservationist movement appealed to those on the left as an enlightened ecological policy. If reserves had been the brainchild of a hunting elite, identified with the imperial right, national parks were the inspiration of the new environmental lobbyists, the forerunners of the 'Greens'. The reactionary preservation had become the visionary conservation.

With the arrival of Cohen in Uganda, events moved fast. A Uganda National Parks Act was formulated and passed in March 1952. The

Kinloch large-scale park had won acceptance against the Uganda National Parks Committee's small-scale model. The Queen Elizabeth National Park (formerly Kasinga, later Ruwenzori) in the lakes area had a total area of 764 square miles, while the Murchison Falls (later Kabalega) National Park in the north covered 1,504 square miles. The Attorney-General of Uganda, Ralph Dreschfield, who became the first chairman of the national parks board of trustees, described the parks as being designed 'for the recreation and edification of the people of Uganda'. In fact, like most of the African parks they were to prove much more significant in the recreation and edification of international tourists. But Dreschfield's phrase helped to identify some of the 'native authorities' of Uganda who opposed the creation of the parks as reactionary forces.

Rennie Bere offers interesting insights into the opposition of Africans to this development and the way their objections were overridden. As Provincial Commissioner of the northern province he persuaded the Acholi tribal council to accept the creation of the park. The Acholi, as Bere himself describes, had a long-standing tradition of organised tribal hunting which ensured that too many animals were not killed and that no area was hunted over too frequently. They had long been critical of the government's policy on game, particularly the moving of people in the name of tsetse control. To win them over Bere had to deliver the assembled chiefs an impassioned lecture. Similar apprehension came from the Toro district administration, already anxious about other developments, such as commercial fishing on Lake George, the copper mine at Kilembe and the expatriate tea and coffee estates. George Rukidi, later the ruler of Toro, was opposed to the park, but he was soon won over and supported it with all the enthusiasm of the converted.[32] The parks board was duly set up, and the trustees included prominent sportsmen and aristocratic members of the SPFE.

Nevertheless the contrast between the old policies of preservation, hunting and control and the new concept of conservation with access was emphasised in the separation of the national park boards and administrations from the game departments. This ocurred in Kenya, Tanganyika and Uganda. The game departments were government organisations concerned with enforcing the game laws, protecting crops and maintaining the remaining reserves and controlled hunting areas. In Uganda the Game Department was also concerned with the development of the lake fisheries. It had taken on this responsibility in 1933, and in 1949 its name was changed to the Department of Game and Fisheries.[33] The implication was that the department was concerned with animal stocks for their potential exploitation as a resource, while the national parks were in the business of absolute protection.

[ 275 ]

Their functions and responsibilities, however, clearly overlapped, and in Uganda it was not long before there was a clash over their supposed alternative philosophies.

When Ken Beaton, the first Director of Uganda's National Parks died in 1954 he was succeeded by the ex-provincial commissioner Rennie Bere. Bere was anxious to distance the parks from the Game Department, believing that the latter was unpopular and that any association with it would hinder the public acceptability of the parks. There seems, moreover, to have been a clash of personality between him and Bruce Kinloch. By 1956 the policy of protection had led to an explosion in the hippo population of the National Parks.[34] There were said to be 14,000 of the animals in the Queen Elizabeth alone. They were overgrazing the grass cover, with two effects: the food source of other species was being destroyed, putting them at risk, and serious problems of erosion were becoming apparent. Uganda was now firmly in the ambit of the international wildlife organisations. American zoologists on Fulbright scholarships and associated with the American Committee for International Wildlife Protection and the American Wildlife Management Institute were active in game studies in the colony and recommended large-scale culling of hippos. Since this suited Game Department practice, Kinloch and his staff approved. Bere and the national parks trustees were anxious about an outcry from the conservation lobby and clung to their founding concept of protection. But their objections were overborne under the weight of scientific opinion and the growing evidence of the destructive scale of the problem. Through game management the practices of the two branches of wildlife protection were forced to converge.

The final years of colonial rule in East Africa witnessed the extension of conservation policies. The East Africa Wildlife Association was founded in 1956. In 1958 the Kidepo game reserve was proclaimed, covering 500 square miles of the remote Karamoja region of Uganda where traditional hunting and cross-border raiding had continued until recent times. In 1961 an East African wildlife conference was held at Arusha in Tanzania.[35] Julius Nyerere, the President of the newly independent republic, signed the Arusha manifesto (not to be confused with the later Arusha Declaration), which pledged the new government to the continuation of wildlife policies (appendix IV). This was given practical expression in the proclamation of four new parks in Tanzania, Lake Manyara, Ngurdoto Crater (later Arusha), Ruaha and Mkumi, all previously game reserves and game-controlled areas. Africanisation of the game department was pushed forward at a speed which alarmed the old colonial conservationists, but Kinloch was instrumental in founding in Tanzania a College of African Wildlife Management,

[ 276 ]

which opened in 1963 with the object of training game staff from a number of African countries.

The history of wildlife conservation in the post-colonial period lies beyond the scope of this study. However, a number of figures serve to illustrate the extent to which the continuation of colonial game practices seemed to make good economic sense. At independence the tourist industry contributed £8 million to the Kenyan economy. In the late 1960s the value of tourism in Kenya, Uganda and Tanzania together totalled £20 million. Tanzania maintained 70,000 square miles of its land area as reserves and national parks. In 1969, in the pre-Amin era, 37,666 tourists visited the Murchison Falls Park while 18,719 went to the Queen Elizabeth (renamed Ruwenzori) National Park.[36]

In other words, game helped to convince the inheritor governments that tourism was a worthwhile sector of the post-colonial eonomy. The debate among economists on the benefits and disadvantages of tourism to developing economies can therefore ultimately be linked to twentieth-century ideas on conservation. Perhaps in this context it should be remembered that the creation of many of the game reserves had been rooted in the sequence of disasters of the 1890s, involving the loss of cattle from nagana or rinderpest, the contraction, dispersal and exclusion of human populations, and that these reserves had in turn been extended and frozen as wildlife sanctuaries and objects of international tourism. In fact the fortunes of many parks were to go through severe vicissitudes in the aftermath of decolonisation. Some became a haven of dissidents and resisters in civil wars, others the sanctuary of guerrillas operating against white rule in southern Africa. Once more game became a resource in human conflict, and the parks represented political and military frontiers rather than recreational areas for urban populations.

*Asia*. The history of conservation in the British Asiatic possessions is somewhat less complex than that in Africa. This is partly because there were no ecological crises and controversies on the scale of those relating to the tsetse, nagana, sleeping-sickness and other diseases, partly because conservation carried fewer implications for human settlement and partly because, in the absence of hunting tourism, Asia received a great deal less attention. As a result, imperial legislation was less extensive and complicated, and the application of conservationist ideas was delayed. Indeed, in the case of India, modern conservationism became the policy of the independent republic rather than of the imperial authority. The rest of this chapter surveys the development of conservationism in Malaya, Ceylon, Burma (about which there is very little information) and, at somewhat greater length,

[ 277 ]

India.

*Malaya.* The development of game protection, sanctuaries and national parks was greatly complicated by the administrative divisions of the region. As well as the Straits Settlements (Penang, Malacca, Singapore), directly administered by Britain, there were the Federated Malay States (Pahang, Selangor, Perak and Negri Sembilan), which had a close administrative relationship with the British , and the unfederated Malay States, which were merely under British protection. The first relevant legislation in Malaya dated from 1884, when an ordinance of the Straits Settlements gave protection to wild birds. In 1896 Pahang afforded protection to the elephant, seladang, or Indian bison, and rhinoceros. The first major piece of legislation, the Wild Animals and Birds Protection Enactment of 1911 was widely regarded as a dead letter because it was inadequately enforced. Licences were issued to cultivators for crop protection and a provision forbidding the transfer of such licenses was readily flouted. It was claimed that the seladang was virtually wiped out in Pahang, and European hunters found many seladang and elephant in Negri Sembilan already wounded from indiscriminate shooting. There can be no doubt, however, that crop protection was essential, while European planters complained that elephants loved the bark of rubber trees and could rapidly destroy an entire plantation. Some revenue was derived from licences under the 1911 ordinance, but there was no game department and no separate expenditure on enforcement officers.[37]

Conservationist pressure produced a new Wild Animals and Birds Protection Enactment in 1922. The Act included provision for licences, a ban on killing immature animals, the need for keeping game records, and the possibility of proclaiming game sanctuaries and the appointment of a game warden. But it was a long time before the latter provision was implemented. It was alleged that little game survived in Selangor and Perak, although areas suitable as game reserves could be found in Pahang and Negri Sembilan. In the five States outside the federation a variety of arrangements could be found. The State of Trengganu had 'an efficient game enactment'; Kelantan protected some animals which could be shot only under licence; Kedah, Johore and Perlis paid little attention to game proection. By 1925 there were four game reserves, one in Negri Sembilan and three in Pahang. The Serting reserve in Negri Sembilan and the Sungei Lui reserve in Pahang were adjacent, making a compact block of 130,000 acres, while Pahang's other two reserves were Krau (135,000 acres) and the Gunang Tahan (36,000 acres). Each of the Federated States appointed honorary game wardens, all of whom, except one, had very little time to devote to game.[38]

The exception was Theodore Hubback, who was resident in Malaya from the 1890s and was the leading exponent of game preservation in the territory. Born in Liverpool in 1872, he entered the service of the Public Works Department in Malaya in 1895, and spent a period as Director of Public Works in British North Borneo. At the end of the First World War he was commissioned by the natural history museums in South Kensington and New York to secure specimens of a rare sheep, ovis dalli, in northern Alaska. In 1920 he settled in Pahang and devoted the rest of his life to game preservation. When appointed honorary game warden of that State he was therefore able to devote himself to the work full-time. His activities did not meet with universal approval. Planters felt that their operations were incompatible with the survival of elephants and other forms of game (mainly seladang, pig and deer). He aroused 'a wave of indignation' and was accused of working to make Pahang 'a place fit for elephants to live in'. The SPFE, prodded by Hubback, made representations to the Colonial Office about the situation in Malaya and raised the subject when a deputation met the Under-secretary for the Colonies in 1924. A new game law was passed in 1926, and Hubback was appointed to a commisssion to investigate the preservation of game in 1930.[39] He was asked to consider the value of the existing regulations, the possibility of establishing a national park, the effectiveness of the game reserves, and the allegations of damage to agriculture caused by wildlife.

Hubback and a government assessor received commissions to carry out investigations in the four Federated and five unfederated Malay States. They travelled 7,264 miles and eventually produced a three-volume report running to 1,089 pages. They argued that there was a consensus in support of game protection, although peasant cultivators seem to have entertained some doubts:

> In a few places, chiefly in Pahang, peasant witnesses, who may have been labouring under the delusion that this enquiry was primarily appointed to deprive them of the admitted rights to protection, or who may have been afraid that they might be asked to pay for something which at present they take for nothing, were hostile towards any steps for conservation.[40]

Some witnesses, indeed, felt that all animals which damaged crops should be exterminated. The report suggested the appointment of game wardens and supporting staff in each State, a game commissioner to cover the Straits Settlements and all States in a supervisory role, the distribution of 'propaganda' with regard to game, the establishment of a Wild Life Fund, and a total prohibition on the commercialisation of wild life. The existing sanctuaries should be constituted under secure tenure, a national park shuld be established at Gunang Tahan, and the Krau game reserve should be turned into a park. Hubback also pointed out that there was a considerable disparity between the revenue and expenditure accruing from wild life in the years 1928-30. Hubback's report was the first of several. As usual, the private sector in the shape of the SPFE commissioned reports too. Just as the society had sent travelling commissioners to African territories in the early 1930s, they sent Sir Thomas Comyn-Platt to various Asian territories.[41] In 1937 he produced reports on fauna preservation in Ceylon and Malaya.

It was some time before the Malayan authorities responded to Hubback's proposals, but when they did he himself was given the title of Commissioner of Wild Life. A chief Game Warden, E. O. Shebbeare, was appointed in 1938 and in the same year the King George V National Park was created, covering territory in Kelantan, Pahang and Trengganu. The park headquarters were established at Kuala Tahan, with a resident superintendant and thirteen rangers. Seventy thousand Straits dollars were spent before the war.[42] The establishment of a game administration and development of the park were brought to a halt by the Japanese invasion in 1941. Theodore Hubback was murdered in 1944 by a Malay who presumably had a grudge against him. The best Malay game ranger in Negri Sembilan, Zinal, was executed by the Japanese while attempting to stick to his post. But the game survived the Japanese occupation because the invaders imposed the death penalty for the possession of firearms. In fact, Shebbeare wrote in 1945, it was under greater threat when the British returned in 1945, since officers and troops were keen to get what sport they could. The military authorities found it necessary to register sporting weapons and start the issue of licences at a temporary Game Department office in Kuala Lumpur. The Game Department was reconstituted in 1947. Arrangements for the appointment of trustees and the promulgation of the rules of the park were made in 1948, but the development of the King George V Park and the newly established Templar Park were again held up, this time by the outbreak of the Emergency, which was partly fought over the park's domain.[43] Templar was finally established in 1954 and retained its name after independence, though the George V was renamed the Taman Negara National Park. Malaysia now has six parks (four of them in the Bornean States) covering a total area of over 2,000 square miles.

*Ceylon.* Ceylon had been the happy hunting ground of Sir Samuel Baker and his acolytes. Baker himself charted the drastic decline of game during the period he knew the island. As elsewhere, anxieties were first translated into legislative action in the 1880s. An ordinance for the protection of wild birds had been introduced in 1886.[44] In 1889 the Conservator of Forests, Colonel Clarke, pressed for conservation measures and two ordinances were passed in 1891. One of these, ordinance No. 10, made provision for the prevention of the wanton destruction of wild elephants, wild buffaloes and other game. In 1907 rules were framed under the Forest Ordinance forbidding all native hunting methods and establishing two game sanctuaries, the Yala in the southern province and the Wilpattu in the north central region. Together they covered some 360,000 acres (562.5 square miles). Of these two, Yala received a lot of attention, but Wilpattu was largely neglected. In fact the Yala sanctuary seems to have been gazetted somewhat earlier, for it is recorded that in 1903 one H. E. Engelbrecht, a Boer prisoner on the island during the Boer War, was appointed guardian, a somewhat ironic appointment in a number of respects. The Game Protection Society of Ceylon, one of the earliest of colonial conservationist bodies, had been founded in 1894 and it provided 'watchers' to guard the sanctuaries. The Yala 'Surround' adjacent to the reserve was a controlled hunting area open to sportsmen shooting under licence. Legislation and regulations were consolidated in the Game Protection Ordinance of 1909, and in 1912 the Game Protection Society made representations about the decline in wild buffalo, already ravaged by rinderpest, and a ban on shooting them was introduced. There were the usual tensions between preservationists and cultivators. The members of the society alleged that the protection of crops was used merely as an excuse for killing game for meat. In their view animals were in fact being destroyed for the sale of their meat and skins.

Tensions within the European community surfaced in 1928.[45] The government Veterinary Department considered the Yala sanctuary overcrowded, creating problems for nearby cultivated land. To the consternation of the Game Protection Society a culling programme was begun. The society managed to enlist the support of the Governor, Sir Herbert Stanley, who had been Governor of Southern Rhodesia, and who was said to be sympathetic to game preservation. In fact a new reserve was planned in the Central Highlands, and the 1930s were to see further advances in preservation. In 1930 the forest administration came under the control of the Minister of Agriculture and Lands, the Hon. D. S. Senanayake, who seems to have been interested in game issues. He appointed a Fauna and Flora Advisory Committee, and the Game Protection Society undertook a campaign to ensure that the provisions of the 1933 Convention on African game were introduced into Ceylon.

In 1938 a major Fauna and Flora Protection Ordinance, following the 1933 principles, was passed, under which a whole range of 'preserves' of differing status was established. The Wilpattu sanctuary became the Wilpattu National Park, covering 212 square miles. Yala was declared a 'Strict Natural Reserve' at 150 square miles. A small park of fifty-three square miles was created in the Buttawa zone, the western part of the Yala Surround. The various reserves were scattered in the low, mid and mountain regions in order to preserve the species of the different ecologies of the island. The total area in each category was as follows:

|  | Acres | Square miles |
| --- | --- | --- |
| Strict natural reserves | 183,392 | 286·6 |
| National parks | 169,852 | 265·4 |
| Intermediate zones | 355,760 | 524·6 |
| Sanctuaries | 208,619 | 326 |
|  | 897,623 | 1,402·5 |

The total figure represented 5·54 per cent of the land area of the colony.[46] Hunting under licence was permitted in the intermediate zones. Before the war a start was made on the establishment of a game department and on making the parks accessible by the provision of motor roads. This policy continued to be developed until independence in 1948.

*Burma*. As in India, game preservation was established under the forest laws. A game warden, H. C. Smith, was appointed in 1928 and annual Game Department reports were issued thereafter. By 1931, when Smith resigned, there were four game sanctuaries in the territory, the Pidaung (260 sqare miles), the Schwe-u-Daung (126 square miles, of which forty-six were in the federated Shan States), the Kahilu (sixty-two square miles, created primarily to protect the rare *Rhinoceros sondaicus*), and the small Maymyo (forty-nine square miles) near the European hill station. In his 1931 report Smith proposed that the first two should be converted into national parks and urged the foundation of a Wild Bird and Animal Protection Society. Steamship and railway companies could, he hoped, put Burma on the wildlife tourist trail. He also reported on the numbers of 'vermin' shot in 1930-31, which makes a fascinating list. They included 374 tigers (492 in 1929-30), 829 leopards (1,242), and 1,018 bears (1,119). Four hundred and fifty-five elephants were captured for domestication (ninety-three died) and 104 elephants were killed for crop protections, under sporting licences or in self-defence. There were also two game sanctuaries in the Shan States. Smith was succeeded by E. H. Peacocke in 1931, but after a few months the post was laid down as part of the financial retrenchment measures of the period. By 1935 game reports were again being issued and another sanctuary, in the Moscos Island (nineteen square miles) had been established. The Burma Wild Life Protection Bill, a major piece of legislation, became law in Octber 1936.[47]

*India.* The statute book of British India was notably lacking in game legislation. Despite the importance of hunting in the life of the imperial elite in the sub-continent, despite the great richness and variety of the Indian fauna, there is nothing comparable with the complex series of enactments on game and hunting characteristic of the African colonies from the 1890s. There are, perhaps, several reasons for this. The most spectacular of India's game – wild elephants, rhinoceros, tigers, gaur (Indian Bison) and wild buffalo – inhabited relatively wild and inaccessible regions (usually under the control of the Indian Forest Service) that could be reached only by a small, and necessarily senior, hunting elite. Second, with the possible exception of Kashmir and Nepal (both outside the jurisdiction of British India), there was very little in the way of tourist shikar in the sub-continent. Third, many of the most important game areas were in the Indian princely States, which lay beyond the writ of imperial legislation. Many of the princes were enthusiastic preservers for sport. Their autocratic authority, their own hunting and shooting tastes, and their jealous restriction of access to a visiting elite, ensured that poaching and tourist hunting were kept to a minimum. Certain forms of the Hunt, like pig-sticking or tiger shooting from elephant-back, were so complex in organisation and highly ritualised as to be accessible only to very specific social groups. Finally, the shooting of antelope and deer in cultivated land, much the most 'democratic' of hunting pursuits in India – in so far as it was indulged in by the common soldiery and lower officialdom of Anglo-Indian society – could readily be depicted as crop protection.

In fact the first attempt to regulate access to game was made under the Indian Forest Act, No. VII of 1878. Under this Act forest produce was deemed to include the skins, horns, tusks and bones of wild animals. The delegated provisions of the legislation enabled the Forest Department to make regulations which would restrict the hunting rights of the indigenous forest inhabitants, and confirm the position of the forest officer as the protector of their stock and crops; and, later in the century, to administer the hunting resources of the forests by dividing them into shooting blocks which would be opened and closed in turn, depending on the apparent fluctuations in the faunal population. This technique was to become the prime instrument of conservation in India in the twentieth century. There were, however, other pieces of legislation. The Madras Act to prevent the indiscriminate destruction of wild elephants, 1873, was later extended to Mysore, Orissa and Assam. The central government's Elephant Preservation Act of 1879 restricted the capture of wild elephants, and prohibited their hunting and killing except in self-defence or in cases of damage to property (presumably including crops). Before an elephant could be shot it had to be officially proclaimed as falling in one of the dangerous categories. In Madras, Act No. II of 1879 defined various categories of game and established the authority to fix a close season for shooting in the Nilgiris. In 1887 these provisions were extended to the whole of British India by Act No. XX of the central government.[48] This Act for the Protection of Wild Birds and Game was also concerned with the sale of plumage and furs and contained provision for Municipal Orders and other local government powers. The permissive character of much of the legislation reflected the diversity of conditions and the range of authorities in British India. There was no imperial uniformity and central government found it impossible to legislate on game in the manner that was to become commonplace in the African colonies.

The twentieth century did see some extension of this legislative activity. Evidence of over-shooting led to the introduction of conservation measures and shooting regulations in Kashmir in Edwardian times. In British India the Wild Birds and Animals Protection Act of 1912 consolidated the nineteenth-century legislation, though in a very brief form. There were further forest Acts in 1927 and, after independence, in 1950, and 'sporting' principles were given legal sanction through the introduction of 'shooting rules' in various provinces – for example, in Bihar and Orissa in 1930.[49] An individual species was protected in the Bengal Rhinoceros Preservation Act of 1932. Bhopal and the United Provinces introduced Wild Birds and Animals Protection Acts in 1930 and 1934 respectively. Independence brought a considerable quickening of legislative activity on conservation and there was a sequence of national park Acts in the 1950s. Indeed the main thrust of the international conservation movement was fully felt only in the post-independence period.

The 1912 Act, the main piece of legislation of British India, was comparatively short. It merely set out the opportunity for local governments in the Indian provinces to declare close seasons, with penalties for killing in the closed period or selling the flesh or other parts of animals killed at that time. There were exemptions for scientific purposes and self-defence. The Act was open to criticism for its zoological inexactitude, the fact that it said nothing about immature beasts, and was, in the last analysis, purely permissive. In fact the main preservationist task remained with the Forest Service in this period. The forests of India covered 245,612 square miles, or a quarter of the land area of the Indian empire. In addition there were 128,300 square miles of forests in the Indian States. From the turn of the century the Forest Department began to create game sanctuaries. These could be formed in two ways: an area could be closed until the head of game had become satisfactory, after which shooting would be regulated and no further closure would be necessary; or an area could be automatically closed and reopened for certain periods of years. In the latter case it was thought that three years' closure was sufficient to permit the temporary recovery of the game. In the former it would be expected that the closure would be for a longer period.

The forests of the Central Provinces had the most developed system.[50] Some sanctuaries created in 1902 were still closed in 1912. Through the temporary closure of forest blocks sanctuaries were automatically formed on a rotating basis. In addition to the closure and opening of specific blocks only a certain number of head of any particular species might be shot, and the permit of each sportsman was endorsed with the number he might shoot. One of the senior forest officers, E. P. Stebbing, pointed out that the system might not protect species with a long gestation period and slow maturation like the rhino.[51] He suggested a more diverse set of sanctuaries in some of which specific species might be absolutely protected or in others all shooting halted in perpetuity. It followed, of course, that adequate policing arrangements would be required.

In the 1920s it was alleged that the game legislation of India was virtually a dead letter.[52] There were few officials specifically charged with protection, although some 'watchers' had been appointed to a few sanctuaries and preserves. There were very few convictions. There had been a considerable growth in the number of firearms in the hands of Indians since the granting of licences for crop protection had been liberalised – as the threat of revolt receded – in the twentieth century. Forest guards, who were charged with preventing poaching in the government forests, found it difficult to argue with armed poachers and might also be amenable to bribery. Moreover the demand for leather in the First World War had led to the opening of many more tanneries and an increase in the supply of hides from a range of sources that were not enquired into too closely. After the war there was little sign of a decline in the tourist market for shikar trophies, horns and skins, and merchants in the port cities were eager to supply these items to those who did not hunt. A complex network of illicit hunting and trading lay behind such sales. European officers, civil, military and forest, continued to hunt with some at least of their old enthusiasm, and motor vehicles had made many areas more accessible. There were also reports of shooting from cars and other wheeled vehicles as well as night shooting with bright lights.

It was in the late '20s that the SPFE turned its attention to India. The society began to press for the study of the Indian fauna, its decline and preservation, the tightening of the game laws, the appointment of appropriate officials and the establishment of protected areas. Conservation was by no means new to India. There are stories of the protection of game in Indian mythology. Ashoka's Fifth Pillar Edicts of the third century B.C. gave protection to fish, game and forests.[53] Local people had for long recognised some animals at least as a resource and conserved them for more effective exploitation. Peasants in one area of South India, around Lake Vedauthangal, had carefully preserved birds for the guano which they used as a fertiliser. Both the Mughals and the British had indulged in game preservation for sport, and the British had encourged the preservationist activities of the princely rulers, many of whom represented the Mughal inheritance in modern India. Among the Hindus certain birds and animals, like the blue pigeon, peafowl, nilgai and monkeys, had long been given religious protection as sacred beasts.

The 1920s saw the shift from the concept of game to that of wildlife, from the notion of preservation to that of conservation. Under its president, Lord Onslow, the SPFE began to receive alarmed accounts of the destruction of the Indian fauna and commenced a programme of representations to the British government that matched their earlier lobbying of the Colonial Office. It so happened that three viceroys in the period up to the Second World War, Irwin (Halifax), Willingdon and Linlithgow, were fervent hunters and eager conservationists. Willingdon's son, indeed, was to become president of the Fauna Preservation Society in the 1950s while Linlithgow's father had led the British delegation at the 1900 conference on African wildlife. Irwin was one of the leaders of the British hunting cult, who later used his hunting interests as a cover to visit the Nazi leadership when he was Foreign Secretary. In 1928 Irwin submitted a memorandum to the society on wildlife preservation.[54] He agreed that 'issuing licences for firearms has been pursued with progressive liberality', but argued that it was impossible to reverse the policy because of the risk of antagonising

Indian public opinion and because the police and revenue staff could not cope with wildlife protection in inhabited areas. In any case, the problem did not seem to be of sufficient importance to justify the adoption of special measures. Despite their interest in game, British officials were at first reluctant to become involved in a movement which might disturb the peace at a sensitive time in the rise of nationalism.

Despite Irwin's complacency, many observers were testifying to the decline, if not disappearance, of game in cultivated areas. A. Dunbar-Brander suggested that early in the century herds of antelope were constantly in view on 200 miles of the Bombay–Allahabad railway line.[55] By 1928 they had almost completely disappeared. The Viceroy therefore acknowledged contemporary reality when he went on to suggest that the only practicable preservation would be in the forest areas. In other words the separation of human and faunal habitats was already well advanced. The Inspector General of Forests estimated that 105,000 square miles could be regarded as game preserves.[56] Some areas had been given the status of sanctuaries, particularly in Burma, Assam, the Central Provinces, Madras and the Punjab. When the government of India had circularised all provinces in 1926, the United Provinces, Bihar and Orissa, Bombay, Coorg and Bengal had responded that existing regulation offered sufficient protection. Nevertheless, the Inspector General of Forests was anxious to appoint a game warden to the forestry establishment of each province. For the rest the Viceroy proposed that the Home Department should be careful to issue firearms licences only to the 'so-called shikari castes', maintained that the existing legislation was adequate, and suggested that a campaign of public education should be instituted. Landlords should persuade their tenants to protect wildlife and local societies should be formed.

Pressures now built up for a ban on the sale of trophies and shikar meat, for the limitation of gun licences, the abolition of the reward system for certain animals, and the development of public propaganda on the subject. The United Provinces Game Preservation Society was indeed founded in 1932, with Jim Corbett as its secretary, and there was a flurry of legislative activity in the early '30s.[57] In January 1935 the Viceroy, Linlithgow, convened a wildlife conference at Delhi, partly under the auspices of the UPGPS.[58] This conference was charged with examining the extent to which the provisions of the 1933 African Convention could be applied to India. It was attended by representatives of all the provinces, from many of the Indian States, the Forest Department and the pressure groups, including the SPFE. The conference produced a series of resolutions which may be summarised as follows:

1. There should be special protection for a number of animals, including all kinds of rhino, the wild ass of Sind, the Sind ibex, the Kathiawar lion, musk deer, cheetah, buffalo, monitor lizard (except in the Punjab), pangolin, caracal and certain types of duck.

2. The revenue from shooting, fishing and game licences, together with fines for breaches of the game laws, should be earmarked for the protection of game and the payment of rewards.

3. Nature study shuld be encouraged in schools, with a better provision of texts, museum services, lantern slides and cheap publications in the vernacular. Societies and Boy Scouts corps should promote this work, and care should be taken to see that the treatment of animals was properly represented in cinema films.

4. Village cattle should be inoculated against rinderpest (as had already been done in Madras and experimentally in Bihar and Orissa) to protect both cattle and deer.

5. The sale of game animals or any parts of them should be prohibited. There should also be prohibitions on hunting techniques at both ends of the technologial scale – netting, trapping, snaring, or noosing on the one hand, and shooting from motor vehicles or by artificial light on the other. Special agencies should be established to protect particular species, and trade in their products should be treated as contraband.

6. All forms of licensing should be tightened up and licences for crop protection should be restricted to single-barrelled, smooth-bore muzzle-loaders. Ammunition for protection should be limited to a definite number of rounds.

7. The government of India should adhere to certain obligations laid out in the 1933 Convention, but the convening at that time of an Asiatic conference on wildlife was considered premature.

Curiously, the conference seems to have had little or nothing to say on the establishment of sanctuaries or national parks. Yet it was in this area that the most notable developments in Indian wildlife conservation were taking place in the 1930s.[59] As we have seen, the Forest Department had since the end of the nineteenth century divided its territory into closed and open shooting blocks in order to allow the recovery of game populations. Certain areas had been declared preserves, but were not granted absolute protection. Senior officers and visiting royal parties still shot in them. This was particularly true of the Indian States. In 1904, for example, the Chamarajanagar State forest of Mysore had been declared a game preserve in the charge of a game supervisor and two watchers.[60] In 1917 part of it, fifteen square miles in area, was declared the Haradanahalli Tiger Preserves and the shooting of tigers was halted. In June 1935 the State of Mysore regarded the central part of the Chamarajanagar preserve as a sanctuary, just under 100 square miles in extent, and all shooting was halted. In 1941 the whole area, lying midway between Mysore City and Ootacamund, became the Venugopal Wildlife Park, the inner part of it being known as the Bandipur Sanctuary. In 1935 the Maharajah of Travancore, also in South India, established the Periyar sanctuary on the shores of the lake of that name, which had been first created about 1900 for irrigation purposes.

The United Provinces, which had previously opposed the creation of sanctuaries, bowed to the pressure of its local lobby, notably the Preservation Society and Jim Corbett, and passed the UP National Parks Act in 1934. Under it a block of 165 square miles in the sub-montane area of Kosi and Ramganga was first closed to shooting and hunting and then established as a national park. At first it was known as the Hailey National Park, but in 1957 it was renamed the Corbett National Park. Maharashtra created the Taroba game sanctuary in 1935, upgraded to park in 1955. There were proposals to turn the Banjar Valley, a celebrated hunting ground in the Central Provinces into a national park. This later became the Kanha National Park, ninety-seven square miles in extent. Elsewhere there were moves to protect specific species, although efforts in this direction were not always uninterrupted. In the 1920s an area of the Kirthar range, sixty miles north-west of Hyderabad, had been declared a sanctuary for the Sind ibex. In 1930, however, the watchers were removed and many of the ibex were shot by local people for trophies and meat. Growing alarm about the status of the Indian rhino led to the creation of the Jaldapara sanctuary on the river Torsa in northern Bengal, close to the Bhutan border, in 1941. There were also anxieties about the Kathiawar lion, which had been reduced to near extinction, the Cutch ass, and several other species. As part of the programme of education and propaganda the Bombay Natural History Society held a major exhibition on wildlife in Bombay in 1939.

These relatively piecemeal efforts were engulfed by the war and the events leading to independence and partition. Within a few years of independence, however, the conservation movement was making rapid strides. Conservation had become fashionable with the left, and just as British Labour politicians like Sidney Webb (Lord Passfield), Ramsay MacDonald and Clement Attlee took an interest in conservation, both in Britain and in the Empire so did Jawaharlal Nehru and other leaders of Congress.[61] Moreover, through the foundation of the International Union for the Conservation of Nature and Natural Resources, an offshoot of UNESCO, in 1947, conservation had also become part of post-war internationalism. The accession of the Indian States and the continuing explosion of the human population had led to the destruction of many private forests and game preserves, the shooting out of animals, and the decline in the numbers of certain species, particularly those with skins that commanded high prices on the world market. Shikar companies had cashed in on the new interest in international tourism. By the 1950s wildlife management had become part of the five-year planning of the Indian State. The central government created the India Board for Wild Life. In October 1953 this body met in the Kanha sanctuary (formely the Banjar Valley reserve) and proposed the establishment of eighteen national parks in fifteen States with an expenditure of forty lakhs of rupees, or about £300,000. In particular it advocated the conversion of the following sanctuaries into parks:

| | |
|---|---|
| Assam | Manas sanctuary |
| | Kaziranga sanctuary |
| Madhya Pradesh | Kanha sanctuary |
| | Taroba sanctuary |
| Madras | Mudumalia sanctuary |
| Mysore | Bandipur sanctuary |
| Rajasthan | Siraska area in Alwar district |
| Saurasthra | Gir Forest |
| Travancore-Cochin | Periyar sanctuary |
| Uttar Pradesh | Rajaji sanctuary |
| Vindhya Pradesh | White Tiger area. |

These more urgent projects were regarded as part of the planning process of the period.[62]

There was a flurry of wildlife protection Acts in various States in the early 1950s and several national park Acts in 1955. Each State established its own wildlife board, and there were wildlife associations, some of them to regulate sport, as in Kerala, Madras, Bengal and Assam. The Wild Life Preservation Society of India became active in the world conservation movement and issued the magazine *Cheetah*. By 1965 there were nineteen wildlife sanctuaries in India, eight of which were adjudged to be of particular importance. Several of the princely game preserves, like the Gir Forest (where the Indian lion made a successful come-back from a mere 100 animals in 1900), the Keoladeo Ghana bird sanctuary, formerly the shooting ground of the ruler of Bharatpur,

Sariska in Rajasthan, Dachigam in Kashmir, Shivpuri, formerly the preserve of the rulers of Gwalior, Bandipu in Mysore, and Periyar in Travancore, all became game sanctuaries. But the total area of all the sanctuaries and national parks came to little more than 2,600 square miles of territory, in other words only a fraction of the size of the single Selous game reserve in Tanzania.

It became obvious in the 1970s that the Indian government was anxious to establish itself as a leader of international conservation. In 1969 the IUCN meeting in Delhi declared the tiger an endangered species and the World Wildlife Fund raised $1,800,000 for Operation Tiger. An Expert Committee to establish the plight of tigers was constituted by the Indian government in 1970 and a census in 1972 concluded that there were only 1,827 left. Under the Wild Life (Protection) Act of 1972 a total ban was placed on hunting and shooting the tiger, and all States surrendered rights of related enactment to the Union government so that the legislation could apply to all India. A Directorate of Wild Life Preservation was established, empowered to impose punitive fines and terms of imprisonment. Reserves were established. Nepal, formerly the most celebrated tiger-shooting kingdom, where Queen Elizabeth II and the Duke of Edinburgh had attended a shoot as recently as 1961, also set about the protection of the tiger, particularly in the Royal Chitawan National Park. In the early '70s there were estimated to be not many more than 170 left in Nepal. In February 1979, by which time populations were recovering rapidly, a major international symposium was held in New Delhi.[63] Technical papers examined every aspect of the behaviour and environment of the tiger as well as its often problematic interaction with humans. A succession of messages to the symposium from all the senior politicians indicated the continuing commitment of Indian governments to wildlife preservation. Ironically the vanquishing of the tiger, which had been seen as an imperial obligation and vital social rite of British India, had been transformed into the rescue of the tiger as a symbol of the independence and environmental awareness of modern India.

The story of Indian conservation activities down to modern times provides an interesting contrast with the African precedent. In India hunting was a crucial part of imperial display, military training, and intelligence. There the Hunt was so restricted in social access – apart from the guarding of crops from pigs, antelope and deer – that conservation measures were not deemed necessary until well into the twentieth century. When they did occur only small areas of land were set aside to supplement relatively ineffective legislation. It was left to the government of independent India to be more systematic in its application of the principles of the 1933 Convention. Even then, the land reserved as wildlife habitat was miniscule in area compared with the vast tracts of Africa devoted to the same purpose. National Parks have become important to the tourist policies of the Asian States, particularly Malaysia, but although their history has aroused some peasant opposition, the extent of dispossession nowhere matches that experienced in Africa.

## Notes

1 A brief account of the remarkable career of Theodore Hubback is contained in John Gullick and Gerald Hopkins, *Malayan Pioneers*, Singapore, 1958 (Malayan Biographies series, No. 2), pp. 78-85.
2 See, for example, R. H. Compton, 'The National Parks of the USA', a report presented to the Visitors' Grants Committee for South Africa of the Carnegie Corporation of New York, Pretoria, 1934.
3 J. Stevenson-Hamilton, *Our South African National Parks*, Cape Town, 1940, pp. 7-9.
4 J. Stevenson-Hamilton, *National Parks*, p. 9.
5 J. Stevenson-Hamilton, *South African Eden*, London, 1937, pp. 211-12, 265.
6 Stevenson-Hamilton, *South African Eden*, pp. 122-3.
7 Stevenson-Hamilton, *South African Eden*, pp. 178, 194, 206-7; C. Selwyn Stokes, *The Story of the Kruger National Park*, Cape Town, 1934, pp. 6-7; J. Stevenson-Hamilton, *The Kruger National Park: the Game Sanctuary of South Africa*, Pretoria, 1928.
8 Stevenson-Hamilton, *South African National Parks*, pp. 43, 47-51.
9 Stevenson-Hamilton, *South African Eden*, p. 225.
10 Stevenson-Hamilton, *South African National Parks*, pp. 57, 67; Stevenson-Hamilton, *South African Eden*, pp. 200, 232-3, 267.
11 Thomas Barbour and Margaret D. Porter, 'Notes on South African Wildlife Conservation', 1935, p. 13; 'Lions in the Kruger National Park', photographic studies by Bertram F. Jearey, Cape Town, n.d.
12 Stevenson-Hamilton, *South African National Parks*, and various articles in the *JSPFE*.
13 Compton, 'National Parks', p. 13.
14 Barbour and Porter, 'Notes', pp. 9. 22-24, 31.
15 Carl Akeley took care to have sport with the gorillas before pressing for the national park. He killed half a dozen on one expedition. *In Brightest Africa*, London, 1924, chapters XI- XIII.
16 Rennie Bere, 'The Story of Uganda National Parks', unpublished typescript, RCS Library, chapter 6, pp. 2-5.
17 Agreements concluded at the International Conference for the Protection of the Fauna and Flora of Africa, London, 8 November 1933, Cmd 4453; *JSPFE*, XXI (1934), XXXIV (1938), XXXVII (1939), p. 9; C. R. S. Pitman, *A Game Warden takes Stock*, London, 1942, p. vii.
18 R. W. G. Hingston, 'Proposed British national parks for Africa', *Geographical Journal*, LXXVII (1931), pp. 401-28. *JSPFE*, XII (1930), pp. 21-57.
19 *JSPFE*, XIII (1931), p. 11.
20 *JSPFE*, XIX (1933), pp. 8-9; C. R. S. Pitman, *A Report of a Faunal Survey of Northern Rhodesia with Special Reference to Game, Elephant Control, and National Parks*, Livingstone, Northern Rhodesia, 1934.
21 *JSPFE*, XIX (1933), p. 9.
22 *JSPFE*, XVII (1932), pp. 8, 27-48, XVIII (1933), pp. 32-45; XIX (1933), pp. 21-34.

23 Keith Robbins, *The Eclipse of a Great Power: Modern Britain, 1870-1935*, London, 1983, pp. 148, 224, 228.

24 *JSPFE*, LI (1945), pp. 10-14; LX (1949), pp. 14-19, *Oryx*, I (1950), pp. 71, 173-86.

25 For the foundation of some of the Southern Rhodesia reserves see *JSPFE*, XXII (1934), p. 10; XXVI (1935), pp. 29-46, 57-8. A useful account of the establishment and development of these reserves is contained in the *Guide to Rhodesia*, Salisbury, Rhodesia, 1972 pp. 180-4; Ted Davison, *Wankie*, Cape Town, 1967.

26 Extract from the Report of the Game and Tsetse Control Deparment, Northern Rhodesia, 1951, *Oryx*, I (1950-52), pp. 349- 52; *Northern Rhodesia Handbook*, 1950, pp. 155-71; 1953, pp. 181-99.

27 *Northern Rhodesia Handbook*, 1953, p. 183.

28 *JSPFE*, LX (1949), pp. 14-19; Ian Parker and Mohamed Amin, *Ivory Crisis*, London, 1983, *passim*, Bruce Kinloch, *The Shamba Raiders*, London, 1972, *passim*.

29 Kinloch, *Shamba Raiders*, p. 281, 338, *Tanganyika Guide*, 1948, pp. 65-71. For the progressive expansion of the Selous reserve see Gordon Matzke, 'The development of the Selous game reserve', *Tanzania Notes and Records*, No. 79 and 80 (1976), pp. 37-48.

30 Bere, 'Ugandan National Parks', and Kinloch, *Shamba Raiders*.

31 Kinloch, *Shamba Raiders*, p. 288.

32 Bere, 'Ugandan National Parks', chapter 6, pp. 13-14.

33 Kinloch, *Shamba Raiders*, pp. 208, 325; Bere, 'Ugandan National Parks', chapter 6, p. 14.

34 Kinloch, *Shamba Raiders*, pp. 325-32.

35 Kinloch, *Shamba Raiders*, pp. 343-5.

36 Kinloch, *Shamba Raiders*, p. 318 and *passim*; some idea of the importance of wildlife in the thinking of modern African governments can be derived from their various national development plans.

37 Theodore R. Hubback, 'Game in Malaya', *JSPFE*, II (1923), pp. 20-6. Letter from Theodore R. Hubback, *JSPFE*, IV (1924), pp. 60-3.

38 Theodore R. Hubback, 'Conservation of Malayan fauna', *JSPFE*, VI (1926), pp. 35-43.

39 The announcement of the Hubback Commission in Parliament was reported, with its terms of reference, in *JSPFE*, XII (1930), pp. 57-8.

40 Hubback Commission, interim report, *JSPFE*, XIX (1933), p. 39.

41 'A Report on Fauna Preservation in Malaya' by Sir Thomas Comyn-Platt, *JSPFE*, XXX (1937), pp. 45 ff.

42 Annual Report of the Game Department, Federated Malay States, for the year 1938, *JSPFE*, XXXVIII (1939), pp. 32-5.

43 E. O. Shebbeare, 'News from Malaya', *JSPFE*, LI (1945), pp. 39-41; E. O. Shebbeare, 'Malayan National Parks', *JSPFE*, LI (1945), pp. 41-5; Malayan Wild Life, Game Department Report, 1949, *Oryx*, I (1950), pp. 83-5; A. H. Featherstonhaugh, 'Malaya's national park', *Oryx*, I (1950), pp. 198-203; E. C. Foenander, 'A game department for Malaya: some views and suggestions', 1943, Rhodes House, Oxford, MSS Ind. Oc. s. 23.

44 G. M. Crabbe, 'Ceylon game sanctuaries', *JSPFE*, XIV (1931), pp. 14-17; Memorandum on Ceylon Game Protection, 25 November 1928, *JSPFE*, IX (1929), pp. 95-9; R. L. Spittel, 'Fauna preservation in Ceylon', *JSPFE*, XXXV (1938), pp. 16-19; J. C. W. Pereira, *The Laws of Ceylon*, 2 vols., Colombo, 1904, Vol. I, pp. 241-2.

45 A. C. Tutein-Nolthenins to the president of the SPFE, 21 October 1928, *JSPFE*, IX (1929), pp. 103-6.

46 *JSPFE*, XXXV (1938), pp. 17-18.

47 Extracts from reports on game preservation, Burma, for year ending 31 March 1931, *JSPFE*, XV (1931), pp. 53-66, and for year ending 31 March 1935, *JSPFE*, XXIX (1936), pp. 21-5.

48 General Acts of the Governor General in Council, particularly Vol. V, 1885-90; Acts of Madras; Acts of other presidency councils.

49 P. D. Stracey, *Wildlife Management in India*, New Delhi, 1966, contains a useful list of Indian legislation, p. 62. The text of the 1912 Act, consideration of its provi-

sions and criticism of it can be found in E. P. Stebbing, *The Diary of a Sportsman Naturalist in India*, London, 1920, pp. 269-79.

50 J. W. Best, *Indian Shikar Notes*, Lahore, 1931, contains an account of the Central Provinces' system of shooting rules and blocks, pp. 222-88.

51 Stebbing, *Diary*, pp. 264-8.

52 A. A. Dunbar-Brander, 'Game Preservation in India', *JSPFE*, XIV (1931), pp. 23-35.

53 Stracey, *Wildlife Management*, pp. 1-2 and *passim*.

54 Memorandum received from the Viceroy, *JSPFE*, IX (1929), pp. 98-101. For the development of the SPFE agitation on India, see *JSPFE*, IX (1929), p. 11.

55 Dunbar-Brander, 'Game Preservation', p. 26.

56 The Irwin memorandum, 1928, and see also Sir Sainthill Eardley-Wilmot, *Forest Life and Sports in India*, London, 1910.

57 F. W. Champion, 'Wild fauna preservation in the United Provinces', *JSPFE*, XVIII (1933), pp. 19-29; introduction by R. E. Hawkins to *Jim Corbett's India*, Oxford, 1986, pp. 1-11.

58 *JSPFE*, XXIV (1935), p. 9; All-India Conference, Delhi, 28- 31 January 1935, *JSPFE*, XXV (1935), pp. 23-33.

59 Stracey, *Wildlife Management; Wildlife Sanctuaries in India*, New Delhi, 1965.

60 *JSPFE*, XXIV (1935), pp. 9-11; 'The Chamarajanagar Sanctuary, Mysore', *JSPFE*, XXVIII (1936), pp. 36-43.

61 J. Ramsay MacDonald had been keenly involved in the conservation movement and became an honorary member of the SPFE, *JSPFE*, XV (1931), pp. 45-6; XVIII (1933), p. 7. See also C. L. Boyle, 'What of India?' *JSPFE*, LVIII (1948), pp. 41-2.

62 *Oryx*, I (1950-52), pp. 224-7; II (1953-54), pp. 144 ff. *Wild Life Sanctuaries in India;* Kailash Sankhala, *Wild Beauty: a Study of Indian Wildlife*, New Delhi, n.d. *National Parks and Wildlife Sanctuaries in Maharashtra State*, Bombay, 1971. By 1971 there were fifteen wildlife sanctuaries and forest parks in Maharashtra alone.

63 *International Symposium on Tiger*, New Delhi, 1979.

# CHAPTER ELEVEN

# Shikar and safari: hunting and conservation in the British Empire

The exploitation of wild animals has long been recognised as a prime impulse of European expansion. Yet hunting in all its economic, social and cultural manifestations has never received its due share of scholarly attention. In 1925 Hugh Gunn wrote that 'the early training and the instincts of the hunter have had much more to do with the expansion of the Empire than is generally realised'. The British have been extolled, Gunn went on, for their sea sense as hard navigators, but the spirit of the chase had been equally responsible for adventures and enterprise, trade and commerce, exploration and settlement in 'unknown and pagan lands'.[1] The British always liked to portray themselves as uniquely competent – it was a necessary myth of global power – but Gunn's remarks were equally true of the French and the Russian empires.

The hunting imperative took different forms in various parts of the world. The assault upon the fur-bearing animals of Siberia and northern and western Canada created a commercial dynamic which was the driving force of continental expansion. In North America, European enterprise initially inserted itself into, and stimulated, indigenous hunting activities. The Hudson Bay Company, for example, used both native and immigrant trappers, while the company's factors acted as the channels to the international shipping and marketing system. The balance between local and European trapping activity, however, soon began to shift in favour of the latter. As settlement moved to the plains, Europeans began to arrogate all hunting rights to themselves. In this the original American colonists had shown the way. They had been eager to secure a more democratic access to game than prevailed at home, but had been unprepared to extend such access to the Indian population whose lands they acquired. Farther west it was European hunters, in league with meat canning and hide-tanning interests, which destroyed the great bison herds in the United States and Canada.

While North America was a region of faunal abundance, Australasia was marked by its relative poverty. By the time Europeans arrived in Australia and New Zealand wild animals seemed to be so important as an underpinning of colonial enterprise that colonists set about introducing them. In New Zealand in particular an extraordinarily diverse zoological cocktail was introduced through the 'acclimatisation' policies of the nineteenth and early twentieth centuries.[2] The release of animals into the wild had begun with Captain Cook's introduction of pigs and continued with several species of deer from Europe, North America and Asia, wallabies, possums, rabbits, wild goats, and many others, quite apart from the introduction of domestic animals (notably the sheep) for farming or sentimental reasons. The increase in the range of fauna was designed to provide a source of food in the wild, a potential

[ 296 ]

economic resource through skins, and also sport. In North America fears about the extermination of indigenous fauna led to the introduction of national parks. In New Zealand national parks were created partly to protect the newly introduced fauna and encourage their spread. In both cases environmental engineering had serious implications for the indigenous peoples. The American Yellowstone Park of 1872 was followed in the British dominions by Banff in Alberta, Canada (1885), and Tongariro, New Zealand (1887). Both were symbolic of white encroachment and indigenous dispossession.[3] The Stoney Indians of Alberta, weakened and reduced in numbers by a smallpox epidemic, were denied access to their old hunting grounds, which became a region of controlled hunting and fishing for white tourists. Maoris, anxious about the spread of settlers into lands of special spiritual significance, persuaded the government to take them into national care, but as the concept spread in the early decades of this century they found themselves denied the right to hunt the very food source the Europeans had introduced.

Africa and India both had a highly diverse and prolific fauna. In Africa particularly it fulfilled all the conditions the New Zealand settlers set out to create by acclimatising animals. Ivory, hides, skins, horns and meat were available in abundance. But whereas the New Zealanders, like zoological sorcerer's apprentices, unleashed a biological explosion they found difficult to control, the conquerors and settlers of Africa were able to exploit existing game resources to the full. In southern Africa the incompatibility of settlement and wild animals was apparent from the start. The first priority of settlers at the Cape was to wrest control from the larger herbivores and the great predators. But game was both an opportunity and a threat. The proceeds of the trade in ivory and other animal products could be invested in the farming economy. Game was also useful in recouping the individual fortune. Andrew Steedman met a colonist called Thackwray who had encountered financial difficulties and was forced into elephant hunting. It was a 'wearisome and hazardous occupation' but the 'readiest means of extrication' from his straitened circumstances.[4] On the other hand Thomas Pringle offered a graphic description of the struggle of the occupants of a 'solitary farm-shieling' at the upper extremity of the White River valley. The proprietor's wife told him that elephants 'came out of the forest by night, trod down her little corn-field, devoured her crop of maize, pulled up her fruit trees . . .' They were', she said, 'too big to wrestle with'.[5]

But elephants always presented a particular problem. Smaller game could indeed be successfully wrestled with. All settlers are, initially, asset-strippers. Throughout southern and Central Africa settlers established themselves by living off the land. They used the meat of available game and sold skins and horns. Wild animals underpinned the transition period until farms could become fully productive. Farther into the interior exploration, missionary endeavour, survey, conquest, town and railway building were also accomplished through the prodigal use of animal resources. Meat was used to sweeten relations with African peoples through whose lands Europeans passed – the 'system of penetrating the country by feeding the natives', as W. D. M. Bell put it.[6] Meat also constituted an important component of or substitute for wages to African labour in this early period. Ivory and skins produced a direct subsidy, meat an indirect but no less significant one, for conquest and settlement.

As the need for this subsidy fell away, imperial rulers began to restrict social access to game even within the European community in the interests of 'sport'. The killing of animals lost economic and achieved ritual significance. Sportsmen began to decry the excessive destruction of animal stocks and argued for preservation measures to promote the survival of species and continued hunting for sport. Much of the blame for declining game resources was pinned on Africans, and the prime concern of legislative action was to destroy African hunting. As in the ancient, medieval and modern European worlds the plain man's hunting had to be frustrated. In Africa this may well have removed a very important source of protein from the diet of many African peoples. What was new was the justification of science. The natural history establishment, many of its members hunters, gave full support to pressure groups and imperial authorities concerned with this process.

In India hunting fulfilled three functions from the start. An extensive deer population, large numbers of India's only antelope, the nilgai, and a rich avifauna were widely dispersed in settled areas and provided a welcome addition to the imperial diet. At first Europeans used the services of Indian shikaris, but they soon appropriated both name and activity themselves. Increasingly they hunted for 'sport', introducing big-game shooting in forests and mountains and adopting the spectacular elephant-borne hunts of the Mughals. To these they added the hunting of foxes and jackals and the most distinctive of all imperial sports (though with ancient antecedents) pig-sticking. Third, they turned the shooting of tigers and panthers, in some areas elephants, into a symbolic system of dependence, appropriating for themselves the protective function formerly offered by specialist Indian shikaris.

In both India and Africa indigenous hunters were transformed by the end of the century into 'poachers'. This was achieved through game and forest laws, gun laws, administrative action, and the separation of human and animal habitats. In Africa such separation was engineered by the creation of reserves and shooting policies in unreserved areas. In some places it was emphasised by human resettlement or game culling associated with tsetse control, the first, significantly, a characteristic of non-settler territories, the second of settler societies. In the latter habitat separation was re-emphasised by a racial division in land apportionment. In India separation occurred primarily through the sheer pressure on the animal resource. Animal populations in settled areas were progressively destroyed as the Indian population increased, marginal lands came into cultivation, and Europeans hunted more destructively. As a result hunting and shooting increasingly became an activity pursued in forests, mountains and princely States.

The development of restricted access, the increasing categorisation and regulation of hunting sports, the appearance of 'preservation' on the European aristocratic model, and the exclusion of local hunters were all closely bound up with the development of a hunting 'code'. This code touched so closely on all aspects of hunting and conservation that it deserves extended treatment.

In the first half of the nineteenth century many of the hunting writers described indigenous techniques in a largely neutral way. They themselves often fired into herds, shot females, and indulged in night shooting at water holes. They were relatively indifferent to the escape of wounded beasts. As the century progressed these activities were increasingly frowned upon. As we have seen in chapter four, Livingstone disapproved of shooting at water holes and admired Oswell because he declined to use dogs in his hunting in the profligate way that Gordon Cumming had exploited them. But it was not until the end of the century that the code was fully established. Many writers referred to its provisions, but Denis Lyell, in his several books, offered it in a highly developed form.[7] The hunter should appreciate the beauty and respect the life force of the animals he set out to shoot. He should never succumb to 'buck fever' or ever fire indiscriminately into herds. The true hunter spoored and stalked his prey to a point at which the age, sex and quality of the trophy of the animal could be identified, a point which would offer the best chance of a mortal shot. Females and their young should be left alone, and it was the essence of the code that the hunted animal should have a 'sporting chance'. If any animal were merely wounded, then the hunter should follow to deliver the *coup de grâce* at whatever cost in time and discomfort to himself. He should never expect an African tracker or gun bearer to do it for him. No one should shoot from railway carriages, river steamers (except at crocodiles, which were always fair game), motor vehicles or aeroplanes.

As the code was formulated in India the old indiscriminate practices were refined. By the 1890s pig-stickers only rode boars and regarded it

as a heinous offence to attack sows (though the latter of course constituted just as great a threat to crops). Even the almost universal practice
of shooting tigers from machans or tree platforms came to be doubted.
Lyell and other hunters in Africa found it a dubious practice, indicating
that a great deal of Indian big-game shooting could not match the
ruggedness or danger of that of Africa. Indian hunters occasionally
agreed. Braddon regarded it as a 'somewhat questionable form of
shikar'. He felt he was an 'unworthy foe – a mere assassin – and . . .
that the performance, however beneficial, was distinctly inglorious'.[8]
The point was, of course, that the tiger did not have a 'sporting' chance
and the sportsman did not endanger himself as he did on the ground.

Moreover the true sportsman was a natural historian and a scientist.
Killing was in a sense legitimated by his understanding of the quarry,
its environment and its anatomy, and his knowledge of firearms and
ballistics added an extra scientific dimension. The hunter had become
a member of an exclusive club, its rules defined by Western technology
and science. The code, though transgressed by many white hunters,
from Theodore Roosevelt downwards, served to exclude Africans and
Indians. It underpinned game legislation which attempted to eliminate
'cruel' African or Indian practices. By these means the club's rules
became national laws. Since the 'clean kill' was the prime provision
of the code, African and Indian hunting techniques involving the use
of traps, snares, poisons and, in the absence of modern firearms, older
technology like bows and arrows, spears and flintlocks could be readily
described as 'unsporting'.

The 'poacher' was defined by object (utility), technique (primitive)
and approach (ease of effecting kill and self-protection). Again Braddon
expressed the distinction. After the passage quoted above he went on:

> The peasants whose cows or wives or sons were killed by tigers were
> other-minded. They were not disposed to criticise methods so long as
> the tiger was destroyed. They even approved of murder by strychnine . . .
> They saw no merit, no good point whatever, in a tiger, which I, rightly
> or wrongly, regarded as the veritable king of beasts, and far more worthy
> of this style and title than the over-vaunted lion. Those benighted
> peasants were eaten up by prejudice as well as by tigers.

There is a certain amount of self-mockery in this, but the conflict in
attitudes was real enough. Needless to say, the most efficacious way
of destroying predators, poison, was regarded as the ultimate in
unsporting techniques.

The question arises, where did this code come from? Did it emerge
from the 'revolution in sensibilities' identified by Keith Thomas as
occurring by 1800, closely associated with natural history studies and

bourgeois romanticism? It may well be true that doubts about animal cruelty emerged at this time, but the evidence presented in this book indicates that it was almost another century before they were formulated into 'the code' and several more decades before it was given full legislative form. During the period when the exploitation of animals was necessary for conquest and settlement in Africa or the initial domination of India, including the provisioning of troops and imperial officials, the inhibitions of a code were generally not allowed to obtrude. Moreover, defensive hunting, hunting for survival and vermin destruction were imperatives (the latter sometimes more perceived than real) which could not accommodate such a code.

It is true that anxieties about animal suffering can be found in a few, though a minority, of the sources, but such sensitivities were often overlaid by Darwinian concepts. Evolutionary ideas were indeed accommodated within the code. Crocodiles representing an earlier stage of evolution and universally hated, were fair game for slaughter, and infringements of the code were consequently permissible in their case.[9] More highly evolved animals deserved greater consideration. A few hunters regarded the shooting of primates with distaste. Hunters also anthropomorphised animals. The rhino, for example, was described as witless, choleric, dyspeptic, unsociable, and its virtual extermination in southern Africa was often explained, and by implication justified, on the grounds of its unpleasant temperament. Other animals were provided with personalities, and the most 'wary' among them, the most difficult to hunt and kill, were described as the most sporting, while those which most vigorously resisted death were 'plucky'. Hunters readily transferred evolutionary ideas from the natural historical to the human sphere. Concepts of sexual selection were applied to home societies and notions of survival to the problem of race and imperial expansion.[10]

Just as adherence to the code varied according to the position of the animal on the evolutionary scale, so was the code abandoned with regard to inflicting injury and death on Africans in the period of generalised colonial violence. Humans were subject to inexorable laws, just as unevolved, non-adapting animals were. In chapters 6 and 7 we saw the tendency of Count Teleki, Richard Meinertzhagen, Sir Claude Champion de Crespigny, Colonel Alderson and Robert Baden-Powell to elide human and animal 'bags' in East Africa and in the campaigns against the Shona and Ndebele in Zimbabwe. Indeed, the sporting officers of these campaigns frequently used hunting metaphors to describe their conflicts with Africans. Moreover hunters in Africa were often cavalier about the safety of their African auxiliaries, and injury or death among beaters and gun bearers was a frequent occurrence. It was also relatively common in India and was treated by some white hunters with indifference, even in a light-hearted manner, when they complained of the compensation, tiny as it was, which they paid out to relatives. In Kenya in 1909 Theodore Roosevelt and his son Kermit were treated to a spectacle specially arranged for their entertainment, in which Africans took on lions with nothing more than spears and shields. Two of them were seriously mauled.[11]

This approach to the life and limb of hunting auxiliaries must of course be placed in the context of racial notions of the day, the alleged capacity, for example, of Africans to endure pain more readily than 'higher races', together with their supposed indifference to the death of relatives or friends. In any case, racial hierarchies implied judgments about the quality and value of life itself. There is ample evidence that the juvenile literature which constituted the staple reading matter not only of the great hunters but also of the majority of the reading public of the late nineteenth and early twentieth centuries made much play of these racial distinctions with regard to injury and death. If hunters were motivated by more refined sensibilities when facing the injury and death of animals, they did not always extend such considerations to human life.

The code was surely influenced by two principal developments, the economic transition inherent in the changing character of imperial rule and the emergence of new technology. The code was only fully formulated and held up as a sporting ideal once the practical requirements of hunting were in decline. The code was symptomatic of the transition from utility to sport. It was inappropriate, or at least difficult to put into practice, while hunting was concerned with the primary financial subsidy of ivory, rhino horn or skins. Those intent upon personal aggrandisement or imperial ventures, missionary, commercial or administrative, were unlikely to be diverted from their purpose by fixed rules of behaviour. Nor were they likely to impose them on the African agents whom they armed for the same purpose. The same was true of the secondary meat subsidy. As Lugard wrote when the code was in its infancy 'We were butchers not sportsmen'.[12] Once these stages of the hunting advance into Africa had achieved their objects, and the desire to frustrate African hunting had become paramount, then the sporting considerations of the Hunt, valuing difficulty, animal resistance, accuracy in marksmanship, and the 'fair chance' needed the regulation of a code. In India the transition was, perhaps, more functional than economic. The adoption of a codified shikar was important to imperial display and the myth of power. This too required that indigenous hunting be frustrated.

But it was perhaps technology that had the most significant influence on the emergence of the code. Until at least 1850 hunters were using smooth-bore muskets, casting their own lead balls, using individual charges of powder, and going through all the complex paraphernalia of muzzle-loading. Both accuracy and penetration were in doubt and with many animals, particularly buffalo, hippo, rhino and elephant, the initial mortal shot was virtually impossible. In consequence hunters had to lame the animal, slow it down or disable it, so that more lead could be pumped into it until death ensued, often from loss of blood. A large battery, all loaded in readiness, and steady gunbearers were required. Dogs distracted the prey from its human aggressor and kept the angry animal at bay while this lengthy process could be achieved. All the early hunters describe the need to inflict multiple wounds before the animal is brought down.

The early rifles were primitive affairs, muzzle-loaded, and still presenting problems of accuracy and penetrating power. A spherical bullet was used which necessitated the use of a mallet to force it into the rifling of the barrel, and it was believed that accuracy could be obtained only by burning a small charge of powder. As with the musket a complicated set of accessories was required. As Sir Samuel Baker described it

> The outfit required a small mallet made of hardwood faced with thick buff leather, a powerful loading rod, a powder-flask, a pouch to contain greased linen or silk patches; another pouch for percussion caps; a third pouch for bullets. In addition to this combersome arrangement, a nipple-screw was carried, lest any stoppage might render necessary the extraction of the nipple.[13]

Baker described himself as introducing the rifle to Ceylon in 1845. Other hunters there had been using a large-calibre smooth-bore shotgun, loaded with a double charge of powder and a hardened ball. With this instrument several good shots in Ceylon had killed hundreds of elephants. But Baker brought a massive rifle of his own design, with a thirty-six inch barrel, weighing twenty-one pounds, firing either three ounce spherical belted bullets or four ounce conical bullets on a massive charge of sixteen drams. With this he secured, so he claimed, great penetrating power and much hunting success. It was a celebrated firearm which other hunters referred to with awe. Baker still required a large back-up battery. He also hunted with large packs of dogs and

[ *303* ]

often killed the deer brought to bay with a knife, a feat he even achieved with a red-deer stag in Glent Tilt in Scotland.

By the later 1860s the small and medium bore Express rifle was coming into use offering a lower trajectory and a higher volocity for a lighter projectile with the additional advantage of minimum recoil. This was accompanied by breech-loading which at a stroke made reloading much simpler. These rifles were in general use by the late 1870s. Magazine rifles appeared for the first time in the late 1880s and by the end of the century the high-velocity cordite rifle was the preferred weapon of hunters. Smokeless powder ensured that the hunter was no longer enveloped in the dense smoke produced by the charge in his firearm. Range and accuracy moved forward by a quantum leap and the safety of the hunter was greatly improved. The single mortal shot for almost any animal, including the elephant, became not only a possibility but the prime objective of the sporting hunter. This pulled two ways with regard to the code. On the one hand it made adherence to the rules a practical propositon; on the other it made long-range firing at distant animals – with less chance of instant success – a possibility. The full implementation of the code was therefore made feasible by the high-velocity rifle; it was also rendered necessary by that rifle's capacity to wound at very long range without any chance of following up. The sporting code was thus influenced by chronological, functional and technical factors. It became fully effective when the decline in utility coincided with an increase in technological sophistication. All of these considerations helped to resolve the dilemmas thrown up for elite members of the European hunting fraternity in the nineteenth century, the unresolved conflict between sensibilities towards animals and practical requirements subject to technical limitations.

The code offered opportunities to judge not only indigenous hunters, but also other imperial powers. Hunting and adherence to the code were the true signs of the virile colonial power, and the British had a tendency to judge fellow imperialists according to their capacity in the Hunt. The Germans shared the palm with the British as the most confident and effective hunters. The Americans had subdued their own continent by hunting and were perfectly capable of turning their attention to other parts of the world. Theodore Roosevelt was the political expression of the American pioneering and hunting stereotype which he established in his many books. His admiration for the British as hunters helps to explain his ardent Anglophilia. The British, Germans and Americans all linked their hunting to natural history study as their specimen-collecting, museums and publications indicated. The

Portuguese on the other hand were neither great hunters nor natural historians. For Frederick Selous, Ewart Grogan and others it showed in their empire. Denis Lyell deprecated the manner in which the Portuguese expected Africans to do their hunting for them.[14] Spanish imperial decline was accelerated, according to one hunter, when the Spanish aristrocracy gave up hunting and bullfighting and became 'frenchified and effeminate'.[15] The French and the Belgians, with a few individual exceptions, were not among the first ranks of hunters either. Dugald Campbell and Marcus Daly gave every indication of despising them when they hunted in their territories [16] and ivory poachers took pleasure in raiding across their borders.[17] They were too epicurean, the stereotype ran, waxing fat on food and wine, avoiding manly exertion, preferring the sexual expression of consorting with African concubines to the sexual sublimation of the Hunt. Colonel Haywood thought that the French in West Africa considered him slightly mad to travel so far to hunt.[18]

Diet was also seen as an essential part of the masculinity of the hunter. Hunting explorers, campaigners and settlers were perforce highly carnivorous and made a virtue of necessity by extolling the importance of meat-eating. Even David Livingstone, an ambivalent hunter, was driven to hunt by his craving for meat and his belief that it was essential for the maintenance of health in Africa. When Stevenson-Hamilton moved to the low veld of the Transvaal to develop the Sabi game reserve, the future Kruger national park, he found it impossible to get vegetables. Their consumption, he wrote, was thought to savour of effeminacy. 'Meat and whiskey were the correct supports for the proper he-men'.[19] An African vegetable grower was duped and his business destroyed when he tried to establish himself in the area. Europeans were fascinated by African beliefs about the properties of different parts of the animals' anatomies – the heart should be eaten for courage for example – and practised a form of it themselves. All hunters insisted on a sumptuary law of meat, the finest cuts to themselves because these were necessary to their more refined teeth and digestions and provided the energy necessary to their position of command and leadership. These attitudes were not unique to the Empire. Any examination of the menus of great country houses, superior hotels, the first class of ships at sea will reveal how strongly carnivorous was the diet of the elite in the late nineteenth and early twentieth centuries. Consumption was an essential element of the hunting ethos.

Preservation, the first stage of conservation, must be set into this context of elite access and dietary privilege. It marked the extension into the Empire of restrictions imposed for centuries in the mother country in one form or another. The protestations of the preservationists with regard to the decline and near-extinction of certain species were sincere enough, and in some cases based on genuine dangers, but their laying of the blame on 'native' and 'ungentlemanly' hunters merely reflected the commercial pressures and the taste for trophies induced by the dominant culture. Indeed the scramble of museums to secure specimens of rare species furthered the process of extinction. Just such a scramble had helped to destroy the remaining stock of great auks earlier in the century, rendering them extinct, and had a serious effect upon the white rhino among other African species. None of the early preservationists were in the anti-blood sports lobby, small as it was at that time. Most were fervent hunters, followers of the newly formulated code, and anxious that access to game should be restricted to the practitioners of its laws. Almost all such adherents defined themselves by ethnic origin and social class (Indian princes gained honorary admission) as members of an exclusive imperial club. It was a club which incorportated and was legitimated by the natural history establishment.

But as preservation moved towards conservation, reserves towards national parks, the unexpected happened. The new rage of game *viewing* secured public support. The railways, but more particularly the internal combustion engine, increased the access of town dwellers to remote game areas. As whites became more urbanised, and comfortable international tourism a more significant force, the game parks became the African, later the Asian, equivalent of the lost rural idyll. The idea spread from North America and Australasia to South Africa. At first all visitors to the Kruger national park brought rifles, convinced they would be necessary for self-defence. The staff had to find ways of sealing them. Within a few years no rifles were brought and all shots were achieved with the camera. There were other unexpected developments. Lions, which had formerly been categorised as vermin and shot at will (they were after all competitors for game meat) became a prime attraction. They turned out to be the most tolerant of cars, the most amenable to the good photographic shots.

This development did not run counter to the interests of the hunting elite. The animals were preserved; a wider social circle was introduced to a new code of behaviour associated with game viewing; indigenous hunting was more effectively frustrated; and controlled hunting areas, often stocked from adjacent parks, were available for elite hunters who could afford to hunt in them. By the 1930s conservation had become an almost unarguable creed. The shift from preservation to conservation had taken it through the political spectrum from right to left and given it great power in the process. In East and Central Africa, most notably, reserves spread dramatically, often into land vacated by humans as a result of the disasters of the late nineteenth century or the warfare of the twentieth. Concerns about the decline of game stocks and the endangering of species, very real in southern Africa, were transferred to eastern and central Africa where they were largely groundless. But such concerns also fitted neatly ideas about settlement segregation, human and animal, black and white, which were central to imperial policies.

As international tourism grew dramatically in the post-Second World War period, particularly with air travel from the late 1950s, so did the national parks. By the 1960s conservation in the interests of such tourism had made another political shift. Some of the new nationalist governments in Africa inherited it from their mentors on the left, even if their own people often had other ideas. Many national parks were to become the hunting grounds of 'poachers', dissidents, and guerrillas.

Yet as the conservation movement gathered force the reaction set in to the hunting cult which had spawned it. Expressions of regret at the deaths of animals became more prominent in the hunting books. As a new breed of administrators, more educated, more middle-class, began to arrive, many ceased to hunt. It was in any case no longer a practical imperative. New forms of the camera, so much less cumbersome than their forebears and using modern film, began to take over. The BSAC native commissioner and poet, Cullen Gouldsbury, declined to hunt.[20] The missionary Donald Fraser became, according to his wife, increasingly sickened by it.[21] The keen hunting governor Sir Geoffrey Archer, when livening up an address to the Royal Geographical Society with some hunting stories, found himself tartly admonished by the President that gentlemen hunted only with the camera.[22] Sir Kenneth Bradley, a district officer in Northern Rhodesia and later Director of the Commonwealth Institute began his career as an eager hunter, but by the 1930s he was tired and disillusioned of the chase and carefully omitted hunting references from his memoirs.[23] George Orwell, famously, reacted against the hunting obligations placed upon him during his service in Burma.[24] The Boy Scouts began to tone down the hunting imagery in the inter-war years. Publications stressed that Baden-Powell believed that it was as meritorious to hunt with the camera as the gun. Baden-Powell and his associates hoped that moral training could be effected by using all the techniques of the hunter while removing the emphasis on the ultimate kill.

Hunters fought a rearguard action. Several like Denis Lyell denied the equality of camera-hunting, which lacked the element of danger posed by the wounded animal, the unflinching courage, swift reactions and essential endurance of the Hunt. Lyell dreaded a time when youth would fail to respond to the 'call of the wild' which he inseparably connected with hunting.[25] Baden-Powell lamented the fact that sub-alterns in India were giving up pig-sticking for 'poodle-faking at the hill-stations'.[26] Claude Champion de Crespigny saw the craze for dancing, night clubs, and the 'pernicious cocktail habit' as the greatest sappers of the moral fibre of the young in the 1920s.[27] Others continued to think in social Darwinian and eugenic terms. Marcus Daly believed that certain Central African species were at risk because they permitted defeated males to continue to run with the herd.[28] The weakest characteristics, he believed, always predominated. Similarly, allowing the weak to survive at home and the removal of opportunities for gaining virility and strength through pioneering and hunting would ultimately extinguish the British race. Lyell also saw the incipient welfare state as the prime threat to the British as a virile and imperial nation. Civilisation 'with its false policy of nurturing the diseased and unfit' was upsetting 'the balance of nature'.[29]

However, though their trade declined, the great hunters began to enter European myth and fable, just as they had done in African societies in the past. Hunting remained the image of war, calling forth qualities of courage, judgment, knowledge of terrain and the ability to inflict violence and death. Yet it was an old-style war that was evoked, a war of rules and 'sporting' attributes. Until the 1930s at least hunting continued to be idealised for popular consumption, through juvenile journals, popular stories, the boy scouts, and above all the cinema. It was uniquely the sport of princes and aristocrats, military men and imperial rulers, natural historians and an elite band of gentlemanly professionals, the very groups that the readers of popular literature were encouraged to emulate. As the twentieth century advanced a few hard-bitten safari leaders, mainly based on Kenya, continued to revel in the myth.[30] They maintained the hunting tradition, if only in the service of rich tourist hunters, celebrating their predecessors, glorying in their injuries as the emblem of their craft and proof of outstanding courage. While the popular interest had largely fallen away they were still able to serve the passions of Texas oilmen, the German nouveaux riches, the occasional French president, various forms of multi-nationalist wealth or leisured and superannuated aristocrats. The conservationists generally tolerated them, as they will not tolerate the universally hated 'poacher' discredited in the twentieth century by the appearance of highly armed professional gangs, because they stick to the code and because inutility somehow lends respectability to their trade. Tourist income lends even more respectability and it is this which keeps some African countries firmly wedded to national parks policy combined with controlled hunting for the elite.

In 1977, however, all tourist hunting was banned in Kenya, for long the centre of the big-game cult. The Kenyan government had become alarmed at the great increase in the killing of elephants – probably the result of the lethal activities of the poaching gangs – and at a stroke put many of the professional hunters out of business. Neighbouring Tanzania, however, eager for foreign exchange, and with one fifth of its land surface turned over to big game, continued to encourage international elite hunting and some of the safari companies re-established themselves there, devoted by now to a highly sybaritic form of the Hunt.

Hunting remains important to those who continue to exercise global power. The highly charged symbolism of the gun for both the individual and the state guarantees its hallowed status in the United States. Many Americans are avid hunters while in the Soviet Union the topmost echelons of the political elite, at least until recently, were enthralled by the Hunt. This may well reflect the historic importance of hunting in the territorial expansion of both continental powers. In South Africa hunting continues to be the mark of and the potential protection for a white ruling minority. There hunting remains the image of defence. In 1985 there were thirteen million guns registered in South Africa and a gun dealer, commenting on the increasing popularity of classses in marksmanship, pointed out that 'we are a hunting nation'.

But in Britain the hunting ethos, though still practised, has declined in status and public acceptability with the end of Empire. This decline is perfectly reflected by the changing relationship of the royal family towards it. Edward VII, George V, and Edward VIII hunted as an act of imperial state. For the Duke and Duchess of York, the future George VI and Queen Elizabeth, the ideal honeymoon in 1924-5 was a shooting safari in East Africa. In these ways members of the royal family not only reflected the interests of the contemporary elite but also displayed themselves as incarnations of the Raj. But in recent decades, when hunting has ceased to be a significant act of state, the royal family has

[ *309* ]

bent to public opinion. This was made apparent by the sequence of events in royal visits to South Asia in 1961 and 1986.

In 1961 Queen Elizabeth II and the Duke of Edinburgh visited India and Nepal. After their arival in Delhi they went on a shooting trip with the Maharajah and Maharani of Jaipur. The Duke shot a tiger. There was world-wide outrage and the British press suggested that the Queen's presence had indicated her approval. The royal couple moved on to Nepal where the King had set up the tiger shoot of the century. The ground had been carefully prepared, the tigers marked down, the elephants marshalled. But the Duke arrived with an allegedly infected trigger finger so that he could not participate. Lord Home, the accompanying secretary of state, was to shoot the tiger. He failed and it was eventually despatched by a member of the Duke's staff. Newspaper opinion was again hostile and although the event was filmed the BBC declined to transmit it. The film was eventually shown in 1986 and it must be said that the distaste of the Queen is apparent.[31] In that year the Queen and the Duke again visited Nepal, but the nearest they came to big-game shooting was to witness the tranquillising of a rhino called 'Philip' so that it could be fitted with a radio device. Here was the perfect symbol for the replacement of the hunting by the conservation ethos, imperial power by post-colonial environmental concerns. A rhino called 'Philip' had become a new form of trophy.

## Notes

1 Hugh Gunn, 'The sportsman as an empire builder', in John Ross and Hugh Gunn (eds.), *The Book of the Red Deer and Empire Big Game*, London, 1925, pp. 137-8.
2 Alfred W. Crosby, *Ecological Imperialism: the Biological Expansion of Europe, 900-1900*, Cambridge, 1986, chapter 10.
3 John M. MacKenzie, 'Conservation in the Commonwealth: origins and controversies', in a volume ed. Richard Maltby and Peter Quartermaine to be presented to Shridath Ramphal, forthcoming.
4 Andrew Steedman, *Wanderings and Adventures in the Interior of Southern Africa*, London, 1935, Vol. I, p. 65.
5 Thomas Pringle, *Narrative of a Residence in South Africa*, London, 1935, p. 97.
6 W. D. M. Bell, *The Wanderings of an Elephant Hunter*, London, 1958, p. 168.
7 John M. MacKenzie, new introduction to Denis D. Lyell, *The Hunting and Spoor of Central African Game*, Camden, N.C., 1987.
8 Sir Edward Braddon, *Thirty Years of Shikar*, Edinburgh, 1895, p. 183.
9 For the fate of the crocodile see Mwelma Musambachime, 'The fate of the Nile crocodile in the African waterways', *African Affairs*, 86 (1987), pp. 197-207.
10 For an elaboration of these points see John M. MacKenzie, 'Chivalry, Social Darwinism and ritualised killing: the hunting ethos in Central Africa to 1914', in D. Anderson and R. Grove (eds.) *Conservation in Africa*, Cambridge, 1987.
11 Theodore Roosevelt, *African Game Trails*, London, 1910 pp. 350-1.
12 F. D. Lugard, *The Rise of our East African Empire*, London, 1893, Vol. I, p. 352
13 Sir Samuel W. Baker, *Wild Beasts and their Ways*, London, 1890, Vol. I, p. 1.
14 C. H. Stigand and Denis D. Lyell, *Central African Game and its Spoor*, London,

1906, p. 3.
15 Sir Claude Champion de Crespigny, *Forty Years of a Sportsman's Life*, London, 1925, pp. 182-3.
16 Dugald Campbell, *Wanderings in Central Africa*, London, 1929. Marcus Daly, *Big Game Hunting and Adventure, 1897-1936*, London, 1937.
17 Derek Temple, *Ivory Poacher*, London, n.d. (1930s).
18 A. H. W. Haywood, *Sport and Service in Africa*, London, 1926, p. 132.
19 J. Stevenson-Hamilton, *South African Eden*, London, 1937, p. 69.
20 Cullen Gouldsbury, *Rhodesian Rhymes*, Bulawayo, 1932.
21 Agnes Fraser, *Donald Fraser*, London, 1934, p. 148.
22 Sir Geoffrey Archer, *Personal and Historical Memoirs of an East African Administrator*, Edinburgh, 1963, p. 15.
23 Kenneth Bradley, *Diary of a District Officer*, London, 1943; *Once a District Officer*, London, 1966.
24 George Orwell, *Shooting an Elephant and other Essays*, London, 1950.
25 Lyell, *Hunting and Spoor*, p. 16.
26 R. S. S. Baden-Powell, *Pig Sticking or Hog Hunting*, London, 1924, p. 34.
27 Crespigny, *Forty Years*, pp. 295-6.
28 Daly, *Big Game Hunting*, pp. 279-80.
29 Denis D. Lyell, *Memories of an African Hunter*, London, 1923, p. 19.
30 Jeremy Gavron, 'A dying breed', *Daily Telegraph*, 18 July 1987. I am indebted to Jeffrey Richards for this reference.
31 BBC TV, Newsnight, 18 February 1986.

# APPENDICES

## Appendix I. Game legislation

This brief list contains some of the principal laws from selected territories.

### Cape Colony

Game Law Proclamation, 1822
Act for the better preservation of game, No. 36, 1886
Act to consolidate and amend the game laws, No. 11 of 1909 (consolidating the 1886
    Act, an amendment ordinance of 1893 and the Game Act No. 11 of 1908)
National Parks Act No. 56 of 1926 (Union of South Africa)

### Kenya

Game Regulations, 1898, 1899 and 1900
Game Ordinance No. 19, 1909
Game Ordinance, 1921
Game Bird Protection Ordinance, 1926
Ordinance for the Protection of Game Animals and Game Birds, No. 38 of 1937
(There were many amendments to these ordinances.)

### Nyasaland

BCA Game Regulations, 1902
Game Ordinance No. 66, 1911
Ordinance relating to Game and Wild Animals, No. 1, 1927
Game Ordinance No. 17, 1929

### Southern Rhodesia

Cape law obtained until the Regulations to provide for the better preservation of game,
    No. 198, 1898
Ordinance to consolidate and amend laws for the better preservation of game, No. 6, 1899
Ordinance to consolidate and amend laws for the better preservation of game, No. 13,
    1906
Ordinance . . . preservation of game and fish, No. 35, 1929
Act for the preservation of the fauna of the Colony, No. 41, 1938

Other principal pieces of legislation included Natal, Act to consolidate and amend laws
on game, No. 8, 1906; Northern Rhodesia, Ordinance for the preservation of game, No.
19, 1925; Somaliland, Game Preservation Ordinance No. 2, 1907, and Game preservation
ordinance No. 5 of 1920; Sudan, Preservation of wild animals ordinances, 1927, 1930
and 1936; Tanganyika, Game preservation ordinance, 1921 (and many amendments in
the 1920s and '30s); Uganda, Game regulations, 1900, and Game ordinances, No. 11,
1902, No 10, 1904, and No. 9, 1906.

### India

Madras, Act to prevent the indiscrimiate destruction of wild elephants, 1873
Madras Act No II, 1879
Bombay, Act No IV, 1887
Indian Forest Act No. VII, 1878
Elephant Preservation Act no. VI, 1879
Act for the Preservation of Wild Birds and Game No. XX, 1887

Wild Birds and Animals Protection Act, 1912
Forest Acts, 1927 and 1950
Wild Life Protection Act No. 53, 1972

## Appendix II. Northern Rhodesia, Ordinance No. 19 of 1925

This is a fairly typical colonial game law, though less complex than those of Kenya or the greatly elaborated legislation of the 1930s. It will be observed that, under clause 6g, Africans were allowed to take out game permits, a right denied then in Kenya, but African techniques were largely prohibited under clause 24. The 1900 treaty between the British South Africa Company and King Lewanika protected African hunting rights in Barotseland, though they were subsequently eroded.

In His Majesty's name and on his Majesty's behalf, I assent.
                    H. J. STANLEY, *Governor.* 30th May, 1925

An Ordinance to consolidate and amend the law making provision for the preservation of game within the Territory.

Enacted by the Governor of Northern Rhodesia with the advice and consent of the Legislative Council thereof.

  1. This Ordinance may be cited as "The Game Ordinance 1925."
  2. In this Ordinance where not inconsistent with the context—
  "Hunt" shall include killing, capturing, or wilfully molesting by any method and also all attempts to hunt, kill or capture;
  "Schedule" means a schedule to this Ordinance;
  "Game" means any animal or bird not being domesticated mentioned in the First, Second or Third Schedule, and any animal bird or fish which may be added thereto by the Governor under the powers conferred upon him by this Ordinance;
  "Sell" includes barter and all attempts to sell or barter, and hawking and exposing for sale or barter;
  "Game Reserve" means any tract of land declared under the provisions of this Ordinance to be a Game Reserve;
  "Licence" means a licence issued under the provisions of this Ordinance to hunt game;
  "Licence holder" means a person holding a licence issued under the provisions of this Ordinance to hunt game;
  "Game Heads" means the heads, skulls or horns of any game but shall not include the tusks of elephant;
  "Port of Exit" means a port of exit appointed by or under the provisions of this Ordinance.
  3. The Governor may by notice in the *Gazette*—
(a) declare any tract of land to be "a game reserve" and define or alter the limits and boundaries thereof;
(b) declare as to the whole or any specified part of the territory that any game or any variety of or sex of game specified in the order, shall be protected and not hunted for a period of time to be mentioned in the order;
(c) suspend the operation of this Ordinance or any part thereof either as to the whole of the Territory or as to certain districts or portions thereof;
(d) alter and amend any of the schedules by adding thereto or removing therefrom the name of any species, variety or sex of any animals, bird or fish or by transferring any

name from one schedule to another, and may if he think fit apply any such alteration to the whole Territory or confine it to any district or other area;

(e) prescribe from time to time conditions as to the numbers, age or sex of the game which may be hunted by virtue of a licence either in the Territory as a whole or in any part thereof;

(f) prohibit or limit at any time as to the whole Territory or any part thereof any method employed for hunting any animal bird or fish which appears to him to be unduly destructive;

(g) prescribe from time to time the close time or fence season within which it shall not be lawful to hunt any game, or any species or variety or sex of any game to be mentioned in the order; and prescribe that such close time or fence season shall apply—

(i) to the whole of the Territory, or

(ii) to a district or group of districts within the Territory, or

(iii) to a part of a district or parts of several adjacent districts;

(h) establish a reward fund for the reward of persons bringing to any Magistrate, Native Commissioner or other authorised official any male or female or young or eggs of any of the animals or birds mentioned in the Fifth Schedule and regulate the conditions of payment and manner of proof of any claim for such reward.

4. The Governor may exempt any person from all or any of the provisions of this Ordinance for such period and subject to such conditions as he may think fit to impose.

5. The Governor or the officer or other person duly authorised to issue any licence may by endorsement on such licence make such special conditions as to the Governor may seem fit; provided that such conditions are within the powers exercisable by the Governor under section *three* of this Ordinance.

6. (a) No person shall hunt any of the game mentioned in the First Schedule unless he is authorised by an Ordinary Licence;

(b) No person shall hunt any of the game mentioned in the Second Schedule unless he is authorised by a Special Licence;

(c) No person shall hunt any of the game mentioned in the Third Schedule unless he is authorised by a Governor's Licence:

provided that the holder of a Governor's Licence shall be deemed to be also the holder of an Ordinary and a Special Licence and the holder of a Special Licence shall be deemed to be also the holder of an Ordinary Licence;

(d) No person except as hereinafter mentioned shall sell any game unless he shall be authorised by a Licence to sell game.

The provisions of paragraph (d) shall not apply to any *bonâ fide* traveller who, while on a journey, barters game lawfully obtained by him for food which is the produce of the Territory for consumption either by himself or by his employees: nor to the barter of game lawfully obtained for food or other native produce where both parties to the transaction are natives of the Territory;

(e) Except as hereinafter provided in respect of licences granted under the provisions of this Ordinance there shall be payable such sums of money as the Governor may by order prescribe. In prescribing the amount payable in respect of any licence the Governor may differentiate between persons who are ordinarily resident in the Territory and persons who are not ordinarily resident in the Territory;

(f) If a licence holder shall be authorised to hunt game in the Barotse Magisterial District under the provisions of section *ten* of this Ordinance half of the amount paid in respect of such licence shall be paid by the Government of Northern Rhodesia to the Paramount Chief of the Barotse Nation.

(g) Notwithstanding anything in this Ordinance contained a native of any sub-district may be granted a native licence which shall authorise him to hunt within the limits of such sub-district but not elsewhere any of the game mentioned in the Fourth Schedule. The fee payable in respect of a native licence shall be two shillings and sixpence: provided that for a period of five years after the taking effect of this Ordinance such licence may be issued without payment of a fee to any native except a native of the Barotse Magisterial District who would not have required a licence to hunt game prior to the taking effect of this Ordinance and thereafter such licence shall continue to be issued without payment of a fee to any such native until the Government shall by notice in the *Gazette* prescribe the fee not exceeding the sum of two shillings and sixpence which shall thereafter be payable in respect thereof by any such native. Nothing contained in this paragraph shall be deemed to render a native ineligible to be a holder of any of the other licences specified in the Ordinance.

7. (1) Licences granted under this Ordinance shall be—

(a) annual and expire on 31st December of each year;

(b) not transferable;

(c) endorsed with any general conditions imposed under section *three* hereof or any special conditions imposed under section *five* hereof;

(d) revocable on conviction for any breach of the provisions of this Ordinance or of any such general or special conditions;

(2) (a) Every European licence holder shall produce his licence for inspection on demand made by any European member of the Police or by any Magistrate, Native Commissioner or Justice of the Peace.

(b) Every native licence holder shall produce his licence for inspection on demand by any of the persons entitled to demand the production of a licence from a European licence holder and in addition on demand by any native policeman or native constable.

8. (1) A Governor's Licence may be issued by the Governor at his discretion and an Ordinary Licence or Special Licence or a native licence or a licence to sell game by any Magistrate or other person authorised thereto by the Governor.

(2) Any person authorised to issue a licence may in his discretion refuse to issue the same and shall not be bound to give any reason for such refusal.

(3) At any time while any Ordinary Licence continues in force it may with the leave of any Magistrate or other person authorised by the Governor to issue Ordinary Licences and Special Licences be exchanged for a Special Licence on payment of the difference between the fees chargeable for ordinary and special licences repectively, but the substituted licence shall expire on the day upon which the original licence would have expired.

9. During a close time or fence season prescribed by the Governor under the powers conferred upon him by sub-section (g) of section *three* of this Ordinance for any district or area in respect of game, no person shall hunt game, and after the expiration of one week from the commencement of such close season no person shall possess or sell game, in such district or area. If the close time or fence season be limited to certain species or varieties of game or to game of one sex, no person during such close time or fence season shall hunt, and no person after the expiration of one week from the commencement of such close time or fence season shall possess or sell game of such species or varieties or sex.

A person shall not be deemed to be in possession of game, within the meaning of this section, owing to the presence of live game on any land owned or occupied by him.

10. No person shall hunt any animal or bird within a game reserve without the permission of the Governor and subject to such conditions as the Governor may impose on granting such permission save as in this Ordinance or in a Governor's Licence may be expressly allowed: provided that except in the case of Europeans officers of the Administration authorised by the Governor to hunt game solely for consumption by themselves and their employees, the Governor shall not give permission to any person to hunt in the Barotse Magisterial District, which is hereby declared to be a game reserve, unless the Paramount Chief of the Barotse Nation shall have signified his consent.

11. No person shall without the special written permission of the Governor which may be granted for any scientific or other purpose mentioned therein wilfully remove disturb or destroy any eggs or the young of any bird included in the Third Schedule. Every such written permission shall distinctly state the number and denomination of such eggs or young of birds which the holder is entitled to obtain or take.

12. (1) Every person who shall under cover of such written permission as is mentioned in the last preceding section obtain or authorise or cause to be obtained eggs or young of birds greater in number or of denominations other than such as shall be specified in the permission granted to him or who, without the written sanction of the Governor shall sell any eggs or young of birds obtained under a written permission shall be guilty

of an offence and shall on conviction be liable to the penalties hereinafter provided.

(2) Where any person is found in possession of any eggs or of the young of any bird included in the Third Schedule, such person shall be deemed to be guilty of an offence against this Ordinance unless he proves that the same were not obtained in contravention of the provisions of this Ordinance.

(3) Where any person is convicted of an offence with respect to the eggs or young of any bird included in the Third Schedule the Court before which he is convicted may in addition to any other penalty order that such eggs or young shall be forfeited.

13. (1) No person shall hunt the immature young of the elephant or the female of any animal included in the First, Second or Third Schedule when accompanying her young without the special written permission of the Governor.

The immature young of the elephant is defined for the purposes of this section as being an elephant carrying tusks of less weight than twenty-two pounds the pair.

(2) If any person is found in possession of the tusk of an elephant weighing less than eleven pounds or of any ivory being in the opinion of the Court part of an elephant's tusk which would when complete have weighed less than eleven pounds, he shall be deemed to be guilty of an offence against this Ordinance unless he proves that the tusk or ivory was not obtained in breach of the provisions of this Ordinance.

(3) No person shall export from the Territory the tusk of an elephant weighing less than eleven pounds, nor any ivory being in the opinion of the Court part of an elephant's tusk which would when complete have weighed less than eleven pounds.

Provided that the Governor, within twelve months of the taking effect of this Ordinance may authorise the export from the Territory by any person of any tusk weighing less than eleven pounds or of any ivory being part of such a tusk, if satisfied that the same was obtained by such person prior to the taking effect of this Ordinance and was not obtained in contravention of the provisions of any law.

(4) Where any person is convicted of an offence with respect to the immature young of an elephant, the Court before which he is convicted may in addition to any other penalty order that any tusk or ivory in his possession which in the opinion of the Court was taken from such immature young shall be forfeited.

(5) Notwithstanding anything contained in this section, it shall be lawful for the Government of Northern Rhodesia to export from the Territory at any time any tusk or park of a tusk.

14. Any Justice of the Peace if he has reason to believe that any portion of any game hunted in contravention of any of the provisions of this Ordinance is in the possession or under the control of any person may search or cause to be searched by warrant under his hand any place where he has reason to believe any portion of such game to be and may seize and detain the same until he shall be satisfied that such game was hunted in conformity with the provisions of this Ordinance and not otherwise and in default of such proof may declare the same to be forfeited and it shall be forfeited accordingly.

15. In all cases of conviction for any offence against the provisions of this Ordinance, the Court may order that any live game and any heads, horns, tusks, skins or other remains of game found in the possession or under the control of the person convicted shall be forfeited, unless proved to be the property of another person who was not a party to such offence.

16. It shall be lawful for any person being the holder of an Ordinary or a Special Licence or Governor's Licence to export free of duty game heads and skins of any game which may have been hunted under the authority of such licence not exceeding three heads of skins of such variety of such game.

17. Upon every pound (avoirdupois) of elephant ivory exported from within the Territory there shall be payable a duty of two shillings and sixpence and on every pound (avoirdupois) of hippo teeth or of rhinoceros horn so exported a duty of twopence: and on every otter skin or portion of an otter skin exported from within the Territory a duty of one shilling and sixpence. Subject to the provisions of the last preceding section upon game heads exported from within the Territory there shall be payable a duty of – ten shillings per head for game included in the First or Second Schedule.

Notwithstanding anything contained in this section no duty shall be payable upon any elephant ivory, hippo teeth, rhinoceros horn, otter skin or portion of an otter skin, or game head exported from within the Territory by the Government of the Territory.

**18.** The duties mentioned in the last preceding section shall be paid to the Magistrate of the district in which the port of exit is situate through which it is intended to export the elephant ivory, hippo teeth, rhinoceros horn, otter skins or game heads, or to such other person as the Governor may appoint who shall give his receipt for the same.

The production of such receipt at the port of exit shall be full and sufficient authority for the export of the elephant ivory, hippo teeth, rhinoceros horn, otter skins or game heads therein mentioned.

**19.** The ports of exit for the purposes of this Ordinance shall be as follows –

Livingstone, Abercorn, Feira, Ndola, Fort Jameson, and such other places as the Governor by notice in the *Gazette* may appoint.

No elephant ivory, hippo teeth, rhinoceros horn, otter skins or game heads shall be exported from the Territory save through a port of exit.

**20.** (1) Any person who shall export or attempt to export any game head or otter skins from within the Territory without payment of the duty imposed by this Ordinance and any person who shall export or attempt to export any game head or otter skin except through a port of exit shall on conviction be liable to a fine not exceeding fifty shillings for every such game head or otter skin exported or attempted to be exported and in default of payment to imprisonment with or without hard labour for a period not exceeding one month and the Court before which he is convicted may order that the game head or otter skin shall be forfeited.

(2) Any person who shall export or attempt to export any elephant ivory, hippo teeth or rhinoceros horn from within the Territory without payment of the duty imposed by this Ordinance, and any person who shall export or attempt to export any such elephant ivory, hippo teeth or rhinoceros horn except through a port of exit shall on conviction be liable to imprisonment with or without hard labour for a period not exceeding six months or to a fine not exceeding one hundred pounds in respect of each offence and the Court before which he is convicted may order that the elephant ivory, hippo teeth or rhinoceros horn shall be forfeited.

**21.** In any prosecution for exporting or attempting to export any elephant ivory, hippo teeth or rhinoceros horn, game heads or otter skins, without having paid the export duty prescribed by this Ordinance, the Court before which the case is heard shall on proof being given that the accused or his agent failed to produce on demand the receipt mentioned in section *eighteen*, presume until the contrary is proved that the accused had not paid such duty.

**22.** (1) No person except as hereinbefore provided by section *sixteen* shall export or attempt to export from within the Territory without the written permission of the Governor, the carcases, skin, fat or any part (fresh or prepared) of any game mentioned in the First, Second or Third Schedule.

(2) No person shall export or attempt to export from within the Territory any live animal, bird, or fish mentioned in the schedules or any live animal, bird or fish which may be added thereto by the Governor under the powers conferred upon him by this Ordinance without the special written permisssion of the Governor and subject to such conditions as the Governor may impose, which may include the payment of such fee as the Governor may direct.

**23.** No person whether he be the holder of a licence to sell game or not shall sell or attempt to sell and no person may purchase, barter or export any horns, skins, tusks, teeth, feathers or flesh of any game obtained in contravention of the provisions of this Ordinance.

**24.** No person shall –

(a) make or use any pitfall, snare, trap or engine or other contrivance for the purpose of killing or capturing any of the animals mentioned in the First, Second or Third Schedule;

(b) use dynamite or other explosives or any poison for the purpose of taking fish without the written permission of the Governor;

(c) except as hereinafter provided employ any native to hunt any game: provided how-

[ *317* ]

ever that a licence holder when hunting game may employ natives to assist him, but such natives shall not use fire-arms.

**25.** Nothing contained in this Ordinance shall entitle any licence holder to trespass on private property except in pursuit of any animal wounded outside the boundaries of such property, and subject in such case to the provisions of section *twenty-eight* of this Ordinance.

**26.** Nothing contained in this Ordinance shall make it an offence for any person to pursue, capture and if necessary to kill any game damage feasant or to kill any game when necessary to do so for the preservation of human life; but in all such cases the onus of proof shall be on the person claiming exemption.

**27.** The owner, lessee and also the manager (if any) of any farm may hunt any game mentioned in the First Schedule on such farm without obtaining any licence under the provisions of this Ordinance.

The onus of proof shall be on the person claiming that any game hunted by him was so hunted on the farm of which he is owner, lessee or manager as the case may be.

**28.** If the owner or occupier of any farm shall have given notice or warning either by letter or by advertisement in the *Gazette*, or in a local newspaper or by notice boards on such farm that he is desirous of preserving the game thereon then any person who shall enter thereon in pursuit of game without his permission shall be guilty of an offence and shall be liable on conviction to a fine not exceeding five pounds for a first offence and not exceeding ten pounds for a second offence in respect of the same farm: provided that in the case of a farm which is not fenced or enclosed a person shall not be deemed to have entered thereon in pursuit of game in contravention of this section unless it shall be proved that he was aware that the owner or occupier of the farm had given notice in accordance with this section of his desire to preserve the game thereon.

**29.** Nothing in this Ordinance contained shall relieve any person from the obligation of taking out any licence which for the time being is required by any other law to be taken out for the possession or use of a gun.

**30.** All Magistrates and Native Commissioners may in respect of persons over whom they have jurisdiction impose and enforce summarily every penalty and forfeiture and revocation of a licence provided for by this Ordinance.

**31.** The Magistrate or Native Commissioner before whom any person shall be tried for an offence under this Ordinance may direct that any portion not exceeding one half of the penalty imposed and recovered shall be paid and awarded to any person who may have given information which shall have led to the conviction of the offender provided that such person be not an accesssory.

**32.** (1) Notwithstanding anything in this Ordinance contained when the members of any native tribe or the native inhabitants of any village appear to be dependent on the flesh or skins of wild animals for their subsistence or the gardens belonging to the inhabitants of any village appear to be in danger of being destroyed by wild animals the Magistrate of the district may with the approval of the Governor by order in writing authorise the tribesmen or inhabitants as the case may be to kill animals within such area as he may think fit.

(2) Notwithstanding anything contained in section *twenty-four* of this Ordinance the Magistrate of the district may authorise any of the inhabitants of any native village to make pitfalls, snares, traps or engines for the protection of their gardens from game at such place or places of such character and subject to such other conditions as he may deem expedient.

**33.** (1) Notwithstanding anything in this Ordinance contained the Governor may authorise any person duly licensed under this Ordinance to employ a native to hunt all or any game for the time being comprised in the First Schedule without a licence for the consumption of food by such person or his servants and may authorise such native being provided with a gun and ammunition upon such conditions as the Governor may see fit to impose, which may include the payment of a fee.

(2) Any contravention of the provisions of this Ordinance or of any condition imposed under this section by any native who shall be so employed with the sanction of the Governor shall also be deemed a contravention thereof by his employer.

**34.** Any person convicted of a contravention of the provisions of this Ordinance shall be liable to the penalties following that is to say:

(a) for contravention of sub-section (a) of section *six*, section *eleven*, section *twelve* or section *twenty-four*, for a first offence a fine not exceeding five pounds and for a second offence a fine not exceeding ten pounds.

(b) for contravention of sub-section (b), or sub-section (c) of section *six* or of section *ten* or section *thirteen*, for a first offence a fine not exceeding fifty pounds and for a second or subsequent offence a fine not exceeding one hundred pounds, or where the offence relates to more animals than two to a fine in respect of each animal not exceeding in the case of a first offence twenty-five pounds and in the case of a second offence fifty pounds;

(c) for contravention of sub-section *(d)* of section *six* or of section *nine* for a first offence a fine not exceeding twenty-five pounds and for a second or subsequent offence a fine not exceeding fifty pounds.

(d) for contravention of any of the provisions of this Ordinance or of any order, notice, declaration, prohibition or condition made by the Governor or with his approval by virtue of the powers conferred upon him by his approval by virtue of the powers conferred upon him by this Ordinance where no penalty is otherwise prescribed by this Ordinance in the case of a first offence a fine not exceeding twenty-five pounds and in the case of a second offence a fine not exceeding fifty pounds.

**35.** In default of paymment of any penalty imposed for any contravention of the provisions of this Ordinance or of any order, notice, declaration, prohibition or condition issued or made under the powers hereby conferred the person convicted of such contravention shall in the absence of other provision in that behalf herein contained be liable to imprisonment with or without hard labour for the respective periods following:

for a period not exceeding one month if the fine imposed shall not exceed five pounds;

for a period not exceeding three months if the fine imposed shall exceed five pounds and shall not exceed ten pounds;

for a period not exceeding six months if the fine imposed shall exceed ten pounds and shall not exceed fifty pounds;

for a period not exceeding twelve months if the fine imposed shall exceed fifty pounds.

**36.** With the exception of the provisions contained in section *one*, in sub-sections (3) and (4) of section *thirteen* and in sections *seventeen* to *twenty-one* inclusive, the foregoing provisions of this Ordinance shall not apply to the Barotse Magisterial District so far as natives under the tribal rule of the Paramount Chief of the Barotse Nation are concerned.

**37.** With the exception of the provisions contained in section *one*, the foregoing provisions of this Ordinance shall not apply to the Paramount Chief of the Barotse Nation so far as the Barotse Magisterial District is concerned and notwithstanding anything in this Ordinance contained ivory of elephant killed in the Barotse Magisterial District, may be exported by him without payment of the export duty herein prescribed.

**38.** Notwithstanding anything hereinbefore contained, at the request in writing of the Paramount Chief of the Barotse Nation or of any Chief or Induna nominated by him and approved by the Governor, a Special or an Ordinary Licence may be issued without payment of any fee which may have been prescribed in respect therof under the provisions of section *six* of this Ordinance by any person thereto authorised by the Governor to any native mentioned in such request who is resident in the Barotse Magisterial District and is under the tribal rule of the said Paramount Chief. The said Licence shall authorise such native to hunt game in any adjacent Magisterial District which may be specified therin in accordance with and subject to the provisions of this Ordinance.

**39.** A licence issued under the provisions of Proclamation (North-Western Rhodesia) No. 1 or 1905, or of Proclamation (Northern Rhodesia) No.6 of 1923 subsequent to the thirty-first day of December, 1924, shall cease to be operative and of any effect upon the expiration of two months from the date of the taking effect of this Ordinance, provided however that from the fee payable in respect if a licence issued to any person under the provisions of this Ordinance there shall be deducted the amount (if any) paid by such person in respect of a licence which has ceased to be operative owing to the provisions of this section, or if the amount so paid shall equal or exceed the fee payable in respect of the licence issued under the provisions of this Ordinance, such last mentioned licence shall be issued free of charge.

**40.** The Government Notices and Proclamations specified in the Sixth Schedule to this Ordinance shall be and are hereby repealed together with all rules or regulations made thereunder.

## FIRST SCHEDULE
### Animals which may be Hunted under an Ordinary Licence.

| | | | |
|---|---|---|---|
| Buffalo | Hippopotamus | Puku | Sitatunga |
| Bush buck | Mpala | Reed buck | Tsessabe |
| Eland | Kudu | Roan | Water buck |
| Hartebeeste | Lechwe | Sable | |

Wildebeeste (except white tailed) Zebra (except mountain Zebra) and any antelopes or birds not mentioned in the Second or Third Schedule.

## SECOND SCHEDULE
### Animals which may be Hunted under a Special Licence.

Elephant                                        Rhinoceros.

## THIRD SCHEDULE
### Animals which may be Hunted under a Governor's Licence.

| | | |
|---|---|---|
| Giraffe | West African Duiker | Secretary Bird |
| White tailed Wildebeest | Ostrich | Rhinoceros Bird |
| Gemsbok | Vulture | Nyala |
| Mountain Zebra | Owl | White backed Duiker |

## FOURTH SCHEDULE

| | | | |
|---|---|---|---|
| Bush buck | Hartebeest | Mpala | Puku |
| Duiker | Lechwe | Oribi | Reed buck |

Wildebeest (except in the portion of the Territory formerly known as North-Eastern Rhodesia)
any other small buck or birds not mentioned in the other schedules.

## FIFTH SCHEDULE

| | | | |
|---|---|---|---|
| Lion | Hyaena | Baboon | Pythons |
| Leopard | Jackal | Destructive Monkeys | Poisonous Snakes |
| Cheetah | Hunting Dog | Crocodiles | |

Large birds of prey except vultures and owls.

## SIXTH SCHEDULE

| Number and date | Short title |
|---|---|
| Government Notice (North-Eastern Rhodesia) No. 9 of 1902 | The Game Regulations 1902 |
| Government Notice (North-Eastern Rhodesia) No. 6 of 1903. | |
| Government Notice (North-Eastern Rhodesia) No. 7 of 1903. | |
| Government Notice (North-Eastern Rhodesia) No. 1 of 1909. | Export Duty Regulations (Otter Skins) 1909. |
| Government Notice (North-Eastern Rhodesia) No. 10 of 1909. | The Export Duty Amendment Regulations 1909. |
| Proclamation (North-Western Rhodesia) No. 1 of 1905. | |
| Proclamation (North-Western Rhodesia) No. 16 of 1906. | |
| Proclamation (North-Western Rhodesia) No. 29 of 1910. | |
| Proclamation (Northern Rhodesia) No. 6 of 1923 | The Northern Rhodesia Licence and Stamp (Amendment) Proclamation 1923. |

## Appendix III. The membership of the Society for the Protection of the (Wild) Fauna of the Empire, 1907

The presence of the colonial establishment within the ranks of the SPFE is apparent from this list and, if anything, became even more pronounced in subsequent years.

### Vice-Presidents

Cromer, The Right Honourable the Earl of, G.C.B., G.C.M.G., K.C.S.I., British Agency, Cairo.

Grey, The Right Honourable the Earl, K.G., G.C.M.G., P.C., 22 South Street, Park Lane, W.

Milner, The Right Honourable Viscount, G.C.B., G.C.M.G., P.C., 47 Duke Street, St. James's, S.W.

Curzon, The Right Honourable Baron, of Kedleston, G.M.S.I., G.M.I.E., P.C.

Minto, The Right Honourable Earl of, G.C.M.G., P.C., Government House, Calcutta.

### Honorary Members.

Bourke, E. C., Pretoria, Transvaal.
Butler, A. L., Khartoum.
Coryndon, R. J., Administrator, North-West Rhodesia.
D'Alva, The Duke, Marlborough Club.
Evans, Col. J. D. Bryon, C.B., A.D.C. to Governor-General, Winnipeg, Manitoba, Canada.
Garston, Sir William, K.C.B., Cairo.
Gravenitz, Baron, St. Petersburg.
Hamilton, Major H. Stevenson, Koomatipoort, South Africa.
Hawker, Captain, Dongola.
Hinde, S. L., Fort Hall, Nairobi.
Hodgson, Lieut. H., Soudan.
Hoyos, Count, 4 Hoyos Gasse 5, Vienna.
Jackson, F. J., Mombasa, Africa.
Jackson, Col. H. B., Dongola.
Kitchener of Khartoum, Lord, G.C.B., G.C.M.G.
Lagden, Sir Godfrey, K.C.M.G., Johannesburg, Transvaal.
Lawley, Capt. the Hon. Sir Arthur, K.C.M.G., Government House, Pretoria, Transvaal.
Liechtenstein, Prince Henry, Schüttel Strasse, No. 11, Vienna.
Linder, Baron H. de, Svarta, Finland.
Lugard, Lieut.-Col. Sir Frederick, K.C.M.G., Abinger Common, Surrey.
Lyttelton, Rt. Hon. Alfred, 16 Great College Street, Westminster.
Merriam, Dr. C. Hart, Washington, U.S.A.
Milton, Sir William, K.C.M.G., Salisbury, Rhodesia, South Africa.
Orr, R. A. W., Resident, Northern Nigeria.
Palmer, T. S., U.S. Dept. of Agriculture, Washington, U.S.A.
Perceval, A. Blayney, Nairobi, East Africa.
Roosevelt, The Hon. Theodore, President of the U.S.A.
Rooth, E., Pretoria, South Africa.
Sadler, Lieut.-Col. J. Hayes, C.B.
Sharpe, Sir Alfred, K.C.M.G., British Central Africa.
Wigram, Major, Kashmir Game Preservation Dept., Srinagar.
Wingate, Major-General Sir Reginald, K.C.B., Cairo.

### Ordinary Members

Aberdare, Right Hon. Lord, Duffryn, Mountain Ash.

Adeane, C., Babraham, Cambridge.
Alington, Charles, Little Barford, St. Neots.
Ashley, Wilfred, M.P., 32 Bruton Street, Berkeley Square, W.
Austen, E. E., Natural History Museum, S.W.
Avebury, Right Hon. Lord, D.C.L., 6 St. James's Square, S.W.
Bailey, Lieut-Col., 7 Drummond Place, Edinburgh.
Baird, J., British Embassy, Paris.
Baring, Cecil, 8 Bishopsgate Street, E.C.
Baring, Godfrey, M.P., Nubia House, Cowes.
Baring, Capt. the Hon. Guy, Tanglewood, Godstone.
Barnard, T. H. Kempston Hoo, Bedford.
Barneby, Theodore, Saltmarshe Castle, Bromyard.
Beauclerc, Lord Osborne, Brooks's Club, St. James's, S.W.
Beaumont, H. R., Brooks's Club, St. James's, S.W.
Bedford, The Duke of, K.C., Woburn Abbey, Bedford.
Bedford, The Duchess of.
Berry, Capt. E., 3 Hyde Park Gate, W.
Blücher, Count, Wellington Club, S.W.
Brooke, H. Brinsley, Foreign Office, S.W.
Brown, H., Windham Club, St. James's Square, S.W.
Bruce, Major the Hon. C. G., M.V.O., Abbottabad, Punjab.
Bryden, H. A., Down View, Gore Park Road, Eastbourne.
Buck, Walter, Jerez de la Frontera, Spain.
Buxton, A., Knighton, Buckhurst Hill.
Buxton, Edward North, Knighton, Buckhurst Hill.
Buxton, G. F., The Bank, Norwich.
Buxton, T. F. V., Woodredon, Waltham Abbey.
Buxton, Right Hon. Sydney, M.P., Newtimber Place, Hassocks.
Campbell, W., Mount Edgcumbe, Natal.
Chapman, Abel, Houxtey, Wark-on-Tyne, Northumberland.
Chapman, W. J., Fruitless Head, Appleby, Westmoreland.
Christy, S. H., Crudwell House, Malmesbury.
Church, Percy, Windham Club, S.W.
Cobb, E. P., Nythfa, Brecon.
Cobbold, J. D., Holywells, Ipswich.
Coke, Hon. John, Guards' Club, Pall Mall, S.W.
Colvin, Col. R. B., C.B., Monkham's, Waltham Abbey.
Coryndon, R. T., Administrator, N.W. Rhodesia.
Cranworth, Lord, Letton, Shipdham, Norfolk.
Crossfield, E., Little Acton, Wrexham.
Cuningham, Captain Boyd, Redburn, Irvine, Ayrshire.
Davies, David, Plas Dinam, Montgomeryshire.
Dawnay, G. P., The Hon., Guards' Club, Pall Mall, S.W.
Delmé-Radcliffe, Lieut-Col., C.M.G., M.V.O., United Service Club, S.W.
Douglas, Greville, 27 Wilton Crescent, S.W.
Drake-Brockman, P. E., Berbera, Somaliland Protectorate.
Du Cane, A., Brooks's Club, St. James's, S.W.
Dutcher, W., 525 Manhattan Avenue, New York, U.S.A.
Elphinstone, Lord, Carberry Tower, Musselburgh.
Fagan, C. E., Natural History Museum, Cromwell Road, S.W.
Fawcus, W. J. P., 4 Queen Victoria Street, E.C.
Findley, M. de C., C.M.G., Counsellor of Embassy, Cairo.
Frederick, H., Burgh Hall, Great Yarmouth.
Frewen, Moreton, 37a Great Cumberland Place.
Gardyne, A. D. Greenhill, Isthmian Club, Piccadilly, W.
Gardyne, Major A. W. J., Castle Hill Barracks, Aberdeen.
Gillett, Frederick, Junior Carlton Club, S.W.

Godman, F. C., 10 Chandos Street, Cavendish Square, W.
Gray, A., K.C., House of Lords, Westminster, S.W.
Greenfield, Captain, Orleans Club.
Greville, Captain Hon. Alwyn, 52 South Audley Street, W.
Greville, Hon. Louis, Heale House, Woodford, Salisbury.
Grey, Right Hon. Sir Edward, Bart., M.P., Falloden, Chathill, Northumberland.
Grey, George, 3 Queen Anne's Gate, S.W.
Guest, Hon. Ivor C., M.P., Ashby St. Ledgers, Rugby.
Gurney, Eustace, Sprowston Hall, Norwich.
Hamilton, The Marquess of, M.P., 15 Montagu Square, WW.
Hanbury, J. M., The Brewery, Spitalfields, E.
Hart-Synnot, Ronald, South-Eastern Agricultural College, Wye.
Harvey, Sir Robert, Langley Park, Slough.
Helmsley, Right Hon. Viscount, M.P., 48 Pont Street, S.W.
Hewitt, Harold, Saham Mere, Watton, Norfolk.
Heywood, N. A., Glevering Hall, Wickham, Market.
Hibbert, Hon. A. Holland, Great Munden, Watford.
Hill, Sir Clement, K.C.B., Whitehall Court, S.W.
Hindlip, Right Hon. Lord, Hindlip Hall, Worcester.
Hobhouse, Charles, M.P., House of Commons, S.W.
Hodgson, Lieut-Col., 142 Tilehurst Road, Reading.
Humbert, A., Rutland Court, S.W.
Hunter, Sir Charles, Bart., Mortimer Hill, Mortimer, Berks.
James, William, West Dean park, Chichester.
Jarvis, Lieut-Col., A. Weston, C.M.G., 2 London Wall Buildings, E.C.
Jenner, J., Digby, Nova Scotia.
Johnston, Sir H. H., K.C.B., 27 Chester Terrace, Regent's Park, N.W.
Jones, Walter, c/o E. Crossfield, Esq., Little Acton, Wrexham.
Kenmare, Right Hon. Earl of, 49 Egerton Gardens, S.W.
Kirk, Sir John, K.C.B., Wavertree, Sevenoaks.
Lankester, Prof. Ray, Natural History Museum, S.W.
Leatham, Capt. R.N., The Admiralty, S.W.
Le Breton, C. M., K.C., 263 St. James's Court, S.W.
Legge, Hon. Gerald, 37 Charles Street, Berkeley Square, W.
Leigh, Capt. Chandos, D.S.O. K.O.S.B., Egypt.
Loder, Sir Edmund, Bart., Leonardslee, Horsham, Sussex.
Lovat, Right Hon. Lord, Beaufort Castle, Beauly, N.B.
Lowther, Lieut-Col. H. C., Lowther Lodge, Kensington Gore, W., and British Embassy, Paris.
Lumsden, Col. D.M., Oriental Club.
Lydekker, R., Natural History Museum, S.W.
McNeil, Capt. Malcolm, Dun Grianach, Oban, N.B.
Millais, J. G., Comptons Brow, Horsham.
Mitchell, F. J., Knorren Lodge, Brampton, Cumberland.
Mitchell, T. Chalmers, Zoological Gardens, N.W.
Monk-Bretton, Right Hon. Lord, 16 Princes Gardens, S.W.
Morgan, S. Vaughan, 37 Harrington Gardens, S.W.
Montgomery, Col. J. A. L., St. Columb's Moville, Londonderry.
Morpeth, Right Hon. Viscount, M.P., 36 Draycott Place, S.W.
Morrell, C., Penarth, Cardiff.
Newport, Right Hon. Lord, 83 Eaton Square, S.W.
Norrie, Major G. M., 62 Queen's Gate, S.W.
Oppenheim, Capt. L., Brooks's Club, St. James's Square, S.W.
Patterson, Col., D.S.O., Cavalry Club, Piccadilly, S.W.
Peach, W. S., 24 Elm Avenue, Nottingham.
Pease, Sir Alfred Bart., Pinchinthorpe, Guisbro.
Percival, Percy, Manor House, Berrow, Burnham, Somerset.

[ 323 ]

Phelps, J. M., Castle Connell, County Limerick.
Phillips, E. Lort, 79 Cadogan Square, S.W.
Phillips, Mrs. E., Vaughan House, 22 Moreland Road, Croydon.
Rees, J. D., M.P., Hillmedes, Harrow.
Renshaw, Dr. Graham, Bridge House, Sale, Manchester.
Renton, Major A. L., 53 Sheep Street, Nottingham.
Renton, Major W. G., 53 Sheep Street, Nottingham.
Ricketts, G. H. M., Foulis Court, Colden Common, Eastleigh, Hants.
Rothschild, Hon. C.N., Tring Park, Tring.
Routledge, W. Scoresby, Conservative Club, Piccadilly, W.
Russell, Harold, 2 Temple Gardens, E.C.
Rutherford, G. M. 31 Sloane Court, S.W.
Sclater, P. L., Odiham Priory, Winchfield.
Selous, F. C., Heatherside, Worplesdon, Surrey.
Seton-Karr, Sir Henry, Bart., C.M.G., M.P., 47 Chester Square, W.
Sigray, Count, Jockey Club, Budapest.
Straker, Alfred H., Orleans Club, St. James's, S.W.
Swinfen Brown, Col., Swinfen Hall, Lichfield.
Tennant, Sir E. P., Bart., M.P., 40 Grosvenor Square, S.W.
Thomas, Freeman, M.P., Brooks's Club, St. James's, S.W.
Thomas, Oldfield, Nat. History Museum, S.W.
Thomas, Peter, Bath Club, 34 Dover Street, W.
Timmis, Sutton, Windham Club, S.W.
Tritton, Claude H., White's Club, St. James's, S.W.
Valentia, Right Hon. Viscount, M.P., House of Commons, S.W.
VanderByl, P. B., The Albany, Piccadilly, W.
Wallace, H. F., 22 Hans Crescent, S.W.
Warner, Sir William Lee, K.C.S.I., AthenÆum Club, S.W.
Warwick, Right Hon. the Earl of , Warwick Castle, Warwick.
Waterford, Right Hon. the Marquess of, Curraghmore, Porthaw, Co. Waterford.
Watney, W. H., Buckhold, Pangbourne.
Wemyss, Major, Army and Navy Club.
West, Temple, The Grange, Crescent Road, S. Norwood.
Whitbread, S. H., M.P., 11 Mansfield Street, W.
White, Major G. Dalrymple, 106 Eaton Square, S.W.
Williams, Alexander, Jerez, Spain.
Williams, Godfrey, Aberpergwn, Neath.
Williams, H. H., Pencalenick, Truro.
Williams, J. C., Caerhays Castle, St. Austell.
Williams, Mervyn, St. Donats Castle, Llantwit Major.
Williams, Morgan, St. Donats Castle, Llantwit Major.
Williams, P. D., Lanarth, St. Keverne.
Wilson, Clarence, 10 Grosvenor Square, W.
Woodward, Henry, LL.D., 129 Beaufort Street, Chelsea, S.W.
Worthington, A. Bayley, White's Club, St. James's Square, S.W.

Rhys Williams, *Hon. Secretary,*
2 Temple Gardens, E.C.

## Appendix IV. The Arusha Manifesto, 1961

A conference on wildlife was held in Arusha, Tanzania, in September 1961, from which emerged a IUCN African Special Project, and a plan for a wildlife training school to respond to pressures for rapid Africanisation. The manifesto represented the commitment of the new government of independent Tanzania

[ *324* ]

to wildlife policies as pursued during the last years of colonial rule.

The survival of our wildlife is a matter of grave concern to all of us in Africa. These wild creatures and the wild places they inhabit are not only important as a source of wonder and inspiration but are an integral part of our natural resources and of our future livelihood and well-being.

In accepting the trusteeship of our wildlife we solemnly declare that we will do everything in our power to make sure that our children's grandchildren will be able to enjoy this rich and precious inheritance.

The conservation of wildlife and wild places calls for specialist knowledge, trained manpower and money and we look to other nations to co-operate in this important task – the success or failure of which not only affect the Continent of Africa but the rest of the world as well.

Julius K. Nyerere
7:9:61

# BIBLIOGRAPHY

*Parliamentary Papers relating to the preservation of wild animals, sleeping sickness, and tsetse:*

Convention for the Preservation of Wild Animals, Birds, and Fish in Africa, signed in London 19 May, 1900, PP, Cd 101 (1900), lvi, 825.

Correspondence relating to the preservation of wild animals in Africa, PP, Cd 3189 (1906) lxxix, 25; Cd 4472 (1909), lix, 635.

Further correspondence relating to the preservation of wild animals in Africa, PP, Cd 5136 (1910), lxvi, 253; Cd 5775 (1911), lii, 521; Cd 6671 (1913), xlv, 759.

International Conference on Sleeping Sickness, PP, Cd 3778 (1908), lxxxviii, 253; further paper, Cd 3854 (1908), lxxxviii, 587.

Report of the Interdepartmental Committee on Sleeping Sickness, PP, Cd 7349 (1914), xlviii, 1; Evidence, Cd 7350 (1914), xlviii, 29.

Agreement for the Protection of the Fauna and Flora of Africa (November 1933) PP, Cmd 4453 (1933), xxviii, 1.

Tsetse Fly, Report of the East African Sub-Committee of the Economic Advisory Council, 1934-5, PP, Cmd 4951 (1935), vii, 297.

Annual Reports of protectorates and colonies in East and Central Africa, FO and CO, issued as PP.

## Journals

(Individual articles from these journals will not be cited in the bibliography that follows.)
*Journal of the Society for the Preservation of the (Wild) Fauna of the Empire*
*Oryx*
*Oriental Sporting Magazine*
*Wild Life*

## Books and articles

(The place of publication is London except where otherwise specified)
Adair, F. E. S., *A Summer in High Asia*, 1899.
Akeley, Carl E., *In Brightest Africa*, 1924.
Alderson, E. A. H., *With the Mounted Infantry and the Mashonaland Field Force*, 1898.
— *Pink and Scarlet, or, Hunting as a School for Soldiering*, 1900.
Alexander, Sir James E., *an Expedition of Discovery into the Interior of Africa* (2 vols.), 1838.
Allen, Charles, *Plain Tales from the Raj*, 1975.
Allen, David Elliston, *The Naturalist in Britain: a Social History*, 1976.
Alpers, E. A., *Ivory and Slaves in East Central Africa*, 1975.
Anderson, Andrew A., *Twenty-five Years in a Waggon: Sport and Travel in South Africa*, Cape Town, 1887, reprinted 1974.
Anderson, J. K., *Hunting in the Ancient World*, Berkeley, Cal., 1985.
Andersson, C. J., *Lake Ngami*, 1956.
— *The Okavango river*, 1862.
— *Notes of Travel in South Africa*, 1875.
Archer, Geoffrey, *Personal and Historical Memoirs of an East African Administrator*, Edinburgh, 1963.
Archer, Mildred, *Tippoo's Tiger*, 1959.
Arnot, F. S., *Garenganze: Mission Work in Central Africa*, 1889.
— *Missionary Travels in Central Africa*, Bath, 1914.
Bailey, Henry, *Travels and Adventures in the Congo Free State and its Big Bame Shooting*, 1894.

Baines, Thomas, *Explorations in South West Africa*, 1864.
— *The Gold Regions of South East Africa*, 1877.
Baker, Edward B., *Sport in Bengal*, 1887.
Baker, Sir Samuel White, *The Rifle and the Hound in Ceylon*, 1884.
— *Eight Years' Wanderings in Ceylon*, 1855.
— *The Albert Nyanza: Great Basin of the Nile*, 1866.
— *Wild Beasts and their Ways* (2 vols.), 1890-91.
Baldwin, J. H., *The Large and Small Game of Bengal and the North Western Provinces of India*, 1883.
Baldwin, W. C., *African Hunting from Natal to the Zambesi, 1852-60*, 1863.
Barbour, Thomas and Porter, Margaret D., 'Notes on South African wildlife conservation', special publication of the American Committee for International Wildlife protection, 1935.
Barrow, John, *Travels into the Interior of South Africa* (2 vols.), 1806.
Beach, D. N., 'The Shona economy', in R. Palmer and R. Parsons (eds.), *The Roots of Rural Poverty*, 1977.
Beachey, R. W., 'The East African ivory trade in the nineteenth century', *JAH*, 8 (1967), pp. 269-90.
Bell, W. D. M. *The Wanderings of an Elephant Hunter*, 1923, reprinted 1958.
Bennett, N. R. *Arab versus European: Diplomacy and War in Nineteenth Century East Africa*, New York, 1986.
Bennett, Scott, 'Shikar and the Raj', *South Asia*, 7 (1984), pp. 72-88.
Bent, J. T., *The Ruined Cities of Mashonaland*, 1892.
Bere, Rennie M., *The African Elephant*, 1966.
Bere, Rennie M., 'The Story of the Uganda National Parks', unpublished typescript (completed 1974), RCS Library.
Bernhard, F. O., *Karl Mauch*, Cape Town, 1971.
Best, J. W., *Indian Shikar Notes*, Lahore, 1920, reprinted 1931.
Blennerhasset, R., and Sleeman, L., *Adventures in Mashonaland*, 1893.
Braddon, Edward, *Thirty years of Shikar*, Edinburgh, 1895.
Bradley, Kenneth, *Diary of a District Officer*, 1943.
— *Once a District Officer*, 1966.
Brown, James Moray, *Shikar Sketches*, 1887.
— *Powder, Spur, and Spear*, 1889.
— *In the Days when We went Hog Hunting*, 1891.
— *Stray Sport*, 1893.
Brown, W. H., *On the South African Frontier*, 1899.
Bruce, C. G., *Twenty Years in the Himalaya*, 1910.
Bruce, David, 'Report of the Sleeping Sickness Commission', Royal Society, No. 16, 1915.
Bryden, H. Anderson, *Kloof and Karroo: Sport, Legend and Natural History in Cape Colony*, 1889.
— *Gun and Camera in Southern Africa*, 1893.
— *Nature and Sport in South Africa*, 1897.
— *Great and Small Game of Africa*, 1899.
— *Animals of Africa*, 1900.
— *Wild Life in Africa*, 1936.
— 'The extermination of game in South Africa', *Fortnightly Review*, 62 (1894), pp. 538-51.
Bullock, Charles, *The Mashona and the Matabele*, Cape Town, 1950.
Burchell, W. J., *Travels in the Interior of Southern Africa* (2 vols.), 1822.
Burke, E. E., *The Journals of Karl Mauch*, Salisbury, Rhodesia, 1969.
Burke, W. S., *Indian Field Shikar Book*, Calcutta, 1920 (fifth edition).
Burton, E. F., *Reminiscences of Sport in India*, 1885.
Burton, R. G., *Sport and Wild Life in the Deccan*, 1928.
— *Tropics and Snows, Travel and Adventure*, 1898.
— *A Book of Man-eaters*, 1931.
— *The Book of the Tiger*, 1933.

# BIBLIOGRAPHY

— *The Tiger Hunters*, 1936.
Campbell, Dugald, *Wanderings in Central Africa*, 1929.
Campbell, John, *Travel in South Africa*, 1815.
Chapman, Abel, *On Safari: Big Game Hunting in British East Africa*, 1908.
— *Savage Sudan*, 1921.
— *Retrospect: Reminiscences of a Hunter-Naturalist in three Continents, 1851-1928*, 1928.
Churchill, Lord Randolph, *Men, Mines and Animals in South Africa*, 1893.
Churchill, W. S., *My African Journey*, 1908.
Clay, Gervas, *Your Friend Lewanika*, 1968.
Cobbing, J. R. D., 'The Ndebele under the Khumalos, 1820-96', unpublished PhD thesis, University of Lancaster, 1976.
Coillard, François, *On the Threshold of Central Africa*, 1897.
Compton, R. H., 'The National Parks of the United States of America', report presented to the Visitors' Grants Committee for South Africa of the Carnegie Corporation of New York, Pretoria, 1934.
Corbett, Jim, *Man-eaters of Kumaon*, 1944.
— *The Man-eating Leopard of Rudraprayag*, 1948.
— *My India*, 1952.
— *Jungle Lore*, 1953.
— *The Temple Tiger and more Man-eaters of Kumaon*, 1954.
— *Tree Tops*, 1955.
Cotton, P. H. G. Powell-, *A Sporting Trip through Abyssinia*, 1902.
— *In Unknown Africa*, 1904.
Crespigny, Sir Claude Champion de, *Forty Years of a Sportsman's Life*, 1925.
Cullen, Anthony, and Darney, Sydney, *Saving the Game*, 1960.
Cumberland, Major C. S., *Sport on the Pamir Steppes, in Chinese Turkestan and the Himalayas*, 1895.
Cumming, Roualeyn George Gordon, *Five Years of a Hunter's life in the far Interior of South Africa* (2 vols.), 1850.
Cunynghame, Sir Arthur T., *My Command in South Africa, 1874-8*, 1879.
Dalleo, P. J., 'The Somali role in organised ivory poaching in north-eastern Kenya, c. 1909-39', *Int. J .Af. Hist. Studs.*, 12 (1979), pp. 472-83.
Daly, Marcus, *Big Game Hunting and Adventure, 1897-1936*, 1937.
Davidoff, Leonore, *The Best Circles: Society, Etiquette and the Season*, 1973.
Davison, Ted, *Wankie: the Making of a Great Game Reserve*, Cape Town 1967.
Decle, Lionel, *Thirty Years in Savage Africa*, 1900.
Dickens, Shirley J., *Grenfell of the Congo*, n.d.
Donovan, C. H. W., *With Wilson in Matabeleland, or, Sport and War in Zambesia*, 1894.
Downes, Mollie Panter-, *Ooty Preserved: a Victorian Hill Station in India*, 1967.
Duffy, Kevin, *Black Elephant Hunter*, 1960.
Dugmore, A. Radclyffe, *The Wonderland of Big Game, being an account of two trips through Tanganyika and Kenya*, 1925.
— *Camera Adventures in the African Wilds*, 1910.
— *Through the Sudan*, 1938.
Dunae, Patrick A., 'British Juvenile Literature in an Age of Empire, 1880-1914', unpublished PhD thesis, University of Manchester, 1975.
Dunbar-Brander, A. A., *Wild Animals in Central India*, 1923.
Dunbary, Gary S., 'Ahimsa and Shikar: conflicting attitudes towards wildlife in India', *Landscape*, 19 (1970), pp. 24-7.
Dunlop, R. H. W., *Hunting in the Himalayas*, 1890.
Edward, Second Duke of York, *The Master of Game*, reprinted 1904 with a foreword by Theodore Roosevelt.
Ehrlich, Cyril, *The Piano: a History*, 1976.
Eliot, Sir Charles, *The East Africa Protectorate*, 1905.
Elphick, Richard, and Giliomee, Hermann, *The Shaping of South African Society*, Cape Town, 1979.

# BIBLIOGRAPHY

— *Khoikhoi and the Founding of White South Africa*, Johannesburg, 1985.

Faulkner, Henry, *Elephant Haunts, being a Sportsman's Narrative of the Search for Dr. Livingstone*, 1868.

Feierman, Steven, *The Shambaa Kingdom: a History*, Madison, Wis., 1974.

Fife-Cookson, John, *Tiger Shooting in the Dun and Alwar*, 1887.

Finaughty, William, *The Recollections of William Finaughty*, ed. G. L. Harrison, Philadelphia, Pa., 1916.

Findlay, F. R. N., *Big Game Shooting and Travel in South East Africa*, 1903.

Finlason, C. E., *A Nobody in Mashonaland*, 1893.

Fletcher, F. W. F., *Sport on the Nilgiris and in Wynand*, 1911.

Foran, W. Robert, *Kill or be Killed: the Rambling Reminiscences of an Elephant Hunter*, 1933.

— *A Breath of the Wilds*, 1958.

Ford, John, *The Role of Trypanosomiases in African Ecology: a Study of the Tsetse Fly Problem*, Oxford, 1971.

Forsyth, James, *The Sporting Rifle and its Projectiles*, 1863.

— *The Highlands of Central India*, 1871.

Fraser, Agnes, *Donald Fraser*, 1934.

Fraser, Donald, *Winning a Primitive People*, 1914.

Fraser, T. G., *Record of Sport and Military Life in Western India*, 1881.

Gilbert, John M., *Hunting and Hunting Reserves in Medieval Scotland*, Edinburgh, 1977.

Gillespie, Stirling, *Celluloid Safari*, Glasgow, 1939.

Glasfurd, A. I. R., *Rifle and Romance in the Indian Jungle*, 1905.

Gouldsbury, C. E., *Life in the Indian Police*, 1912.

Grogan, Ewart S., and Sharp, Arthur H., *From the Cape to Cairo: the first Traverse of Africa from South to North*, n.d.

Gurdon, Bertram Francis, Lord Cranworth, *A Colony in the Making, or, Sport and Profit in British East Africa*, 1912.

— *Kenya Chronicles*, 1939.

Hamilton, J. Stevenson-, *Animal Life in Africa*, 1912.

— *The Kruger National Park*, Pretoria, 1928.

— *The Low Veld: its Wildlife and its Peoples*, 1929.

— *South African Eden*, 1937.

— *Our South African National Parks*, Cape Town, 1940.

Harding, Colin, *Far Bugles*, 1933.

Harris, William Cornwallis, *The Wild Sports of Southern Africa*, 1839.

Haywood, Colonel A. H. W., *Sport and Service in Africa*, 1926.

Hastings, A. C. G., *Nigerian Days*, 1925.

Hawkins, R. E. (ed.), *Jim Corbett's India*, Oxford, 1986.

Hemans, H. N., *The Log of a Native Commissioner*, 1935.

Herbert, Agnes, *Two Dianas in Somaliland*, 1908.

Hill, Ian Barras, *Landseer*, Aylesbury, 1973.

Hingston, R. W. G., 'Proposed British national parks for Africa', *Geographical Journal*, 77 (1931), pp. 402-28.

Hole, H. M., *Old Rhodesian Days*, 1928.

Hopkins, Harry, *The Long Affray: the Poaching Wars in Britain, 1760-1914*, 1985.

Horne, W. O. *Work and Sport in the Old ICS.*, Edinburgh, 1928.

Hume, Allan, and Marshall, C. H. T., *Game Birds of India, Burmah and Ceylon* (3 vols.) Calcutta, 1888-91.

Hunt, Roland, and Harrison, John, *The District Officer in India, 1930-47*, 1980.

Hyatt, S. P., *The Old Transport Road*, 1914.

Iliffe, John, *A Modern History of Tanganyika*, Cambridge, 1979.

Inglis, James ('Maori'), *Sport and Work on the Nepaul Frontier, or, Twelve Years' Sporting Reminiscences of an Indigo Planter*, 1892.

Itzkowitz, David C., *Peculiar Privilege: a Social History of English Foxhunting, 1753-1885*, Hassocks, 1977.

Jack, Rupert W., 'Tsetse fly and big game in Southern Rhodesia', *Bulletin of Entomolo-*

*gical Research*, 1 (1914), pp. 97-110.

Jackson, Sir Frederick, *Early Days in East Africa*, 1930, reprinted 1969.

— *The Birds of Kenya Colony and the Uganda Protectorate*, 1938.

Johnson, Daniel, *Sketches of Indian Field Sports as followed by the Natives of India*, 1822, reprinted 1827.

Johnston, Sir Harry, *The Uganda Protectorate*, 1902.

Johnston, J., *Reality versus Romance in South Central Africa*, 1893.

Kaul, H. K. *Travellers' India: an Anthology*, Delhi, 1979.

Kearton, Cherry, *Cherry Kearton's Travels*, 1941.

Kerr, W. Montagu, 'The Upper Zambesi zone', *Scottish Geographical Magazine*, 2 (1886), pp. 385-402.

Kinloch, Alexander A. A., *Large Game Shooting in Thibet, the Himalayas, Northern and Central India*, 1892.

Kinloch, Bruce, *The Shamba Raiders*, 1972.

Kjekshus, Helge, *Ecology Control and Economic Development in East African History*, 1977.

Knight-Bruce, G. W. H., *Memories of Mashonaland*, 1895.

Lamphear, John, *The Traditional History of the Jie of Uganda*, Oxford, 1976.

Laws, R., *Reminiscences of Livingstonia*, 1934.

Leonard, A. G., *How we made Rhodesia*, 1896.

Leyland, J., *Adventures in the far Interior of South Africa . . . to which is appended a short Treatise on the best Mode of skinning and preserving Birds, Animals, etc.*, 1866.

Livingstone, David, *Missionary Travels in South Africa*, 1857.

Lloyd, J. B., *African Animals in Renaissance Literature and Art*, Oxford, 1971.

Luard, N., *The Wildlife Parks of Africa*, 1985.

Lugard, F. D., *The Rise of our East African Empire* (2 vols.), 1893.

Lyell, D. D., *Hunting Trips in Northern Rhodesia, with Accounts of Sport and Travel in Nyasaland and Portuguese East Africa*, 1910.

— *Nyasaland for the Hunter and Settler*, 1912.

— *Wild Life in Central Africa*, 1913.

— *Memories of an African Hunter*, 1923.

— *The African Elephant and its Hunters*, 1924.

— *The Hunting and Spoor of Central African Game*, 1929.

— *African Adventure, Letters from Famous Big Game Hunters*, 1935.

— *Big Game Shooting in Africa*, Lonsdale Library, Vol. 14, 1932.

Macintyre, Major-General Donald, *Hindu-Koh: Wanderings and Wild Sport on and beyond the Himalayas*, 1889.

MacKenzie, John M., 'Hunting in Central Africa in the late ninetieth century, with special reference to Zimbabwe', in W. Baker and J. A. Mangan (eds.), *Sport in Africa*, New York, 1987.

— 'Chivalry, Social Darwinism and ritualised killing: the hunting ethos in Central Africa to 1914', in D. Anderson and R. Grove (eds.), *Conservation in Africa*, Cambridge, 1987.

— 'The imperial pioneer and hunter and the British masculine stereotype in late Victorian and Edwardian times', in J. A. Mangan and James Walvin (eds.), *Masculinity and Morality*, Manchester, 1987.

— 'Representations of the Hunter in the late Nineteenth and Twentieth Centuries', unpublished paper, British Museum conference 'Making Exhibitions of Ourselves' 1986.

— Denis D. Lyell, a new introduction to *The Hunting and Spoor of Central African Game*, Camden, N. C., 1987.

— Blayney Percival, a new introduction to *A Game Ranger's Notebook*, Camden, N. C., 1988.

— 'Hunting and Juvenile Literature', in Jeffrey Richards (ed.), *Imperialism and Juvenile Literature*, Manchester, 1988.

Mackintosh, C. W., *Coillard of the Zambesi*, 1908.

Maconochie, Evan, *Life in the ICS*, 1926.

[ *330* ]

# BIBLIOGRAPHY

Mangan, J. A., *Athleticism in the Victorian and Edwardian Public School*, Cambridge, 1981.
— *The Games Ethic and Imperialism*, Harmondsworth, 1986.
Markham, Colonel F., *Shooting in the Himalayas*, 1854.
Marks, Shula, and Atmore, Anthony (eds.), *Economy and Society in Pre-industrial South Africa*, 1980.
Marks, S. A., *Large Mammals and a Brave People*, Seattle, Wash., 1973.
Matzke, Gordon, 'The development of the Selous game reserve', *Tanzania Notes and Records*, Nos. 79 and 80 (1976), pp. 37-48.
Maugham, R. C. F., *Portuguese East Africa: History, Scenery and Great Game of Manica and Sofala*, 1906.
— *Nyasaland in the Nineties*, 1935.
Maxwell, M., *Stalking Big Game with a Camera in Equatorial Africa, with a Monograph on the African Elephant*, 1924.
Maydon, Major H. C., *Big Game Shooting in Africa*, 1932.
— *Big Game of Africa*, 1935.
— *Big Game of India*, 1937.
Meinertzhagen, Richard, *Kenya Diary, 1902-6*, Edinburgh, 1957.
Michael, Marjorie, *I Married a Hunter*, 1956.
Millais, J. G., *A Breath from the Veld*, 1899.
— *Far away up the Nile*, 1924.
— *The Life of Frederick Courtenay Selous*, 1918.
Moffat, Robert, *Missionary Labours and Scenes in Southern Africa*, 1846.
Moir, F. L. M., *After Livingstone: an African Trade Romance*, n.d.
Molyneux, E., and Younghusband, Sir Francis, *Kashmir*, 1909, reprinted 1924.
Moore, E. D. *Ivory, Scourge of Africa*, 1931.
Munro, J. Forbes, *Africa and the International Economy*, 1976.
Munsche, P. B., *Gentlemen and Poachers: the English Game Laws, 1671-1831*, Cambridge, 1981.
Musambachime, Mwelma, 'The fate of the Nile crocodile in the African Waterways', *African Affairs*, 86 (1987), pp. 197-207.
Neumann, Arthur H., *Elephant Hunting in East Equatorial Africa*, 1898.
Neumark, S. David, *Economic Influences on the South African Frontier*, Stanford, Cal., 1957.
Nicolls, James A., *The Sportsman in South Africa*, 1892.
Ofcansky, Thomas P., 'A History of Game Preservation in British East Africa, 1895-1963', PhD thesis, University of Wisconsin, 1981, to be published by West Virginia University Press.
Onselen, Charles van, 'Reactions to Rinderpest in South Africa, 1896-7', *JAH* 13 (1972), pp. 473-88.
Ormond, Richard, *Sir Edwin Landseer*, 1981.
Orpen, J. M., *Reminiscences of Life in South Africa*, 1915.
Orr, Willie, *Deer Forests, Landlords and Crofters*, Edinburgh, 1982.
Osten, R. van (ed.), *World National Parks: Progress and Opportunities*, Brussels, 1972.
Oswell, W. Edward, *William Cotton Oswell, Hunter and Explorer* (2 vols.), 1900.
Pakenham, Valerie, *The Noonday Sun: Edwardians in the Tropics*, 1985.
Parker, Ian, and Amin, Mohamed, *Ivory Crisis*, 1983.
Pauling, George, *Chronicles of a Contractor*, 1926.
Patterson, J. H., *In the Grip of the Nyika*, 1909.
Pearson, M. N., 'Recreation in Mughal India', *BJSH*, 1 (1984), pp. 335-50.
Pease, Sir Alfred, *Travel and Sport in Africa*, 1902.
— *The Book of the Lion*, 1913.
— *Half a Century of Sport*, 1932.
Percival, A. Blayney, *A Game Ranger's Note-book*, ed. E. D. Cumming, 1924.
— *A Game Ranger on Safari*, ed. E. D. Cumming, 1928.
Pereira, J. C. W., *The Laws of Ceylon* (2 vols.), Colombo, 1904.
Perham, Margery, *Lugard: the Years of Adventure*, 1956.

# BIBLIOGRAPHY

Phoebus, Gaston, Count of Foix, *The Hunting Book*, 1984.

Pitman, C. R. S., *A Game Warden among his Charges*, 1931.

— *A Game Warden takes Stock*, 1942.

Pollok, Fitzwilliam Thomas, *Sport in British Burma, Assam and the Cassyah and Jyntiah Hills*, 1879.

— *Fifty Years' Reminiscences of India*, 1896.

— *Incidents of Foreign Sport and Travel*, 1894.

Powell, R. S. S. Baden-, *The Matabele Campaign*, 1897.

— *Sport in War*, 1900.

— *The Sport of Rajahs*, Toronto, 1900.

— *Marksmanship for Boys*, 1915.

— *Pig Sticking or Hog Hunting*, 1889, reprinted 1924.

Pringle, John A., *The Conservationists and the Killers*, Cape Town, 1982.

Pringle, Thomas, *Narrative of a Residence in South Africa*, 1835.

Rees, Sir John D., *HRH the Duke of Clarence and Avondale in Southern India, with a Narrative of Elephant Catching in Mysore, by G. P. Sanderson*, 1891.

Renford, Raymond, K., *The Non-official British in India to 1920*, Oxford, 1987.

Rice, William, *Tiger Shooting in India*, 1837.

Richards, Audrey I., *Land, Labour and Diet in Northern Rhodesia*, 1939.

Ritter, E. A. *Shaka Zulu*, 1955.

Roberts, Andrew, *A History of Zambia*, 1976.

Robertson, W., *A Hunter Talks*, 1930.

Rogers, W. A., and Lobo, J. D., 'Elephant control and legal ivory exploitation, 1920-1976', *Tanzania Notes and Records*, Nos. 84 and 85 (1980), pp. 25-54.

Roosevelt, Theodore, *African Game Trails*, 1910.

— *Ranch Life and the Hunting Trail*, 1896, reprinted Gloucester, 1985.

Ross, John (ed.), *The Book of the Red Deer*, 1925; also published in a larger version, ed. Ross and Hugh Gunn, *The Book of the Red Deer and Empire Big Game*, 1925.

Ross, Robert, *Adam Kok's Griquas*, Cambridge, 1976.

Rouillard, Nancy, *Matabele Thompson: an Autobiography*, 1936.

Ruffer, Jonathan G., *The Big Shots: Edwardian Shooting Parties*, 1984.

Rukavina, Kathaleen Stevens, *Jungle Pathfinder: the Biography of Chirupula Stephenson*, 1951.

Rundall, L. B. *The Ibex of Shā-ping*, 1915.

Sanderson, G. P. *Thirteen Years among the Wild Beasts of India*, 1878.

Sattin, Anthony (ed.), *An Englishwoman in India: the Memoirs of Harriet Tytler, 1828-58*, Oxford, 1986.

Schneider, William G., *An Empire for the Masses: the French Popular Image of Africa, 1870-1900*, Westport, Conn., 1982.

Schreiner, S. C. Cronwright-, *The Migratory Springboks of South Africa (the Trekbokke)*, 1925.

Scudder, Thayer, *The Ecology of the Gwembe Tonga*, Manchester, 1962.

Scull, Guy H., *Lassoing Wild Animals in Africa*, New York, 1911.

Scully, W. C., *Further Reminiscences of a South African Pioneer*, 1913.

— *Lodges in the Wilderness*, 1915.

Secord, James A., 'Natural history in depth', *Social Studies of Science*, 15 (1985), pp. 181-200.

Selous, F. C., *A Hunter's Wanderings in Africa*, 1881.

— *Travel and Adventure in South East Africa*, 1893.

— *African Nature Notes and Reminiscences*, 1908.

Serpell, James, *In the Company of Animals*, Oxford, 1986.

Shakespear, Captain Henry, *The Wild Sports of India*, 1960.

Sharpe, Sir Alfred, *The Backbone of Africa*, 1921.

Shorter, Aylward, *Chiefship in Western Tanzania: a Political History of the Kimbu*, Oxford, 1972.

Shorthose, Major W. J. T., *Sport and Adventure in Africa*, 1923.

Siggins, A. J., *Shooting with Rifle and Camera: Filming The Four Feathers*, 1931.

Simson, Frank B., *Letters on Sport in Eastern Bengal*, 1886.
Smith, Andrew, *Illustrations of the Zoology of South Africa* (5 vols.), 1838-47.
Smith, John, *Colonial Cadet in Africa*, Durham, N. C., 1968.
Sparrman, Andrew, *A Voyage to the Cape of Good Hope from the Year 1772 to 1776*, 1785.
Spinage, C. A., 'A review of ivory exploitation and elephant trends in Africa', *East African Wildlife Journal*, Nairobi, 2 (1973).
Stearn, William T., *The Natural History Museum*, 1981.
Stebbing, E. P., *Jungle By-ways in India*, 1911.
— *Stalks in the Himalayas: Jottings of a Sportsman-Naturalist*, 1912.
— *The Diary of a Sportman Naturalist in India*, 1920.
Steedman, Andrew, *Wanderings and Adventures in the Interior of Southern Africa* (2 vols.), 1835.
Sterndale, Robert Armitage, *Seonee or Camp Life in the Satpura Range*, 1877, reprinted 1887.
Stigand, C. H., and Lyell, D. D., *Central African Game and its Spoor*, 1906.
— *Hunting the Elephant in Africa, and other Recollections of Thirteen Years' Wanderings*, 1913.
Still, John, *The Jungle Tide*, Edinburgh, 1930.
Stockley, Lieutenant Colonel C. H., *Stalking in the Himalayas and Northern India*, 1936.
Stokes, C. Selwyn, *The Story of the Kruger National Park*, Cape Town, 1934.
Stone, M. L., 'Organised poaching in Kitui district: a failure in district authority, 1900-60', *Int. J. Af. Hist. Studs.*, 5 (1972), pp. 436-52.
Stoneham, C. T., *Wanderings in Wild Africa*, 1936.
Stracey, P. D., *Wildlife Management in India*, New Delhi, 1966.
Summers, Roger (ed.), *Prehistoric Rock Art of the Federation of Rhodesia and Nyasaland*, Salisbury, Rhodesia, 1959.
Sumner, François, *Man and Beast in Africa*, 1953.
Sutherland, James, *The Adventures of an Elephant Hunter*, 1912.
Swann, Alfred J., *Fighting the Slave Hunters in Central Africa*, 1910.
Tabler, E. C., *The Far Interior*, Cape Town, 1955.
— *Trade and Travel in Early Barotseland*, 1963.
— *To the Victoria Falls via Matabeleland: the Diary of Major Henry Stabb, 1875*, Cape Town, 1967.
Taylor, John, *Big Game and Big Game Rifles*, 1948.
Temple, Derek, *Ivory Poacher*, n.d.
Thomas, Keith, *Man and the Natural World: Changing Attitudes in England, 1500-1800*, 1983.
Thomas, T. M., *Eleven Years in Central South Africa*, 1873.
Thompson, E. P., *Whigs and Hunters: the Origin of the Black Act*, Harmondsworth, 1977.
Thomson, Joseph, *To the Central African Lakes and Back* (2 vols.), 1881.
— *Through Masailand*, 1887.
Thunberg, C. P. *Travels in Europe, Africa and Asia performed between the Years 1770 and 1779* (3 vols.), 1795.
Todd, W. Hogarth, *Work, Sport and Play*, 1928.
— *Tiger! Tiger!*, 1927.
Tosh, John, *Clan Leaders and Colonial Chiefs in Lango*, Oxford, 1978.
Trench, Charles Chenevix, *The Poacher and the Squire*, 1967.
Turley, Charles, *With the Prince round the Empire*, 1926.
Vaillant, François Le, *Travels from the Cape of Good Hope to the Interior Parts of Africa*, 1790.
Vance, Norman, *The Sinews of the Spirit*, Cambridge, 1985.
Vandervell, Anthony, and Coles, Charles, *Game and the English Landscape*, 1980.
Varian, H. F., *Some African Milestones*, 1953.
Waley, S. D., *Edwin Montagu: a Memoir and an Account of his Visits to India*, Bombay, 1964.

[ *333* ]

# BIBLIOGRAPHY

Waller, Horace (ed.), *The Last Journals of David Livingstone* (2 vols.), 1880.

Wallis, J. P. R. (ed.), *The Northern Goldfields: Diaries of Thomas Baines* (3 vols.), 1946.

Walmsley, Leo, *Flying and Sport in East Africa*, 1920.

Ward, Rowland, *Empire of India Exhibition: Illustrated Guide to the Jungle*, 1895.

— *Horn Measurements and Weight of the Great Game of the World*, 1892.

— *A Naturalist's Life Study in the Art of Taxidermy*, 1913.

— *Records of Big Game*, many editions, first 1896.

— *The Sportsman's Handbook . . . to Practical Collecting, Preserving . . . of Trophies and Specimens and Synoptic Guide to Hunting Grounds of the World*, many editions, first 1880.

Wardrop, A. E., *Days and Nights with Indian Big Game*, 1923.

— *Modern Pig Sticking*, 1914, reprinted 1939.

Whitehead, Peter, *The British Museum (Natural History)*, 1981.

Williamson, Thomas, *Oriental Field Sports* (2 vols.), 1808.

Wilmot, Sir Sainthill Eardley-, *Forest Life and Sport in India*, 1910.

— *Leaves from Indian Forests*, 1930.

— *The Life of a Tiger and the Life of an Elephant*, 1933.

Wilson, Monica, and Thompson, Leonard (eds.), *Oxford History of South Africa*, Vol. 1, 1969.

Wolhunter, Harry, *Memories of a Game Ranger*, Johannesburg, 1948.

Wolley, Sir Clive Phillips, *Big Game Shooting* (2 vols.), 1894.

Wood, J. G., *Through Matabeleland: Ten Months in a Waggon*, 1893.

Woodyatt, Nigel, *My Sporting Memories*, 1923.

Youé, Christopher P., *Robert Thorne Coryndon: Proconsular Imperialism in Southern and Eastern Africa, 1897-1925*, Waterloo, Ontario, 1986.

Younghusband, Sir Francis, *Wonders of the Himalaya*, 1924.

# INDEX